the BIRTH DAY BOOK

the

BIRTH DAY BOOK

what the day you were born says about you

SHELLEY VON STRUNCKEL

Aries

MARCH 20–
APRIL 18

Taurus

APRIL 19–
MAY 19

Leo

JULY 22–
AUGUST 21

Virgo

AUGUST 22–
SEPTEMBER 21

Sagittarius

NOVEMBER 21–
DECEMBER 20

Capricorn

DECEMBER 21–
JANUARY 19

Gemini

*MAY 20–
JUNE 19*

Cancer

*JUNE 20–
JULY 21*

Libra

*SEPTEMBER 22–
OCTOBER 21*

Scorpio

*OCTOBER 22–
NOVEMBER 20*

Aquarius

*JANUARY 20–
FEBRUARY 18*

Pisces

*FEBRUARY 19–
MARCH 19*

Introduction

Welcome to this tour of the astrological year.

Everybody's intrigued by astrology—even those who don't "believe" in it. I know this because, having written columns that are published worldwide and in a number of languages, I have learned that the fascination with the 12 signs of the zodiac, and the individual dates within each, is universal.

The columns I write for each star sign focus on the nature of each day for the 12 signs. However, there are shades of intensity and character that shift over the 30 or so days of each sign.

Many don't realize the dates of the signs are linked to the seasons. For example, in the northern hemisphere, the first day of Aries is linked to the beginning of spring; Cancer, to the first day of summer; Libra to fall, and Capricorn to winter. While in the southern hemisphere the seasons are reversed, the dates are still linked to the start of each season.

And as the day of each sign unfolds, elements of its character—its joys, charms, and challenges—arise in a unique form. So while the interpretation for your birthday will reveal insights, reading the interpretation for other days could prove fascinating, if not revealing, as well.

Each day of the year has its own character, but just as with a family, those of the same sign are bound to have similarities.

Also, knowing about the day's character is useful for anybody, whatever your sign, so at the bottom of each page, you will find an entry called This Day for Everyone, which is exactly that—it is the nature of that day for those of any sign; it offers astrological tips for your day, whatever your sign—check it out.

Questions about the dates of the signs? Find out more at shelleyvonstrunckel.com.

Enjoy your journey.

Shelly

Aries

March 20–
April 18

Aries Fiery Aries is the first sign of the zodiac, and being ruled by the warrior planet Mars, you are a forceful character who thrives on challenges in a range of forms. Each adds to your skills, wisdom, and, ultimately, patience. Your plants and flowers reflect that sharpness, from thistles to gladioli, and your spice is, of course, red chile. Your gemstones are red, too—ranging from ruby to coral.

A
R
I
E
S

GIFTS Forthright, Industrious, Athletic

CHALLENGES Impulsive, Demanding, Unbending

NUMBER 5

(2+0) + (3) = 5

Each day I will surprise somebody—and in a wonderfully unexpected way

You

Not only are you an Aries, but you were born on the first day of Aries, which makes you about 150-percent Aries, the most Aries of all. And even if you aren't into astrology, you are probably still proud of the energy and power that come with being an Aries and being ruled by the dynamic planet Mars. In fact, you may even have a stubborn streak that comes as a result of this intense energy.

In your personal life and your personal style, you rarely compromise. However, that can lead to ups and downs, simply because you don't pause to consider whether what you're doing is worthwhile, so it is exhausting, or perhaps it's time to make a change. This enthusiasm, therefore, needs to be balanced with an awareness of what is actually in your best interests, which means pausing in a way that won't necessarily come naturally to you.

Yet when you begin to do this, not only will you enjoy life more, you will also find more subtle joys in your own day, in relationships with others, and in what you do. And you may even find yourself having fun doing things you would once have dismissed as being too dull. And this is your journey as an Aries. It's not just being true to yourself; it is discovering what life itself has to offer and enjoying every second of it. Master that and you will have mastered life's biggest secret.

You and others

As an enthusiastic Aries, you have a knack for getting those who are questioning whether certain ideas or introductions, are worth the effort. While mostly others profit from your encouragement, if they're seriously unwilling, then back off, at least for the moment.

Health and well-being

When you are in the mood to get moving, you're not just enthusiastic, you will tire others. The trick is keeping up the pace. Taking it more slowly may seem like a compromise, but it means you are more likely to continue in the future.

Goals and challenges

Admitting your decisions were unwise may not be easy, but the sooner you do it, the more swiftly you will be able to rethink the plans in question. Ask others for their guidance. They will admire you for being so open about your problems.

THIS DAY FOR EVERYBODY

Obviously, it would be easier if you could deal with the range of changes currently reshaping various elements of your life all at once. Yet not only are things moving too slowly for that, your own perspective is also changing. The trick? Rethink plans, but regard any decisions as tentative.

If things aren't going according to plan, I will figure out why, then learn from it

You

Your enthusiasm is a kind of magnetism that draws people to you. You don't understand why. In fact, because it's something you have had your whole life, you don't even think about it until others mention it. Yet that magnetism starts and stops. It seems to depend on your mood. And this is where your lesson lies, which is important for you: never compromise in what you're doing.

Don't act to please others, unless it is part of an arrangement at work or in a relationship where basically you have to compromise to help each other. But at the same time, be aware that there is very much the possibility of doing too much of a good thing. And when you sense that, you will want to pause and consider whether more of what you are doing is actually in your best interests.

In fact, bizarrely, you can get so into the habit of dressing in a particular way, eating something in particular, or doing something else, that you don't even realize you could make a change. And that is one of your big lessons. When you consider that, you will also begin to be a bit calmer and be able to enjoy life itself and those around you all the more.

This is one of the greatest gifts for you. Your passion for life comes with who you are. The passion to enjoy the life around you and others is one of the skills you will learn.

You and others

As someone who lives full-speed ahead, conducting a relationship, a friendship, a romantic liaison, or even relations with family can be tricky. The secret? Ask others for their concerns and advice, then discuss their views frankly. Everybody will learn from the resulting exchanges.

Health and well-being

Being excited about an activity is great, but even when you are so involved, you must remember to eat or even to rest. Also, you've been so absorbed in an activity or regimen that you were told was beneficial, you will do nothing else. The fact is there can be too much of a good thing, and this is it.

Goals and challenges

You are amazingly self-sufficient, and proud of it. Because of that, you could struggle to accept an offer as exciting as it is unexpected, simply because it was somebody else's idea. There are few greater gifts than being offered to be part of somebody else's project. Say a heartwarming and enthusiastic yes.

THIS DAY FOR EVERYBODY

Others are complaining about the time it is taking you to make simple decisions. They'd be easy if your circumstances stayed the same, but with changes—both minor and major— demanding that you rethink even the simplest of ideas or arrangements, it is nearly impossible to make long-term plans.

A
\
R
/
I
\
E
/
S

When I'm feeling bored, I'll tackle dull tasks I've been ignoring for a long time

You

Every Aries is ruled by the dynamic planet Mars, but in your case, Mars can sometimes be too big a player in your life. Mars is the planet of energy, aggression, and sometimes war, which means that occasionally you can get involved in a plan, get involved in learning something, but itis almost as if you intend to conquer rather than enjoy it. And, of course, what happens after that is you become exhausted and it seems overwhelming.

And then it loses its luster. So for you, the trick is to maintain that amazing enthusiasm that comes with your nature, but also to learn to spread it out in doing more than one thing, or to spend time with someone who helps you recognize when you are overdoing it. Not only is this important because it allows you to keep balance, it also means you have time to enjoy not only achieving those goals, but for life itself.

As you are aware, there are times when you have completely ignored those who are closest to you, perhaps even forgetting an important day or a birthday. Or perhaps you have been madly in love with somebody, but haven't been in touch with them. Whatever the case, the lesson here is to find that balance as well. Do that and the feedback you get, the love you get, and the joy you get, will not only make it worthwhile, it will remind you to do that all the more often.

You and others

With your passion for life, you attract everybody to you. But that doesn't mean you enjoy everybody's company or should make plans with them. If you do so unwisely, simply apologize and back out. This prevents you from making arrangements that are no fun. Better yet, it teaches you to pick and choose carefully those who you spend time with.

Health and well-being

You will often become enthusiastic about eating something you were told was good for you or doing an exercise or a sport because it is recommended. However, these can become routine, and soon, achingly dull. The secret? Make changes just for the fun of it.

Goals and challenges

Finding things that excite you is easy, but getting that excitement to last is another matter. Usually you are eager to move on to anything that is new or exciting. The real challenge is finding the balance that is perfect for you, one that enables you to be true to yourself, which for you as an Aries is crucial.

THIS DAY FOR EVERYBODY

Understanding the need to be patient can be challenging, especially when others are in a hurry to make things happen. Yet at the moment, even you are struggling with the feeling that things should be moving more swiftly. They will. But for now, you are better off taking it slowly.

Instead of doing a single good deed each day, I will aim to do a dozen

You

As an Aries you've probably heard people say that they envy your enthusiasm. However, you will wonder why that is, because for you, this comes so naturally you don't even think about it. Yet at the same time, the range of your feelings, or the amount of energy you have, from being on top of the world to exhausted, has to do with the need to find the center between these two: something that doesn't come naturally to you, and is in fact one of your biggest lessons. This has to do with your energy level and your enthusiasm, but also with the things you get involved in, your work, close relationships, and romance. Also, how you live your daily life and how you organize your routine. Bizarrely, in your enthusiasm you can forget things you need to do, whether it's paying bills or even, occasionally, eating.

While you can't always make notes about this kind of thing, what you can do is deal with one of the greatest challenges and joys for you. That is to pause every once in a while, take a deep breath, and realize how wonderful it is just to be you and just to be alive. And if you're with somebody, have a brief chat about that. Once you begin this, and once you begin to do it more often, you will not only enjoy the swings between the excitement and the stillness all the more, you'll also enjoy every single breath of life all the more as well.

You and others

The gift that you bring to any relationship, whether it's family, loved ones, or even a neighbor or colleague, is that you're entirely you. In fact, it puzzles you when others put up a fake front. Discuss this, but gently, because it probably means they're shy, nothing more.

Health and well-being

While sometimes you will throw yourself into a way of eating or exercising that you have been told is good, or which you find particularly rewarding, at the same time you have a tendency to exclude other things. Then you will tire of that regimen and move onto another. Moderation may not come naturally, but it is your best bet.

Goals and challenges

Being passionate by nature, you thrive on excess: overdoing, then being exhausted. So not only is finding balance difficult, you don't really enjoy it. What's more, that inner stillness can be difficult to achieve. Still, at times it's not only wise, it gives you space for recovering from the past and to consider the future.

THIS DAY FOR EVERYBODY

Recent setbacks have freed you from a situation that, while seemingly worthwhile, was increasingly worrying. What's more, as that particular arrangement comes to an end with each passing day, another far better one isn't just increasingly likely, it is showing amazing promise.

A
\
R
/
I
\
E
/
S

GIFTS Candid, Loving, Impulsive

CHALLENGES Self-involved, Unbending, Obsessive

NUMBER 9

(2+4) + (3) = 9

If somebody is dull, I will talk to them, until I realize how amazing they are

You

Those around you will always remark on your enthusiasm and your zest for life—and how involved you get in things. And while it is true, sometimes that involvement can turn into an obsession, to the degree that you actually end up getting bored with whatever it is. You will note this when someone asks if you are still interested in this thing, whether it's a form of exercise, a particular way of eating, or going someplace—and you'll almost have forgotten that it existed because you got so tired of it you moved on to something else.

One of your big lessons in life, therefore, is to find those things that you can be passionate about, but in ways so that passion doesn't overwhelm you. This has to do with activities, but even more, it has to do with how you work and close relationships. It may well be that you've been so passionate about a certain line of activity that you got very well educated and got a degree in, and then found you didn't actually like. Or it could well have been the same with a close alliance, a friendship, or even a relationship. You overwhelmed yourself. Finding that balance for any Aries is challenging, but it is especially important for you. Because when you acquire that skill, it will enable you to enjoy the subtleties in your own life and close relationships, and love in ways that you have not been able to before.

You and others

One of your greatest gifts is the attention you pay to those you meet and those you get to know. However, one of your greatest obstacles is the degree to which that attention can become so intense that you forget there are other things around you. It may be a friend whose company you really enjoy, or, if you're in love, it is usually madly in love. And the gift here is to learn, to take it easy, and to take time with it. This won't come naturally, but it is one of the greatest challenges for you.

Health and well-being

In the same way, your health and well-being require balance—a thoughtful approach as to how you take care of yourself, how you eat, and possibly even moments of questioning or reflection. If you socialize constantly or are a movie addict, it might be time to cut back and, even more, consider what's next.

Goals and challenges

One of the greatest gifts for you is to have problems to solve and obstacles to overcome, each of which forces you to focus on elements of your life you often ignore. Initially, these won't seem exciting, yet while dealing with them you'll learn something very challenging for yourself, which is to live a balanced life.

THIS DAY FOR EVERYBODY

Listening with your heart as much as with your ears is always important, but more so now. While certain individuals are eager to clear up persistent issues, their efforts to discuss these matters are only making things worse. Forget discussions. Instead, make it clear how much they mean to you.

Frustrated by the same tedious task? Get others involved. Do it faster, better

You

One of your greatest characteristics is loyalty. When you believe in something or somebody, you will stick with them through thick and thin. However, the difficulty is, you assume they feel the same. And if they don't behave the way you expect them to, you are not only disappointed, you can get angry—except, of course, the individual in question won't understand why.

This is also one of your greatest journeys as an Aries, and one of your biggest life lessons— to recognize that the intensity of the way you are with others, or an organization, or perhaps a profession, can be overwhelming. It is also about how you negotiate. You can talk things over and in doing so, you will not only resolve those issues, you'll learn a lot about yourself. It is said life is a journey. And for you, that journey has to do not so much with finding that balance, because life is always changing, but with discovering the fact that sometimes you go so far toward the edge, others can't understand where you're coming from.

Begin to talk that over with others and you'll have some of the most important discussions of your life, and find yourself coming close enough to the center that you'll be able to establish warm and stable relationships in your personal life, your romantic life, your working life—and most of all, with yourself.

You and others

Achieving a balance in close relationships is a challenge, and could become one of your greatest skills. You will not only learn patience with those who are frustrating, you will discover that, often, they are a mirror for many of your characteristics. Recognize that, and even serous clashes with others will turn into incredibly useful lessons.

Health and well-being

You want to feel great but are sometimes so overwhelmed you can barely think, still less be enthusiastic. The trick? Make a few changes, health-wise. Find something fun, yet physically challenging along with others. Then do it regularly. A few weeks of that regimen and you will be a new person.

Goals and challenges

For you as an Aries, life is always full of challenges. That's the way you like it. If everything was easy or predictable, you would be bored. Yet for you, choosing the right challenge for the right time is a complex skill—one you will be learning to understand every day of your life.

THIS DAY FOR EVERYBODY

Few things upset you more than being forced to disappoint somebody else. It's not only troubling, you'll find it difficult to discuss the matter in question, so are tempted not to mention it at all. That's understandable. Still, you're urged to talk things over, in detail, and the sooner, the better.

GIFTS Passionate, Motivated, Warm

CHALLENGES Rash, Stubborn, Impatient

NUMBER 2

(2+6) + (3) = 11 = (1+1) = 2

If your goals seem distant, set new ones. For now. Make them challenging but possible

You

You sometimes wonder why people aren't as enthusiastic about life as you are. Of course, it comes naturally to you. But you have a tendency to assume that everybody has it, and they don't. It's for this reason that you also feel frustrated because others don't respond in the way that you hope or expect they will when you are talking about what you're doing, or something you can do with them, or even when you're asking about what they are up to. The important thing to remember about this is that it's not about right or wrong, although there are certain people who will criticize you for being as enthusiastic as you are about life.

It's about being who you are and being true to you. And if someone isn't particularly enthusiastic about a certain activity, or even about spending time with you, it doesn't matter; you can move on. And that's the other skill that you'll be developing during your life: to carefully pick and choose those who you spend time with and the activities you pursue. Just because you're excited about something doesn't mean you need to commit to it for months, or even years. And it's the same with a person. The skill of choosing what and who suits you is a skill that you will be developing every day of your life. One at which you'll be getting better every day. And one that will allow you to enjoy life all the more every day.

You and others

Being a spontaneous fire sign, the idea of carefully selecting the people you hang out with seems strange. Yet you've learned that while some people are fun and even challenge you, others seem more boring by the minute. Selecting the people you spend time with is just as crucial as how you eat and take care of yourself.

Health and well-being

Long ago you realized that you feel better when you eat wisely. Despite that, you occasionally rebel, only to discover that there's a price to pay for indulging yourself. The trick? Make a date to treat yourself a bit on some days, and continue being mindful on the others.

Goals and challenges

It may be that, when you were very young, setting a single, lifelong goal made sense. Since then, however, you've realized just how much there is to do and discover, and the more you fit into each day, the better it is. As an Aries, the more passions you have, the better.

THIS DAY FOR EVERYBODY

Somebody seems determined to corner you into doing something that will serve them well but not you. The real problem is that they haven't asked, thereby recognizing this as a favor. They are manipulating you into offering. Don't. Instead, address this frankly. You won't regret it.

Restless? Ask somebody what they really enjoy doing. Then learn it from them

You

For you, life is full of challenges, not in a negative sense, but it's the way you learn things. Whereas others will often run from challenges, you may ask them to join you in doing something new. To your amazement, they will say they actually aren't interested in altering certain elements of their lives. As an Aries, you were born to enjoy these challenges, to thrive on them. And sometimes they will last for years, or sometimes you'll learn what it is you need to know and move on.

Most of all, you need to recognize that not everybody will share those challenges with you. It's the same with your own activities in the world. It is important for you to find activities—personally and in your job—that allow you to do things in a new way. If not, you will quickly get tired of them, or perhaps it will be that in your personal life you'll find those challenges, even if your work is a bit predictable. You may just decide to reorganize things from time to time so that you are always learning something.

Whatever the case—and it can be different at different times in your life—for you, those challenges, those lessons in doing things in a new way, are like taking a very special variety of Aries vitamins. Once you've learned to do that, you'll not only benefit from it, you will want to do it for the rest of your life.

You and others

As an Aries, discovering that others think very differently from you can be a surprise, if not jarring. Tempting as it is to focus on those who are equally enthusiastic about life, often relationships thrive on contrast. In your case, learning to accept this with others and enjoy them for what they are is an art.

Health and well-being

While you can hurl yourself into certain activities, hoping they will make you stronger and healthier, sticking with it is another matter. Ideally, you should aim to have a variety of activities and, equally, a varied and interesting diet. That way, you can be indulgent on some days, then be more moderate over the next few.

Goals and challenges

The secret is not so much finding the single "right" goal or ambition, as having a series of them: some your current focus, others on the sidelines but by no means forgotten. Some involve other people, a few are yours alone to do. The one thing in common is your passionate feelings about them all.

MARCH

28

A
\
R
/
I
\
E
/
S

GIFTS Strong, Enthusiastic, Loyal

CHALLENGES Impatient, Sullen, Single-minded

NUMBER 4

$(2+8) + (3) = 13 = (1+3) = 4$

Always being told what to do? Irritated? Ask for a list. That'll change everything

You

You don't usually think of this, but you tend to take on more than you can realistically do. As a life enthusiast, anything difficult, new, or challenging is appealing to you. You'll say yes first, assuming you'll fit it into your schedule. While this means your life is rich, it can also be overwhelming, and either you don't have time to do things properly, or you are always catching up, so you're late for everything.

What's more, the idea of cutting back is unappealing. However, there is another approach and that is to pause every once in a while and do something out of character, which is to ask for help. Find a friend, family member, or even a professional who'll review your activities and calendar, and help you examine where your time and, possibly, money are going. This isn't just about practicalities, but where you invest your deepest feelings, and whether it is wise and worth it.

This is because you are also fiercely loyal and will sometimes stick with something simply because you made a commitment, when actually what you need is someone to suggest it's time to say farewell to that particular activity, ambition, or, indeed, relationship. And that is one of your biggest lessons in this life. It's not to pick and choose what you do, but to know when to say farewell to certain things so you can enjoy the rest all the more.

You and others

When you make a commitment to an activity, job, or individuals, whether it is family, loved ones, or even colleagues, you feel that this connection is an important one and you do everything you can to honor it. But others must earn your loyalty. No excuses and no discussion.

Health and well-being

Being able to enjoy life and its pleasures, and enjoy feeling and eating well, is important. However, it is easy for you to overdo things, then adopt an extremely tough regimen of diet and fitness. While balance doesn't come naturally, it is the secret. The trick here is to learn to say no, and at the right time.

Goals and challenges

If ever there were an individual who loves a challenge, it's you. And, what's more, you love achieving those goals. It's just that some of them don't mean as much to you as you thought they would, possibly long ago. It's okay to say no, to back out, and that's the big lesson for you today, and every day.

THIS DAY FOR EVERYBODY

What you are facing requires you to acknowledge the need to be patient, even while others are putting the pressure on to make things happen, and fast. Yet at the moment, you are questioning the idea things should be moving more swiftly. They will. But, for now, you are better off taking it slowly.

Stuck somewhere dull? Ask anybody, even a stranger, where you should go

You

One of your greatest characteristics is your zest for life. Of course, this comes with being an Aries and being ruled by Mars. However, your particular nature is such that it needs new challenges, some small, others bigger, but in every case, it is exciting for you to learn to do something, how to achieve a skill, or even how to have the kind of relationship you want. The trick to all of this, however, is to recognize that some things are simply skills. They aren't challenges and you don't need to put quite as much energy into them. You just need to figure out how to discern. And this is where those closest—family, friends, and even work colleagues—come in.

In the past, you wouldn't listen to their caution that maybe you were doing too much, hurling yourself into one activity. Finally, what you are learning to do is to begin to back off. That isn't just worthwhile, it means you will have time to explore other activities and perhaps even one or two challenges that will be rewarding. But most of all, it will give you time to be with those you care about most, to spend time with the number-one person in your life—you—but equally, with those who add to your life: family, friends, and colleagues whose company you enjoy. And rather than worrying about having to get somewhere, you will be able truly to relax with them.

You and others

It is rare that an Aries depends on another individual to fulfill his or her life. Caring passionately, about people and projects is normal. But putting yourself first is key. That is part of your lesson, and your journey. Do that, and work, live, and love intensely, yet retain that all-important link with your deepest inner self.

Health and well-being

Knowing what is in your best interests seems simple. Yet you complicate it with complex fitness routines and demanding diets. Being good to yourself should be simple, and once you have linked up with your inner wisdom, you will know exactly what to do. Until then, think carefully about whose ideas you embrace.

Goals and challenges

Some say that, ideally, you'll set challenges that are modest. However, not only is that completely out of character for you, if you talk to friends, you will find they are amazed and impressed by what you do on a daily basis. If you like the idea of a challenge, go for it. But knowing it won't prove anything to anybody.

THIS DAY FOR EVERYBODY

Few things are more rewarding than having struggled with difficult people and coming up with a plan that works for everybody. The good news is, that is what you've done. The bad news is, these arrangements will change—before you can regard anything as settled for good.

GIFTS Loving, Dynamic, Spontaneous

CHALLENGES Brash, Unbending, Impatient

NUMBER 6

(3+0) + (3) = 6

Unsure about your life goals? Maybe there is more than one on a path of self-discovery

You

It has always fascinated you when somebody lives in the same home for their whole life, if they have the same job and don't even think about changing it, or they have a particular hobby they stick with—or a combination of all of these. As an Aries, you are passionate about life, and sometimes even you will stick with a single, lifelong passion, but one side of your nature thrives on new experiences that stretch you in a way that is important to you. While you enjoy meeting people and learning about them—and about new ideas—you can get lost in it. You then have to find your way back to yourself.

As an Aries and a fire sign, passion is in your nature. What's more, you are generous, and if someone's struggling or in need, you'll do what you can. In trying to help others, though, you sometimes forget your own needs—home, family, loved ones, or, quite possibly, your work—or you may be avoiding something that you don't enjoy doing.

Your challenge is to balance the two—maintaining that wonderful generous streak, but instead of struggling to ensure that others are happy and to keep up with your own commitments, you'll find you are able to enjoy life in a way you have never really done before. It's an art, but most of all, it will be the greatest gift you could give yourself.

You and others

Finding balance in close alliances, at home and out in the world, is important but can also be challenging. Often, the biggest lesson involves somebody who's your exact opposite. Where you're obsessive and impatient, they're easygoing. This can be at home with family or friends, or out in the world. Achieving this balance is one of life's greatest gifts.

Health and well-being

For many (but not all) Aries, taking care of yourself—that is, your physical well-being and eating well—isn't of particular interest, which is itself an important challenge. The trick to doing it is to keep it simple, but make it exciting, and ideally make it part of your life with others.

Goals and challenges

Goals are easy to define. However, overcoming obstacles is another matter. Instead of battling them, the trick is to define them very clearly, which, as an impatient Aries, annoys you. Tackle this now, and not only will you learn a lot, better yet, what you learn will be an asset for the rest of your life.

THIS DAY FOR EVERYBODY

Some problems can be defined and dealt with swiftly, and then put behind you. However, those you're currently facing are more complex than they seem and so could take days to put to rest. Still, while this will require considerable patience, it will be justified by the result you achieve.

GIFTS Joyous, Strong, Forthright

CHALLENGES Headstrong, Overzealous, Unbending

NUMBER 7

(3+1) + (3) = 7

Are you often late or do you forget something? Try showing up unexpectedly, but with gifts

You

There are two ways of viewing your nature. One is that you're flexible, and adapt swiftly to new and even very unexpected developments. While that means you are comfortable with the twists and turns of modern life, you're also easily bored. So when those around you—family, friends, or colleagues—settle into a routine, you're restlessly looking for something new. Of course, as a fire sign, this is natural.

Still, there is a secret to dealing with this. It's to allow yourself to be swept away by the moment you're in, that is, what you are doing and whoever you are with. You'll either be thrilled by your enthusiasm, even with unfamiliar activities, or will recognize your deep, and touching, response to certain individuals. True, these experiences will be as unsettling as they are appealing, mostly because you've so valued your independence that previously you have brushed off any such feelings. This fresh perspective will shift your approach to the rest of life.

You may have been this passionately involved with your own pursuits, from your career to a challenging activity you enjoy, from sports to a game of bridge. However, this will trigger a top-to-bottom review of your priorities. What's more, because this can't be done in a day, you will find yourself asking questions about almost every area of your life.

You and others

As a fire sign, you have a well of passion waiting to be discovered. Certain situations or individuals will lead the way. And they will take a special place in your calendar, your priorities, and, possibly, your heart.

Health and well-being

Action makes you feel powerful. But learning from others touches your heart. If you slow your pace enough, soon you'll adore time spent in activities and with people who, previously, you barely noticed.

Goals and challenges

You have a restless and inquisitive mind. It needs to be kept busy, ideally with suitable challenges. Physical fitness is okay, but regular mental workouts will do the trick

THIS DAY FOR EVERYBODY

You have been battling with certain individuals about important details. Now that you're looking back, you are beginning to realize you were sidestepping the real issue. Deep down, you know what this is. The challenge is raising it. Once you do, everything else will be easy.

A
\
R
/
I
\
E
/
S

GIFTS Lively, Openhearted, Frank

CHALLENGES Rash, Obsessive, Demanding

NUMBER 5
_____
(1) + (4) = 5

Give yourself the challenge of surprising three people, in three wonderful ways, today

You

Being born on the first of the month brings a fresh energy to the world around you, into your life, and importantly, to your enthusiasm. You need to do things your way. That's typical, but this process of discovering your own approach to life isn't just exciting, it is almost as if you were an explorer on a ship sailing to the New World, and not sure what you were going to encounter. That sense of excitement and vitality fuels your life. Even if you are simply going around the corner to do something ordinary, you never know who you'll run into or what you'll discover. And that enthusiasm rubs off on others, which means that they in turn want to spend time with you. This is a great gift.

However, the lesson is to ensure that you channel your energy into something that doesn't just benefit others, but is also a benefit to you personally—in close relationships out in the world, in your job if you go to one, and in the activities you pursue—but even more than that, these benefits need to come through your feelings, your mind, your heart, and your soul. Because you're so busy thinking about things, you sometimes neglect to embrace those more subtle and more tender moments. The more you learn to do that each day, the more you'll enjoy the day itself and the days to come as well.

You and others

Finding perfect friends, a perfect relationship with family, a perfect way of dealing with others, is so important to you because there really is a belief that there's a kind of high that's possible. You've experienced it and you will want to experience it again. It's just that this comes and goes. And when it comes, it is a very special moment. And when it isn't there, it's important you realize it will come again.

Health and well-being

It's easy to say it is important to eat well. For you, it is simply because you're quite sensitive, and if you haven't had enough to eat, if your diet is out of balance, you can pay a price for it. If you eat too much sugar and then crash, you will struggle. If you don't eat enough, you will struggle, too. Finding a balance is important. It's the same with movement. A brisk walk each day will make all the difference.

Goals and challenges

Life for you is nothing without at least three goals to pursue every day and one challenge to overcome. When you find that and find the perfect balance, you'll also find it's as if you were taking the best vitamins in the world.

THIS DAY FOR EVERYBODY

When you decided to sidestep certain potentially upsetting issues, they were minor, so of little concern anyway. However, now that these are out in the open, you must be frank about your concerns but, also, seek advice. Brainstorm solutions together. You will be amazed how helpful others' ideas are.

Bored? Unsure what you enjoy? Ask what others do for fun, then explore together

You

For you as an Aries and somebody ruled by the passionate Mars, passion is itself a way of being. It is not something you simply feel from time to time.

However, you don't really think about this until you are around those who don't seem to be excited, much less passionate, about anything. Yet at the same time, these individuals are drawn to you because your warmth, your excitement, and your enthusiasm are almost like taking vitamins for them. While this is wonderful, it is also important that you provide your own passion in a way that satisfies you, not others. And it is finding that balance that is important for you.

Also, much of life, close relationships, your job if you go to one, varies every day. Tasks don't necessarily involve that feeling of passion, which means it is important that every day you ensure there's some component of it. Whether it is an activity you love, a variety of exercise that you enjoy, or music. That means a lot. That balance can change from day to day, but for you in particular, as an Aries thriving on this variety of passion, finding ways to fit it in is like finding the right vitamins to take. And once you are sure there is enough of that enthusiasm, passion, zest for life in some form in your life every day, then each day will be a joy.

You and others

You realize that some individuals will never be excited about certain activities—they don't have that kind of nature. They are happier just to sit comfortably and quietly. Hopefully, this means you have given up trying to create that excitement for them and discovered that despite this, often they're good company.

Health and well-being

Here, too, passion is important, but in this particular case, it's your own passion for your well-being, and for ensuring that over a period of time, you are eating well. Some people have an exact routine, but for most Aries, that is too boring. Besides, you need to change things around every once in a while. And it's the same with activities. Ensure that you have plenty to keep you going.

Goals and challenges

For you, a challenge a day is a kind of vitamin. It may be a small challenge or a big one, but the more you embrace these challenges regularly, the better you'll feel about the day, the week, the month, and your entire life.

THIS DAY FOR EVERYBODY

Obviously, you're in no mood to confess that when you withdrew from one particular arrangement, you were dishonest about the reason why. Your objective was to avoid hurting anybody's feelings. Now that everything has come out, you have to be frank. Still, you can speak from the heart.

A
\
R
/
I
\
E
/
S

GIFTS Energetic, Frank, Affectionate

CHALLENGES Single-minded, Hasty, Excitable

NUMBER 7

(3) + (4) = 7

I'll play a game with myself. How many dull tasks can I do before getting bored?

You

If you are familiar with astrology, you will know that you are ruled by the intense, passionate planet Mars, and that you're a fire sign as well, both of which indicate that you have an incredible zest for life. Of course, you don't really think about this most of the time, until you run into those individuals who don't share those qualities. You sometimes wonder what you can do to make life more exciting for them. And the answer is: nothing. They are who they are.

Acknowledging this isn't easy, but it is like acknowledging that certain people are blonde while others have dark hair, some are tall and others short. The trick is recognizing, then learning, to enjoy those differences. While your sheer enthusiasm for life is an amazing gift, it is yours. What you can learn is to enjoy those who are less easily excited or who prefer to live life at a slower pace. It may be family, it may be colleagues, or maybe it is someone you are close to.

Your romantic partner may be like that, and despite their slow pace, you still love them. In fact, it may well be that it is this slower pace and what it brings to your life that makes the relationship, whether it's personal, family, or even professional, so rewarding. Whatever its nature, know that this isn't about changing anybody, but about balance.

You and others

Some relationships are about enjoying time with others. However, for you, often they are an invitation to broaden your horizons in terms of the individuals in question. You are discovering new ways of experiencing life, together and individually. It is a challenging, powerful, and rewarding journey.

Health and well-being

Some say feeling your best is all about what you eat and how you exercise. For you, however, the emphasis is on communication: that is, understanding others. The more you discuss, the greater that understanding will be.

Goals and challenges

Nothing focuses your mind more than an exciting challenge. However, when you're short on facts or the circumstances are unclear, you can become so irritated that you find it impossible to be clear-minded. This is your greatest lesson—and challenge. Patience.

THIS DAY FOR EVERYBODY

Recently, you have struggled to keep certain long-standing arrangements going. And you've succeeded. Yet circumstances and your own priorities are shifting. While these changes are timely, they're also upsetting, because this means rethinking arrangements that, only recently, you struggled to keep going.

GIFTS Warm, Candid, Enthusiastic

CHALLENGES Stubborn, Brash, Self-centered

NUMBER 8

(4) + (4) = 8

Are you always complaining? Ask others to rate your complaints. You'll end up laughing

You

Some say that you were born into a particular sign for a reason; that is, if you are an Aries, you were born to discover the passion that comes with being a fire sign and to benefit from the energy associated with being ruled by the planet Mars. Yet at the same time, there is in every individual the need for balance within you as well. And your particular chart shows that, while it is essential you use your Aries enthusiasm to make the best of it. It is also important for you to discover that slower pace within you. This isn't just about living slowly, it's about being able to slow down so you can listen to and be with those you care about, whether it's family or loved ones, or even those out in the world—friends or colleagues.

This discovery of this slower pace will also enable you to rethink certain elements of your life that have been a source of frustration. You may have kept trying to make things work when actually they aren't meant to be that exciting. Or you may have tried to force them into being worthwhile when actually they aren't. And the greatest gift you could give to yourself is to let them go.

Whatever the case, and the situations will appear from time to time, being able to say farewell to something that doesn't suit you isn't just wise, it may be the nicest thing you can do for yourself.

You and others

It's unusual for an Aries to compare themselves to others, because being born under the first sign of the zodiac, you are always thinking about what you have done in the past, and your future goals. However, you care about those closest, and if they aren't happy, you worry. What means most to them is that you care. That, alone, is enough.

Health and well-being

Taking care of yourself may seem selfish, yet in order to be at your best, it's an important variety of selfishness. Think of that each day, and when you can't be bothered to eat properly, or do a little exercise, or get enough rest, recognize that not only is it a gift to you, it's a gift to others as well.

Goals and challenges

Finding the balance between generosity to others and taking care of yourself is one of your major challenges. However, because it's something you can control yourself, it is also something you can learn to resolve very quickly.

THIS DAY FOR EVERYBODY

A long time ago, your mind set on doing something, going somewhere, or achieving one particular goal. But, despite your efforts, you've achieved nothing. Frustrating as this is, it isn't about what you can actually do, but having a challenge that stirs you up. It's about getting you doing, not getting it done.

A
\
R
/
I
\
E
/
S

GIFTS Robust, Strong, Honorable

CHALLENGES Unbending, Impatient, Thoughtless

NUMBER 9

(5) + (4) = 9

When I am impatient, I'll make it a game to guess how long things will take

You

The theme for your birthday is discovery. What a wonderful theme to have, because it isn't about trying to keep things the same or even trying to make what you have better, it's about recognizing that your life is going to be peppered with all kinds of exciting discoveries. Some things you have been hoping for, others are unexpected.

If there's any challenge, it will be acknowledging those discoveries that you encounter as being important, which you should embrace. If you recognize these as something that will add to your life, then, when they arise, you'll explore them. But in some cases you're much more than this. They will add to your way of thinking, your way of living, maybe your way of working. But in each case, you'll be discovering something new. That's the key to it.

It's interesting because, as an Aries, you're inquisitive, but you can also be a creature of habit and can be rather impatient about having to learn new skills or new ways of doing things. Ironically, some of what you're learning may mean that you meet other people or have new experiences that will themselves be rewarding. And that, again, brings us back to the theme of discovery. Think about it in the past, acknowledge it in the present, and embrace it, and you will have a future full of delightful and rewarding discoveries.

You and others

You tend to want to share discoveries with others. Except each individual is here to learn their own lesson, to have their own experiences. And while there may be times when you're able to share them with those around you, just as often it is important that you enjoy them yourself.

Health and well-being

You will be surprised how unexpected events or encounters teach you new ways to take care of yourself: activities that are worth your while, ways to eat that benefit you. More than that, however, recognize that this is an ongoing part of your life, so there will be further discoveries over the coming days, months, weeks, and even years.

Goals and challenges

Making yourself number one is difficult for you, because you're generous by nature. But when you find that balance between taking care of yourself—and taking care of yourself first—and being generous with others, you will also find that you experience great satisfaction.

THIS DAY FOR EVERYBODY

Unsettling as the revelations you are facing may be, deep down you've known something is amiss. The real shock is the extent of issues and how secretive certain individuals were. From their perspective, this was wise. Yet the gulf between you is wide—so much so, it's unlikely you'll strike an accord.

Today I'll lend my focus and enthusiasm to somebody who needs a boost

You

For you, as an Aries, the secret to making the best of your nature is to make a point of learning from each day. That may sound strange because you learn from all of life. Yet in this particular case, it's about being much closer to the day's events in a way that might be more normal if you were born in the sign next to yours: Taurus, an earth sign, or Virgo, another earth sign, which are both very much into the details of the day, as opposed to the action, which is so much a part of your nature.

While by no means are you lacking the fiery nature of the Aries, you also need to pause, and pause regularly, to look at what you're doing each day. In doing so, you'll think about whether it could be better, whether you need to take a new path. That is important. And this isn't just about achieving what you want. It is also about the time you spend with those around you, whether it's friends or family, and what you're doing for yourself. It might be termed checking in with yourself regularly.

Make a habit of this and you'll find that not only do you achieve far more than you imagined you could each day, you'll also enjoy the day. You will be far more aware of what you have achieved, what has been a pleasure for you, and even those obstacles you have overcome. And each of those will put a smile on your face.

You and others

Often when dealing with others—family, colleagues, neighbors, or friends—it's about keeping the peace and getting along with them. But in your case, you feel the responsibility to keep them happy. While this is wonderful, and shows your generous nature, it is also tricky because some individuals don't want to be happy. Acknowledging that will be difficult for you, but once you actually do this, you'll find it a lot easier to deal with those around you.

Health and well-being

Tempting as it is to spoil others at the expense of your pleasures, finding those little pleasures every day isn't just important, it will add to your life in ways you can't imagine. And it's not just about pleasures in terms of what you eat, it is also the objects around you that add to your life, and even having things that you do, from exercises in a lovely setting to something that is equally rewarding.

Goals and challenges

You have a strange challenge, and that is to learn to be a little more self-centered. This is unusual for an Aries, but as you will be aware, it is an important one for you.

GIFTS Enthusiastic, Passionate, Spontaneous

CHALLENGES Driven, Relentless, Single-minded

NUMBER 2

$(7) + (4) = 11 = (1+1) = 2$

A
\
R
/
I
\
E
/
S

Are certain individuals bossy? Turn it around. Actually ask them to tell you what to do

You

Most Aries think and move swiftly. So swiftly, in fact, that often they won't catch the things that need to be reflected on, thought about, or analyzed. In your particular case, though, this variety of analysis is so rare in your sign that it doesn't come naturally. Sometimes you wonder and worry whether you might actually be missing something.

However, this also allows you to enjoy what you are achieving in a way that isn't common for those who were also born under the sign of Aries. This allows you to slow down. And if there is any challenge, it is being able to pick up and move swiftly when you need to, and to back off from that process of analysis.

Of course, you are ruled by the dynamic and courageous Mars. And if you let that side of you kick in at those times when you need to move quickly, to be dynamic, or possibly even courageous, if you allow Mars to take the lead, if you need to take a stand with somebody, then you will know exactly what to do.

But most of all, you might want to borrow an idea or a concept from the sign opposite yours—Libra—which is all about finding that balance, that analytical side, that helpful side with a passion that is so central to you being an Aries.

You and others

Often when people ask how you are, they don't care. Of course, you do care, and it is one of your greatest gifts. And others need to care about you. It's not that you're secretive, but it does mean that sometimes you need to let others know what's going on inside.

Health and well-being

Making the best of life has to do with its pleasures, but it also has to do with being in both the physical condition and state of mind that allow you to enjoy every day. Ironically, sometimes you can be a bit lazy about that, simply because your mind takes you elsewhere. One of the lessons for you is to turn taking care of yourself into a joy.

Goals and challenges

The passion that you have for life and for everything good is admirable, but sometimes you can take such a long time organizing things that you won't necessarily achieve what you want as swiftly as you might hope. However, if you bring a little Aries passion into that, things would happen more swiftly.

THIS DAY FOR EVERYBODY

The time has come to take a tough line with one particularly tricky individual. While you are usually able to sidestep their maneuvers or stage a diplomatic confrontation, neither of those has worked. Bizarre as it seems, the fact is, they want to talk things through, but are too shy to ask.

GIFTS   Truthful, Dynamic, Lively

CHALLENGES   Hasty, Unbending, Single-minded

NUMBER 3

(8) + (4) = 12 = (1+2) = 3

If you find you don't care about your goals, start making ones you are passionate about

You

If there is anything irritating for you—in the world around you, in the lives of others, and in your own life—it is that things seem to start and stop so much. As an Aries, and somebody ruled by the planet of focus and action—the fiery Mars—when you tackle something, it's natural for you to plunge in. And once you've plunged in, you expect to get things done. In fact, the most difficult thing for you in the world is to begin a task, whether it's something at home, involving a friend, or at work, and then be forced to stop. But every once in a while, you must. Being easygoing in this way is one of your biggest lessons in this life.

What's more, if you battle those situations, you either end up more frustrated or could actually make things more complicated. Instead, try going with the flow. Then you'll realize there are a lot of other things to pay attention to—to do and to enjoy. And that many of those you'd otherwise have missed out on will be a lot of fun, if not a real joy. This is the reason achieving a balance in your life is so important.

While your drive to get things done and to turn your goals into reality is important, focusing on enjoying what the moment offers is a big lesson for you. And what you learn will become increasingly rewarding, so make the best of it.

You and others

Sometimes you feel so impatient with certain individuals you want to explode. After that mood passes, you are more relaxed, and would do anything for them. Then, when you have time to talk and understand what they are struggling with, instead of being annoyed, you understand them much better.

Health and well-being

Few things make you feel better than getting out in the fresh air and moving swiftly. But, frustratingly, that's not always possible. The secret is to find minor ways to achieve that same feeling, wherever you are, and even when there is not much time. It is challenging, but feels terrific when you manage it.

Goals and challenges

When you know what you're going after, there is no stopping you. However, when your options—or worse, your own priorities—are unclear, making decisions can be complicated. True, you could act on impulse. Take time to ensure your decisions are wise ones.

There has been talk of changes in the circumstances of somebody close to you, events that would be as disruptive as they might be exciting. While so far, nothing has happened, suddenly things are moving swiftly. However unsettling this is in the short term, it is in everyone's best interest.

A
\
R
/
I
\
E
/
S

GIFTS Passionate, Forthright, Loving

CHALLENGES Fixed, Demanding, Self-involved

NUMBER 4

(9) + (4) = 13 = (1+3) = 4

Stuck with somebody boring? Ask what is magical in their life. Their answer will amaze you

You

If there is a single lesson for you, Aries, it is summed up in the phrase "less is more." It has long been said that living simply is both wise and a virtue. What's more, there is a growing passion for decluttering.

But this is about more than that. It is actually about recognizing that sometimes what you're already doing or what you have is plenty. Despite that, this can be challenging for you as an Aries, a fire sign, and somebody who thrives on a challenge, because you want something more to do, and often that will translate into creating or acquiring more of what you already have.

The lesson for you, though, is to pause and recognize what you have and enjoy, then to begin to explore. And this is where it can be tricky because again, for you as an Aries and someone who is both passionate by nature and impatient, you'll be eager to do, acquire, or achieve what you have in mind right away.

However, the trick is to take it slowly. Ordinarily, this alone would be frustrating for you. The idea of allowing things to unfold at their own pace is seriously aggravating. The trick? Finding a balance. Do that, and you'll benefit from it in ways you couldn't have imagined possible. And that is the path to joy for you in this particular life, as the very special kind of Aries that you are.

You and others

Often, you're the most enthusiastic person in a relationship, and consequently, whatever its nature—whether it's family, romance, or career—you'll probably be taking the lead. Yet, it's important that you encourage others to express their views or take action, even if their pace is slower than yours.

Health and well-being

The tendency to want to do things with others is so strong in your birthday chart that you'll want to match up to the joys and desires of others. Whether it is the way they like to eat or exercise, it's about teamwork, except you are very much an individual, which means learning to pursue that. Sharing joys is a great art.

Goals and challenges

Sharing life is a gift, and this is a gift that you have. Being true to yourself while you're sharing that life is the challenge for you. Once you learn how to do it, not only will this challenge become a joy, you'll find that you're all the closer to others in your life as well.

THIS DAY FOR EVERYBODY

You have no problem airing your views. And, if challenged, will still make an effort to ensure others understand what's behind those convictions. However, certain individuals are in a tricky mood. So be careful what you say, or minor differences could turn into a major, and completely unnecessary, blowup.

GIFTS Impulsive, Loyal, Generous

CHALLENGES Rash, Impatient, Excitable

NUMBER 5

(1+0) + (4) = 5

Set up a challenge a week and see how exciting life becomes

You

Being born the tenth of any month, which is numerologically a "1" day, underlines the importance of doing things by yourself. This by no means indicates you'll be tackling them solo, but it does mean you must do what is of significance to you. While that can't always be the case due to obligations to family, work, friends, and yourself, at the same time you can find certain activities that are rewarding or mean a great deal to you. These can have to do with your physical well-being and with developing new, and rewarding, challenges. It might be that you decide to become so skilled at a particular pursuit, you will know you've achieved something. It could involve a range of activities; and while it is your decision, it may be something that's visible to others or something you're doing quietly, on your own.

This balance between taking action and getting others involved is always shifting, and those changes are of significance in your relationships. You may not actually discuss this with others. However, the fact you are doing something because it's important to you will substantially alter the way you deal with others and, interestingly, mean you're more easygoing with them and enjoy their company more. What's more, you'll feel less pressure to do things your way just to show you are in control, and that alone will bring you huge joy.

You and others

As a fire sign, you're okay with life's ups and downs, although living with constant tension with others isn't easy. Yet certain individuals like it that way. Acknowledging this seems like a defeat until you realize their problems aren't yours to resolve. It's not about what others think or do, it's about what you do for you.

Health and well-being

You have a tendency to put off taking care of yourself, physically and even the way you eat—your excuse being it can wait until everything else has been dealt with, and everybody else is happy. That will be a long wait. The best approach? Make taking care of yourself your priority now.

Goals and challenges

You realize that your biggest goal is to put yourself first. As an Aries, this is not unusual, because being born under the first sign of the zodiac, you know this kind of individuality comes naturally. But in your case, it is a skill you'll be developing for much of your life.

THIS DAY FOR EVERYBODY

Life would be a lot easier if you could make decisions about certain complex situations, then turn those into lasting plans. However, with the foundation on which these are based shifting so swiftly and dramatically, the more flexible your thinking and your long-term vision, the better.

11

A
\
R
/
I
\
E
/
S

GIFTS Frank, Unconventional, Sincere

CHALLENGES Single-minded, Stubborn, Abrupt

NUMBER 6

(1+1) + (4) = 6

Do you sometimes annoy others? Make it a game. Ask what you can change

You

As an Aries, you were born to face challenges. That may sound like you're in for struggles, but it is the reverse. You are enthusiastic, if not obsessive, by nature about what you want to do. Having been born under this passionate fire sign, you have a gift for turning merely good ideas into something exciting, and equally, overcoming obstacles. Your challenge? Carefully selecting your obsessions. At times you get so involved in something or with somebody that it becomes central to your life.

Only later do you realize that either it is impossible or, if you achieved your goal, it wouldn't be nearly as rewarding as you hoped. This may have to do with an activity, a relationship, or even your physical well-being. But in every situation, it's vital that you pause and consider whether what seems so important to you now will mean as much next month or next year.

Once you're looking at life from a clearer perspective, you will also be able to view many other elements with a new clarity. And this won't just enable you to spot but also consider ending the pursuit of aims or goals that are unrewarding. It will enable you to recognize just how much you've already achieved and how, if you invest more time, energy, thought, and, indeed, heart into those activities, how much richer life will be as the years unfold.

You and others

Finding a balance in relationships is difficult for anybody. But it is particularly the case for you, as an intense and passionate Aries. You will often put others, and their needs, first, and in a way that is out of balance. While relationships are always in flux, one of your biggest lessons is focusing on that balance.

Health and well-being

Looking out for your well-being is an important journey for you. However, unless you consciously decide it will be fun, it could seem seriously dull. Finding a way to make it exciting may take a while, but you will. And, what's more, the results will more than justify the effort you've made.

Goals and challenges

For you, life is dull without challenges, but it is important that they aren't just challenging physically, but that they also lift your spirits. Simply defining that is itself a challenge. But that's the point. Each day and each step will add to your knowledge, and that increases your joy in what you're doing and achieving.

 THIS DAY FOR EVERYBODY

Be watchful of conversations about certain tricky issues. One or two individuals are trying to measure, then compare, the sincerity of others. While this will never work, they need to discover it for themselves. Until then, back off and leave them to their debates, while you busy yourself elsewhere.

GIFTS Affectionate, Loving, Generous

CHALLENGES Excitable, Fixed, Reckless

NUMBER 7

(1+2) + (4) = 7

Learn to make tasks fun. Then you'll be able to enjoy anything and everything

A
\
R
/
I
\
E
/
S

You

As an April 12th Aries, facing challenges isn't so much what you want to do, but each experience strengthens both your identity and confidence. The trick? Finding a balance between your capacity to face those challenges, in your life and the world you are living in, and being able to relax. It is about knowing when to pause. That may sound strange in situations where you felt frustrated. This isn't because of your success or failure, but because your expectations were very different from the actual circumstances.

Yet one of your greatest gifts is your ability to ignore restrictions. Many Aries achieve a great deal doing that, whether it's climbing peaks—both literal, such as mountains, or in business—or creating a happy family under difficult circumstances.

But in your particular case, the trek's about situations where you'll need to be aware that making changes requires you to be persistent. This is also about personal goals, especially being close with others. Sometimes you are a bit impatient, because certain individuals don't understand how much you care about your plans or their ideas differ from yours.

However, the resulting discussions will not only be enormously rewarding, they will also deepen your connection with the individuals in question.

You and others

So often in life, you've wondered if you and those around you were speaking the same language. As an Aries, you're passionate about what you want to do, and about connecting with others, and you are sometimes impatient, because others act at their own, usually slower, pace. The challenge? Being patient.

Health and well-being

Waking up brimming with energy is fabulous. However, that can be complicated. There are all sorts of ways to make this happen, but you get distracted. Or bored. The trick? Do things that boost your energy, well-being, and spirits, and change your routine frequently. This won't just make you feel better, you'll be creating a valuable, and lifelong, habit.

Goals and challenges

Keeping life interesting is no challenge. There is always something or somebody to deal with. Your problem? Once you have dealt with that challenge, major or minor, you need to pause to enjoy your victory and congratulate yourself. This seems pointless, but those good feelings are a variety of essential emotional vitamins, to be taken daily.

THIS DAY FOR EVERYBODY

In raising certain persistent issues, your intention is to speak from the heart. However, the resulting discussions could easily slip into the type of brutally frank exchanges you dread. Tempting as it is to avoid these, don't. Actually, they won't just be timely, they will do wonders to clear the air.

A
\
R
/
I
\
E
/
S

GIFTS Candid, Vivid, Enthusiastic

CHALLENGES Edgy, Unrelenting, Brash

NUMBER 8

(1+3) + (4) = 8

Want to be the best at something but struggling? Tackle another challenge. Then try again

You

As you know, as an Aries, you can be impulsive. In fact, that us one of your greatest gifts: the ability to think and act swiftly and to be authentic and true to yourself whatever the situation. Yet at the same time, there is a tremendous emphasis on the practical side of life and on the doubts that acting with passion raises. This discussion and the resulting process of exploration—either to justify your decisions to yourself, or to explain your thoughts to others—may seem annoying, but, intriguingly, it will bring you closer to others.

The trick, therefore, is not to find the swiftest answer, but to delve deeply, and then to talk with those closest, whether it's family, friends, or possibly even in a work setting. It doesn't matter where. This will go on in various ways, in various elements of your life. And in each case, what you learn when doing it will help you understand yourself better, your priorities better, and it will also deepen the relationship.

Even more than that, this will bring a certain joy to exploring situations that you once might have regarded as almost explosive. While at one point you might be right, now, as you learn more about who you are and about how to discuss even very sensitive matters, you will not only enjoy those discussions, you will deepen the resulting relationships as well.

You and others

As in Aries, you're all or nothing. When you care, it is total, and you're both honest with others and support them, whatever. When there are differences, though, or you can't be there for them, you worry. Sometimes letting go and believing others will survive without you is the challenge. Being there or not, what is most important is how much you care.

Health and well-being

You will sometimes hurl yourself into a diet or exercise with admirable enthusiasm. The problem? Often this doesn't last, because the program in question didn't suit you personally. So you got bored. The secret is recognizing that while many activities are worth your while, you need to search for the right ones.

Goals and challenges

Being comfortable with yourself is essential for you, because it affects your confidence. This creates the foundation for your worldly success at a job, or with plans or projects. Each day will bring progress. Rejoice in this broader, more exciting world, and the powerful insights it brings about the future.

THIS DAY FOR EVERYBODY

Recently, you've not only discussed matters that, at one point, you'd never have dared even mention, you have learned a great deal. Tempting as it is to withdraw and mull things over, you're far better off keeping the lines of communication open. Amazingly, you'll soon begin to enjoy those frank exchanges.

Turn boring commitments into a game. Figure out how to make them fun

You

By nature, you're self-sufficient. Your ruling planet is the powerful Mars, which means you tend to feel it is your duty to deal with everything that comes your way. You are actually really good at that. What's more, you enjoy overcoming challenges, because this process broadens your horizons and you learn about new people, situations, and settings. Even more, it is a measure of your capacity to handle all such matters. Yet certain elements of your life are so important to you, if issues involve them, you will worry—a lot. You will be concerned about doing things right, about the impact of plans on circumstances, or about upsetting others.

And this is the big lesson for you—to understand that the passion you bring to any situation is important, but if you make decisions based on the past, then you are only complicating your life. The trick? It's to shift your focus from managing the present, the here and now, to focusing on the future.

This is especially important for you as an Aries, because you feel it is so important to act swiftly. But if you take a deep breath and reflect slowly on your options, extending your thinking into the future, your perspective will change. And, instead of acting swiftly—but, possibly, unwisely—you will act slowly and with wisdom.

You and others

Sometimes those around you are seriously upset about your plans or ideas. Ordinarily, you would say nothing but proceed, knowing success wins others over faster than words. Still, at times, you have no choice but to listen to others' concerns. What they say is one thing, but a serious exchange of ideas matters even more. The secret? Truly listen to what others are thinking, You'll learn a lot.

Health and well-being

You're happily involved in what you're doing and enthusiastic about life. You are so busy that you don't notice you're tired. Or, because you're living at a swift pace, you forget to eat. That results in a mood that is difficult for you and others. It is easy to forget about these things. But remember, and the rewards are huge.

Goals and challenges

There are many varieties of success. Some are about achieving goals of your own, those at work, or affecting others. You can get so involved in these, you neglect to set your own goals, from each day being a joy to achieving your own personal successes. These goals matter most of all.

THIS DAY FOR EVERYBODY

By being aware of what others are dealing with—sometimes more than they are themselves—but also conscious of the rapid rate of change reshaping so many situations, you have been doing a lot of juggling. Now, however, your maneuvers need to be discussed, and soon.

GIFTS Strong, Spontaneous, Dynamic

CHALLENGES Thoughtless, Rigid, Hasty

NUMBER 1

$(1+5) + (4) = 10 = (1+0) = 1$

Is somebody boring? Ask them questions until you discover amazing facts about them

You

For you, life is a juggling act, trying to balance everything you have achieved and the resulting demands on your time versus the dream of getting rid of it all so you can pause and take a deep breath. These extremes are typically Aries. Juggling your time, having too much that's exciting going on, is typical. Yet there is a remedy other than making everything go away because you are overwhelmed. It's how you deal with it.

As an Aries and a fire sign, ruled by Mars, you are dynamic by nature. You were designed for ongoing excitement. The trick, however, is to know what form that excitement will take, how you will employ that energy, and how you can benefit from your actions. And, equally, you will learn when you need to slow down and cut back on your commitments. This is the tricky thing, because "doing less" doesn't come naturally to you.

This is one of your greatest lessons. First, knowing when you need to slow down. Second, learning how to pause, think about what's next, and decide whether what you're doing would truly be in your best interest. And it's also about cutting back, possibly letting go of familiar plans or even passions. Achieve this balance now, and you will be able to live it out every day. And that is one of the greatest goals for you.

You and others

Your passion for life is natural. You are intense, sometimes overwhelmingly so, even for you. But reducing that vibe isn't easy. And finding common ground between you and others can be challenging. However, it is possible. And doing so will enable you to spend stress-free time with others, from family to close friends or colleagues.

Health and well-being

You want projects to succeed instantly. That includes taking care of yourself, from working out to watching what you eat. And if you aren't successful, you give up. Your challenge? Being patient, but also finding ways to take care of yourself that excite you and you enjoy. Do that, and the rest will be much easier.

Goals and challenges

Some goals can be achieved swiftly. But, as you're well aware, others take much longer. The secret for you is to line up short-term objectives when you're facing something that requires patience, but which you really care about. That simple strategy is the difference between enjoyment and frustration.

THIS DAY FOR EVERYBODY

Certain individuals or, possibly, destiny itself, are trying to take over. Your plans have been disrupted, if not radically changed, and more than once. It may seem you are alone in these struggles. But look around you, and you'll soon realize you're not alone. Everybody is facing similar difficulties.

You can make joy your best friend. It's all about how you decide to live your day—and life

You

Making compromises is difficult for any Aries. It seems as if you are undermining your convictions as an individual. Yet you long ago learned that, in certain situations, your refusal to compromise will only create complications in your plans and, sometimes, life. The challenge is finding a balance between the two. This has to do with how you live, how you think, and even your personal style.

Yet at the same time, you're generous by nature and if what you do makes others unhappy, then you'll work hard to remedy the situation. The trick in all of this is to borrow a characteristic from the sign opposite yours, Libra, and find a balance between your passion for life and your impatience over a willingness to allow others to take the time they need. It's about each understanding the other better. While this is important in close relationships, it is an amazing tool when it comes to life in general. As a fire sign, you rarely struggle with the twists and turns or unexpected events that trouble others. You recognize them as an invitation to experience or learn something new, even if that isn't always clear at the time. And that is the skill in learning to slow down and communicate with others at their pace. Make that your objective and not only will you learn a great deal, you'll enjoy the process.

You and others

One of your greatest challenges is also one of your greatest gifts. That is your ability to inspire others yet also stand up to them. The challenge is recognizing the line between the two. The solution? When you discuss such matters, learn to listen more and talk less. It won't be easy, but it will change everything.

Health and well-being

Sometimes your concerns about things not going as swiftly as they should emerge as being uptight, if not short-tempered with others. This undermines your own well-being. The solution? Back off. Chill. It's the reverse of your instincts, but can improve your mood and lead to inspired solutions as well.

Goals and challenges

Even when you're living life to the fullest, when you have what you want, achieved what you desire, you still have a tendency to want to reinvent things. And that process can steal the joy from the here and now. The way to overcome it? Simply be in the moment, and rejoice in those achievements.

THIS DAY FOR EVERYBODY ⑦

You could easily misinterpret the change in attitude or plans, or perhaps both, by one particular individual as no more than a bad mood, one from which they'll recover swiftly. Actually, they have misunderstood something you said or did. This isn't serious but needs attention, and the sooner, the better.

GIFTS Loving, Dynamic, Strong

CHALLENGES Hasty, Irritable, Passionate

NUMBER 3

(1+7) + (4) = 12 = (1+2) = 3

Make bringing happiness to three other people your project. Then see what happens

You

For you as an April 17th Aries, energy and enthusiasm are your bywords. Yet despite thriving on it, life itself is a stop-and-go affair, and the resulting changes in pace are as sudden as they are unexpected. It's about observing these rhythms. Some are predictable: days and nights, and even more, the seasons of the year, in which nature reminds us about timing.

For you, it's about allowing certain plans, arrangements, and passions to develop at their own pace. This doesn't come naturally to you. Being a fire sign and ruled by the dynamic Mars, your impatience is understandable. Yet one of your lessons is to accept nature's pace and, equally, that projects won't always move at the rate you're planning. The solution? Learn to allow things to grow, and at their own pace. This isn't just important, it is vital.

If you had a vegetable garden, you couldn't pull up a carrot to see if it had grown yet. Instead you'd have to learn to observe its growth. And you'd simply have to wait. In the same way, in certain other elements of your life, you are learning to allow things to grow. Once you understand the process, you will not only enjoy it, and the people involved as well, you will want to do more of it, because that understanding of allowing things to grow, in a garden and in life, is one of the greatest gifts anybody can be given.

You and others

Often when dealing with others, the question isn't what they're doing, but why they are avoiding certain situations—some that involve you, but as many that do not. This question links to a frequent irritation with friends, family, and, if you work, close colleagues. And that is: why do they take so long discussing or dealing with things? There's a simple answer. They're not you. They're not an Aries. Simple.

Health and well-being

As a fire sign, you thrive on life lived in the fast lane. Thinking and moving swiftly are your strengths. The problem? Circumstances aren't always in a cooperative mood, and delays are inevitable. The solution? Don't push. Do something out of character and cool it. This may seem a compromise, until you realize options beyond anything you'd imagined possible have appeared from nowhere.

Goals and challenges

It's said that the greatest advice given to anybody is also the simplest. Be. Here. Now. For you, as an Aries, that can be very difficult, because most of the time your mind is focused on "there": that is, where you're going and not the present. That is your greatest challenge, and achieving it will be your greatest gift.

 THIS DAY FOR EVERYBODY

You've been nursing certain long-cherished plans, ideas, or alliances that once held promise but are increasingly burdensome. Difficult as saying farewell to these would be, the moment you let go of them, you'll create space in your life for the thrilling events or ideas waiting in the wings.

Don't give up on tough tasks. It will be great remembering how you battled to do them

You

Balancing enthusiasm and optimism with concerns or even pessimism is tricky. Of course, you expect your efforts to go well. And because you are full of that marvellous Aries energy, often they do. Yet there are periods when bad timing, minor obstacles, or serious challenges force you to rethink arrangements. However, instead of recognizing that changes are necessary, you could get upset or even back off as if you're almost demanding that nature find a remedy.

The trick? Acknowledge that you are in a period that is forcing you to both slow your pace and rethink things, not just those plans but, possibly, life in general. You could battle those changes or, instead, recognize that something new and exciting, but as yet unknown to you, is developing behind the scenes. You need to recognize, and embrace, nature's pace.

Next, it's about freeing yourself from the past so you can embrace those changes as they take form. You could struggle or embrace this process. If it's the latter, you'll recognize this as the adventure it is. What's more, you'll be in the here and now, and enjoy what you have, without tinkering with things just to keep yourself busy. Take this approach, and without doing a thing you will discover a whole new world in the present.

You and others

There are times in life when you haven't just been overenthusiastic, you've almost bullied others into feeling the way you do. Then you wondered why they were grumpy. This is a real Aries challenge: sometimes your enthusiasm overwhelms others. Still, that shows how much you care. And that's what's important.

Health and well-being

The trick to feeling wonderful is twofold. One is to take care of your physical body, which you do with enthusiasm, but can also forget to do. However, being happy in your head is mostly the result of being contented with life as it is, even if things aren't going as swiftly as you want or you have to rethink plans. Finding that balance is a challenge and a gift.

Goals and challenges

The most important thing for you as an Aries to discover is that life is full of exciting challenges, most of which are goals, but in disguise. Once you discover that, you will think carefully about what the outcome will be. And if you are happy with it, you will hurl yourself into dealing with those challenges, and the sooner, the better.

THIS DAY FOR EVERYBODY

You're eager to take a break from the rather intense discussions of the past few days. But you've learned so much, not only about where others stand on certain matters, but also your own perspective has changed. Continue to talk things through. The results will amaze you.

Taurus

Ruler Venus
Element Earth

Symbol The Bull
Flower Orchid

April 19–
May 19

Taurus   Sensuality and practicality are fundamental to you as a Taurus, the first of the earth signs. While its ruling planet, Venus, accents life's pleasures, it's also about assets, which means you are a gracious individual who lives both well and wisely. That's reflected in your flower, the orchid, and your aromatic spices—cloves and sorrel. Your tree is crab apple, while your stones reflect Venus's pastel shades in both jade and emerald.

T
/
A
\
U
/
R
\
U
/
S

APRIL

19

T
/
A
\
U
/
R
\
U
/
S

Instead of questioning the unexpected, I embrace it with enthusiasm

You

As somebody born under the first day of your sign, you could be termed pure Taurus. You benefit from all of the assets of your sign, but are occasionally bewildered by the rest of the world, especially those who don't see things the way you do. As an earth sign, you're practical and benefit from an ability to enjoy life. And, equally, you have a strong sense of beauty. You appreciate it in life, in food, even in the character of others. What's more, you have a gift for bringing joy to those around you.

This, in turn, benefits your relationships, from family to personal and even more worldly links. Your gift for enjoying the physical side of life extends from your own body to an appreciation of movement and music, possibly even dancing. And then there's food, and often amazing gardens. If there's any challenge, it is differences with others.

You're often puzzled that the values and interests of certain individuals are so at odds with yours. Once that is clear, even challenging relationships with others, and your own comfort with yourself, will grow enormously. We're all here to grow. And one of your most important journeys as someone born under the first day of Taurus is being able truly to savor the influence of your ruling planet, the harmonious Venus, and bring love, joy, and pleasure into your life.

You and others

Venus, your ruling planet, accents harmony in all relations, from family and loved ones to friends and even colleagues. You're not casual about any of them. But it is confusing when others seem determined to do things that provoke clashes. Learning to understand each other is a valuable part of your journey.

Health and well-being

Because Venus accents beauty and abundance, you can sometimes overdo these. The trick? Take care of yourself, but do it luxuriously, whether it's in a gym, on a walk, or dancing. Balance the luscious food you enjoy with activity you love, and you will fit into the beautiful clothing you enjoy as well.

Goals and challenges

For you, once life is organized the way you want, you like to keep it that way. Consequently, sudden events that upset arrangements can be annoying. But not only are these changes vital, they encourage you to rethink what you enjoy and make improvements where they are needed.

THIS DAY FOR EVERYONE

Mostly, you enjoy tackling issues as a team. Yet you're uneasy about trusting certain individuals. This is mostly because you are in unfamiliar territory, so feeling anxious in general. As with all feelings, however, these will pass. Knowing that, get involved, but adopt an uncharacteristically slow pace.

GIFTS Generous, Luxury-loving, Scent-aware

CHALLENGES Uncompromising, Stubborn, Immoderate

NUMBER 6

$(2+0) + (4) = 6$

Increasingly, I recognize the unexpected drawing me into rewarding experiences

You

All Taureans are ruled by the planet Venus, and in fact, your birthday honors Venus, which is named after the beautiful goddess that signifies all of life's joys and pleasures—everything from scent to flowers to eating well. But it also accents what you own and earn, money and any assets.

What's more, the typical Taurean is interested in collecting, but not just anything. It's about acquiring knowledge that expands your appreciation and understanding of what you're collecting. This may not involve objects; it could focus on a garden or a skill. The most important thing is the pleasure they give you. It is the same with close alliances—with those you care about. It's not so much what you might call the quality of the character of the individual, but the place they hold in your life and what you give back to them.

And this is one of your greatest gifts and skills as a Taurus, and somebody ruled by charming Venus. It is not until you observe the behavior of others that you recognize that, often, people simply don't know how to share the experience of being together. For you, it's not only your special gift, it's one you can share generously with others: that is, family, friends, and your broader circle—something that improves your life and theirs and, ultimately, in some ways, the world.

You and others

While spending time relaxing with family and friends is important, it is just as vital that special individuals bring something new into your life. Part of your nature thrives on discovery, on the magic of broadening your horizons. This is linked to your birthday, so it isn't just special; these experiences are like vitamins that supercharge your life.

Health and well-being

You wouldn't necessarily think of health and well-being and sensuality in the same phrase. But for you especially, and your sensual Taurus nature, pleasure in the process is as important as the result. Once you discover how to turn achieving your objectives into a joyous endeavor, the rest is easy.

Goals and challenges

The trick to transforming challenges into a game involves exactly that: finding the fun in them. While, initially, this may not be easy for you, instead of dwelling on getting things done because you must, try focusing on the joy of discovery. Do that, and each task will become exactly that—a joy.

GIFTS Well-presented, Sensual, Loving

CHALLENGES Selfish, Willful, Inflexible

NUMBER 7

(2+1) + (4) = 7

Each time I say "No," I explore what a "Yes" would bring my way

You

As an April 21st Taurus, there are big questions in your life and they are important for you as an earth sign and somebody who appreciates what you have. These questions are: Am I what I possess? Am I what I have created? While you should take pride in that, the question also is whether to go deeper in your thinking and consider if elements of your life that aren't involved with what you, as an individual, have created are as important.

We are in a world that focuses a lot on material things, so it's easy to get lost in conversations about those more practical, financial, or physical achievements. Yet being ruled by Venus, the planet of relationship and beauty, the less tangible, more intuitive side of life is equally important to you. That balance between assessing what you have and what you have achieved, and the nature of your relationship with others, and even with Mother Nature, is important.

In some ways, these support you and feed you in ways that material possessions or even achievements can't. This is an essential component: to examine what you're doing with your time and your priorities, and whether you're getting enough good feelings in the process. If these are lacking, it is not difficult to recognize them. It's simply a matter of spending time dwelling on them each day.

You and others

Family and old friends are important. But, also, those who remind you of the joys that come with life's simple pleasures, with nature, even small yet beautiful possessions, all add to each day's enjoyment. One of the joys of this is that the balance changes as each year moves on, and as you evolve as well.

Health and well-being

You can be a creature of habit. If you have found ways to take care of yourself that work for you, that's great. You'll be eating, living, and moving in ways you enjoy, but that also benefit your mind and body. However, from time to time, some of those habits may belong in the past and need to be rethought, if not radically altered.

Goals and challenges

Few individuals are happier than a Taurus who appreciates what he or she has, and has a few projects in mind or actually happening. Yet as you know, it's easy to settle into a routine and to put off even exciting changes. That's your challenge, and potentially a source of great excitement.

 THIS DAY FOR EVERYONE

Although you are likely to be short of facts about recent amazing developments, that shouldn't keep you from taking action on what you do know. If others say you should organize plans beforehand, thank them politely but ignore them. With things moving swiftly, you'll need to think and act fast.

GIFTS Beauty-lover, Practical, Insistent

NUMBER 8

CHALLENGES Excessive, Insensitive, Single-minded

$(2+2) + (4) = 8$

Just when life seems tough, I realize what an exciting adventure it is

You

You're often described as a sensual Taurus, but that description suggests you indulge yourself broadly. And while it is true, you enjoy your pleasure, another side of your nature, as an earth sign, prefers life to have a certain order, and you enjoy organizing arrangements and setting goals. What's more, you'll ensure the process of achieving those goals will be fun. But you will sometimes put off that gratification until you've achieved everything you have in mind, whether in regard to your personal life, your activities out in the world, or a long-term goal—perhaps something at school or at work.

Similarly, this involves studying, even when you are simply lounging around. You might set yourself the target of learning about art or a particular sport. And for you, this process of making plans and achieving goals is a kind of vitamin. However, finding a balance between this and two other components of your life— close alliances, and simply to enjoy life for what it is—is one of your challenges.

Once you manage to achieve this—linking certain goals with the pleasure of others' company, while learning something new, or simply allowing exciting developments to take over your life for a few days, weeks, or even months—you'll find a balance that will turn a life of objectives into a life of joy as well.

You and others

With Venus ruling Taurus, you care deeply about the happiness and well-being of others. And if you are asked to do too much or someone else is overwhelmed, you will try to achieve a balance. The trick? Recognize that there are cycles—times to receive and to give. Find that balance and you'll achieve peace where, previously, there has been tension.

Health and well-being

Finding a balance when it comes to taking care of yourself can be challenging. While a regimen is tempting, being by nature sensual, you must be able to enjoy it. However, seek out and find a form of fitness or a way of eating that is a joy, and you will achieve both health and happiness.

Goals and challenges

Sometimes you become so addicted to certain challenges and how to face them that you forget to stop and embrace those partway goals, small achievements that become your priority each day. Equally, it is vital that you congratulate yourself on what you have done each day. Do that, and your joys will blossom abundantly.

THIS DAY FOR EVERYONE

As much as you enjoy learning about changes, both in the world around you and those reshaping the lives of others, you are less enthusiastic about changes in your own life. Yet judging by planetary activity, they are unavoidable. Explore what has arisen. Learn more, and you'll be thrilled.

APRIL

23

T / A \ U / R \ U / S

Every day, love appears in many forms, some as unexpected as they are powerful

You

The theme of your Taurus birthday is the appreciation of beauty. It is likely that you are already well aware of the beauty of the world around you, possibly since you were very young, recognizing it in your own toys or the things you saw. It may be that something you viewed in your parents' home or were given that so fascinated you has become a source of interest, if not study. Alternatively, this may have been the starting point for exploration of another variety.

Whatever the case—and there could be a range of situations—as your life has unfolded, you will have learned a lot, not just about those objects, but about the value of time, your own efforts, perhaps even about money itself.

While this is important to you, especially as someone born under the sign that is said to rule money, it is also vital for you to spot and deal with habits that could limit your thinking or your capacity to learn about, or enjoy, new activities. And this form a link to the planet that rules your sign: Venus, also the ruler of the sign of Libra, which is about balance. Make this your objective, your theme—for today and every day. Do this and not only will you enjoy these discoveries, you will also develop a growing awareness of what there is to enjoy in each day of your life.

You and others

You sometimes get short-tempered with family or friends or, if you work, colleagues, wondering why they waste time on unimportant matters when other activities are so rewarding. However, they aren't you and probably aren't Taureans. Your challenge? Recognizing that others live in their own world, and it is completely different from yours. That is the key to true harmony.

Health and well-being

When you are passionately involved in an activity or time with loved ones, the day will go by and you won't even have taken a walk. You may grab a bite or, alternatively, share a delicious meal with others. Great. But then compensate with the gift of getting out, and getting your own energy going.

Goals and challenges

If there is a single word that could sum up your goals and challenges, it's balance. Too much never works, and struggling is no fun. Focus on balancing what you're always seeking and what you already have, today, in the here and now. Achieve this, and life will become far more joyous day by day.

 THIS DAY FOR EVERYONE

Being told you are about to be disillusioned may not sound like good news. Yet when you think about it, you're trading in a fantasy, one that is likely to be disappointing, for the facts. If you're facing any challenge, it is narrowing down your range of options and deciding what you will do next.

Beauty and kindness are easy to recognize but, often, generosity isn't as clear-cut

T
/
A
\
U
/
R
\
U
/
S

You

For you, Taurus, the twist and turns you face during your day, week, or throughout your life can be puzzling, simply because you've worked so hard to organize things, to create the stability that enables you to enjoy life. But then something happens and a plan you've made, your vision, is thrown into disarray, or so it seems. But, actually, it is simply that life is about change. The weather changes, clouds pass in the sky and plants around you grow.

And indeed your own life and relationships with others also change and grow. Still, you'll often put off, if not battle, changes, because you fear the disarray they'll bring. It is true: the process of change, and growth, can be unsettling, if not untidy. Yet making plans is one thing; taking action on them is another. What's more, finding that balance between those plans and allowing space for growth is a crucial challenge—and a skill. Once you understand how it's done, you will also develop the ability to turn the process of exploration into something you enjoy. As a Taurus and the sensual earth sign, life isn't just about being practical. Deep down, you feel that living well is an art. Once you recognize it as such—an art you can enjoy in ways small and large—in every day of your life, everything else will be so much more exciting—and more worthwhile.

You and others

Sometimes you make plans with others, then they change them. You're irritated, then ask why. They will detail sudden changes, which intrigue you. This balance in all close relationships shifts constantly and is always informative. The key? First, ask questions. Second, recognize that twists and turns are normal. Support each other through those, and learn and share together.

Health and well-being

Here, the key to finding pleasure in taking care of yourself is so important. For you, going to a gym where everyone is sweaty may work, but it won't necessarily be as rewarding as taking a walk in the countryside, or even being around those who are doing something that is as energizing as it is worthwhile.

Goals and challenges

You can be a creature of habit. It is predictable, but also comfortable. And you then realize life is no longer exciting. For you the great skill is catching that rut before you become so accustomed to it that any change seems impossible. Actually, you can make those changes right now.

THIS DAY FOR EVERYONE

If you were told you're a creature of habit, you would probably disagree. Yet you're battling necessary changes in elements of your daily routine. What's more, you're aware how beneficial these could be. Consider the possibility those habits are more dominant than you care to admit.

APRIL

25

T
/
A
\
U
/
R
\
U
/
S

My joy comes in new and unexpected ways, making each day an adventure

You

For you as an April 25th Taurus, life is about the principle of balance, living well, and love. It is about finding that capacity to be true to yourself, to enjoy what life has to offer, yet also to love those around you: family, friends, and romantic partners.

However, at the same time, you must face the fact that this requires you to love yourself first. This may sound like psychobabble, but as somebody ruled by the planet of love, Venus, it is essential. This requires a degree of analysis that may not come naturally to you as a Taurus and an earth sign. You are, of course, very logical. But the kind of detached analysis that is so important for any personal growth may take time. Deep down, you feel that you and those you're with will simply understand each other. Often, getting to know others is like learning a foreign language: while you can do it on your own, it's worth getting guidance.

Talking things over gives you a chance to look at what you're doing, and what your priorities are, from a fresh perspective. This also offers a glimpse of new ways of dealing with existing issues and possibilities for the future. Do this from time to time; be reminded that there is always more to discover and more joys to share with those around you, whether it's those closest, those you work with, or those you're about to meet.

You and others

Close alliances are important. However, even these can settle into a routine that's reassuring and easy, but can become restrictive. It can even mean you miss out on opportunities on your own, with others, or to meet new people. Balancing stability with the unexpected is an important skill. Achieve it and you will soon be exploring exciting new activities.

Health and well-being

True, habits are important. Theoretically, you needn't change worthwhile habits. Yet both in relationships and in taking care of yourself, breaking habits can introduce a new magic into your life. Tempting as it is to get into a reliable routine, be bold. Make changes just to make them. You'll soon realize how exciting taking care of yourself can be.

Goals and challenges

Discovery is the key here. When you begin to recognize how much there is out there for you to not only experience but also enjoy, instead of settling into a familiar routine—which as a Taurus, you can do—you'll make a deal with yourself to discover something new and wonderful every single day of your life.

 THIS DAY FOR EVERYONE

Every once in a while, life is good—so much so that there's no need to query ideas or offers. All that is necessary is that you respond to events as they arise. Yet certain well-meaning individuals are warning you that things are just too easy. At other times, that might be true. But not now.

What is least expected is increasingly the highlight of my day

You

From your point of view, you are a straightforward person—someone who loves life, beauty, and who tries to use your time wisely. However, destiny seems determined to make this difficult for you. There is a secret to this. It's about achieving balance in several areas of your life. It's about what you intend to do and those things that pop up that often distract or annoy you. Then, eventually, you realize that, actually, these unexpected events are an invitation that is taking you into new territory.

While this may involve your daily routine, it is about your social life, from family and relationships to your job and pursuits you're passionate about. Unsettling as those twists and turns may seem, they're about breaking habits, which in turn lead to unexpected discoveries. While often, planning ahead is important, this is about organizing your life so you can spot and embrace the unexpected. Go with the flow, and you'll discover how much fun you can have venturing into the unknown.

Yes, it's out of character. However, both those relationships and activities—and even certain once burdensome duties—will be more fun every day. In fact, you might even find yourself going off in new and rewarding directions and enjoying them before you even realize it.

You and others

Often, talking to certain individuals is such hard work that you wonder why you bother. However, others don't think this. They expect less than you do. While obviously finding those individuals with whom you have a special "spark" is vital, enjoying others is an essential skill. Discover that and, bizarrely, you'll have the key to the joy you're seeking.

Health and well-being

Every Taurus has experienced the feeling that when they're doing one thing, they should be doing something else. While you might say it's because you have a rich imagination, it could also be because you're avoiding getting out and about when you're so comfortable. The secret? Take that imagination out for a brisk walk, and ask your body to come along.

Goals and challenges

In general, your goals and challenges are what we have been talking about here. Familiar habits are holding you back. Note those, and each day break a habit—a little one maybe, then a medium-sized one, and once a week a big one. Not only will your life be a lot more fun, the results could be miraculous.

THIS DAY FOR EVERYONE

Sometimes even the simplest of plans takes a long time to organize. Yet now and over the coming days, things will move with astonishing swiftness. This is wonderful. Bear in mind, however, that you'd better have all the details beforehand, because you'll have no opportunity afterward.

APRIL 27

T / A \ U / R \ U / S

Making plans boosts my sense of control, yet the unexpected brings magical moments

You

If there were a single motto for your life, it would be summed up in the hopeful phrase, "One day everything will work out." As a Taurus, ruled by Venus, the planet of beauty and exactly that—order—it's understandable that this is your ideal. But the fact is, each day the sun rises and each evening it sets; the world changes—and so do you. So while that idealistic order you're seeking may be achieved on one particular day, with the world itself changing, life itself must shift, change, and on occasion reform itself as well.

And that's the big lesson for you—in general, and very much as the future unfolds. Appealing as the thought of getting things organized perfectly may be, you'll be far better off simply accepting the disarray in which events unfold, and to find the beauty in that.

As someone ruled by Venus, once you can discover beauty in anything, including the way things unfold, then you will also have answered all the questions and dealt with all the obstacles that otherwise would seem to keep popping up. You will see the beauty in growth. And that, as a Taurus, is essential for you. Doing that, you will be able to tackle even the tricky situations and difficult individuals with a delight that previously wouldn't have been possible. And you will also have the key to planning the future.

You and others

As desirable as creating and maintaining harmony in relationships is, sometimes you learn most, and gain a greater understanding of others, when you're working out differences, if not truly at odds with others. The trick? Pause, review what you have learned, and if any apologies are due, make them then.

Health and well-being

When you were very young, there was everyday life and everyday eating, and then there were treat times. These occurred during seasonal holidays, when away on a trip, or, of course, as part of a birthday or celebration. The secret is to include those mini-treats as part of your everyday life, enough to lift your spirits and remind you how special life can be.

Goals and challenges

From your earliest days, you were probably asked what you wanted to be when you grew up. Since then, a lot has changed—for you, but also for the world. However, there may still be a part of you that feels you really should be pursuing that childhood dream, however unappealing or inappropriate it is. If so, the best time to say farewell to it is now and, equally, it is time to embrace the future.

THIS DAY FOR EVERYONE

Most questions have relatively straightforward answers. However, several aren't just perplexing, you're under pressure from certain demanding individuals to come up with fast answers. They're being unrealistic. Explain diplomatically but firmly that there's no way you can fulfill their demands.

While changes can be puzzling, I welcome a thrilling surprise

You

For you, as an April 28th Taurus, living well and with joy is a priority. That may sound strange, because you would imagine everyone thinks that way, but they don't. This also means that if you intend to spend time with those around you, whether it's family, friends, or colleagues, it is your responsibility to organize things. While that's sometimes annoying, it also means those arrangements will be far more interesting than if you left plans to others.

Yet being a Taurus and ruled by Venus, which also rules Libra, the relationship sign, it's all about collaboration. Getting others involved in plans is an art. What's more, those around you may have very different views about what they'd enjoy. In fact, when they come up with something, you may wonder what on earth they're thinking. Actually, they're revealing their point of view to you.

Recognizing this is part of your journey. The more you listen to, learn about, and experience what others find joy in, the better you'll understand them, and ironically, you will gain better understanding of yourself as well. While you could sit back and try to figure things out, your birthday is linked to learning. The more you explore and the more you experiment, the more you'll discover—and the more joy you'll have with every passing day.

You and others

As a Taurus and an earth sign, you're often the person everybody expects to make decisions. However, sometimes you're too cautious. That is one of your biggest lessons. Make a deal with yourself to take a chance, on your own and with others. You'll not only learn a lot, but even seemingly challenging relationships will suddenly begin to be fun.

Health and well-being

Life is about breakthroughs. Once, you enjoyed doing certain things and eating foods that were good for you. But you have changed, times have changed, and those habits need to change, too. It's all about experimentation. Take chances—with eating, with what you do, and with how you live. What you discover will be as unexpected as it is exciting.

Goals and challenges

The biggest challenge for you is to resist settling into a familiar activity. Instead, do something new—if not every day, then at least once a week. Get yourself into this routine, and what you discover, who you meet, and the delights you encounter will feed you in ways beyond anything you'd imagined possible.

APRIL

29

T
/
A
\
U
/
R
\
U
/
S

I recognize that disappointments are often thrilling surprises in disguise

You

As a Taurus and an earth sign, you're a collector. You may actually collect objects, but also you will collect experiences. In the same way, you collect friendships with people. And some of them—those objects, and even those people—stay in your life for a long time, and this familiarity gives you a kind of comfort.

At the same time, every once in a while you need to allow changes to roll in your life. And it would appear that finding a balance between these two, between creating a collection of people and activities that are rewarding and ensuring these changes take place, is a skill that is important for you to develop as you live through the days and months and years of your life.

This is especially significant, because otherwise, you could easily settle into something that is appealing, but when changes arise, as is inevitable in life, that could lead to complications. You'll either worry that something's wrong and try to go back to the way things were. Or you'll realize that, every now and then, life is not about merely dealing with changes, but embracing them—and as a result, thinking and living in a new way. Once you have developed this skill, you will be able to enjoy these changes, enjoy the changes in the lives of those around you, and enjoy the changes in your world all the more.

You and others

Being close to others—from family and friends to certain special individuals—is important. So when they act unpredictably, you worry or may be upset. The key? Discuss this, and everything else, often. They may question this. Fine. Slowly, they, too, will realize how much they're benefiting from these changes. They might even begin to enjoy them.

Health and well-being

For you, habits are natural. And they're reassuring. Once something works for you, you will stick with it. However, it may be that 20 years have passed, or your life has changed, yet you're still doing the same thing, the same way. Make a point of discovering things, and regularly. You will be glad you did.

Goals and challenges

Sometimes a goal seems uncomplicated. Often, it is. Learning a sport such as tennis, or appreciating jazz, perhaps. But as important are shifting goals, some long-standing. Each day, say something new and try something new and agree to something unexpected, and you'll soon realize how rewarding this is.

THIS DAY FOR EVERYONE

It doesn't matter whether the issues in question are personal or involve others. They are unsettling, and therefore not easy to discuss. Despite that, the time has come to raise them. It won't be easy. Still, once you do, you'll notice how grateful others are that you had the courage to bring these up.

GIFTS Perfume-aware, Good Host, Practical

NUMBER 7

CHALLENGES Uncooperative, Stubborn, Arrogant

$(3+0) + (4) = 7$

There is no wrong way to be thankful, yet it is a skill to receive gratitude

T
/
A
\
U
/
R
\
U
/
S

You

For you, the art of reviewing is an important one. This may seem strange, because most of the time, we focus on what we do. However, this is actually about pausing to review what you've done recently and, equally, thinking about times in the past when it seemed as if things worked better, or life was easier. This may well have been true, but it could also be that, in your imagination, you remember things being easier, simply because you've forgotten the parts that were difficult or challenging. This process of review isn't about idealizing the past, but remembering the challenges and what you learned from them.

Every so often, life throws a twist or turn your way. And if you consider these to be a nuisance and do all you can to stop them, then life could turn into a battle. If, on the other hand, you remember times in the past when those twists and turns became joys, then you'll recognize that, even though what you're doing is unsettling, it, too, will become a joy.

It is the same with close alliances with others. Sometimes it may take a bit of imagination to picture where things are going, especially when you're having difficulty with family members or with somebody close. Yet, at the same time, every once in a while, you've had to break through those difficult times and will be learning from them in amazing ways.

You and others

Your instincts say an ideal life—relationships with close friends or partners—is guided by destiny. Some go back a long time, and you've grown close slowly, while with others there was instant magic. However, things move on. Understand that, as you recognize changes are like the seasons, and not only will you enjoy them, you'll discover how enriching they are.

Health and well-being

Yes, feeling well in life has lots to do with how you eat and how you live. But, even more, it is about enjoying every minute. This may sound absurdly idealistic, but sometimes life seems an uphill climb. And the trick is to recognize that often these challenges are gifts in disguise.

Goals and challenges

Sometimes goals are clear-cut. However, often they come in the form of a challenge at the gym, sticking to a diet, or undertaking studies. And those goals aren't always clear. So if you notice the challenge, then you'll be aware that, at its conclusion, you'll have achieved far more than you would have dreamed possible.

THIS DAY FOR EVERYONE

Exciting as recent ideas or offers were, they're taking you into unfamiliar territory. As much as you enjoy new experiences, you prefer to undertake them when it is convenient. Now, however, events have made the decision about timing for you. Simply go with the flow. You'll be glad you did.

MAY

01

T
/
A
\
U
/
R
\
U
/
S

Increasingly, I'm surprising myself at my joy when the unexpected shakes things up

You

For you, being a May 1st Taurus brings a complex range of options, opportunities, and joys. May Day is one of the happiest days of the year—a celebration of spring, flowers, beauty, and joy. It's a wonderful theme for your birthday. And it's also about the joys of family and friends and colleagues and loved ones: being able truly to enjoy time with them, and the pleasures that come with that.

However, there is a part of you that's very much about the first of the month, about action and getting things done. Except some of those joys take time, just as being able to understand somebody doesn't happen in a hurry. The flowers that are so much a part of the spring take a while to blossom. If you've planted something, it may not yet be in flower.

The lesson for you is to recognize that the passion you bring to the moment sometimes needs to be balanced with patience. And occasionally, you need to remind others to do this as well. In fact, it may be that they are making demands on you to move more swiftly, or be more passionate, in ways that are unwise, if not impossible. They want you to care more about what they're doing in the ways they want. This is a valuable part of the journey, one that enables you to discuss differences and to learn from them, and in doing so, to deepen those relationships.

You and others

One of your greatest challenges is the conflict between your desire for harmony—and understanding of others—and certain issues that aren't easily resolved. Yet, this is a rewarding lesson. It is the simple acknowledgement that those differences are a great gift. At last, you will enjoy them for who they are, and they will enjoy you as well.

Health and well-being

Often it's assumed that everybody's happy to pursue health and well-being by eating in one particular way and heading off to the gym. But there is also simply enjoying what each day brings and the company of others. When you find that single joy, the rest may or may not follow, but it won't matter nearly as much.

Goals and challenges

Some say that life's greatest joy is achieving your goals. But others say it is about savoring what the day brings. Certainly making that your priority will mean you will have a smile on your face when you wake up, and when you go to bed at night.

THIS DAY FOR EVERYONE

The time has come to let go of familiar but restrictive arrangements. From time to time you have considered making changes but decided it would be too much bother. Now events are forcing your hand. Tempting as it is to do the minimum, you'd regret it. Muster your courage and plunge in.

Daily, I worry less, and my understanding of the power of kindness and generosity grows

You

True, you were somebody born under the sensual and sensible earth sign of Taurus. However, to a certain degree, you share the sensibilities of Libra, the other sign associated with the planet Venus, which is always trying to balance things and make everybody happy. While you certainly want others to be happy, you'd never sacrifice plans just for the sake of a good mood. And as an earth sign, you have a strong instinct about what will work and what won't, and have found often that if you stick with those feelings and talk things through with others, you will not only achieve an accord with them, you will also figure out a way to do whatever needs to be done wisely and well. Better yet, you'll deepen the relationship with those individuals.

You will also enjoy the process of creating something, which is so central to being an earth sign and being a Taurus. It may be anything: creating an object, a home, or a business. Whatever the case, it can be small or large. For you, it's an art. And it's also the art of sharing with others in a way that allows you to exchange ideas and to recognize that often they see things very differently to the way you do.

This recognition brings a certain peace in what may have been tricky relationships in the past and promises more in the future.

You and others

Being ruled by Venus means relationships are important to you. But finding a balance when it seems others are almost trying to create disarray isn't easy. However, their views about life and relationships differ from yours. The secret? Get them to listen more, then you do the same. Instead of getting lost in those differences, you will build a beautiful bridge between you.

Health and well-being

There are two perspectives on your health and well-being: one is purely about how you eat and take care of yourself. But the other, inner point of view, accents the joys in your life, those that bring a happiness that includes, but is beyond, the physical. The simple idea of inner well-being is key.

Goals and challenges

Setting goals is important, but turning them into challenges can make them difficult. Yet there is another way, and that is joy in exploring these goals. You then focus on bringing that vision to reality. Better yet, this is a variety of magic you can use every day.

Inevitably, certain changes will mean leaving elements of the past behind. While in some situations this is a relief, others bring a pang of regret. If so, pause to reflect on what you've done, enjoyed, or accomplished, then say farewell. At the moment, life's about discovery, not dwelling on the past.

MAY

03

T
/
A
\
U
/
R
\
U
/
S

What seems an insurmountable obstacle today will become tomorrow's joy

You

As a Taurus, you are often easygoing and, being ruled by Venus, you have a unique charm that's appealing to everyone. Yet as a May 3rd Taurus, you can sometimes be on edge, if not impatient with yourself. You want things to work well, and you have ideals—yet you can't quite figure out how to make these happen. The resulting impatience can lead to making plans which, because they are done in haste, are unpredictable and unreliable.

The trick to dealing with this is to spot that impatience and recognize that it won't make things happen any more swiftly. However, it does suggest that you could unintentionally do things that, ultimately, you will regret. First, you need to think about the past, and previous situations that seemed to turn out brilliantly, often because you gave them a certain special attention. It's the same now. And in fact, this isn't about getting things done quickly, but about what you learn about yourself and this variety of patience.

These are some of your greatest challenges. However, not only will you overcome them, but what you learn will turn into a skill. It is also about allowing your imagination to work, which means giving it time. This is all about trust, but when you do this and trust in this way, you'll find a new joy, not only in every day of your life, but in being you.

You and others

Every once in a while, you find yourself wondering why others behave as they do. Also, it is puzzling why they argue about matters when it is clear what is right. However, their view of life differs from yours. It's as if you each see life the same but from a different angle. Recognizing that makes everything else a lot easier.

Health and well-being

Feeling positive isn't just about eating well and exercising; it's about being able to relax. Often you put so much pressure on yourself, you are on edge with others. Both cause stress. Instead of analyzing those problems, focus on something beautiful. Do it often. Gradually, you'll exchange those tensions for a smile.

Goals and challenges

Sometimes goals are very specific and challenges can be defined. But often, you're impatient, and either obstacles are slowing your progress or there are problems with others. These happen. And sometimes you can't control them. But you can decide to relax and see what happens. There may well be progress without you having to do a thing.

 THIS DAY FOR EVERYONE

For weeks you've kept quiet about unsettling issues, thinking others weren't ready to discuss them. While that is true, you were relieved to avoid them, too. Now that circumstances are forcing these out in the open, waste no time on analysis. The faster you begin discussing them openly, the better.

GIFTS Well-presented, Loving, Good Host

CHALLENGES Stubborn, Excessive, Arrogant

NUMBER 9

(0+4) + (5) = 9

Wise ideas guide the way, but laughter makes persistence easy—and a joy

You

For you, Taurus, as an earth sign ruled by Venus, the planet that has to do with beauty and balance, figuring out a plan is essential. Once you know this, then you can think about each stage—what you will do and also about others' responsibilities. Then you can relax. While this makes sense, it is likely minor events or unexpected developments could trigger doubts, or even undermine your plan. It has happened before, so you may wonder if there is a flaw in your thinking. Actually, you are approaching things perfectly. These doubts can overshadow the here and now if you let them. Tempting as it is to focus on past experiences, it often means you're stuck with the familiar when it s better to take chances—although not in a way that triggers those previously mentioned doubts.

   Important as making plans may be, ensure that they are flexible. They may have to do with your personal life, close alliances, your work if you have a career, or how you organize long-term plans. In every case, it is about knowing what you want and setting goals, but also including a kind of flexibility that you sometimes regard as being weak. Most of all, learn to view making plans and life itself as a great adventure. The more chances you take, the more fun you will have—and the greater your rewards will be.

You and others

Being ruled by Venus, for you, relationships are precious. Whether it's family, friends, or loved ones, you want others to know how important they are to you. Yet sometimes, their way of looking at things differs from yours so much, you have no idea what to say. The trick? Recognize how very differently each individual see things. Acknowledging that alone will change everything.

Health and well-being

Looking after your health is one thing. If you do, that's great. However, stress can be unsettling, and even interfere with your sleep. But you aren't always sure what's causing that stress. Amazingly, you don't need to know. Just employ a trick designed for Taureans, which is to take a deep breath, and, as you do, simply accept life as it is, even if just for that moment.

Goals and challenges

We have things to learn. What is most important is living a happy life. This requires patience. You'd think as a Taurus, you'd be easygoing. But you put lots of pressure on yourself, in terms of how you live, work, or even your style. Actually, the highest achievement is simply living each day with joy.

THIS DAY FOR EVERYONE

There are few things as bitter as being disappointed by somebody you've trusted. Before you draw any conclusions, however, ask a few questions. And be forthright. The odds are good that they were dealing with issues of which you were unaware. Once you learn about these, all will be forgiven.

GIFTS Flower-lover, Sensual, Generous

CHALLENGES Excessive, Headstrong, Unbending

NUMBER 1

$(0+5) + (5) = 10 = (1+0) = 1$

I'm learning to ask whether those who are giving advice are, themselves, happy

You

As a Taurus and an earth sign, you don't particularly think about life being about cycles, but as a May 5th Taurus, life isn't just about cycles. It is about new discoveries and the excitement that comes with them. This can be in terms of people or activities, then the process of learning about those—and the doubts and concerns that arise. Perhaps, in some cases, you are even feeling disillusioned—and then doing it all over again.

This journey is important to understand, because it is actually about life. In life itself, there are seasons. There is spring, when you were born, when everything is bursting with bloom. There's summer heat; and then there is fall, when the blooms vanish and the leaves fall from the trees. Then there is the stillness of winter and then spring again. In your life,too, it is about this cycle.

When you become comfortable with that, then you will also understand that important as certain relationships are, they will have their ups and downs. As exciting as certain discoveries are, whether it's personal goals or activities out in the world, each will be about a journey that may occasionally be easy, but often will have twists and turns. You'll also discover how exciting and rewarding these are. Once you do that, you'll have learned one of life's most important lessons.

You and others

Few things upset you as much as when somebody you have trusted disappoints you. The big question is, have you learned that the issue is not their actions, but your own expectations? There may have been a misunderstanding or an unexpected problem. It has happened to you, and will again. The secret is to realize that mistakes are human and there is nothing to forgive.

Health and well-being

While it is good to eat well and move well, stress can be one of the most challenging elements of your life. Learning to undo that stress is one of the major themes for you as a May 5th Taurus. The trick is to disentangle yourself from situations that ordinarily you might get upset about, and learn to be relaxed.

Goals and challenges

Having goals is important, as is spotting challenges. Learning how to dance around those goals is the biggest trick of all. This is the lesson for you: to recognize that it isn't about getting things resolved on any particular day, but enjoying what each day brings.

THIS DAY FOR EVERYONE

Life is full of minor disagreements that often lead to valuable discussions and rewarding new ideas. Now, however, you are taking one particular issue too seriously, mostly because it involves a matter about which you have intense feelings. Admitting this won't be easy, but it is essential.

GIFTS Values Investments, Persistent, Tough

CHALLENGES Willful, Uncooperative, Immoderate

NUMBER 2

$(0+6) + (5) = 11 = (1+1) = 2$

I am drawn to elegance, yet am increasingly aware of the beauty of wisdom

You

As a May 6th Taurus, you will find that every once in a while you face a puzzle, one that's more or less unique to you. It's not unusual, because as a practical earth sign—and also what is termed one of the fixed signs of the zodiac, that is, the signs born in the middle of each season—once you understand a situation or figure out a plan, you stick with it. Yet you frequently seem to encounter individuals who have an entirely different approach to certain situations.

If you make suggestions but are ignored, this can be puzzling, if not a very real challenge. The trick is to realize that your understanding of how things work is yours and yours alone. The perspective of others about the same thing can be very different. Acknowledge that, and the resulting exchange of ideas can bring amazing insights.

This is actually about broadening your horizons. Why? Because another point that's key to your birth date is the importance of being flexible, to rethink plans and alter goals as you go along. While you may make arrangements based on the past—which makes sense because they've already worked—if you use that approach now, with things having changed, you could miss a whole new world of discovery, excitement, and experiences just waiting for you to become part of it.

You and others

You have decided to embrace a new, flexible approach to life. Great. What about others? Forget about discussion and just live it, day by day, and see what happens. Your concerns may be about old habits you are changing anyway. You may even welcome ideas you've dismissed as unrealistic or unwise. Better yet, you create a new way of being together, one that is all about discovery.

Health and well-being

This tension can undermine your health. You may be doing what you need to do—you may be eating right, you may be out and about—but if you are uptight, this can overshadow the simple health and well-being you've created. Finding this balance and ensuring it includes joy is one of your biggest challenges.

Goals and challenges

While some challenges have to do with finding that joy, in general, being able to roll with ups and downs is the most important component for you. In some cases, this will mean going along with what others think. Initially, you might question it, but soon you will discover just how clever they were.

As much as you enjoy talking over intriguing ideas, ensure that others understand you are doing no more than exploring possibilities. Certain individuals will mistake your enthusiasm for serious interest in getting involved. Explain that clearly and you'll avoid misunderstandings, if not hurt feelings, later.

MAY

07

T
/
A
\
U
/
R
\
U
/
S

Seeking the perfect final plan tempts fate, whereas a flexible vision welcomes it

You

The theme for you as a May 7th Taurus is building your best life. Of course, as a Taurus and somebody ruled by the elegant Venus, this is nothing new. Except in your particular case, it is, because your ideas about what is best are themselves shifting. There is a part of you that's impatient. Once you get things organized, if they aren't quite as good as you'd hoped, you'll need to change something—and then you'll change something else.

It seems like one thing after the other changes and you are never quite satisfied. Yet the joy actually comes from what is inside you. It is being able to savor the process of making those changes, whether it involves you on your own, whether it has to do with your relationship with Mother Nature, whether it has to do with family or friends or even a business. It may be a range of these. Whatever it is, it is also recognizing the role you are taking on your own or with others in those changes, and that's the greatest discovery for you.

When you do that, also, you will be in touch with a creative side of your own nature, and it is easy to miss out on in a time that emphasizes chatting about things and doing things so much. Your love affair with Mother Nature is one of the most important aspects of your life. This encourages you to explore it.

You and others

Your theme is teamwork, but not as you have thought of it previously. It's spotting those who are struggling with something, but an issue that's very different from what you're facing. The trick is not to focus on the goal, but to turn each day's challenges, however minor, into a lesson. Together, you'll learn to master them, then turn them to your advantage.

Health and well-being

There are all sorts of formulas for waking up with a spring in your step, including exercise, vitamins, and the right diet. However useful these are, there is a secret rarely mentioned—and that is to expect the best, and in turn, ensure that is what you give to others. Simple. And it works miracles.

Goals and challenges

Some people are obsessive list-makers, but everybody makes a list at some point in their lives. Really, you only need one thing on your list. To choose the most exciting, promising approach to any task, then tackle it right away. That alone will ensure you get everything done, with a few adventures along the way.

THIS DAY FOR EVERYONE

After a fast-paced and exciting period, things are slowing down, and you are able to focus on the practical side of things. You will realize that you're just in time. And if you don't act swiftly, certain obligations or financial issues could become troublesome. The sooner you tackle these, the better.

Sometimes I seek others' advice, when I could simply ask them for a hand

You

As a May 8th Taurus, the big question for you revolves around the pleasure you take in what you do, or in what you acquire. True, you have no choice about many elements of your life. However, you have a range of options in terms of timing, the people involved, or the extent of your commitment. This isn't about money, investment, or status; it's about the quality of your experience, so even simple arrangements are appealing, if not just plain wonderful.

That different kind of satisfaction has less to do with settings, situations, or objects and more to do with lifting your spirits, being quiet, or feeling inner peace. Of course, even thinking this way is new for many, and then organizing your life so events include experiences like this may seem unlikely, if not impossible. Yet you're already recalling certain times this happened, so you know it's possible

Knowing you can do this is one thing. Doing it is another. But when it comes to your everyday life, it may seem that bringing a similar joy would be asking too much, if not impossible. However, it is the feeling behind it all, the beauty in the mood, and the spirit of those involved, even in nature around you, that add to the enchantment. Take that approach, and you'll begin to relax and simply enjoy dealing with a bright day or a sunlit evening, or even with simply taking a breath.

You and others

You are all about the quality of life. Explaining that to others isn't easy, mostly because their ideas will differ from yours. What's more, because you sometimes question your own priorities, discussions with others can be confusing. The solution? If their ideas are unlikely to enrich your thinking, change the subject. Save deep discussions for those who have something to offer.

Health and well-being

Health can be achieved by taking care of yourself, by eating well, by exercising. However, well-being comes with inner peace, and that is about your own journey, as an individual, as a May 8th Taurus. Its also about the kind of discoveries that are so important. Recognize those and you will also find joy.

Goals and challenges

Achieving a goal seems clear-cut. It is about building something, acquiring a certain amount of money, or arranging a successful event. However, enjoying the challenge is something else entirely. That involves balancing those goals with your own nature. Instead of tackling challenges because they're there, first ask yourself how much you care about them to begin with.

THIS DAY FOR EVERYONE

When it comes to certain rather tricky matters, timing is as crucial as your strategy. What appear to be setbacks are actually preventing you taking action now. Frustrating as this is at the moment, you will be more than compensated by what comes your way very soon.

GIFTS Animal-lover, Generous, Realistic

CHALLENGES Unsympathetic, Uncompromising, Idle

NUMBER 5

$(0+9) + (5) = 14 = (1+4) = 5$

Love can be shown with affection or gifts, yet it can be felt from far away

You

For you as a May 9th Taurus, one particularly big question comes to mind again and again. It is actually the core of being ruled by the planet Venus. On the one hand, Venus, the goddess of love, has to do with exactly that—loving those around you, family, offspring, and even loving friends—and sometimes it is about loving what you do. Yet, equally, being a Taurus and therefore conscious of every element of your well-being, living well but wisely is important, too.

One of the questions that often arises is whether this stability is more important, or those loving bonds with others. Which should come first? The fact is, neither. It is about finding yourself, and the center of your being within. This, then, enables you to love life, whatever you're doing. While life has its ups and downs—and even the most careful, thorough, and calculating Taurus will experience ups and downs of nature—learning how to enjoy who you are and, equally, to enjoy those around you is a vital skill.

Ironically, that isn't about passionate love as much as it is about the sheer joy of life itself, and being able to take pleasure in that is one of life's greatest gifts. The skill is learning to enjoy it, whatever the setting and whoever you're with. The more you develop this skill, the happier life will be.

You and others

Often our standards vary. We tolerate one thing from family or close friends, another from neighbors or colleagues, and yet another from strangers. But being ruled by Venus, which accents what you both value and love, the trick is to view these individuals all as fellow human beings. It may seem strange, but it is easier and will make you happier.

Health and well-being

For you, health is one thing, but enjoying life is quite another. That means being so "together" that you don't allow even unsettling events to upset you. That may sound idealistic, because all sorts of things happen. But part of your journey is learning to recognize them as passing, which they will.

Goals and challenges

There is no simple way to overcome a challenge, but there is a very simple way to deal with it—to recognize that, instead of fighting it, you can seek a new approach. When you spot it, you make it possible to exchange the concept of goals and challenges for a creative way of leading life itself.

 THIS DAY FOR EVERYONE

Having dealt with a series of unsettling situations, the last thing you want is more unexpected developments. However disruptive as those coming your way may be, you will soon realize how much you'll benefit from them, and exchange irritation for enthusiasm about changes you dreaded recently.

Certain individuals bring out the worst in me, but what I learn is worthwhile

You

As a May 10th Taurus, you live life with an understated passion. Of course, as a Taurus, you're perfectly capable of free-flowing passion. But, normally, you try to avoid allowing this to dominate your life. You also give considerable thought to what's in your best interest and, equally, the price you'd pay if you allowed that passion to take over. While that is wise, every once in a while it is important that you "let go." This is about the feelings of passion you experience when a plan or project comes together; it could involve anything from a garden to a business, or even a long conversation with another. Once you've experienced this, you'll know it's worth the risk.

Still, finding and maintaining the balance that is so important for you can be difficult, if not actually challenging. The trick is to realize how much you relish and, in fact, benefit from the action, and the heat of it all. But also you will develop the stillness of finding your way back to your own center.

That's the trick, to have that passion in some element of your life, yet to stay connected to your center. Do this, and you will have accomplished one of the greatest lessons of this life, one that is about being who you are, being a passionate and intense individual, yet one who also retains a powerful link to your fundamental nature as a grounded Taurus.

You and others

Obviously, relationships matter. While many are easygoing, those involving certain individuals take a very special role, and demand a particular kind of attention. In these, you try to figure them out, to anticipate—if not control—their behavior. Yet it's actually about caring about them, and living in the moment: enjoying it for what it offers, even if it is not what you expected.

Health and well-being

Talking about life's tensions, you will find that in achieving a balance in those stressful elements of your life, you need to work less at being comfortable, and more on being healthy. Those ups and downs can take a toll or be an excuse for not taking care of yourself.

Goals and challenges

You have set so many different goals, most focusing on achieving those objectives, and in the way you planned. However, your challenge is recognizing that, as the world changes, so must those goals. Letting old ones go clears the way for new, and potentially more rewarding, aims and objectives.

THIS DAY FOR EVERYONE

Certain individuals regard change as worrying, if not an enemy, something to analyze at length. You avoid such discussions. Now, however, you must keep these individuals updated on your plans. Explain your intentions concisely, and in a manner that invites neither comment nor discussion.

GIFTS Practical, Flower-lover, Affectionate

CHALLENGES Excessive, Inflexible, Selfish

NUMBER 7

(1+1) + (5) = 7

MAY

11

T
/
A
\
U
/
R
\
U
/
S

Practical decisions bring pleasure, while helping others brings a more lasting joy

You

The theme for your birthday is the joy of order. As a Taurus and an earth sign, you appreciate the beauty of life in so many ways. You appreciate the beauty of nature, but also the beauty of kind gestures and beautiful objects. They don't necessarily need to be valuable, but simply something that brings joy to your heart. At the same time, you also need for your own life to be in order.

Obviously, it is nice if what's around you is in order, but the pace of events and the role those around you play are also important. Yet, things don't always work out as you expect. When you're so busy it is impossible to be organized, you will still try to be orderly. However, at times, that temporary chaos becomes a permanent variety of disarray.

Bizarrely, often that disarray can lead to a fresh viewpoint on elements of your life you hadn't realized need to change or, alternatively, introduce new activities or objectives that hadn't previously crossed your mind, possibly because you were so focused on what you were already doing. The key is to balance your pleasure in life's beauty, but also to recognize that, occasionally, what seem to be unsettling changes are actually breakthroughs—changes that won't just be useful, but will add to your life in ways that you couldn't possibly have conceived of when those events first arose.

You and others

Hoping for relaxation, order, and joy with others is wonderful. It's just that this may means something entirely different to them than to you. Discuss it? Maybe. But that, too, can create confusion. The solution? Recognize their views are, and always will be, different to yours. Find a middle ground, one that holds the promise of joyous times together.

Health and well-being

It is easy to blame stress—from others or from things that aren't working—for undermining your enthusiasm for life. True, challenges can be overwhelming. The solution isn't battling them but simply stopping for a moment, taking a deep breath, and being still. It is by far the best strategy.

Goals and challenges

Whatever your lifestyle—at home, working, or juggling lots of duties—everybody needs a goal. Challenges are important, too, although undoubtedly there are times when you wish they'd vanish. Approach these as offering you the potential to celebrate achievements, major and minor, and you will be amazed how much you learn from each.

THIS DAY FOR EVERYONE

Tensions with loved ones or close friends aren't easy. They've been behaving oddly but made no explanation, so you assume they'd rather keep things to themselves. Perhaps. Yet it is just as likely they don't realize how much certain concerns have altered their behavior. A frank discussion will do wonders.

GIFTS Well-presented, Persistent, Gardener

CHALLENGES Unbending, Opinionated, Immoderate

NUMBER 8

(1+2) + (5) = 8

Justifying your decisions to those who are critical achieves little

You

Many think of profit in financial terms. But often it is said you've profited from dealing with, and overcoming, a serious challenge—one you have dealt with by employing thought, analysis of others' perspectives, and, most of all, patience. Profit doesn't always have to refer to finances; you will have learned how time, effort, and a willingness to wait, watch, and learn from others can also be profitable. What's more, this reminds you that the time, effort, energy, and even heart you put into whatever you're doing creates the end result.

This, in turn, highlights the importance of the word "joy," which is often used in ceremonies such as weddings, and the wonder of holidays. Here it has to do with a leap in your heart, a real and personal joy that comes from having done something you know will benefit you, others, and, possibly, even the world. With this as a theme for your birthday, it is also important you find a balance between doing what you need to do and being able to savor life's joys. True, often it is believed the world isn't designed in this way.

Dealing with finances involves dull duty and challenges. However, in your particular case, the capacity to get things going and to bring money and joy into your life—and at the same time—is both a skill and an art, and one that you are always learning about and refining.

You and others

Making the best of life is one thing, discussing it with others is quite another. When at your best, you have a talent for creating magic. What's more, it is important to share this gift with those who you were destined to be with—family or loved ones or friends. While there isn't a single right way to do it, every effort adds its own magic.

Health and well-being

We all have moments when things just don't feel right. That can mean you need to rest or you have a touch of something. But just as often it is because you're worrying and don't realize it. The key? Pausing long enough to find the joy in your life. That, in turn, will give you a clearer sense of what is needed to restore your health and well-being.

Goals and challenges

Often people are encouraged to set very specific goals, then make a list so they can achieve them. While at times this is useful, it can also be restrictive. And for you as an individual, not only is that restrictive, it interferes with using your intuition not only to achieve those goals, but to remind you how to celebrate them.

Don't be shy about saying what you want, from others or even from life itself. This may seem bold, if not downright selfish. However, this forces you to go from distant and perhaps vague dreams to define exactly what you have in mind. It's a vital first step to achieving those dreams.

MAY

13

T
/
A
\
U
/
R
\
U
/
S

Some insist that being kind is weak. Still, do it anyway

You

For you, Taurus, as an earth sign, imposing order on life is important. Even if there is disarray, you like to know where you are standing, what needs to be done to impose order, what comes first, and perhaps, even what you can put off until next week or next month. Yet at the same time, there are twists and turns that can upset your plans. The trick is to recognize how much you can achieve, or not, on any one day. Then, take a deep breath, knowing that the rest simply has to wait.

Yet there is a part of you that truly enjoys this challenge. Without it, life can be dull, if not predictable. You may complain about those challenges, but the creativity they bring out is important. What's more, they expose you to new ideas and new people, which bring very real rewards.

So the challenge is learning to recognize how much you benefit from the resulting twists and turns and, in doing so, possibly complaining less, too. The problem with complaining? It prevents you from viewing difficulties as challenges that you can actually conquer, and in the process, learn from. Better yet, when you have conquered them, you can celebrate not only your conquest but also what you've learned. Abandoning complaints may seem strange. Still, once you do, it will be like clouds vanishing, leaving you with sunny sky.

You and others

We all face practical challenges. But you may encounter somebody who enjoys creating obstacles—possibly a family member, friend, or colleague. As a determined Taurus, your instinct is to stand up to them. Yet, this only complicates matters. Back off. Let them be who they are. This may seem weak, yet you'll soon discover the peace it brings to your life.

Health and well-being

While there are all sorts of diets and regimens to follow, true inner well-being is another matter. It is about allowing certain individuals, or even circumstances, to be the nuisances they are meant to be. You enjoy battling to make improvements, even if it means facing one battle after another. By simply letting them unfold, you will give yourself peace.

Goals and challenges

You wouldn't think achieving goals begins with stillness. But this variety of reflection prepares you to fight for what you intend to achieve. True, this may not come naturally to you. But once you realize achieving that stillness is the challenge you're meeting, then you'll not only enjoy it—you'll be proud of yourself for doing it.

THIS DAY FOR EVERYONE

Usually you'd check out the facts before getting involved in life-changing arrangements, personal or professional. Yet things are moving so swiftly, it's a matter of now or never. Waste no time debating the pros and cons. It will only confuse you. At moments like this, your instincts are far more reliable.

GIFTS Good Host, Fashion-lover, Tough

CHALLENGES Extreme, Selfish, Uncompromising

NUMBER 1

(1+4) + (5) = 10 = (1+0) = 1

MAY

14

T
/
A
\
U
/
R
\
U
/
S

Ignore others' maneuvers— and have a grand time anyway

You

For you, the process of planning—of imposing order on life, or turning ideas into reality—isn't just about getting things done. It is a pleasure, and even more, it is one of your real gifts as a Taurus. While you are a practical earth sign, born with the relationship planet Venus as your ruler, you have a talent for managing such matters naturally. Yet there is also a challenge. Once you've organized a plan and made things happen, it feels like a letdown, because you no longer have a project.

The question is, what will you do next? Organize another plan, plant a garden? The fact is, you can do any of that. Your journey is about being able to exercise your creative muscles in every way, and even more, to experience the joy of that creativity every day, in how you live, how you think, and your plans and projects.

As an earth sign, you tend to focus more on the physical world around you. One of your greatest challenges is to go within while still enjoying what nature offers you. Find the balance between the two, and every day will be a joy. You will enjoy the plants around you and the heavens in the sky. What's more, you will enjoy the love of those you care about all the more. While you can't weigh or measure these, they're still deeply touching. Achieving that balance can be one of your greatest gifts.

You and others

You take an understandable pride in the fact that those around you—family, colleagues, even neighbors and friends—rely on you. They come to you for support, they ask questions. As a clever earth sign, you've got solutions. Yet, while you're delighted to lend them a hand, it doesn't boost your spirits. Learn to embrace others' joy and discover your own.

Health and well-being

There is all sorts of advice out there about taking care of yourself. However, the best starting point is whatever excites you and gives you a sense of promise. It may simply mean exercising in the way you want, by walking or going someplace lovely, or it may be having a beautiful meal or a massage. Whatever it is, it's something that is just for you.

Goals and challenges

Life, your background, school, and, if you work, your job, will all have given you clear information on how to achieve. None of it is about enjoying yourself. But increasingly, it is time both to deal with life's practicalities and be excited by what each day brings. The starting point? Be generous with yourself.

Ordinarily you'd be uncomfortable handing a task that's your responsibility over to somebody else. Except, at the moment, that individual is both eager to deal with the matter in question, and perhaps, better equipped than you are. Knowing that, waste no time on debate. Simply leave it to them.

GIFTS Values Investments, Practical, Insistent

CHALLENGES Rigid, Excessive, Contrary

NUMBER 2

(1+5) + (5) = 11 = (1+1) = 2

T
/
A
\
U
/
R
\
U
/
S

Those who insist I show my love in a certain way don't know how to receive it

You

For you, the path to joy can be a confusing one. That may seem a strange statement, because you have a talent for making life seem easy. Even when you are facing challenges alone, somehow you manage to help guide others past the obstacles they're facing. Often people tell you how much they envy you. It's true: you're accomplished at this.

Actually, it isn't until you notice how much others struggle with certain practicalities that you realize what a knack you have for dealing with even very tricky situations. Of course, some would say that being charitable with others is important. However, you do so much. In this particular case, it is about you and you alone—and recognizing what brings you joy. That may be the challenge—because you've focused so much on others, you are not really sure what you, personally, want to do or what will bring that special kind of joy.

The solution? Waste no time on discussion and experiment. Where to begin? Think small. Maybe it is about studying something that interests you. Maybe it's about taking a walk, thinking about how or what you eat, or even taking time alone or with a certain individual. Whatever the case, this part of your journey is one of discovery, and what you have learned about yourself during the process will benefit you now, and for the rest of your life.

You and others

Often, when you speak, it is about a hope. You say, "If only I could …" followed by ideas about helping a particular person, or rethinking certain past arrangements. Some are possible; most are not. Your path has reached a fork. You can continue focusing on impossible situations, or forget them and employ your mind, energy, and effort in the future those where you can make a difference.

Health and well-being

There is a tendency to feel that if you take care of yourself adequately, then you should be fine and happy. But in your particular case, life is about discovering ways of thinking and activities that lift your spirits. Focus on these, and on making them a part of your life every day for a week, or a month, and note how much things change.

Goals and challenges

It is easy to turn big challenges into big ongoing projects. But with these, a sense of achievement is in the distant future. Try adding everyday tasks, some easy, others challenging. They're like taking daily vitamins. They enrich your well-being, day by day. Do both. That is the skill and the challenge.

THIS DAY FOR EVERYONE

Having struggled to get the attention of one particular individual about certain concerns and complaints, you are exasperated. You're both annoyed and concerned about the situation in question. Soon you will have a chance to confront them. But you must act on it—and fast.

GIFTS Luxury-loving, Sensual, Stylish

CHALLENGES Lethargic, Self-indulgent, Willful

NUMBER 3

(1+6) + (5) = 12 = (1+2) = 3

There is no greater gesture of love than that which is as sudden as it is unexpected

You

As a Taurus and an earth sign, you have a knack for managing the physical world—from finances to acquiring beautiful and often valuable possessions. You also benefit from a powerful and analytical mind. Yet it isn't only about what you think; the direction your mind takes you is also of considerable significance, because while you are smart and good at thinking things through, you can sometimes get lost in those thoughts.

There is a fine line between being creative—that is, using your excellent mind to come up with ideas—and doing what might be called daydreaming, and allowing your mind to wander off in all sorts of directions. And, on occasion, you come back 15 minutes or even an hour later, feeling relaxed but wondering where you have been.

While this is okay, in your particular case, learning to master that capacity to create visions, not just to relax but for your benefit, is a powerful and important part of your journey. And one that, as your awareness of it grows, will become exciting. It will open the door to ideas that may have been on the fringe of your thoughts, but will take center stage. Next, you'll think about making them reality, and even part of your way of living, working, or loving. Do that, and you will discover joys that once seemed far beyond your reach.

You and others

You have an imaginative and rich side to your nature. Yet, it is difficult to describe, so you have shared it with few people. Mostly, with others, you focus on more "Taurus" topics—the world, what you enjoy, your achievements. However, certain individuals share that imaginative vision. Talk to them about it. Those discussions won't just be enriching; you could create some projects together.

Health and well-being

While often health and well-being is thought of as fitness—what you eat and what you do—sometimes it is more about your capacity to realize a vision. And that's very much the case for you. Ironically, sometimes if you get involved physically walking while envisioning your desires, you'll be able to combine that vision with taking care of yourself.

Goals and challenges

Figuring out what's next from a practical point of view is often wise. But as you are increasingly aware, sometimes you need to allow your imagination to shape your thinking. Do that, and you'll be shaping the direction you'll be taking now, over the coming days, weeks, months, and possibly even years.

THIS DAY FOR EVERYONE

Usually, you stick with who or what you believe in, through thick and thin. Yet even you could discover that you're unable to ride out the coming weeks' tricky events without making changes. No matter how much of a compromise this seems at the time, those changes are in your best interest.

MAY

17

T
/
A
\
U
/
R
\
U
/
S

The love that comes from a flower or a newborn can help you express your feelings

You

For you as a Taurus, the idea of turning concepts into action may be an appealing one, but being a thorough Taurus, naturally you'll check out the facts. However, these days, with things moving so swiftly, or being so different from elements of the past, there really are no facts to check out. You can talk to other people about what they have done. But, mostly, you need to trust another element of your nature: your intuition. While you're well aware of it, you're sometimes reluctant to even mention it, just because you are unsure of the reaction you'll get. Yet, increasingly, you are learning to rely on it, even with practical matters. What's more, this is very much what your journey as an individual is about.

It is about combining that amazing ability to enjoy life's pleasures and to manage its demands. When necessary, you employ your intuition, which can often bring a fresh view to arrangements. Yet at the same time, in certain situations, you to want to plan ahead. And this is where it gets tricky, because when you are using your intuition, often half of what you're envisioning is based on the past, while the rest has to do with a future that hasn't yet taken place. This is where the process of developing your trust and true vision comes in. As you master this, you'll embrace a rewarding skill, and deepen your wisdom about life itself.

You and others

Your gift for understanding others is wonderful, although you don't always realize how much your knack for knowing what those around you are working on, dealing with, or passionate about means to them. Better yet, you know what to say, and when. The irony is, your kindness or patience don't always extend to yourself. That is your next project.

Health and well-being

Sometimes the emphasis on health is on physical well-being alone. In your case, the emphasis is also on your mental and even emotional well-being. As much as you care about others, sometimes that concern becomes worry, which can undermine your mood. Learning to spot that, and where appropriate, shift your focus, is a vital skill.

Goals and challenges

Some would say putting life in order and outlining what needs to be done are vital. And often they are, but in your particular case, because you have such a strong practical streak, your instincts will tell you when to get in touch with somebody, when to rethink a plan, or when to undertake something new. Trust those feelings; they're a powerful gift.

THIS DAY FOR EVERYONE

It seems you need only say yes and a series of brilliant events will unfold. Yet appealing as this is, it is sudden enough that you have no time to consider. Judging by the pace of events, however, you won't have the luxury of such reflection. In fact, it's now or never.

If you debate the rights and wrongs of joy, it becomes an impossibility

You

For you as a Taurus and an earth sign—and somebody who likes to get things organized— life should be fairly straightforward, except you have a tinge of the sign next to you. It's Gemini, which has to do with having a different kind of vision; having a lively mind; noticing what's going on in the world around you; noting what people are talking about, and new ideas.

Sometimes you don't even realize you've done that. Yet at the same time, it is all about a kind of discovery that is important simply because occasionally those insights, completely unconsciously, add to your life and come up as ideas later, and you don't even know where they came from. Being able to take advantage of them is the important thing. And the trick is to refuse to get caught up having to explain or justify them, or to come up with facts to support them. Simply dive in. That may seem unwise, but you have done it before.

And you'll do it enough now that you'll be increasingly aware of this very special skill— to swing from being a solid Taurus to being inquisitive, a visionary, which is what you can be at times. And it will be, the more you recognize it. This is an important part of your journey. The more you embrace this visionary part of you, the more you will accomplish, and the more you will enjoy life itself.

You and others

There have been many times that you've been confronted by those who are so narrow-minded that there is no point in even discussing ideas different from theirs. Still, their persistence can undermine your confidence. The fact is, part of the challenge is to trust yourself and your feelings over those who seem determined to raise doubts.

Health and well-being

Your passion about certain ideas or activities can mean you forget obligations, including taking care of yourself. While it is unusual for a Taurus, you're borrowing that from the sign next to yours, Gemini, which tends to get so absent-minded they forget to eat or sleep. The solution? Return to your core nature, and take care of yourself, like a good earth sign.

Goals and challenges

For you, life is about discovery. While one side of your nature is tempted to stick with something that is safe and familiar, you thrive on new ideas and even unfamiliar settings. The more you venture into that new territory in terms of ideas and activities, even passions, the more you will get the most out of life.

THIS DAY FOR EVERYONE

Don't be surprised if certain individuals aren't as enthusiastic about new ideas or potential changes as you are. While you've already explored these possibilities in depth, they're new to others. Knowing that, invest time in explaining exactly what's behind your feelings of enthusiasm. That should do the trick.

GIFTS Loving, Good Host, Musical Sensitivity

CHALLENGES Uncooperative, Rigid, Insensitive

NUMBER 6

$(1+9) + (5) = 15 = (1+5) = 6$

You move fewer muscles when you smile than when you frown, so it's more relaxing

You

The theme running through your life, Taurus, is "rediscovering yourself." You were born sharing the influence of Taurus, one of the most down-to-earth signs, and the creative, restless, imaginative Gemini. And with that toughness of Gemini in your nature, you're always aware of future possibilities. This insight prevents you from getting overly stuck in Taurus activities alone, as important as they can be. However, it can also mean that you sometimes get caught off-guard. It could be that you are thinking about a new idea or possibly swept away by something exciting. An encounter will have inspired you or you have a vision of something you really must do.

The problem isn't yours. While those closest are aware of these two sides of your nature, if somebody knows only the down-to-earth Taurus side, the individual in question could misunderstand you. Yet talking with others— using those Gemini vibes and discussing new ideas—with those who, like you, share these wonderful qualities of practicality and vision, will be fun. There are those who understand you. And as much as you enjoy the company of others, of family and friends, there will always be a few whose company not only inspires you, but gives you the kind of appreciation that is heartwarming. It is almost like a type of vibrational vitamins.

You and others

Dealing with others is easy if you employ your Taurus side, which is as charming as it is practical. But as you've learned increasingly over the past years, you have a visionary side, too. And it's almost as if you are speaking two different languages. The trick? Learn to live with both sides of your nature, then share it with others. They'll benefit, and so will you.

Health and well-being

Contending with pressure from others is nothing new. Mostly, they need to be convinced that your plans or ideas have promise or will actually work. But, in every case, struggling achieves nothing. Instead, it is about relaxing and allowing things to come together in their own time. This may seem difficult, but once you take a deep breath, those ideas will begin to fit—like magic.

Goals and challenges

You have a tendency to get bored. The remedy? Explore. If ever there were a time to begin, it is now. Learn the art of doing what you need to, and the art of exploration, and not only will you enjoy life and achieve a lot, you will begin to live your vision.

THIS DAY FOR EVERYONE

If ever there was a time to take certain ventures you're passionate about further, it's now. The planets' favor is likely to take the form of certain extremely helpful individuals. You've already done all you can. So sit back and allow those who are both able and eager to give you a boost.

Gemini

Ruler Mercury
Element Air

Symbol The Twins
Flower Lavender

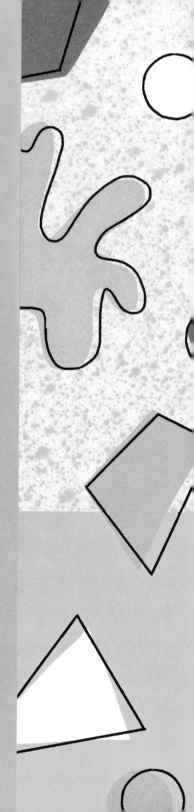

DATES

May 20–
June 19

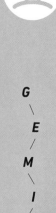

G
\
E
/
M
\
I
/
N
\
I

Gemini The first of the three
inquisitive air signs, Gemini, the
twins, benefits from the rule of
restless Mercury, the god of
communication, charm, and,
especially, a lively mind. You are
an endlessly curious individual,
often with many sides to your life,
interests, and tastes. Your flower is
lavender, your herb is savory
marjoram, and your tree is the
hazel. Your stone is agate, with its
endless range of colors.

GIFTS Traveler, Versatile, Communicator

CHALLENGES Mercurial, Tardy, Skips Details

NUMBER 7

(2+0) + (5) = 7

The power of a golden moment of insight changes your life forever

You

You are the very essence of Gemini, born on the day the sign starts. You carry the clever wit and enthusiasm of your ruling planet, Mercury, and of the theme for your sign, which is communication—it's about ideas, not only communicating with others, but paying attention to what is going on in the world around you and learning from that. Sometimes, however, that enthusiasm can turn into impatience, so you may take action or even commit before your know all the facts.

Of course, you don't think about this until later, when you find you must extract yourself from certain arrangements or commitments, personal or even of a business nature—that's part of your style as a Gemini. It is said that many of you born under this sign live several lives, with a range of activities, and in many settings. Certainly your symbol—the twins— suggests that you may even live all of those lives at one time.

The trick to making the best of this is to enjoy the diversity, and to take advantage of it. There may be those around you who are jealous, but it's yours to live. And your own day isn't just about experiencing all those ideas, it is about making them a part of your life. Focus on these and not only will you be spectacularly good at them, you will enjoy what each and every day brings your way.

You and others

You don't just enjoy the company of others, often your life is built around those you're close to—family, friends, even neighbors and colleagues. However, this can mean that often you're the one who is creating all the excitement. The secret? Encouraging them to learn how to add magic to their own lives. You'll be doing yourself, and them, a favor.

Health and well-being

As you're aware, sometimes you can be tired or hungry and not even realize it. That's because you get so involved in what you're doing, and in your enthusiasm for life itself, you forget to eat. On the other hand, you can eat so much that you feel exhausted. Finding that balance is a challenge, but once you do, you will feel much better.

Goals and challenges

This has to do not so much with life out in the world as your life within, and the challenges you set for yourself and the ways in which you explore those happening. This isn't about a single day or challenge, or even a single year. It's about finding a way to live that allows you to use your active mind and your energy to set up challenges that aren't just worthwhile, they bring you personal satisfaction as well.

G
\
E
/
M
\
I
/
N
\
I

For every step you take forward, you are leaving something behind. That may seem obvious, yet you're fighting that fact now, in one situation you've strong feelings about. While letting go of both that emotional attachment and certain arrangements won't be easy, it is essential that you move on.

GIFTS Quick-thinking, Listener, Smart

NUMBER 8

CHALLENGES Procrastinates, Undependable, Scattered

(2+1) + (5) = 8

G
\
E
/
M
\
I
/
N
\
I

Discussing ideas can be informative. Listening to others' words can be life-changing

You

Your birthday theme is "inquisitiveness." You'd think this comes naturally to every Gemini, but actually, you benefit from a special if not unique variety of interest in the world around you, and the people in it. You enjoy each day for what you learn. You love collecting ideas and the experiences you have as a result of the circumstances you are in. And even more than that, you love learning about what people are doing, not so much because you intend to become close friends or involved with them, but simply hearing about what they have in mind is enchanting.

At the same time, finding your own center, and finding people you can exchange ideas with are just as important. These discussions are also a major part of what might be called your "personal vitamins." This has to do with you, as an individual, but also with your activities out in the world, your work, in your community, or with your family. Here, too, while you will listen to what others have to say, the exchange of ideas with them is what is most important to you.

As a result, your world becomes a broader and more exciting place. Not only do you pursue exciting goals, you could even take up something new. This isn't just important; this approach to life brings you a variety of joy in the present and promise for the future.

You and others

While relationships are important, when that word is used, it doesn't just apply to everyday relationships. Yes, it's about friendships, family, and even neighbors. But it is just as much about those individuals you meet who add enormously to your life, and in fact, you add to theirs, too. Recognize that, and the richness of the links between you.

Health and well-being

On occasion, something hits you that doesn't just slow you down, it "flattens" you. It may seem you're ill, but actually it's fatigue. As a Gemini, you are both restless and endlessly inquisitive, so often you don't realize you've forgotten to eat or are exhausted. Recognizing this involves simply noticing when you need to relax, then doing exactly that.

Goals and challenges

For you, as an inquisitive Gemini, a life without challenges, without something to learn about, would be very dull indeed. Yet, you often get so involved in others' projects that you forget about your own. The remedy? Every once in a while, make a list. Then, from time to time, check it out, and ensure that you are putting on your own goals first.

 THIS DAY FOR EVERYONE

It is worth considering the fact that while some decisions can be made once and will last forever, others really must be regarded as tentative. This means that, for now, things are settled, yet at the same time, you will have the freedom to explore the rather intriguing ideas or offers coming your way.

Insights can appear in surprising settings. Often, what is least expected turns out best

You

There are vitamins you take, and there are vitamins in food. But for you, as an inquisitive Gemini, there are what might be termed vitamins in ideas, and your active mind needs to be fed with them. This isn't just about ideas, though; it also has to do with people, being out and about, or finding yourself in situations where your restless need to know what's happening in the world is satisfied. Some get involved in a hobby. And while you might have one, observing others satisfies your desire to learn about what's happening around you, often by simply observing what people are doing. Also being in situations that are unfamiliar gives you an opportunity to broaden your horizons.

You are an inquisitive Gemini, but your character is a balance between simply learning what you can and taking action. While you might decide to turn some of what you discover into a part of your life, simply learning about what is going on around you, with others and in the wider world, is vital and rewarding. Whatever you're doing, explore. That simple process, of exploring for the sake of what you experience, can itself become a rewarding part of your life, something you do with friends, a vocation, a career, or even a passion. The most important thing is to realize the joy in discovery that is core to your nature.

You and others

True, often you are more aware of what's going on than those around you. Yet at the same time, others' experiences and the places they will take you add to your life. Once you recognize how vital this is, and how those experiences add in wonderful ways, you'll ensure there are always one or two individuals who can add to your life in this unique way.

Health and well-being

As a Gemini and an air sign you are easily distracted, and rapidly become impatient with dull routine when taking care of your health or eating. As a result, you can overdo things until you're exhausted. The trick is to turn potentially beneficial activities into fun. Whatever it is, if you enjoy it, you'll do it.

Goals and challenges

Being by nature an inquisitive Gemini, you always need something new, and that could very well have to do with what's next in your life. Some people stumble over these, but for you, the process of searching for it is as important as the discovery. What's more, being excited about what's next makes today's tasks more fun, too.

THIS DAY FOR EVERYONE

When you offered to help somebody, you had no idea of the complications involved. Now that you know more, you have a choice. Tempting as it is to ignore this, hoping it will resolve itself is unfair and unwise. Either do the best you can, or back out of the arrangement, explaining why.

GIFTS Multitalented, Fair, Adaptable

CHALLENGES Sporadic, Forgetful, Preoccupied

NUMBER 1

$(2+3) + (5) = 10 = (1+0) = 1$

MAY

23

G
\
E
/
M
\
I
/
N
\
I

Every day, exchange an old habit for a more upbeat one. Your life will take on a new glow

You

While you may not think about this, as a Gemini and somebody ruled by the planet Mercury, you have a sister sign, Virgo, which is also ruled by Mercury. It's an earth sign, and it's all about order. And your particular Gemini character has a touch of that Virgo need not only to create order, but to organize your life in a way where you appreciate the beauty of what you're doing—far more than the ordinary Gemini would. You appreciate the ideas, and once you've created a balance, you will also know how to create situations and a lifestyle that give you the activity and excitement you thrive on. Also, this is about joy in terms of living well, which includes knowing interesting people and having an exciting life.

However, that earth-sign aspect of your nature, linked to Virgo, is as important as the Gemini side. It's analytical. It considers what those you spend time with bring into your life, from rewarding ideas and activities to sheer fun. It's not that you demand anything specific from them, but simply that because you offer so much as a friend or a colleague, you want others to bring something to the experience, too. The challenge? That tough analysis. Sometimes you are too generous. This isn't easy, yet it is one of your most important tasks, as a Gemini with a touch of Virgo.

You and others

Those around you, the individuals you're with regularly, are important to you. This includes friends, family, colleagues, or even just close acquaintances. Each adds something, because each lives a life or has access to facts unfamiliar to you, so they are fascinating. Not everyone understands this. Don't bother trying to explain. Just continue to enjoy people for who they are.

Health and well-being

As a Gemini who is influenced by Virgo, you'll analyze what's good for you, then worry about whether you are doing the right thing or not, and then end up doing nothing. The trick? Try things out, from new ways to eat and exercise to relaxation. See how they feel and, importantly, whether or not you want to stick with them. They'll keep you from getting bored.

Goals and challenges

For you, setting goals is important. While you often set far-reaching goals, minor goals for a month, a week, or even a day are as important. They are a form of vitamins for you. As you begin your day, choose one goal, and by the day's close, you may have accomplished it, but you'll have done other things, too.

THIS DAY FOR EVERYONE

There is a difference between things going wonderfully and events being what you've planned or anticipated. Ironically, what's least expected could turn out best in the long run. Knowing that, explore absolutely every idea and offer that comes your way. You won't regret it.

A lively exchange of ideas is exciting. Learning what others feel touches your heart

You

The message for you as a May 24th Gemini is that every day is a new experience. This may seem obvious, but it's not the case for others. Many people set up their lives so that each day is basically the same thing, day after day. That would drive you crazy. As an inquisitive Gemini, but especially one born on this day, you have a need to discover. While obviously there are certain things that are essential to your daily routine, if you set up things so that you have something new to do every day, then you'll have a sense of accomplishment.

Whether it's taking a new route somewhere, trying a new food, or talking to somebody you've never met, it doesn't really matter. And in fact, you may do it spontaneously. But each will add to your life. Some experiences may be memorable. Some may be forgotten almost immediately. But each will increase what might be termed your memory box of experiences.

Better yet, this gets you in the habit of searching for things that will be rewarding. And here again, rather than trying to figure out why something in the past wasn't that rewarding, instead of worrying, you'll forget about it, and will instead derive great joy from the actual process of searching. And that's the key to being a Gemini born on this day: not just to search, but even more to enjoy the process of discovery.

You and others

Often when people meet, they'll exchange questions, sometimes discreetly, sometimes forthrightly, about their lives or background. For you, that's natural. But it is important that you talk about yourself, too. This adds to your life and theirs. And sometimes, that exchange will grow, and become an essential and rewarding part of your life.

Health and well-being

For you as a Gemini, serious workouts can be dull. But if you're able to find those activities that lift your spirits, from eating well to fun exercise—maybe salsa dancing—you'll exchange boredom for enthusiasm and feel more energetic. Better yet, do it with someone whose company you enjoy. Do that, and even jogging at home will bring you pleasure.

Goals and challenges

Many people love setting goals. But you will think about such matters, then get distracted, and end up doing a bit of this and a bit of that. One of your biggest challenges is remembering to set goals for yourself. Once it becomes a habit, you'll not only benefit from it, you'll enjoy the process as well.

GIFTS Clever, Unbiased, Communicative

NUMBER 3

CHALLENGES Flighty, Forgetful, Mercurial

$(2+5) + (5) = 12 = (1+2) = 3$

MAY

25

G
\
E
/
M
\
I
/
N
\
I

The more you try laughing, the more powerful you will realize it is

You

If you're into astrology, you will know Gemini is an air sign, which symbolizes thought and ideas. And it's true: most Geminis live in a world of concepts and possibilities, that is, thinking about what they could be doing, what they've done in the past, the ideas they've exchanged with others. But you also focus on the tangible side of life—that is, the world around you. That includes what you actually see, possibly the objects you own, the colors around you that create texture in your life. And, equally, it is about the food you eat and the feelings you experience around others or when doing things. Each of these brings its own excitement to your day. The challenge? It's getting others to understand that— because, to your surprise, not everybody is as aware of that special variety of joys.

Gradually, though, you will connect with those who do appreciate that, and they'll become friends, or possibly colleagues. The activity could become a hobby or even an element of your work. Your restless side needs a range of interests. Some will become a temporary obsession while others will draw you in more. This could turn into a lasting hobby, from gardening to collecting something about which, gradually, you become expert. And it could become a second career, one you don't just enjoy, but also share with others.

You and others

One major focus is deepening your link with others. Some Geminis are just happy talking with people, including those closest. However, it is important that you find deeper links, those you can develop. This may be in terms of a personal relationship, but one that also extends into the world. In every case, ensure you devote enough time to these enriching connections.

Health and well-being

The key here isn't what you do, it's how you approach it. Do something—say, workout at a gym—solely because it's good for you and soon you will be unenthusiastic. If instead, you're excited, whether it's salsa dancing or tennis, you will actually do it. And whatever it is, it will be helpful for you.

Goals and challenges

The real challenge for you is exactly what we've been discussing—to make sure that you're able to appreciate that tangible side of your life. That it excites and inspires you. These feelings may not come naturally, but the more you practice, the more you will benefit from it, and the more you'll enjoy whatever it is you are doing.

THIS DAY FOR EVERYONE

It would seem that while problems cause dissent, everybody would agree that there are golden opportunities to be taken advantage of. Unfortunately, that is not the case. In fact, if you are to make the best of what comes you way, you may need to compromise, at least in the short term.

Be the student who discovers the perfect, yet unexpected, solution

You

While everybody sees the world around them in their own way, as an inquisitive Gemini, you see a world that is wider than most. You're unusual in the sense that you don't just observe events, you experience them in a very personal way. However, you may not be aware of that, unless you compare notes with others about what you see versus what they experience.

Of course, this becomes an important part of your life at home, and equally, you'll view the world around you with joy and pleasure as you take a walk or look at a garden. Yet for many Geminis, this is actually part of your work, something you do that allows you to analyze something, anything from fashion to architecture, even to observing or being involved in something as mechanical as how a car is built. Looking at and enjoying the world is one thing, but the process of discovery is also exciting. If you notice yourself feeling critical or uncomfortable about one particular matter, simply stop and back up to the point at which you began to think about and appreciate the matter, idea, or activity in question.

Do that, and you'll discover the joy that is very much a part of this side of your life. And even more, you'll discover the joy that comes with being able to spend time with and talk to others who view life in this way.

You and others

For you, being able to hang out with others is so important. But often you find people overwhelming and enjoy being alone. The trick is achieving a balance. Ensure those around you add what might be called "vitamins" to your life, especially enthusiasm vitamins. That way, you don't just have a good time, your spirits get a very real boost.

Health and well-being

The funny thing about dealing with your own health and well-being is that it is influenced by the pleasure you take in taking care of yourself. If what you're doing is no fun, you're unlikely to do much of it. Find a setting or an activity that satisfies your need for quality and beauty, and you actually go, and will enjoy it.

Goals and challenges

Your challenge is living life a little bit better than others do. That may sound strange, but many people can't be bothered to make the effort you do to ensure that every day has its wonderful moments. As you do that, what you learn will add to your life, to your relationships, and lead to achievements.

Sooner or later you will need to disentangle yourself from an arrangement that once made sense but no longer does. The problem is, the actual process will involve facts, figures, or the kind of formalities you loathe. Tempting as it is, putting it off achieves nothing. The sooner you tackle this, the better.

GIFTS Explorer, Listener, Fair

CHALLENGES Scattered, Late, Easily Distracted

NUMBER 5

$(2+7) + (5) = 14 = (1+4) = 5$

MAY

27

G
\
E
/
M
\
I
/
N
\
I

Your busy mind seeks ideas—unaware that the best ideas emerge from stillness

You

Your theme as a May 27th Gemini is actually the result of being ruled by the restless and inquisitive Mercury, and that is "Keep moving." Of course, there are lots of ways to do this. Your body can keep moving. You can take a walk. You can do exercise. But much of your nature as a Gemini is your constantly roaming mind. It is circulating around any room you're in. It's wandering, thinking about what you will be doing next. And sometimes it is moving around the world.

While many Geminis benefit from a restless mind, your vision and your mind's capacity to wander are both a joy and a skill. True, if you allow your mind to wander too far or into thoughts that don't profit you, it can be exhausting. And this is very much the focus, because being aware of those mental journeys and of their impact on you is a challenge—and a skill that will enable you to direct your mind along more rewarding paths. It allows you to think about what you need to organize and do as well as to find what you enjoy.

Ironically, even when you are doing something you enjoy, your mind can wander and dwell on something that is less joyous. So for you, this process of learning to stick with the thoughts that elevate you isn't just useful, it's something that can actually reshape your life and bring true joy.

You and others

You may not think of it this way, but at times the negative attitude of others can be infectious, in the sense that, after being around them a short while, you don't just feel lousy, you are questioning why you're there—and with good reason. You can ensure the visit is brief. Also you can actually learn how to improve on the vibes of the situation.

Health and well-being

Being in an upbeat mood is one thing; however, feeling well physically adds its own light to your life. Yet you sometimes get lost doing things you don't enjoy, even eating unwisely, and don't know why. Forget analysis. Simply change your habits. The payoff will come in how wonderful you feel.

Goals and challenges

The challenge for you is accepting the fact that you are an eternal explorer. You may stay in the same place, you may even remain in the same job, but that process of exploration is a wonderful part of your nature and one to be noted, discussed with others, and savored each and every day.

 THIS DAY FOR EVERYONE

You have been concerned and upset by sudden developments. Since then, you've learned a lot, which has both surprised and delighted you. Remember this when other, as dramatic, developments arise over the coming weeks and instead of battling them, you will focus on exploring what they offer.

GIFTS Smart, Fluid, Communicator

CHALLENGES Preoccupied, Undependable, Mercurial

NUMBER 6

$(2+8) + (5) = 15 = (1+5) = 6$

Helping others comes naturally to you. Accepting thanks doesn't

You

You don't think of yourself as being restless until you compare how you live and think to others, and then you realize that while those you're talking to may be doing the same things, living the same way as they were a month, a year, or possibly several years ago, you'll have explored all sorts of ideas. You'll have met people, gone places. This restless side of your nature comes naturally, but also there's a part that is seeking a single perfect moment in a day, a perfect link with others and possibly even the perfect activity.

This isn't simply about moving around or being restless, it is about a search. Yet, the trouble is, life itself changes, which means that when you find that perfect activity, that link with somebody that brings a new glow to your life, you may well find that the next day it's not quite the same, which of course is natural.

And this is the lesson for you: to recognize that what seems like restlessness is a genuine and enthusiastic and what might be termed golden curiosity about life. Those perfect moments are wonderful, but they can't last, because life itself changes. Day comes, then night comes. Spring comes, is replaced by summer, and then fall and winter. Each of these is about the changes. Don't be surprised when those golden moments leave. They're simply clearing the way for the next ones.

You and others

Relationships, whether family, friends, or close emotional ties, can be confusing, simply because, for you, the need for variety is as natural as breathing. Yet certain individuals need to do things the same way, day in, day out. Obviously, this drives you a little crazy. The solution? It's not changing them. It is developing a sense of humor. That is the secret to many of life's crises, including this.

Health and well-being

That restless part of you, as you can imagine, needs a lot of different things to do with your mind, but also with your body. Your sense of well-being comes not only from physical movement and choosing wisely what you eat. Even more crucial is a positive mental attitude. This is about improvement. Once you find that center, you are able to continue exploring.

Goals and challenges

One of your greatest challenges is not allowing other people's negativity to influence you. You wouldn't think it would actually have that much of an impact, but you'll find that if you can manage to avoid, if not shut off, discussions with individuals of that nature, not only does life seem a lot better, you'll feel a lot better as well.

THIS DAY FOR EVERYONE

Life often brings surprises. Often those you remember best are those that were challenging. Yet the surprises that are coming your way now will be memorable for other reasons. While you may be short of reassuring facts to begin with, once you get involved, you'll recognize just how promising they are.

GIFTS Bright, Debater, Easygoing

CHALLENGES Inquisitive, Flighty, Skips Details

NUMBER 7

$(2+9) + (5) = 16 = (1+6) = 7$

MAY

29

G
\
E
/
M
\
I
/
N
\
I

Turn setbacks into opportunities— it is easier than you imagine

You

Your birth message is inspired not only by your ruling planet, Mercury, but also the Roman god Mercury himself. He is renowned for being swift of mind and fleet of foot. His influence accents these elements of your character, especially with your May 29th birthday, because you share those characteristics of being quick-thinking and fast-moving. If you've seen the images of him, you'll know he wore a winged helmet. And, just like him, you, too, have ideas that, when you release them, can fly in so many directions, offering inspiration, insights, and, on occasion, helping somebody resolve issues.

But his capacity to bring ideas is just as important, and this is your gift as well. It's just that it comes so naturally to you, you don't even think about it. At the same time, you're always trying something new, which for you seems normal, but certainly individuals around you may complain about it and that's simply because they don't have your inborn gift of being inquisitive.

Don't let complaints about your inquisitiveness bother you. This is your special gift—in fact, many people appreciate being with you because of that enthusiasm. The more you appreciate yourself and the more you allow it to shape your life and your activities, the better.

You and others

Being an inquisitive Gemini, you're interested in a wide range of topics. For you, being fascinated by events is as natural as breathing, and the more you explore, the better. In some cases, you'll go one place, then another. But in others, you don't need to go any further. These will be a part of your life, forever.

Health and well-being.

As often as we're told it's good to get involved in a routine, the trick for you is to find a range of people to spend time with and, equally, activities. Similarly, you need variety in your way of eating. All of these are vital, and in fact, this variety comes naturally to you.

Goals and challenges

Setting a single goal seems crazy and, in fact, for you, it is. It's vital that your life is organized around what might be termed "mini-goals," that is, modest aims and challenges. But ensure you have one or two long-term, if not lifetime, goals. Combine those and not only will you enjoy every day of your life, you'll be amazed at how swiftly you move toward achieving them.

THIS DAY FOR EVERYONE

The adage goes, "Never say never," and rarely was such advice more apt than now. In the past you may have said there were certain things you wouldn't consider or even certain individuals you'd do anything to avoid. But that was then, and times have changed—and so have you.

GIFTS Flexible, Versatile, Listener

CHALLENGES Sporadic, Procrastinates, Changeable

NUMBER 8

(3+0) + (5) = 8

Often the most rewarding joys are entirely within your mind

You

As a May 30th Gemini, one of your greatest gifts is your broad interest in the world around you, in ideas and discussions and, especially, in people. However, you don't realize how wonderful and, indeed, unique this is until you begin to talk with somebody and realize they don't ask questions of any variety.

For you, this process of exploring the world around you and what people do and the resulting discussions are like special vitamins that nourish you in the present. And, even more, often those ideas you hear about will add to your awareness. While you may well collect things—anything from art to photographs and books—you are also collecting memories that will enrich your life, even when you aren't around the actual objects that you have in mind.

True, it's very easy for you to get so involved in the process, you get overwhelmed. This is partly because, with your inquisitive mind it's satisfying, it can expand. You may begin collection number one and then find you have collections number two, three, and four, and that's when it can overwhelm your life.

This is where balance is so important to you, because that process of discovery is so wonderful and deepens your feelings so much, but even more important is recognizing how much being with people alone benefits you.

You and others

Whether it's family, friends, colleagues, or neighbors, people add to your life. However, if you depend on them too much, you can forget about the pleasures of going solo. What's most important is to find that center within yourself, which, quite simply, enjoys life: what you're doing now. Your most important relationship? The one you have with yourself.

Health and well-being

Health is one thing, well-being another. They're separate, in the sense that you can feel terrific, even if you're tired, or you really should be eating better, simply because that sense of well-being comes from living an interesting and worthwhile life. However, it is vital that you balance the two, and manage to eat well and take care of yourself. This brings a certain lightness to your day.

Goals and challenges

Often people are told to list their goals, but because you are by nature so inquisitive, things don't always work that way. Rather, you discover one thing and then another, and then another, and then you eliminate something. While that's one approach, it also means that you may not fit in with everyone else's idea of listing goals and challenges.

THIS DAY FOR EVERYONE

Being interested in others is one thing. But there are one or two individuals who seem to think you'll be there for them, whatever your other commitments. Thus, saying a firm "no" can be very difficult indeed. That is, however, exactly what you'll have to do, or face yet more unrealistic demands.

GIFTS Multitalented, Fluid, Just

CHALLENGES Easily Distracted, Tardy, Unsettled

NUMBER 9

(3+1) + (5) = 9

G
\
E
/
M
\
I
/
N
\
I

True love? You'll being thrilled by what you discover because of it

You

The birthday theme for you—imagination—is something you rarely focus on, because it is so much a part of your way of thinking and living. You're imaginative; rather than simply dealing with change swiftly, you benefit from new experiences and exposure to ideas that stimulate your thinking. Yet at times, your mind can run away with you—you will go from simply organizing plans to imagining getting away from the everyday, taking off to somewhere far away. The trick here isn't what you imagine, but reining in your mind, to focus on facts and potential solutions, and then on exploring new possibilities.

It may well be that you are intrigued by certain new ideas, but you didn't pursue them because you didn't know enough, there wasn't someone to do it with, or you were distracted. Yet at the same time, for you as an inquisitive Gemini, delving more deeply into these ideas and potential activities lifts your spirits. That, in turn, leads to meeting people with similar interests. True, this could mean rearranging your life. If so, it's worth beginning that process of broadening your horizons, which, in turn, boosts your feelings and ultimately, brightens your life.

Turn your imagination into an asset and whatever else you're doing, your way of living, activities, or work, will benefit enormously.

You and others

Your links with others, from family to friends or colleagues, are dances. Each has its own rhythm and style. Some are like a stately waltz, others rock 'n' roll, possibly with frequent shake-ups. The resulting variety means you're never bored, and what's more, it encourages others to find, and live, according to their own rhythm. Nothing could be better than that.

Health and well-being

For you, as a restless May 31st Gemini, following others' rules is nearly unbearable. Yet you need the energy that comes with eating well. There is a secret. Stock up on all sorts of nutritious food so that you have a choice, but having a healthy diet or routine will boost your spirits and your intake of vitamins.

Goals and challenges

Some people set goals for a year, even several years, ahead. You do, too, but because you're creative, you also need to be able to rethink your objectives, and often. Achieving a balance between planning and indulging the spontaneous side of your nature is itself a challenge, and one you'll actually enjoy wrestling with.

THIS DAY FOR EVERYONE

It may seem you're stuck in a rut. But actually you've been restricted by circumstances. Now, happily, those are about to change. So when sudden and unsettling events shake things up, welcome events, as they're a first step to new, and timely, changes—and better yet, rewarding if unexpected adventures.

GIFTS Communicator, Adaptable, Quick-thinking   NUMBER 7

CHALLENGES Erratic, Scattered, Argumentative $(0+1) + (6) = 7$

Discussing ideas wakes up your mind.
Reflecting on life's joys delights your soul

You

Your birthday theme is "fresh start." This is natural because, of course, it's the first of the month. But, also, being ruled by Mercury, you are inquisitive by nature, so every day is about discovery. In fact, you fear getting stuck in situations where you are prevented from exploring new ideas. For you, this is like breathing. However, you can unintentionally catch yourself in restrictive habits. It's because they're so familiar that you don't realize their influence. The trick? Be aware of the moments when you feel you "must" do something. It's about balancing the discomfort of making frequent changes, doing things in a new way, yet being so organized you can deal with events in your personal life, in your career if you have one, and in close relationships. Ideally, this means you're not always doing things at the last minute.

   While this may seem a lot to think about, once you've organized a routine, knowing what's next actually frees you. If that routine includes giving you the space to do things differently, then finding the balance in your thoughts and actions becomes a real joy. It may not be the way others want to live—and they may question this odd balance between freedom and your own version of a routine— but then, they don't have to live your life. You're doing a very good job of it.

You and others

You'd like to deepen links to others, but don't always do it. The reason? You're lively and inquisitive, and some criticize you for that. If it's family, simply agree to disagree. If it's friends, variety is crucial. They don't need to be like you. But it's vital they rejoice in who you are and enjoy being themselves with you.

Health and well-being

As you know, in the past you've sometimes been so uptight that even if you're eating well and exercising, you're still unsettled. Knowing this, aim to balance health and well-being with your way of thinking. Do that each day, and gradually you'll end up eating better and sleeping better without a strict routine, but simply because you're more balanced.

Goals and challenges

As a Gemini, setting goals is one thing, but because of your changeable nature, those goals tend to evolve as you do. They tend to do what might be termed "morph," something that is important for you. As those goals change, you will have the option to rethink plans, in the unique way that is one of your greatest strengths.

G
\
E
/
M
\
I
/
N
\
I

Financial issues have been on your mind for weeks. While you've managed to resolve several, one or two require the cooperation of a particular individual. Not only has that not been forthcoming, they wouldn't even discuss it. Try again. Recent events are forcing them to take such matters seriously.

GIFTS Fluid, Fair, Easygoing

NUMBER 8

CHALLENGES Skips Details, Forgetful, Late

$(0+2) + (6) = 8$

02

Good ideas can bring relief, but laughter broadens your horizons

You

As a June 2nd Gemini, you tend to be a bit of a collector. While you may collect objects, what you really collect are ideas—that is, memories of wonderful times, from places you've been and of people you've been with. When you are reminiscing, you'll sometimes compare them to the here and now. That's risky. It is easy to focus on everyday struggles, then compare them with pleasant memories from the past.

However, you'll have forgotten about the challenges you faced back then, from difficult people or puzzling obstacles. This is the key for you to making the best of your life, to recognize that often you will recall the past as having been rosier than the present. And, often, you'll anticipate great joys for the future. However, actually achieving joy in the here and now is another matter, and can be a real challenge.

You're not alone in this, and in fact there are plenty of others who will join you in complaining. They will merrily talk about how awful things are, to the extent that, if you don't begin the conversation in a bad mood, by its end, you will be. The lesson? Recognize that this is about where you allow your mind to go. Use the power of your unique Gemini vision, as if you were directing a movie, and you'll create a happy and productive here and now—and ultimately, the future as well.

You and others

As a Gemini, you're sometimes influenced by those you feel a link with. You can tend to agree, unthinkingly, with what they say. Do that, however, and you can be drawn into their world—one that may not suit you. Sometimes you have to "agree to disagree." Whatever the nature of the relationship, ensure you can be who you are.

Health and well-being

You have a knack for taking care of yourself wisely. You get moving and, equally, eat the right things. Yet, there are times when your joy vanishes, and a glum mood takes over, often influenced by others. Learning to acknowledge and deal with this, and create emotional links with others, especially if they're being moody, is a gift, and mastering it will bring you lifelong joy.

Goals and challenges

Sometimes goals can be listed, one by one. But in your particular case, your goal and challenge are to learn to enjoy every moment for what it is. Worldly achievements are exciting. However, perhaps the greatest achievement for you is developing the ability to enjoy each and every moment of life, from its shadows to its sunniest moments.

THIS DAY FOR EVERYONE

Sometimes setbacks are exactly that. However, what seem like problems are actually events prompting you to reconsider arrangements that have been a part of your life for such a very long time, you wouldn't otherwise question them. But you must. Once you begin, you'll realize why changes are crucial.

Analyze what's wrong and needs fixing—or what you can learn from it

You

The planet Mercury isn't just your ruler, it's dominating your birthday reading. The ancient Roman god Mercury was a clever young man but also a trickster, with a reputation for surprising people with what he would or wouldn't do. For you, life can be like this. You'll commit to a situation, then change your mind, then discover certain people are upset. Or alternatively, it may be that those around you make the changes and you have to deal with the resulting fallout. In every case, however, it's about recognizing that, just as day inevitably follows night, long ago a part of you recognized that no matter how carefully you figure out details, things won't necessarily go according to plan. The irony is, in some cases, those changes are an improvement.

Ignore those who are upset by those unexpected developments. Instead, focus on figuring out a new way to work with what's happened versus what's necessary. Once you're doing that, you'll begin to use the creative side of your Gemini nature and, even better, the creative influence of Mercury.

You'll come up with plans far better than you'd have imagined possible. Live out your life, knowing that even unexpected twists are allowing you to trigger this wonderfully creative side of your nature, and you'll not only make the best of it, you'll enjoy it as well.

You and others

Life is about change and evolution, especially in relationships, whether it's with friends, neighbors, or colleagues. These changes are the result of decisions but, as often, shifts in circumstances or others' needs. Their complaints? Agree they're inconvenient, then say no more. Why? Because what seems most worrying in the short term may actually be a thrilling opportunity.

Health and well-being

Unsettling periods and sudden changes aren't just stressful; you'll sometimes forget about taking care of yourself. The trick is to recognize that while life has twists and turns, you as an individual have a stable core that is important to take care of. That has to do with how you sleep, how you eat, and finding the joy that is there in every moment.

Goals and challenges

Your greatest challenge is being able to recognize that, when things aren't going as you expected, there is an opportunity to create a breakthrough, a genuine golden moment. Focus on that, and not only will you become increasingly good at it, there will be more and more of those shining moments in your life.

Obviously, you can't ignore the questions of certain individuals or the advice others insist on offering you. But you can explain you are busy and so would prefer to speak to them when things are a bit quieter. This allows you to make your own decisions, and without justifying your plans to anybody.

JUNE

04

G
\
E
/
M
\
I
/
N
\
I

Self-love can be confusing—savoring others' love is easier and more fun

You

As a June 4th Gemini, you have a remarkable capacity for finding things to do, from exciting activities to interesting encounters. This a gift. But it is also a challenge, because when you are looking for that special something that will fulfill your objectives, it can mean you miss something closer to home, if not right in front of you. And that might be even better.

This is about balancing the restlessness of your inquisitive Gemini side and the gift of being able to spot what works in the here and now. However, those things you're familiar with may not be as exciting as you had hoped. What's more, there is always something thrilling about a new activity, something exotic about going to a new place. While that's true, the trick is reining in your inquisitive side, which wants to explore, so the part that needs to be in the here and now can focus on practical matters as well.

That may not sound exciting but, ironically, what you learn and who you meet when dealing with those practicalities could be more rewarding than what you gain from the activities or alliances you once thought would add so much to your life. For you, change is like breathing. However, the only time you can actually take a deep breath is in the present, and that is the reason it is so important that you learn to enjoy what you have.

You and others

There's no doubting the excitement of meeting somebody new, and the joy of getting to know an individual who adds welcome inspiration to your life. Even more important, however, is enjoying your own company. You often assume others are more exciting. Achieve a balance between these, and you'll find amazing peace.

Health and well-being

In a way, dealing with health is easy. Eat well, live wisely, and exercise in some way. However, if you're worrying about the future, or brooding about the past, you are gradually undermining your well-being. That is the big lesson for you. Yes, take care of yourself physically, but even more, ensure that you feed your mind with nourishing thoughts.

Goals and challenges

Long ago, you realized that a good challenge gets you going. Yet, if things are predictable, you'll sometimes create a "do-it-yourself" challenge, deciding changes are urgent or that you must explore a new idea. While this brings welcome excitement, the trick is recognizing you needn't explore, because what you are seeking is right there in front of you.

 THIS DAY FOR EVERYONE

Timing is important in all of life. But in tricky situations involving those you're close to, personally or professionally, the moment you undertake certain discussions is crucial. Instead of focusing on analysis, trust your instincts. You'll find they prove far more reliable than you expect.

GIFTS Versatile, Just, Smart

CHALLENGES Argumentative, Flighty, Forgetful

NUMBER 2

(0+5) + (6) = 11 = (1+1) = 2

Can you plan for joy? No. But be ready for it, and embrace it when it arrives

G
\
E
/
M
\
I
/
N
\
I

You

For you as a June 5th Gemini, balance is the key to your life. You may already have sensed this because, at times, you've felt terrific, then something came along and your sense of well-being vanished. On the other hand, when you're worried, or even perhaps feeling a bit grim, an event boosts your spirits. This is an element of your Gemini nature, the two aspects of your personality and mood.

While these ups and downs can be unsettling, you have a rich range of feelings, much broader than most. What's more, you can actually take advantage of these ups and downs, in terms of your interests, activities, and emotional life.

You understand the feelings of others better than most. In fact, you'll find that certain individuals will join you in exploring these feelings. This process will enrich your life and deepen crucial relationships.

Whatever it is, rather than struggle to counter those "down" feelings, when you're ready, you will simply give yourself a big dose of whatever shifts your focus.

It's not so much a case of things being better, it's more the way you are looking at them. Often, simply capturing that moment is what's important—and being able to do that is an essential skill.

You and others

Certain individuals lift your spirits, others don't. You already know that. But you don't necessarily realize there's a cost in spending time with those who are "downers." True, sometimes people like that can be puzzling. However, it is the same with what you eat. Balance indulgent food with fresh goodness—and take the same approach with those whose company you keep.

Health and well-being

There's a tendency for you to put off dealing with dull practicalities, but you must. Then, when you're feeling great, you'll revert. But, as a Gemini, you thrive on variety. The secret? Recognize that the simple act of eating a little better and doing something ordinary, such as taking a walk, will actually add enormously to your day, to your week, and to your life.

Goals and challenges

As much as you enjoy achieving your goals, you have a short attention span, so you'll often redefine your objectives midway. While that keeps things more exciting, it's vital you let others know about changes. They may complain or, equally, be delighted. What's most important is keeping in touch.

THIS DAY FOR EVERYONE

Often, when making a decision, discussion isn't just wise, it's essential. While you may need to go to others for facts, one particular matter is complex. Practicalities alone aren't enough. And you'll soon realize why you must ignore those facts and rely entirely on your own views and feelings.

GIFTS Flexible, Communicator, Traveler

CHALLENGES Preoccupied, Unsettled, Sporadic

NUMBER 3

(0+6) + (6) = 12 = (1+2) = 3

G
\
E
/
M
\
I
/
N
\
I

Every sunrise is a special moment that lifts your vision in a new way, for a new day

You

As a Gemini, you're one of three air signs. Along with Libra and Aquarius, you live in the realm of vision, thoughts, and ideas, and all three are clever, quick thinkers. Plus, because your ruling planet is Mercury, which is about communication, you have a gift for learning about, and discussing with others, life and the world around you. Every sign accents a certain part of the body, and for Gemini it's your shoulders, arms and hands. Often Geminis will use these, both to express themselves but also in sports. Just as much, it is important that you focus on how you handle things, and whether you want people to be close or not, or, in fact, if you want to keep them at what some would call "arm's length," and this is the other element of your nature.

As an air sign, while you're very much about communication, you also like to keep certain ideas to yourself and discuss them only when you're ready to. What's more, if you spend time with those who ask too many questions, you can feel uncomfortable. Yet at the same time, often these individuals will have good ideas, some that are worth listening to. An important part of your journey is to discover who is of benefit to you, and who isn't. And, equally, who you feel like linking your Gemini arms with, to play, to explore, or to go on a longer journey.

You and others

On rare occasions you describe somebody as a "true friend." However, there are real questions about what truth and friendship mean. Is it convenient for the moment, or lasting? What's more, it is worth considering whether in certain situations, you are doing more giving than receiving. What you learn could lead to timely discussions, if not changes.

Health and well-being

In order to feel well, you need to eat wisely, and will benefit from getting outside and moving. But the other question is whether your time with others is worthwhile, and do you benefit from the challenges? The trick for you as a Gemini is your attitude toward all of this. Decide to be upbeat, and within a moment, your mood will soar.

Goals and challenges

Everyone benefits from a challenge from time to time. But they can seem overwhelming. It's not necessarily what's happening but that others have taken over, and their plans benefit them, not you. Standing your ground won't be easy, at least at first. But soon, it will be natural and you will handle things wisely and will feel a tremendous sense of accomplishment.

THIS DAY FOR EVERYONE

Nobody minds sudden and exciting ideas or offers. Thrilling as what's happening may be, though, it could undermine arrangements you worked hard to organize. Seek some form of compromise, and you'll find that, with a combination of persistence and creativity, you're able to achieve great things.

GIFTS Multitalented, Listener, Unbiased

CHALLENGES Procrastinates, Inquisitive, Erratic

NUMBER 4

(0+7) + (6) = 13 = (1+3) = 4

Solving persistent dilemmas is easy, but finding the path to inner stillness isn't

G
\
E
/
M
\
I
/
N
\
I

You

Your own ruling planet, Mercury, accents ideas and discussion. However, you sometimes get lost in those ideas. Equally, you can become so interested in discussing possibilities that you lose track of time. What's more, you enjoy gathering facts and analyzing what you've learned. Yet fascinating as these are, that's not all you need to know, because decisions involve feelings as much as facts.

Your usual approach to such matters is to get more information. That's often helpful, yet some matters require a different approach—shifting the focus to your own priorities. You may not be as clear about these as you imagined. Often there is no need to dwell on these until pivotal moments arise, as they sometimes do. These accent the importance of being aware of what, and who, you put first.

If you rely on others' views, those decisions are unlikely to last. So put your own priorities first, rather than going along with others. As a flexible Gemini, finding a balance can be challenging. Once your mind is clear, the resulting choices will be less complicated as well. From that point onward, the trick is to avoid being distracted by intriguing, but unreliable, ideas and, equally, individuals, and stick with what, and who, brings stability and happiness to your life. Do that, and suddenly everything else will make sense.

You and others

The trick to dealing with situations involving you and others is to be alert to those where you're almost seduced by going along with others. You want their support or approval, or, perhaps, you're anxious about your own decisions. However, the only way you'll learn if your ideas will work is by giving things a try. And that's the message from the planets for you. Put yourself and your ideas first.

Health and well-being

For you, this should include the unsettling feelings you experience when struggling with indecision. Yet it's also about learning to rein in your mind rather than allowing worry to take over. The solution? Take a walk, do yoga or some form of meditation. That leads to relaxation, unwinding, and, ultimately, sleep.

Goals and challenges

Of course, life would be very dull without challenges to take on, or goals to meet. You'd be a lot more comfortable with those periods when there are twists and turns to deal with. Bear this in mind when those challenges arise, too, and recognize that they're giving you an opportunity to use an important muscle in your character, and not only will you use it well, you'll use it wisely.

THIS DAY FOR EVERYONE

The time has come to take a stand with somebody whose attitude or actions have been a constant source of irritation. You've mentioned this, but they've ignored you. Bring it up again, but be both frank and precise about what's bothering you. They've no idea what they're doing is so annoying.

JUNE

08

G
\
E
/
M
\
I
/
N
\
I

You debate ideas for fun—ensure others know what you stand for and believe

You

Your birthday theme is finding ways to use your energy wisely. That may seem strange, because as a Gemini and somebody ruled by the planet Mercury, your mind's more active than your body. In fact, directing your amazing mental energy can be a challenge. As a Gemini, you're an air sign, and live in the realm of thoughts and ideas. While that means you sometimes forget to eat, you occasionally struggle with mental exhaustion.

However, there's a solution that is about a union of the mind and body. Your challenge—and lesson—is balancing your physical and mental energy. While taking up certain sports, such as tennis, or, say, fencing, will do the trick, walking is also great. Add a setting that requires concentrating on balance or agility, and do it with a friend. It could be a serious walk in the countryside, or hiking. The urban version is shopping, a variety of hiking, just from one store to another. What's more, if you're trying on lots of clothes in the process, that, too, requires agility.

The trick is to be in an appealing setting, and to keep moving. This can turn a walk around your neighborhood into a joyous experience. Learn to employ your mind and body together, in your day-to-day life, and in doing so, you'll begin to discover how the combination brings you joy and confidence.

You and others

Friends, colleagues, even family can be more of a distraction than a pleasure. You may enjoy family events, but relaxing can be quite another matter. This is a challenge: learning to consider what you want to do, then selecting your companion accordingly. That ensures you'll have a good time. It's not obvious but, once you know what to do, it is easy.

Health and well-being

Focusing on how you eat is important, as is being attentive to your physical well-being. Yet you sometimes forget to eat altogether, and it's the same with physical activities; if they're boring, you just want to escape. The trick? Discover something exciting that keeps your attention. Once you do this, the rest will come.

Goals and challenges

Often setting goals is vital. However, with your roving mind, you're an expert at many areas—so many that you fear being trapped in one. While others have single goals, you have many, and they change. Actually, that's perfect. Don't let those whose minds, and lives, are narrow corner you into thinking or living like them. Commit to learning something each day, and the next, and the next one after that. That's your ideal life plan.

THIS DAY FOR EVERYONE

Promising developments can be as exhausting as they are exciting, as you're currently discovering. One of the biggest challenges you're facing is the recognition that as you embrace the future, elements of the past must go. You could struggle to keep these afloat but, deep down, you know it's unwise.

Some difficulties can transform your vision of what's possible every day

JUNE

09

G
\
E
/
M
\
I
/
N
\
I

You

As a June 9th Gemini, for you the challenge is having too many options. That may not sound like anything to worry about, but there have been times in your life when there has been so much going on, you've felt overwhelmed. The issue may have been the people around you, things you were doing, or even ideas that came your way. However, the confusion was a result of a single issue, and that is having too much on your mind—that, combined with the sense of being unable to assess the situations in question or get a grip on the ideas involved.

That is the secret for you. The key isn't figuring things out; it's learning to balance advice you're given, what you're told by others, including experts, with your own knowledge and experience. As a Gemini, you're inquisitive, and as an air sign, you thrive on debate. What's more, you enjoy analyzing what you hear about and observe. Then you have to weigh things. You don't think in terms of things being interesting, but whether they're worth learning about—or not. And that's a skill you'll develop year by year.

It may have to do with your activities, the people you like to spend time with, or even who or what you put first. In every case, achieving that balance isn't about how interesting it is but, rather, how worthwhile it is to you, now and in the future.

You and others

While getting to know people is endlessly fascinating, it also drives you crazy. You'd rather create your circle, then get to know who's who. Yet because you're inquisitive, the list of people you'd like to get to know grows every day. The secret? Stick with long-term core friends. Ultimately, it's better than spending time with somebody new, only to discover how truly dull they are.

Health and well-being

You're one of those Geminis who has a natural kind of health and well-being, except when you get anxious about decisions. The trick is to take a break from decision-making and to learn from others. Do that, and the rest of you will start to thrive in the process.

Goals and challenges

One of the challenges in your life is that you're always working toward a goal, and because of that, you are rarely happy with your current achievements. This is, in fact, your biggest lesson: first, to enjoy what you have right now. And then, while you're doing that, you can begin to think about what might be your next project.

Ordinarily, it would be wise to analyze sudden changes before you get involved. However, with things moving so swiftly, there is no time. Just as important, what you learn from even seemingly bizarre experiences will offer insights that will prove vital when the time comes to make lasting plans.

GIFTS Agile, Quick-thinking, Fair

NUMBER 7

CHALLENGES Inquisitive, Late, Undependable

(1+0) + (6) = 7

JUNE

10

G
\
E
/
M
\
I
/
N
\
I

Talking to others is fun. Time spent with those you needn't talk to is a luxury

You

While every Gemini is ruled by Mercury, the planet that is associated with communication and a quick mind, it is especially strong for you. The benefits include your broad interests and capacity to discuss new ideas and discover exciting people and places. Yet at the same time, your mind sometimes runs away with you. Of course, as an air sign, this lively mind is one of your greatest gifts, and also indicates your ability to come up with intriguing ideas.

However, at times you also have a need for stillness: that is, being free to concentrate on one thing, perhaps a plan or, in certain cases, a particular individual. The trick is being able to recognize that while your quick mind can be an asset, it can also break away, to the extent you need to rein it in. This is a lifetime skill, one you'll learn, then over the years, refine, until you are able to quiet your mind and access calm inner moments.

And it's then that, often, you have your greatest discussions and enjoy the here and now. The trick is to live with both sides of your nature, allowing each to emerge at the right moment. It is a skill—one you will master gradually. You can undertake activities that keep you in the present. Ultimately, you'll enjoy those moments of liveliness and of peace, which is an achievement for anybody, but especially for a Gemini.

You and others

On one hand, you are the best company in the world. You're genuinely interested in others, and the questions you ask demonstrate that fascination. Yet you move swiftly from one topic to the next. For you, lasting connections with others demand that the individual in question be as passionate about life and certain interests as you are. Those interests may differ, but your passion for them won't.

Health and well-being

Knowing who you are is an art, especially for a changeable Gemini. While you link up easily with others, if those connections dominate your way of living, working, or thinking, you can lose track of your true self. This involves how you live, eat, take care of yourself, and your sense of well-being. Each is an essential part of your nature.

Goals and challenges

The irony is, you have an amazing knack for achieving goals others struggle with. Yet at the same time, you have your own battles, some as frustrating as they are persistent. While they're annoying, seeking solutions for them broadens your circle, and you meet fascinating people and encounter exciting new ideas—so exciting they make up for those struggles.

THIS DAY FOR EVERYONE

You take great pride in standing up for what and who you believe in. You'll support those you care about and causes you regard as significant. However, there is one particular personal matter in which you're compromising. True, admitting this might be challenging. Once you do, the rest will be easy.

Your radar for those who are argumentative for the sake of it is good. Still, be wary

You

As a Gemini, you're an air sign, and because of that, are very good with ideas. You're inquisitive, and in fact, you enjoy collecting things, not just because of the actual object but because the story behind it interests you.

The fun comes in learning about where they came from, what they're made of, or, perhaps, how they're used. This can be from something small, such as jewelry, or cars. It can involve the outdoors; nature, from plants to crystals; or even recipes. Whatever the case, the real fun is the sheer joy of learning about them. As an air sign, you'll find it's not about owning them but that looking at them brings back the story that came with them.

Rewarding as these interests or pursuits are, and however much they add to your own story, try changing your daily routine. You can become a creature of habit, doing the same things, in the same way, every day. While this streamlines your activities, try balancing that efficiency with changes that spice things up in your daily life. This is vital. Yes, shaking things up is unsettling, but that's the point. Altering your routine can actually mean you enjoy life more. Simply undertaking routine activities in a different order can make an amazing difference. Try it. Even minor shifts will add a new fizz to your day and a new, and welcome, excitement to your life.

You and others

Many relationships are lasting—because of family links, or perhaps they go back years, possibly to school. However, as an inquisitive Gemini, when you meet somebody who shares your interests, you'll click, and those links will last as long as you're both involved. Yet over time, you'll discover another, deeper link, and a special understanding that brings a joy that nothing, and nobody, can replace.

Health and well-being

There are two types of Gemini. If you're the type who lives in your head, you're interested in fitness because you want to look good and be energetic, but nothing more. Other Geminis, though, view sports as a mental exercise; some may even become professional. Whatever the case, this is an all-or-nothing relationship for a very few—it's a true passion.

Goals and challenges

As much as you enjoy meeting new people and having new experiences, if you do too much, you become overwhelmed. Finding a balance between routine and new pursuits is itself a challenge. However, once you do, not only is life more interesting, those around you profit from your inquisitiveness, and in many ways.

GIFTS Debater, Adaptable, Bright

CHALLENGES Changeable, Unreliable, Tardy

NUMBER 9

(1+2) + (6) = 9

There's a sense of warmth that's bringing wonderful changes into your life

You

For you, life is about discovery, a new relationship with change. Most Geminis have a fairly short attention span, so ensure they have lots to do and experience. However, you tend to settle into habits, so changes and challenges need to stimulate both your mind and, even more, your imagination; it is like devising solutions for intriguing puzzles, and you enjoy tackling life's puzzles. These can be a part of your personal or working life. Ideally, however, you'll seek a range of settings, as stimulating as they are diverse.

It's the same when it comes to taking breaks or vacations—as a Gemini, you thrive on variety. Even if you go to the same place, you'll vary the routine, checking out unfamiliar settings or new additions. The fun is in the discovery of what's new. Ideally, even relaxing won't just be fun, it will challenge your mind in ways you're unfamiliar with.

But, whether you're away or living everyday life, you thrive on new ideas, experiences, and interesting people. What's more, this links with another challenge. It's confronting the part of you that gets stuck with routine.

Here, too, the trick is the discovery that you could do things, live, or love differently. The less restrictive your thinking and the more you explore, the more magical your life will be.

You and others

Being understood by others is wonderful, yet it's something Geminis struggle with, mostly because family and colleagues view life from a different perspective. Despite your knowing this, every once in a while the realization comes as a shock. When making plans, this demands careful discussion, and exploring with others why they enjoy or benefit from your ideas. It's not easy, but it is vital.

Health and well-being

Because you streamline your time, you're likely to devise a formula for health, too. Do that, however, and you could find yourself doing the same thing regularly, and unenthusiastically. While you may feel better and fitter, you'll also be increasingly bored. The trick? It's discovering new activities, from jumping rope to flamenco dancing, complete with castanets.

Goals and challenges

You've achieved goals that others only dream of. However, you're restless, and need new challenges, from personal to more worldly pursuits. Your biggest challenge is actually enjoying what life brings you. That's very much about refusing to allow the routine that you've established to dominate life, to make every day an adventure.

THIS DAY FOR EVERYONE

Rethinking plans is one thing. But revisiting the foundation on which certain arrangements are made may seem strange, if not impossible. Despite that, raise it with the individual in question and you'll find that you're not only able to clear up confusion easily, you'll discuss future plans with equal ease.

GIFTS Smart, Communicative, Just

CHALLENGES Scattered, Argumentative, Sporadic

NUMBER 1

(1+3) + (6) = 10 = (1+0) = 1

Strengthen your connection with your inner self so you know what's best

G
\
E
/
M
\
I
/
N
\
I

You

The theme for your birthday is the balance between organizing things in a way that makes life almost routine and having freedom. This is unusual for a Gemini, because normally you value freedom above all other things.

However, because in the past you've found yourself in situations where you neglected one detail or another, you've developed a way of dealing with plans, but in a manner that leaves you little option to get creative or, and this is what's important to you, to make mistakes.

The trick is now to be less exact, and give yourself more space to deal with those tasks, and to enjoy life in a way that you probably haven't for a while. However, this is also about finding that balance between being organized, which is terrific, and being creative, allowing the moment to take over, especially if it's something that excites you—when you have encountered something new, or met someone who seems interesting to know.

If your plans are flexible enough to rethink things, initially for the time being, you'll be free to explore your options, and, if necessary, consider making serious changes. So while achieving this balance takes effort, the reward is the freedom it gives you to explore. This isn't just about the here and now. It's also about what you'll be considering as the future unfolds as well.

You and others

You don't think about it, but when life's too predictable, you'll stir things up, reorganizing existing arrangements or making changes. True, they'll be timely and beneficial, but others may complain. Explain, but briefly. Then, next time around, discuss your ideas as you proceed. This may seem a distraction, but in the long run it will save you time and stress.

Health and well-being

You could easily have a fixed relationship with your diet and activities, never eating certain things, and always working out in a particular way at a particular hour. Except there's another kind of well-being, which involves self-awareness, the variety that's about truly feeling life's joys, and that can mean being more easygoing, whatever it is you're doing.

Goals and challenges

Because you're always thinking about what's next, you sometimes forget to look back, and consider what you've done, the challenges you've met, and skills you've mastered, many amazingly. And, happily, there are more challenges to keep you busy. But there's another, even more important challenge, which is being able to enjoy every minute of life itself, from its challenges to its joys.

JUNE

14

G
\
E
/
M
\
I
\
N
\
I

Those who give unsolicited advice are well-meaning but questionable advisors

You

One of your greatest assets, your quick mind, can also be a liability—as you well know. True, you benefit from being ruled by the planet Mercury, whose legendary swiftness brings worldly skills that are employed in everything from politics to media and all forms of communication. However, if that active mind of yours isn't busy, it can overshadow life's joys. This can turn minor irritations into major concerns. Yet, when distracted by a new project—or passion—those worries vanish.

Getting lost in doing things works for a while. But even a rewarding social life or a job you really enjoy won't calm your restless mind, which can be as much of an adversary as an ally. The secret is to find and maintain interests and alliances that don't just nurture you, but that are consistent, that you can rely on.

These can range from healthy habits, from eating well—many Geminis forget to eat— and doing some variety of exercise, to having people whose guidance you trust nearby. Once those stabilizing habits are formed, you exchange the ups and downs that can become a way of life. Instead, you'll exchange them for a variety of balance rare these days, especially for Geminis. Once you conquer it, and calm is yours, life becomes a very different, and rewarding, adventure—less lived on the edge, and more centered in joy.

You and others

Finding friends and forging close emotional ties with people who are as inquisitive as you are isn't easy. But it's a skill you'll acquire, and you'll keep them close. Getting along with those whose company you can't choose, from family to colleagues, is an art—one that takes effort but is worth learning.

Health and well-being

Yes, you forget to eat. Some envy this, but it takes a toll on both your mood and energy level. The irony is, while lots of Geminis are gourmets, unless you train yourself to enjoy them, both eating and taking care of your physical well-being can be more of a chore than a joy.

Goals and challenges

Your active mind is an asset—you're inquisitive. That means you notice more, and can enjoy all sorts of places and people, in your social life and work. Yet it's about ensuring there's variety, and that dull tasks are mixed with stimulating activities and companions.

THIS DAY FOR EVERYONE

Although you wouldn't describe yourself as being generous with others, it's true. This isn't about money as much as it involves thinking carefully about who and what matters to certain individuals—and doing what you can to enable them to connect. And, amazingly, often you'll do it in secret.

GIFTS Clever, Easygoing, Versatile

CHALLENGES Easily Distracted, Forgetful, Scattered

NUMBER 3

(1+5) + (6) = 12 = (1+2) = 3

Celebrating before a victory indicates an excess of optimism and a lack of patience

G
\
E
/
M
\
I
/
N
\
I

You

Others tell you how much they envy your easy charm and clever mind. While you enjoy being admired for some things, this is strange if not annoying. Why? Because these characteristics are as much of a nuisance as an asset. True, you've a knack for dealing swiftly and cleverly, with a wide range of difficulties. But, ironically, it means there's not much excitement in managing tricky situations or difficult people.

You have an amazing instinct for what to say or do to defuse very complex problems. However, problems and practical matters are one thing. Those matters that involve close relationships, that call on your deeper feelings, your heart, and intuition, are more complex.

However, what you're learning isn't just how to manage a tricky issue, it's about being closer to those who matter most. Knowing you could distract everybody is a good idea, combined with your legendary Gemini charm. Or you could go deeper, and talk things over. True, others may be uncomfortable and you could struggle. But what you learn about the situation in question—and the individuals involved—could allay these concerns. And it could create a new understanding and a new way of having relationships in general. You can make these changes at any time. You needn't wait for a drama. And the minute you begin, life will be a lot more fun.

You and others

Many Geminis are surprised by the number of people who regard them as best friends, or "part of the family." This is both heartwarming and puzzling, because you don't feel the same closeness. The confusion? Your interest in them. For you, these emotional links come with time. They're not nearly as skilled at it, so you being involved means all the more.

Health and well-being

Many Geminis benefit from the lanky body type that thrives on physical activity, from physically challenging activities or games. However, other Geminis tend to be round. Both find eating regularly, and wisely, a challenge. The trick? Turn it into a hobby, one you can share and enjoy doing with everybody from family to friends.

Goals and challenges

You wouldn't think your quick mind is a problem. However, because you take on and overcome challenges easily, much of the time you are in what might be termed mental "high gear," which means if there's no crisis to focus on, you'll feel the need to find one or, on occasion, you'll become absorbed by others' unending dramas. Escaping this isn't easy. Once you do, you'll be relieved and grateful.

THIS DAY FOR EVERYONE

True, recently you've achieved a great deal. But it's come at a cost to other plans and pursuits, and also caused a fair amount of aggravation with certain individuals. Now, finally those matters are dealt with, which means those worries are gone and you can relax.

GIFTS Multitalented, Debater, Unbiased

CHALLENGES Skips Details, Flighty, Mercurial

NUMBER 4

(1+6) + (6) = 13 = (1+3) = 4

JUNE

16

G
\
E
/
M
\
I
/
N
\
I

True wisdom is modest. It arrives quietly, waits until you're ready, then moves on

You

The theme for your birthday is expansiveness. While on one hand this is about exploring the broader world, it is also about discovery. And that occurs when you get away from a familiar setting. Whether it is making local journeys or going further afield, you benefit from being in a different environment and doing things in a new way. You need to be well away from your everyday life.

This form of balance is important for you, because while you love having lots of plans organized, you are sometimes anxious about getting stuck in exactly such plans. Geminis thrive on new ideas and activities. Repetition is boring for you. The trick is balancing the two—what you must do, with activities that are about discovery, from new places to things you've never done before.

Tempting as it is to organize plans based on past experiences, there is a world waiting for you to discover it. Stick with the familiar, and you're committing to one destiny, dominated by the past. Take a chance on the unknown, and you'll make breakthroughs that aren't just important, they are like breathing. Once you begin to make them, and discover how to step into this new world of the unfamiliar, not only will you be glad you did, you'll become expert at embracing the unexpected and begin having an enthusiastic affair with destiny itself.

You and others

Dealing with others is part of life and, mostly, fun. But decisions can be tricky. The views of others can be a challenge. You don't think of yourself as being rigid in your thinking. However, this isn't just about plans, it is about getting to know people in a whole new way. That not only deepens your understanding of them, it will broaden your world.

Health and well-being

When life is demanding, you'll stick to a well-being regimen. However, you thrive on variety, so need options; otherwise you'll rebel and do nothing. The answer? Avoid a demanding schedule; instead, loosen up and explore. The more intriguing options you have, the more fun you'll have experimenting, and the more you will explore and enjoy it.

Goals and challenges

While it's easy to reduce life to certain goals and challenges, for you it's really about how you explore and embrace life itself. It's as if you were having a romance with destiny and discovering what it brings you each day. Take that approach. Not only will you learn a lot, you will indeed enjoy every day of the process.

THIS DAY FOR EVERYONE

Once you are committed to something, you rarely need prompting to take action. On the contrary, you sometimes have to battle your tendency to be single-minded. Still, your feelings about one particular situation or individual have become are so intense you could be regarded as obsessed.

GIFTS Versatile, Fair, Listener

NUMBER 5

CHALLENGES Unpredictable, Preoccupied, Last-minute

(1+7) + (6) = 14 = (1+4) = 5

Fewer joys are greater than spending time with somebody you know loves you

You

If there is any challenge for you as a June 17th Gemini, it's the conflict between the drive to take it easy and the drive to broaden your horizons, to think about new ideas, to do more, and to explore the world that always seems to be calling to you. The settled and the restless are each genuine, legitimate sides of your nature. Previously, you tended to focus on one, then the other. You've either been out there in the wider world, discovering things, or you might simply have been talking with those individuals who are knowledgeable about ideas, people, or places that you aren't.

It doesn't matter where you have been or what you've been thinking, but that your mind has been active, if not working overtime. Yet, there have been periods when you haven't just relaxed, you have totally kicked back. The trick is to learn to blend the two. This may sound difficult, if not challenging.

However, even thinking about it will get your mind going. That's the key: to realize that this doesn't relate to anything you've done before. Actually, it is taking everything that you've done and putting those experiences into one glorious package of discovery and adventure. As a Gemini, you were born to do exactly that—to explore, to discuss ideas, and, from time to time, to reinvent yourself. That's exactly what you are doing.

You and others

When you need practical help or your spirits need a boost, you know who to call on. And often the individuals in question will achieve miracles. But, in a bizarre way, others are no help at all, and sometimes undermine your confidence. The problem? Discerning between the two. Find that one person whose clarity is unfailingly accurate. Ask their guidance. End of problem.

Health and well-being

There is a tendency for people to say, "When everything is settled, then I'll take care of myself." And, often, you are one of those people. Finding a way to take care of yourself, a regimen that's easy enough to do, and a way of eating that is not too complicated, can be very difficult. However, if ever there were an investment to make in yourself now, it's that.

Goals and challenges

This makes it sound as if there is a final goal in life, and once you have done that, things will be finished. But of course, life is all about discovery. As long as we are breathing, there will be goals to achieve. What is most important for you is to recognize the joy in the goals you're currently exploring. Once you do that, everything else will be easy.

THIS DAY FOR EVERYONE

You're by no means a control freak. Yet when certain decisions you've made routinely for a long time are given to others to deal with, you're unhappy. You may be tempted to battle to restore arrangements. Don't. You'll soon have other, far more intriguing activities to think about.

JUNE

18

G
\
E
/
M
\
I
/
N
\
I

With family and friends, you speak in a kind of shorthand. But a heart-to-heart is vital, too

You

As a Gemini, you were born under one of the cleverest and most versatile signs. You rarely think about this until you're talking to somebody who has no imagination. While usually your inquisitiveness is a gift, it can also mean that when you need to focus or make decisions, you're drawn into exploring other possibilities: some very real and worthwhile.

But more often than not, pressures on time or practicalities mean you've got to stick with one particular plan. This isn't just annoying, it can be frustrating, especially if you have other ideas. Learn to recognize when it's not about doing more, it is about moving on. For you, remembering that is crucial; it is the difference between struggling or accepting things as they are. Challenging as this is, once you've learned this, you'll also have learned how to sidestep other frequent struggles in your life, all of which have to do with settling on a plan, decision, or commitment, acknowledging that, then firmly moving on.

You will then discover that there is a bridge to the next thing to do, the next plan, project, or encounter. The trick is to hurl yourself into whatever is next, knowing that there will be new discussions and discoveries. And new decisions. Those exciting moments appear regularly. The trick is to be free from the past, and ready to embrace the future.

You and others

Relationships can be both tricky and deeply nourishing. Those you get to know over time become trusted friends, people you talk things over with. Yet sometimes it is vital to discuss things less and venture out more. You have known certain people for so long, there are no surprises. Balance is key. Sustain long-standing links, while you are exploring new ones.

Health and well-being

You don't think of yourself as extreme. This applies to how you eat and take care of yourself. In fact, when you are stressed, it's likely that you'll embrace a strict routine, when thinking will clarify your mind. Yet if ever there was a time to be kind to yourself, it's then. Being kind to yourself is the best approach to any challenge.

Goals and challenges

Setting goals is exciting. Meeting them can sometimes be difficult, simply because you set those goals so high, it's unlikely that you will be able to achieve them. Yet you keep trying. That is one of the gifts as a Gemini— your inquisitiveness. You'll take a chance, just for the fun of it, to see what happens. There is no better approach to the new, unfamiliar, and exciting than that.

THIS DAY FOR EVERYONE

The time has come to do your math. And this doesn't just refer to who owes what to whom. It is about the effort you've made on behalf of certain individuals. While some acknowledge what you've done and a few try to return the favor, amazingly, others just seem to take it for granted.

Meditators speak of stillness—and, as every Gemini knows, a quiet mind is bliss

JUNE

19

G
\
E
/
M
\
I
/
N
\
I

You

For you, your birthday is all about living many lives: not just the two lives that are known as the Gemini twins, but also many different worlds, living in many different realms, and in some ways, being very different to other people. And, what's more, these won't necessarily come together, nor do they need to.

In fact, if everyone who knows you came together in a single room and were talking, each would describe a different, and often unique, side to your nature. This is both fun and vital for you, because it allows you to explore ideas and experiment as an individual, in a way that is beneficial. But even more, you'll be discovering things that, otherwise, you wouldn't have encountered.

Experimenting in this way is essential, and in fact, it is a theme for your approach to life. It is not about finding the single way to do anything but, rather, it's about learning from every experience and taking chances in the process. This allows you to make the best of your inquisitive nature, the part that thrives on having lots of interesting options to explore.

It's the same for people and activities. The trick is to trust some and recognize that others may involve taking a chance, but know that you will be learning from each of them. Most of all, it's about recognizing the joy in discovery, because that's what it's all about.

You and others

Spending time with those around you is important. However, you can easily allow their ideas, thoughts, views, or concerns to influence your thinking. Listen and learn, but remember your priority is being true to yourself, views, and commitments. The process of discovering who you are never stops. But when you are around certain individuals, that process of growth accelerates. Learn to spot those periods.

Health and well-being

Are you looking for the secret formula for staying on top of things when you're feeling overwhelmed? You've tried dealing with every detail, and that doesn't work. The trick is to take things a day, or even an hour, at a time. Do what you can. As a quick-minded Gemini, you'll be amazingly relaxed, and actually enjoy every twist and turn.

Goals and challenges

Often when we speak of goals, the focus is on whether there is a single, distant final objective you have in mind, perhaps as a heritage. Yet for you, goals are about actually being able to enjoy what every day offers. That is the most important thing for you during this particular cycle, and during your entire life.

THIS DAY FOR EVERYONE

It's unlike you to sidestep the responsibility for important decisions. But with the circumstances on which they'd be based shifting, you need time to think and to ask questions. What you learn will make you realize you're not alone in facing changes that are more complex than they seem.

Cancer

Ruler The Moon
Element Water
Symbol The Crab
Flower Lily

June 20– July 21

Cancer The only sign ruled by the Moon, Cancer accents cycles— both nature's rhythms, especially the oceans and tides, and those in our lives. The symbol, the crab, is linked to water, as are your sign's flowers: the lily and the lotus. Your herbs are aromatic, tarragon and verbena, and your tree is the maple. Your jewel, the pearl, not only comes from the sea, it mirrors the Moon's form.

C
/
A
\
N
/
C
\
E
/
R

I'll remember that the Moon shines on even dark nights—and so can I

You

You benefit from two signs. You benefit from the influence of the sign next to yours, Gemini, and your own sign, Cancer.

This is an unusual blend, because the Gemini part of you is a rather clear-minded air sign, while the Cancer side is not only an intuitive water sign, but benefits from the influence of the rulership of the Moon, the heavenly body that has to do with cycles.

And for that reason, your intuition is very strong. You sense when it's time for things to grow, both in nature, but also in individuals. You sense when stillness is important. This balance in yourself means that you're able to be a good friend, both to family and loved ones, but also that if you go to a job, to those at work as well.

You manage to give advice in a way that doesn't seem like advice, but it almost seems more like you are listening to others.

For you personally, however, finding that kind of nurturing is important. That has to do sometimes with family, but often it will be with that special friend who knows what you're thinking and who is able to encourage you to sit quietly and talk with them.

Most of all, it's about recognizing the powerful cycles that shape the world around you, and even more importantly, shape your own life.

You and others

The formula here is about giving and receiving. That seems simple, but as you've discovered when dealing with those around you, all too often you tend to end up doing a lot more giving and much less receiving. The trick is knowing when to stop, and even more, when to ask.

Health and well-being

Being a Cancerian, your mood is as important as how you take care of your body, and when you recognize that it is time to stop and to rest, it is as significant as what you eat or what you do or the way you exercise. Pausing in this way is an important gift for yourself.

Goals and challenges

While what you do in the world is important, what goes on within is just as important, and there are times when you wrestle with your right to go after things you dream about or what you want to achieve. The most important part of the process is to pause and consider what, personally, is most important to you.

THIS DAY FOR EVERYONE

Obviously, you're not thrilled about admitting you made an unwise decision, especially because this involves a matter where you battled to have things your way. However, the circumstances have changed. Acknowledge that you dislike admitting you got it wrong, apologize, and move on.

GIFTS Inviting, Empathetic, Warm

CHALLENGES Takes Offense, Hypervigilant, Moody

Nature's power to grow, even in unlikely places, will inspire me

You

To a certain extent, you tend to feel responsible for others, for their happiness, for whether they're enjoying life. This isn't something you think about. It's natural, and it's a wonderful quality. However, the challenge for you is recognizing when you feel responsible, when actually, you're meant to be encouraging them to look after their own interests.

And equally, it's time for you to focus on what you need. In some cases, this is time for yourself. In other cases, it's pursuing what's important to you, whether it's a hobby or an activity, or simply being able to be alone. For you, joy—true joy—comes from within. You know this, but you don't always give yourself the gift of time to share that for yourself, and the balance between what you want to give to others and the gift of that time for yourself is one of the most important gifts for you in life.

Once you begin to recognize that, you'll also have a clearer sense of what you need to do to bring joy in your life. You may have a job or even activities at home that are rewarding, but the important thing is for you to seek out that single passion that lifts your spirits, that you look forward to. It may be one thing. It may be a number of things. It may evolve. But the most important thing is, it's entirely yours.

You and others

You are a natural diplomat, but that isn't always the best way for you to deal with those around you. Being persuasive is one thing, but there are times when either frank discussions or getting others to just talk about their own issues openly is what is most important. That is the big lesson.

Health and well-being

When it comes to health and well-being, your tendency is to think that you can be either self-indulgent or austere. However, there is something in between that has to do with being able to enjoy each day and find activities that make you happy. It may be a walk. It may be exercising. It may be indulging yourself in eating something, or eating less. Whatever it is, it's finding it that's important.

Goals and challenges

There isn't a single shift that has to do with achievement. It has to do with finding that balance between being happy with what you're achieving and what you're not.

For a long time you've managed to keep one particularly tricky issue under wraps. It hasn't been easy, but you've felt strongly that this was nobody else's business. Now it is and, in fact, you'll need to ensure that certain individuals are aware of the full facts, including why you've said nothing until now.

GIFTS Caring, Visionary, Persistent

CHALLENGES Evasive, Procrastinating, Jumpy

NUMBER 1

$(2+2) + (6) = 10 = (1+0) = 1$

When I'm a bit down, I'll imagine the power of the Sun emerging from behind a cloud

You

Your initial instinct when there's something to talk about is to pause and reflect and figure out what you need to say. This can have to do with conversations with others, with your own activities, with your job if you go to one. And then you think once you've got it all figured out, you will talk things through. The trick is to recognize that those around you are also on what might be termed a journey, and they, too, are figuring things out. If you spent too much time on the thought, you might miss benefiting from what they have to say. What's more, by asking others what they are thinking about and what they're learning, you will all broaden your horizons. This process of discussion is an important one, because it also allows you to remove the burden from your shoulders to figure things out.

For you, finding joy on your own and with others is a journey. It's not something you figure out on a single day, but it is a skill that you develop over time: a skill that, as each day passes, you become better at; and a skill that allows you to enjoy what life offers all the more. As a Cancerian and a water sign, life isn't so much about what you have or what you own, or even about your relationships, as much as how you feel each day, and if, when you wake up in the morning, you're looking forward to what the day holds.

You and others

You're well aware of your role in supporting others, but you're less conscious of the need to allow them to support you. That exchange is an essential part of it. It's almost as important as breathing. Recognize that, and you'll find and sustain that all-important balance.

Health and well-being

It would be nice if you could find a single routine that you could stick with, but for you, joint exploration is important. That's a kind of exploration that is about doing things together—and taking advantage of those who have a knack for introducing you to new activities and new pursuits.

Goals and challenges

Sometimes people are encouraged to make a list of things they want to accomplish. However, because you're intuitive by nature, it may well be that you're not fully aware of what is most important until suddenly you're facing that opportunity, and in doing so, know you have found the moment to say yes.

THIS DAY FOR EVERYONE

There's no wrong way to refuse an offer you find unappealing, or which simply doesn't work. If the individual behind the offer takes offense at your words, bear in mind they may be playing a game, one in which they'll use guilt to lure you into doing what they want. Politely but firmly ignore them.

GIFTS Wise, Tenacious, Considerate

CHALLENGES Supersensitive, Clinging, Wary

If a dream seems unachievable, I'll remember others that seemed just as impossible

You

For you, there is a real appeal to having order in your life, knowing what you're going to be doing on any day, possibly next week, or possibly even a year from now. Being ruled by the Moon, the heavenly body that itself changes constantly, your instincts are telling you that that kind of somewhat rigid way of organizing things actually could be frustrating, and that's true. In fact, you will have found that, often, if you try to organize things too much, you just have to reorganize them at the last minute.

Your lesson is, indeed, to understand that cycles exist: in nature, in the world around you, and in your own life, and especially in relationships with others—personal relationships but also out in the world. Once you are able to embrace that, then instead of worrying about things going the way you want, you'll find that you encounter something exciting.

And because both your thinking and your planning are more flexible, you're able to explore that. This then allows you to do more things in a day, in a week, and in a month than you would have imagined possible, and it's that flexibility that is the greatest gift you can give yourself, as a Cancerian and somebody ruled by the Moon, the body in the heavens that teaches us all about those cycles.

You and others

Sometimes you feel like you need to take a role in dealing with others. This can be tricky, but at times, it's useful, because if an individual, family, a friend, or even a colleague is being difficult, you can lead them to what they need to learn. But when it comes to those closest, the most important thing is to speak from the heart.

Health and well-being

The idea of seeking a stable way of doing things is wonderful. However, for you, what is most important is to be enthusiastic about what you're pursuing. That means changing things around from time to time. This may mean undertaking something new or simply altering the order in which you approach such matters.

Goals and challenges

The word "challenge" tends to imply a single situation on a single day. However, if you think of those challenges as opportunities, a chance to do something new, to learn something, to challenge yourself in a new way, then instead of worrying about them, you will plunge into them with joy.

THIS DAY FOR EVERYONE

Usually, there's no wrong way to express concern about a matter somebody is struggling with. However, currently, one particular individual is presenting an upbeat façade to the world, and would be upset if they thought you saw through it. What they need, however, is somebody to do a lot of listening.

GIFTS Prudent, Warmhearted, Sentimental

CHALLENGES Nervous, Defensive, Gets Upset

At those moments when I feel like a vulnerable child, I'll wrap myself in loving warmth

JUNE

24

C
/
A
\
N
/
C
\
E
/
R

You

There is a part of you that feels that if you can just get things figured out, then everything will be okay. However, being a Cancerian and someone ruled by the Moon, the heavenly body whose cycles are so powerful and so obvious, there is a lesson for you.

And that is that there are periods in life and during the month when it's about growth, when it's about stillness, and when it's about rest. While that is something you may understand intellectually, there is a part of you that still feels as if you are always supposed to be doing something.

If you're not pushing yourself to get something done, you're encouraging someone else. And of course, the lesson here—and, in fact, the gift to yourself—is to recognize that you are allowed to stop.

And just as at the time of the New Moon when there is stillness, stillness in nature, you will also be still. The irony is, during that time of stillness you will have time to reflect, and there comes great joy in that moment simply because it allows you both to question what you are doing and to consider your options, but also to consider the idea of broadening your horizons in terms of the people you spend time with, what you're doing, or what you're seeking for your own life, in the present and in the future.

You and others

The question for you and others is, are you responsible for the bad mood of those around you? There seem to be certain individuals who think that's the case. And if you allow them to convince you that's true, then you will have a problem. This may require taking a tough line, because the fact is, every individual is responsible for their own well-being.

Health and well-being

Cycles are the subject for you. And this is, of course, natural, being a water sign. Yet you have a tendency to feel that when it comes to your health and well-being, you will do better if you have a regimen. The important thing is to recognize that deep within you lies a need for cycles. Pay attention to that and make that the basis on which you make decisions.

Goals and challenges

Your most important goal when it comes to organizing your life and your goals isn't what you actually achieve but what you learn in the process. Make that your priority, and everything else will fall into place.

THIS DAY FOR EVERYONE

There is a difference between making tentative plans, which is what this period is all about, and lasting commitments. The problem is, one individual views every arrangement as final. Gently but firmly help them understand that, at the moment, anyway, plans that are flexible will be better all around.

I know I am connected to nature's powers. It's just sometimes, I have to remind myself

You

There is a secret to being you, and that is to pause and review what you're happy with and what you're not. This is important, not because you're going to get things organized perfectly, which is a powerful instinct you have, but rather, to recognize what you'll have fun figuring everything out. There aren't problems that need to be fixed so that they're perfect, but being ruled by the Moon, which waxes and wanes every month, you'll realize that certain things develop in cycles, and that while certain elements of your life and activities are quiet, others will be growing.

This doesn't just have to do with you and what you're doing—with your activities, your passions, or your job It also has to do with your relationships with others and ensuring that, at times, they're thriving, but that at other times, you give yourself space. Similarly, you may develop a new hobby and be obsessive about it for a month or even a year, and then decide it's not nearly as interesting and move on.

This isn't just important. It is natural, and if those around you wonder why you're moving on, simply smile at them and say it's because it is indeed the most natural thing for you to do. That capacity to discover new activities and be passionate about new pursuits is one of life's greatest gifts.

You and others

Life can be enormously rewarding. However, certain individuals around you seem to think that it's your job to make it rewarding for them, too. Recognizing that this isn't your obligation may be difficult, but you don't have to say it. You simply need to disappear at the appropriate moment.

Health and well-being

There are those who regard health and well-being, that is, how you eat and how you take care of yourself, as a bit of a science. But for you, it's a matter of discovering what feels good. That changes, and it is something that you needn't discuss with anybody at all.

Goals and challenges

Much of the world seems to think that there's one particular goal, and it has to do with achievement and money. While you may be interested in those things, what's most important is to find the challenges that you want to achieve, that are your challenges and what you alone wish to pursue.

THIS DAY FOR EVERYONE

Few things are more precious than time with loved ones. Now, somebody you care about is putting others first. Before you get hurt or angry, ask what's going on. The odds are good they have an obligation they haven't mentioned. Once they explain, you will understand what it is they're dealing with.

GIFTS Compassionate, Constant, Kind

NUMBER 5

CHALLENGES Avoidant, Stuck, Hurts Deeply

$(2+6) + (6) = 14 = (1+4) = 5$

Good times are fun, but lasting joy comes from an endless well, deep within my being

JUNE

26

C
/
A
\
N
/
C
\
E
/
R

You

Your birthday chart shows how important others are in your life. The individuals around you, whether they're family or friends or colleagues or even people you know, perhaps from the past, are part of your own growth. Their ideas, their activities, and in fact, their complaints all contribute to your understanding of what makes the world go around. It is important to recognize this doesn't mean you're responsible for making them happy. However, you may end up doing a lot of listening, and as a result, you will discover things within yourself that you want to explore. And this is the irony of it.

While those around you will play an important part in your life and lead you to think and grow—and of course, certain individuals will bring you great joy—the actual joy comes from the you who is within you, who you discover when you're in the midst of all of those individuals, or equally, having gotten away from those individuals for a while, this may have to do with the you who is able to take a walk alone.

In every case, as a Cancerian and somebody ruled by the Moon, your life is about cycles, and discovery comes in that way. Just as when plants are flowering, they'll grow, and then the flowers will fall off and they'll pause. Give yourself the gift of time to pause as well.

You and others

There are many who say that keeping a routine is an important thing, but from your point of view, keeping your own rhythm is even more important. If you want to share doing things with others, do so, but if they want to stick to that routine and you don't feel like it any more, it's absolutely okay for you to say no.

Health and well-being

It's funny how some people think of food as more of a science, where as a Cancerian and somebody who's well aware of their feelings, you well understand that this is as much about your mood. Being able to indulge yourself when you want, choosing to be austere when you want to be, and being able to do whatever you decide at the moment that's right are most important.

Goals and challenges

The trick to understanding the cycle of challenges arising is to recognize that, rather than worrying about them, challenges are to be welcomed, because they're an invitation to a variety of growth you might not otherwise experience and may even lead to acquiring one of life's greatest skills or experiencing one of life's greatest joys.

THIS DAY FOR EVERYONE

Sometimes, you're in a rush. As often, however, it's pride that prevents you from allowing others to deal with certain crucial arrangements. You have no choice but to hand over a range of such matters. And the sooner you talk this over, the more swiftly you can let go. That should win over the doubters.

GIFTS Empathetic, Nurturing, Cautious

CHALLENGES Delaying, Homebound, Emotional

NUMBER 6

$(2+7) + (6) = 15 = (1+5) = 6$

Although nobody takes lessons in how to love, we all have an endless ability to share it

You

For you, being born in a world where achievement is often measured in possessions, in money, or in the title you have as a Cancer, is a paradox. While you may enjoy having good things, you also have a deeper knowledge of what might be termed inner values—that is, those feelings that come with being happy with others, but even more, with being true to yourself.

Of course, if you're living a busy life, despite being a juggling act, it can be joyous. The trick is to manage to find that time that's so important to be yourself, even if you are in the midst of doing exciting things or being distracted by those you care about. And that is the art. It isn't what you have or what you earn. It's the way you own your time and your joy.

That may seem selfish, but intriguingly, those around you witnessing you embracing that joy will not only be happy for you, they will begin to learn from you, and this is what's best. This variety of joy is infectious. It is something that you share, not because you talk about it, but because you live it. This is one of your most important journeys as a June 27th Cancer: not only to experience that joy, but in experiencing it, to share it with others.

You and others

Helping those around you comes naturally to you. You don't even think about it. When you extend yourself, receiving help from others, their support, their goodwill, is more difficult for you. The lesson? If you understand that this is like breathing, that accepting is as important as giving. Then you won't struggle with receiving any more.

Health and well-being

Often, regimens are not only boring, they suggest that you're unhappy. Search for a formula that works. The trick is to find something that isn't extreme, and in fact, that goes with your natural flow.

Goals and challenges

Those around you may have lots of ideas about what you should be doing. If so, thank them very much, then ignore them. Their version of advice isn't advice. It is actually somebody trying to impose their will on you. The most important goal that you could possibly follow is a goal of your own.

Exciting ideas are in the air. While you're eager to explore, others are wary and fear wasting their time or being disappointed. Forget about trying to win over the individuals in question and, if necessary, get involved on your own. Then you can discuss your own experiences.

There is no fee for kindness yet the wealth of joy it gives is endless and timeless

JUNE

28

C
/
A
\
N
/
C
\
E
/
R

You

You love a challenge. A challenge gives you an opportunity to exercise the muscle of your mind, the muscles of your body, but also the muscle of your feelings, of what inspires you. If there's any challenge in this, however, it's that there's a tendency for those around you to measure your success at meeting such challenges in more worldly ways, whereas for you, it's actually more about your intuition and what you learn and being able to hone those worldly skills, but also to go within.

The trick, of course, is recognizing that not everybody even has an inner world. These individuals won't understand what you are talking about when you refer to a sense of personal achievement, and still less about inner peace. But for you as a Cancer, that combination of achieving what you want in the world around you, but also achieving that inner peace, is one of the things you were born to do or to discover.

While you may not be able to talk to others about it, you can be an example of how to live that way, and that's also important. Often, it's not what you say, but it is the peace others recognize in you that becomes something they would like to experience and may come and sit by you simply to experience that peace. If so, you will know that you have achieved your goals.

You and others

There's a temptation to do whatever is necessary to keep others happy. Hopefully, you have already discovered that while theoretically that's easy, it's about the most draining thing you could possibly attempt to do. The secret is an exchange. Do something for them, but then get them to do something for themselves.

Health and well-being

There are those around you who will be happy to give you advice about what you should be eating, how much, and when, and equally, how you should be moving your body. However, as a Cancerian, you have the greatest instincts in the world. Pay attention to those, and ignore what others have to say.

Goals and challenges

It's impossible not to discuss what you're doing, and therefore, to discuss with others your own goals. They may offer to analyze things for you, because that's what people consider to be conversation. However, the important thing for you to remember is that by no means do you have to pay attention to that analysis.

THIS DAY FOR EVERYONE

Just when you thought that once troublesome issues had been dealt with and can be regarded as in the past, sudden changes have put them at the forefront of everybody's thinking and discussion. Worrying as this seems now, be bold. Speak from the heart. The warm response you receive will amaze you.

Healing occurs when hope meets need in a setting that allows for the miraculous

You

As a Cancerian, you have an instinctive understanding of the difference between learning in the normal way, that is, learning when you go to school, and learning a skill. Whether it's a professional skill or a sport, you need to get out and do it. Understanding is another matter, however, and that comes from reflection, from sitting, from thinking about things, from talking to those who you admire, and understanding will also shape what you do and what you learn.

Many people don't realize this, and those you're talking to—about what you're doing or the possibility of rethinking things, the possibility of pursuing something new—may think that everything they understand will come from taking action instead of this particular variety of reflection that is so important for you as a Cancer.

The fact is, if they don't understand how important it is, you probably won't be able to teach them, in which case, you'll remain friends with them, or perhaps you'll remain a member of their family, but when it comes to reflecting on what you're doing, the rewards you're getting at, what you want to seek more of, these may not be the people to talk to. Gradually, you'll begin to discover those who share this understanding with you, and those individuals will become your true family.

You and others

Discussing what makes you close to someone else can itself be a very tricky thing. The most important thing is to analyze whether you feel comfortable with them and whether you want to see them again. Make that your assessment of who is close.

Health and well-being

There are those who are absolutely dedicated to a particular well-being regimen, whether it's eating in a particular way or something they do. However, they're not you, and being a water sign, you're much better off doing what feels good, rather than what someone else says is right.

Goals and challenges

You have an instinctive sense of when it's time to set a new goal, and equally, when it's time to leave something behind you. But what's most important is to recognize those activities that touch your heart. This is because, being a water sign and ruled by the Moon, you understand that more deeply than anybody else.

THIS DAY FOR EVERYONE

While you have an easygoing attitude about the remarkable events taking place, others aren't nearly as comfortable with them. Once you understand that, everything will make sense. You will not only know why certain individuals are determined to do things their way, you'll back off and allow them to do so.

GIFTS Inviting, Constant, Empathetic

NUMBER 9

CHALLENGES Procrastinating, Taking Offense, Annoyed   *(3+0) + (6) = 9*

Those who say there is a "right" way to love have entirely missed the point

JUNE

30

C
/
A
****
N
/
C
****
E
/
R

You

As a water sign, it is important that you note something about your character, and that is that it is your instinct to try to help where you can, to try to fix situations where it's possible.

In fact, you can end up putting this first, particularly in circumstances involving others. Of course, the trick is to balance that, to balance the importance of your own life and remedying things you need to do yourself.

You may tend to put off your own needs later, until you recognize the importance of establishing what might be called a give-and-take ratio. That is, you give—it's important for you. But also, there are times when you take assistance from others, or times when you're on your own and you put yourself absolutely first.

The irony of that is, you find that the more you do that—the more you put yourself first—the more you will be celebrated by those around you.

That is simply because in taking this approach, you'll be recognizing how important it is that you nurture yourself, and that alone will be the kind of lesson you've been wanting to give to those around you. Even more than that, it will allow you to discover your next set of goals and set you off on that path with enthusiasm.

You and others

Not everyone gets along all the time, and there are moments when there have been tensions with others, if not very difficult situations. The trick to dealing with this is to recognize that there are occasions when you need to disagree with others, and sometimes those disagreements mean saying farewell.

Health and well-being

There are kinds of extreme exercises people get involved in which suit them, and that may suit you. But in this particular case, the kind of extreme health and well-being you need to get involved in is doing what's absolutely true to you and nothing else.

Goals and challenges

Every once in a while, somebody comes along and you begin discussing what you want to do. This gives you advice without even asking if you'd like it. You may want to listen to them, but what may be most important is to be so selfish that you will do only what pleases you. There could be no more important goal in life.

THIS DAY FOR EVERYONE

You've hoped to sidestep one particular demanding situation involving an element of your way of living or working. But recent events made it clear you'd have to go along with others' decisions. Worse, there's no room for negotiation. Grim as it seems, don't argue. Ultimately, this will benefit you hugely.

Trusting my instincts is easy, until I try to get things right. Then they often go wrong

You

Numerologically, the first of every month signifies the number one, new beginnings. In fact, this is all about you discovering your own rhythm. However, it's important to recognize that this isn't about a single rhythm.

It's about your own ups and downs, not in the sense of negativity, but in the sense that there are times when you're bursting with energy, as if there is a spring bubbling inside you, and there are times when you need to be still. These are all important.

In fact, those still moments give you time to rest and reflect. These are mirrored by the seasons, and also, when you're reflecting, new ideas will grow, ideas that might possibly not have grown had you not taken that time for stillness.

The trick, therefore, is to ignore those who are encouraging you to get out and about when that isn't what you want to do. This is important for everybody, but for you, as a Cancerian and somebody who is ruled by the Moon, the planet which has its own cycles, the message is very clear. Pay attention to when you want to be still and do that, and then, when you're stirred by passion to do something, to achieve something, to go someplace, or in fact, to fall in love with something or somebody, do it, and do it just at the moment you feel is best.

You and others

It seems strange to recognize that those around you don't have the sense of cycles you do, but the fact is, they don't. When they want to go along with you, recognize that they may not be following the same rhythm you are, and if so, simply allow them. Step back and be who you are. Let them be who they are.

Health and well-being

There's a single message for you, and that message says move. Walk, dance, hop, jump rope—whatever it is, feel your body. Feel the muscles in your body, indeed, moving, and not only will you feel that. You'll feel the sheer joy of being alive.

Goals and challenges

Sometimes, challenges are just that, but for you, challenges are about defining the hill you want to climb and then climbing it. Then having gotten to the top, recognize that there are plenty of other hills you could climb and embrace the joy of knowing you can climb each of them.

Somebody seems determined to reveal flaws in your thinking. While you acknowledge you can get it wrong, you're confident that in this case, everything is accurate. Still, explore what is being said. At the least, you'll learn something. But the odds are good you'll discover that others are correct.

GIFTS Visionary, Loving, Accommodating

CHALLENGES Irritable, Worrying, Overextending

NUMBER 9

(0+2) + (7) = 9

Lively get-togethers are fun, but life's joys are found in the least likely of settings

C
/
A
\
N
/
C
\
E
/
R

You

Your birthday theme is a balance between your own life and your own stories and the lives of others and their stories. While you may care a lot about what they are doing—and in fact, in situations where you care about others you'll be thrilled by their activities—by no means does that suggest you need to get involved.

You can be involved—by caring about it—but you and your own interests must come first. As a Cancer, you tend to feel that in order to show you care, you need to be out there with others, and often, those around you will be delighted if you come, but the fact is, looking after yourself and your own interests is an important part for you as a Cancer.

Being born under the sign of nurturance, that balance between being interested in and caring about others, but also caring about yourself, is always an important one. It's also one you're always learning because you're changing and the world around you is changing, and that balance itself changes.

Perhaps the most important thing to keep in mind is that this isn't selfish. This is also showing those around you that they, too, can live a life that's exciting and full of activities and caring, but also ensures that they are looking after their own best interests. That's the secret.

You and others

There is a single phrase that defines your role when it comes to you and others. It's give and take. That means in both cases, the individual in question must recognize what the other is interested in and enjoy that. This always shifts. There is no fixed recipe.

Health and well-being

The important thing for you to remember is that there is a difference between a routine—that is, doing something—and doing the same thing. For you, taking care of yourself should be a routine. It's important. However, doing the same thing week in and week out doesn't qualify. Enjoying life is the best routine for your health and well-being.

Goals and challenges

It's easy to list what you need to do and what you want more of, but what may be most important for you to do is to note, and follow what lifts your spirits, and what challenges you in the best-possible way. Make that the center of your goals, and the rest will fall into place perfectly.

THIS DAY FOR EVERYONE

Few things are more upsetting than clashes with those closest over issues that really shouldn't be a problem. Or so you think. Begin delving into the source of those differences. What you learn won't just be surprising. You'll realize that a number of matters need to be discussed. And the sooner, the better.

Those who insist there's a right way to give a compliment have missed the point entirely

You

For you as a July 3rd Cancerian, discussing life and plans and projects with others can be tricky. This is simply because you'll be talking about what you want to do, and you'll be eager to hear what others have in mind.

The difficulty is that others will want to be helpful and give you advice, except you'll be well aware that what they think is a good idea isn't necessarily going to suit you, and this is where tact comes in.

You may find yourself being drawn into what they're doing, simply because they seem so determined to be helpful and you find it difficult to say no. And this is one of your challenges—to differentiate between those who think that they're offering something wonderful, but don't fully understand that you actually function in a very different way than they do. This is because they aren't an intuitive water sign, and you are.

If there is any skill, it is the skill of being able to withdraw from the offers of others who think that if you do what they say, then you will thrive. The secret is, appreciate who they are and help them appreciate who you are, and that relationship will thrive. And even more than that, you will live out each day appreciating life's joys all the more and, equally, appreciating what they brought into your life.

You and others

Some people are naturally generous, and they have an instinctive sense of what will benefit you. Others are well-meaning, but just plain selfish. They will organize your life so they will enjoy things, and that's one of your big lessons. You'll learn to say this single word firmly: no.

Health and well-being

The trick with this is to be able to recognize the difference between regimens that make others happy, but which, basically, are about depriving you of life's joys. The fact is, you can do what's good for you, but it doesn't need to take away from your everyday joys. It's about making the choices that add to your life in every way.

Goals and challenges

It's so easy to be distracted, if not drained, by goals that have made others successful, yet being able to say to them, "That's wonderful, but I'm not interested," can be one of the most difficult things in the world, especially for you, as a sensitive Cancerian. Practice saying no, just as you might practice something else, and you will benefit for the rest of your life.

JULY

03

C
/
A
\
N
/
C
\
E
/
R

Everybody has to deal with issues of some nature. It's just that those you're facing seem both more complex and more frequent than usual. This is mostly because changes, while beneficial in the long term, are chaotic. Be patient. The results will more than justify the disruption you're currently facing.

The problem isn't what those who are unkind say, it's that you pay attention to their words

JULY

04

C
/
A
\
N
/
C
\
E
/
R

You

It's said that planning ahead is good, and that's true. However, you have to consider what you're getting involved in—whether it's new territory in terms of activities, in terms of ideas, in terms of the culture you might be in, or the people you'll be around. If that's the case, it's almost as if you were learning a new language.

You may indeed actually have to, but it could also mean that you'll need to take time to figure out what's going on. You may feel that you're supposed to be bold and just plunge in, but this particular variety of moving into new territory is about a kind of discovery, and once you recognize that, then you'll actually enjoy taking care of yourself.

You'll treat yourself as if you were a very special kind of tourist, moving into a new kind of experience, into a new setting, a new country, a new way of thinking, and once you do that, you'll also begin to enjoy what you're doing.

The trick is to abandon that feeling that you're supposed to figure it out on your own, and instead treat yourself as the very special being that you are, the individual who deserves to be tutored when you're entering new territory, and in being tutored, will become very skilled at living in that setting and living very well indeed.

You and others

The message for you is to be aware of certain individuals who are what might be termed chronic complainers. Whatever it is that's going on, they'll find something wrong, and they'll expect those around them, possibly you, to remedy that. The fact is, they're just spoiled, and you and your needs come first.

Health and well-being

There seems to be somebody around you that has very strict do's and don'ts for taking care of yourself. That might work for them, but being ruled by the Moon, the heavenly body that has cycles, that kind of thing isn't your style. In fact, the more you align with your own rhythms, the better.

Goals and challenges

There's a single phrase for you when it comes to goals and challenges, and that's "Don't let others take over." They may mean well, but in doing so, they're trying to impose their interests and values on you. If others try to do that, say thank you, then give serious thought to who and what are most important to you.

THIS DAY FOR EVERYONE

The time has come to talk things over. True, with so much going on, the last thing you're in the mood for is in-depth discussion of minor issues. However, those differences aren't nearly as insignificant as they seem, something which will become clear as others reveal why they're concerned.

GIFTS Loyal, Romantic, Caring

NUMBER 3

(0+5) + (7) = 12 = (1+2) = 3

CHALLENGES Defensive, Cranky, Overcommitting

The formula for ending suffering? Dwell on love until there's no room for anything else

JULY

05

You

You like planning ahead, because it makes life easier, but at the same time, you hope for the unexpected. This is so you're able to think quickly and come up with new ideas, which actually is as much fun as making plans.

This is because you have a strong inquisitive side to your nature, and that inquisitive side responds well when you have to take care of sudden twists and turns or perhaps meet people who will help you resolve the surprising developments that have arisen.

Not everyone understands this, which means that there can be those around you who will try to convince you simply either to go with the flow or make more solid plans.

But this is very much your own journey— and if you try to take the advice of those who want to make plans and have you stick to them, then you'll simply be following their theme.

This shows the inquisitive side of your nature as well, the part that thrives on discovery, the part that enjoys those twists and turns and, in fact, recognizes that the unexpected allows you to exercise a muscle that is unique to you, one that is about embracing the unfamiliar and about discovery and about the joy of learning something new, ideally every day. Embrace that, and you will be making each day a joy.

You and others

The trick is to do something that seems odd and that is to have two sets of routines. One is for others and will enable you to go along with what they want, but your own is for those discoveries that make life itself exciting, and those are the adventures.

Health and well-being

For you, as a Cancerian, mood is as important as the time of day or what you are doing. Being ruled by the Moon, you have an understanding of the importance of this, but others don't, so don't try to explain. You will never be able to.

Goals and challenges

Beware of borrowing the goals of others. They will be delighted to share them with you, but that doesn't mean it's wise. This is the most important thing for you to discover. You pursuing their goals will make them happy, not you.

C
/
A
\
N
/
C
\
E
/
R

Currently, it may seem life is like a chess game, in that you can only move so far, and only under certain circumstances. Frustrating as that is, it's forcing you and others to pause and reflect on your priorities with every step. This prevents you being pressed into making hasty decisions.

GIFTS Nurturing, Warmhearted, Persistent   *NUMBER* 4

CHALLENGES Delayed Reaction, Grouchy, Nervous   *(0+6) + (7) = 13 = (1+3) = 4*

Sometimes it is only when a heart is broken that true love can find its way in

C
/
A
\
N
/
C
\
E
/
R

You

Do you ever wonder why some people seem to make life so difficult, they turn ordinary situations into something unpleasant, or pick up on unnecessary challenges? Well, it's not about you. It's about them. The fact is certain individuals seem to be programmed that way.

The skill for you is to notice that and, unless it happens to be a child you're raising or a very close friend, to acknowledge that that's just what makes them tick, that's how they look at the world. Then back off and know that you're different, and that by no means should you let them undermine your thinking or your life. This has to do with the individuals around you, but it also has to do with life in general and any setbacks you're facing.

As a Cancerian and a water sign, you can be sensitive and can often turn seemingly unimportant situations into something that has to do with you personally. That may indeed have to do with your mood.

That's one of your greatest lessons—to recognize those moments when the choice lies entirely with you, whether you'll enjoy what life brings you or turn it into a drama. You could even turn those dramas into something exciting and enjoyable. After all, many people go to the theater to do exactly that. You're able to do it in your own life. And better yet, you're able to direct how the play goes.

You and others

Beware of the stories that others tell you about what they're trying to do, especially what they're trying to do for you. While they may have good intentions, putting you first is probably the best way to get what you want to accomplish and done in your own timing.

Health and well-being

It's said that dieting and working out with somebody else is great. However, in certain situations, the individual you have in mind may want you to do things their way, in their routine, eat what they need to eat, as opposed to you looking after your own needs. Think about this and think about it carefully.

Goals and challenges

Making lists about what you want to do is important. However, what's more important is to follow your instincts. As a Cancerian and a water sign, these are powerful—more powerful than those of others—which is the reason that those around you don't necessarily encourage you to listen to what your instincts tell you.

THIS DAY FOR EVERYONE

Admitting you're wrong is no problem. However, certain individuals insist their facts are right. The real problem is that they're looking for a battle and have chosen their topic, which involves you. Say nothing. The individuals in question will soon turn their attention elsewhere.

Nobody decides what kindness is. Only the recipient can say, and even then, it changes

You

As a Cancerian, you seek security and stability. Yet at the same time, in life you need new challenges—not just to have things organized but something new to think about. On occasion, this will involve others and their support, which is important.

But what's most significant for you is to put what you need to do and your own objectives first, then get others involved if you feel like it. Most of all, you need to recognize that what you learn from setting your own goals isn't just about life itself, but constitutes an opportunity to review what's worked and what hasn't and what you want to leave behind.

As a Cancerian, you have an instinctive understanding of the cycles of nature. You are, after all, ruled by the Moon, the heavenly body that is known for its cycles. Yet sometimes you try to make your life fit into the kind of order that others follow.

Recognizing that there are times when, like the Moon, you have more energy, and other times when you need to be still will allow you to use these quiet times to reflect on what you've done, what you are happy about, and what you will want next. Do that, and when it comes time to make major decisions, you'll already know where you stand and what and who is most important—and, even more than that, what brings you joy in life.

You and others

The thing for you is give and take. This is necessary when dealing with others. However, certain individuals are convinced that if you organize things in a way that makes them happy, then everything will work. The secret is to learn to say no, not to debate the rights and wrongs of it, but simply to do what you need to do and put that first. Not by arguing, but simply by putting one foot after the other.

Health and well-being

You're sensitive by nature and need a break from the rigors of life every once in a while, including the rigors of eating well. Yet it's important to balance taking care of yourself with indulgences. These may have to do with something you eat or something pleasurable, and are as important as the vitamins you take—in fact, in some instances, more important.

Goals and challenges

Because you're creative by nature, sensing what will be rewarding is of great significance. That may mean rethinking your goals as you focus on them. In some cases, these will last a week, in some a month, and in some cases they'll last years. But in every case, if that goal comes from the center of your being, from your heart, then you will achieve it.

JULY

07

C
/
A
\
N
/
C
\
E
/
R

GIFTS Compassionate, Attentive, Visionary

CHALLENGES Evasive, Easily Affronted, Anxious

NUMBER 6

$(0+8) + (7) = 15 = (1+5) = 6$

Talking somebody out of a bad idea only delays it. Showing them they're loved ends it

JULY

08

C
/
A
\
N
/
C
\
E
/
R

You

As a July 8th Cancer, you balance a Cancerian desire to get out there in the world and do what you want to do. It may be that world is your home, perhaps in business or travel. You are creative by nature and enjoy doing things that are lasting, that bring you pleasure, and will benefit others. Yet at the same time, being a Cancerian and a water sign, ruled by the Moon, you have ups and downs.

When you are experiencing downs, you want either reassurance from others or need to build up your own sense of ego or sense of optimism about what's next that may involve looking back on what you've done before and the challenges that you've managed to meet. But it also may be doing something that is out of character for you but you don't think of, which is to pause and take a break, to walk, to look at the sky, to recognize that it isn't always about doing or not doing, but about being. This is one of the greatest skills for you.

The point of it is to give you the strength to tackle what's next, because as a Cancerian and somebody who is one of the cardinal signs, the signs that begin each season, starting something new is as much a part of your nature as breathing. Find that balance between the need to be still and nurturing yourself to meet that next challenge, and you will have found the most important balance in your life.

You and others

Rituals are an important part of life and often of those around you. Family or friends enjoy them. You always meet on a certain date and do something in particular. But every once in a while, those rituals can turn into a trap. Being able to set your own, often with new friends, is an essential part of your life.

Health and well-being

It's said that if you get into a routine, you can keep that for life. But actually it's not true. Times change, you change, and what makes you happy changes. But also things can become so routine that you don't even notice what you're doing and you end up getting lazy. Excitement comes from doing something different, learning something with somebody new, and challenging yourself in a way that is as exciting as it is rewarding.

Goals and challenges

Planning ahead is important, but often those plans need to be rethought before they become reality. Yet there's a part of you that worries you didn't think about those things first, that you didn't catch the need to make those changes. Observe how a plant develops new leaves or even flowers. So, too, will your challenges develop and grow.

THIS DAY FOR EVERYONE

Planning ahead may be a virtue and make life easier. But with your ruler Mercury retrograde for a few more days, you're better off regarding even the simplest of arrangements as tentative, if not a bit of an experiment. While things may go as expected, the odds are good there will be several changes.

A smile from the heart can turn a pleasant moment into a profound, and lasting, bond

You

You tend to swing from gathering people and activities, even sometimes objects, to shedding them. Once you've got too much going in your life, you realize it's important to let go. Still, saying the farewells can be very difficult indeed. You may find excuses to put it off.

But this is one of your greatest lessons: letting go of certain elements of your life, even habits. That may mean letting relationships go, but it also may have to do with certain goals that once meant a great deal.

The other element of this is to recognize that being an intuitive water sign, you have what might be termed a rich inner realm: that is, those feelings and perhaps even the mystical side of your nature that senses what's going on in the world around you, in the lives of others, and, importantly, in your own life.

Sometimes you keep feelings of that nature to yourself because you know others won't understand that. But if you have one or two friends or family members who are themselves intuitive and with whom you can talk about those feelings, then it's important to do so.

That's the secret for you. As a Cancerian—and somebody who is on one hand bursting with initiative and on the other goes deep within—it's not what you do or say, but finding the balance that's important.

You and others

Habits are comfortable—at home, with family members or with friends, all make it easy, because you don't have to make decisions. You can do the same thing on the same day or go to the same place. However, that makes things predictable. The secret for you, and one that's important to remind yourself of, is that change is like taking a deep breath and bringing new life into your life and those of others as well.

Health and well-being

Often those who get involved in a well-being routine, whether it's what you eat or getting out and about, follow it in a way that makes it duller by the day. The trick is to turn that into a joy—and an experiment. That may mean you lose individuals who are committed to that strict regimen. If so, that's fine because you'll have more fun without them.

Goals and challenges

It's hard to measure if you've achieved a goal unless it's something specific—writing a book, say, or getting a degree. So it's essential you set your own goals, not measured by others but those that mean the most to you. You may not discuss them with others, but what's most important is that when you achieve them, your spirits will get a boost like nothing else.

It's rare that, when making plans, you lavish attention on details. You long ago learned that because things change, you're better off dealing with such matters at the last minute. Not everyone agrees. Tempting as it is to reassure them, that's unwise. The best strategy is to say nothing.

Sometimes a fierce debate conceals a loving, and passionate, exchange

JULY

10

C
/
A
\
N
/
C
\
E
/
R

You

You often tend to measure your days in what might be called good vibes—that is, if something you're doing lifts your spirits. While that's wonderful and important, not every day brings that kind of thing.

If you measure the success on that and are disturbed if that doesn't happen, then you may not recognize what you've achieved in situations that are less easy to deal with: facing people who are difficult, facing obstacles, or perhaps even having to undo something from the past that may have been difficult to contend with.

Whatever it is, the thing for you to recognize is that often the most important achievements occur in the most challenging of circumstances. This by no means indicates anything is bad. It's just simply that it's a big stretch for you.

As a water sign, and somebody who feels more deeply than the other signs, it's vital that you recognize that sometimes those feelings of struggle are an indication of making an effort, kind of as if you were lifting weights to get stronger. Most of all, recognize that often after those struggles come delights: delights that simply wouldn't have been possible had you not struggled. When you're celebrating in that way, remember that for the next time you face similar obstacles.

You and others

Habits play a big part in your relationship with others. There's a celebration of doing things the same way. However, that can be limiting, and it can be difficult to say no to certain habits. It may take courage, but, bizarrely, once you do, others will agree that it was wise to make a change, and you'll all be delighted, because life isn't just about doing things the same way. It's about discovery.

Health and well-being

Some habits are good. However, some are unhelpful. Also, some pleasures are appealing. In every case, it's isn't how much you enjoy doing something or not. It's about examining where it fits into your life and if it brings you benefit in the here and now. If it doesn't, it's time to say farewell to it.

Goals and challenges

Occasionally, you put off tackling a particular challenge because it doesn't seem the right time. But often it's because the situation or people involved are themselves challenging. Take a deep breath, stand firmly on your feet, and note that not only can you meet that challenge, you can overcome it. And better yet, think about how wonderful you'll feel when you've done it.

THIS DAY FOR EVERYONE

You seem to be caught in one of those tricky situations in which a particular individual will go to any length to avoid taking responsibility for something they did wrong. While this isn't your problem, it is essential you make it clear you had absolutely nothing to do with the matter in question.

GIFTS Warmhearted, Constant, Wise

NUMBER 9

CHALLENGES Overcautious, Annoyed, Frozen

(1+1) + (7) = 9

When hearts are tender, careless laughter can cause deep wounds

You

A long time ago, you got in the habit of fighting to do what you want. While this is important, many of the things you were fighting for at that time are no longer rewarding. Yet because you battled for them, you're keeping them as part of your life, mostly to remember what you've achieved.

Yet times have moved on and, in fact, the kind of review that was once important for you has changed. It's not just about finding new battles, but also exciting and rewarding new activities and possibly individuals in your life.

Habits are important, and they might be viewed as kind of an arbor that holds up roses in the garden. However, in your particular case, those habits can hold you back. The trick is to regard yourself as if you were a plant that bloomed anew each season and that as you bloom, you must choose what you want to be drawn toward, just as a flower is drawn toward the sun.

It may well be that certain activities and goals that were once rewarding actually no longer mean that much. While you're inclined to reach toward others, decide what those are, commit to them, and, within a very short time—months or possibly even weeks—you'll be achieving them.

You and others

Tempting as it is to stick with those you care about, every once in a while you need a break, and that involves doing something with somebody new. It may just be a one-off visit, or it may be someone who will become an important part of your life. But in every case, mixing it up, blending family and friends and those you've known forever with new encounters, will be the tonic you need.

Health and well-being

Maybe you're looking for a quick formula for feeling better or you've heard about one from others, but you've lived in your body for a while and you'll be using it for a while yet. And so, making it comfortable and happy may also take time. Regard it as if you were caring for a beautiful piece of furniture that needed to be cared for over time. Don't rush it into being perfect; enjoy the process of looking after it.

Goals and challenges

It's not about whether you've succeeded or not, but by whose values you are judging. Often those around you will have clear ideas about what you should be doing with your life, which may differ from yours. You're number one in your own life, and you need to decide what you regard as success.

THIS DAY FOR EVERYONE

If it seems that you're running up against people who are either demanding or opinionated. That's no surprise. However, it is worth noting that your views on several matters are equally inflexible. Begin reviewing these, and suddenly discussions with others will go better.

Healing occurs when the power of love outweighs the force of fear

You

Every once in a while, you have a deep conversation with the most important person in your life, yourself, about what you want to do. There may be certain things you'd like to change, or goals you would like to pursue, or there may be doubts you're wrestling with.

While you can go around and around with these, there's also the chance to discuss these matters with others. However, that can be tricky, especially if it's family or close friends you're talking to, each of whom will have their own view about what's in your best interest.

The secret to dealing with all of these is to sit down with yourself and consider what actually brings you joy. True, not everything in life will be joyous, certain situations require plain discipline. Still, the simple act of doing what you need to do is itself joyous.

The trick is to avoid sticking with the old just for the sake of it, or to keep those around you—family, friends, or colleagues—happy, but to explore. And in exploring, discovery's an important part of that. Report back to those around you how much you're enjoying it. Instead of seeking their guidance, invite them to join you in that process of discovery.

You'll be turning destiny around. Rather than seeking others' guidance, you'll be giving it to them. Together, you'll move ahead into a far more rewarding chapter.

You and others

There's a secret to dealing with tricky matters. That is to raise them. And the more swiftly you do that, the better. Once you begin, you'll realize that often those issues were on the minds of others, and they're grateful you brought those matters up. Most of all, say exactly what you want. Here, too, others will be grateful for your bold approach.

Health and well-being

You have a choice. You can have really big ideas about the way you look after your body, then do very little simply because it is overwhelming. Or you can do something radical and take things one day at a time. Do that and you'll not only be acting in your own best interest, you will be setting an example for others as well.

Goals and challenges

You often forget your own achievements, some minor, some major. First, you put them all behind you, then you compare yourself to others. Every once in a while, if not even once a day, it's useful to recall what you've done and enjoy the satisfaction those achievements have brought. Do that—then, when you tackle what's next, you will do so with joy and conviction.

THIS DAY FOR EVERYONE

Having right on your side is reassuring, especially when you're dealing with those who are eager to debate existing plans or priorities. Still, before you challenge others, it would be wise to double-check even seemingly solid facts. Times change so much, you're likely to make several surprising discoveries.

A loving heart always knows what's needed, and without a word being spoken

JULY

13

C
/
A
\
N
/
C
\
E
/
R

You

As a Cancerian and an intuitive water sign, you go back and forth between your practical side that thrives on security and the part that is sometimes described as superstitious. However, that has an instinct of the rhythms of nature and also a clear sense of the degree to which your own way of looking at things and thinking about circumstances can influence both how they flow and the outcome.

Of course, as you've discovered, it's tricky discussing this approach with certain people, and it has even made you a bit self-conscious. Yet if you can blend the two in your activities, in your major goals, and in your everyday pursuits, then you'll find you're benefiting from both, and there will be a new kind of magic in your life. Even more than that, there will be a new kind of joy.

You wouldn't think that this would have anything to do with benefiting you in practical or financial terms. Yet if you think positively about what you could do, you might be surprised. At the same time, being able to look toward those whose company can be challenging in a more positive light can alter that as well.

The trick, therefore, isn't so much expecting magic, but turning your own mind into the tool that makes magic happen. Try that and you'll be amazed at how much you achieve.

You and others

Particular individuals often withhold their approval until you do things their way. Sometimes that may be a game, but often it's a manipulation as well. The most important thing is to recognize when that occurs, and to make a point of making your own decisions and doing exactly what you please.

Health and well-being

Most people speak of changes in the way you eat, or move, or exercise, as a regimen. However, there's another approach, and it has to do with the idea of being nice to yourself. Choose to eat in a certain way that you'll benefit from and to move in a certain way—one that you enjoy. That is a much better approach than any regimen.

Goals and challenges

The term "challenge" itself implies an uphill struggle. However, life is all about cycles—day and night, up and down—and you won't have a goal without a challenge. Bear that in mind, and when those challenges arise, you will view them as climbing that hill, at which point you'll have an amazing view, not just of where you've come from but of what's next. That isn't so much a challenge as it is a goal realized.

THIS DAY FOR EVERYONE

Change is in the air. While it's clear things can't remain as they are, you've been hoping you could discuss and deal with certain tricky matters gradually. But, ironically, the disruption caused by those changes will force others to acknowledge, and join you in tackling, the issues you have in mind.

Often we pray to a divine being beyond us, when in fact, that power lies within

JULY

14

C
/
A
\
N
/
C
\
E
/
R

You

As a Cancerian and a water sign, one of the three signs that are sensitive and highly intuitive, not only do you derive insights from what you sense, but also some of your greatest joys come not so much from possessions or achievement, but your feelings.

This by no means indicates that you don't enjoy acquiring things. In fact, many Cancerians are great collectors. It just means that it is important for you to recognize that whatever you're doing, a portion of that activity is based on those feelings.

If there's anything tricky, it's that those around you won't necessarily hold the same deep feelings. If you try to discuss them with others, they may look at you blankly because they don't understand. So it is important that while you may be close to certain family or friends, you pick and choose those with whom you discuss these feelings.

It also means that sometimes you'll juggle what you say. In some cases, you'll need to be very frank and deal only with the facts, while with others you can talk about feelings. It's like having two languages. But it is also like being a very special person, because not everybody has the capacity to experience life's deepest joys and its deepest feelings in the way that you do as a Cancerian. That's a very precious talent, one to be savored and enjoyed.

You and others

You may be into a routine or perhaps those around you like to do things the same way. Whatever the case, there's a tendency to stick with the familiar. However, changes aren't just great. They allow you to retool things that you didn't even realize needed to be rethought and to make them better, either on your own or along with others.

Health and well-being

Your sense of well-being has as much to do with the state of your mind and your feelings as with the body you're living in. Instead of focusing only on your physical body, your activities, and what you eat, pay close attention to your words and ideas, the way you feed your mind and your feelings. Focus on that and you will feel terrific every day.

Goals and challenges

You need to assess whether your current goals are actually appropriate for the person you are today. Every so often, it is essential to stop and consider whether what you were once passionate about still means as much to you. This may have to do with life out in the world, or your personal life. Whatever the case, ensure that what you care about most is something that you *actually* care about.

THIS DAY FOR EVERYONE

In your efforts to avoid causing offense or seeming overly critical, you've given one particular individual the impression that you've no objection to what they've said or done. But that's not the case. This leaves you little choice but to be frank, and in a way that removes all possibility of doubt.

GIFTS Constant, Tenacious, Kind

CHALLENGES Evasive, Getting Upset, Moody

NUMBER 4

(1+5) + (7) = 13 = (1+3) = 4

When the moment is right, an abrupt "No" can be a statement of love

You

There are many definitions for the word "success." On one hand you are a cardinal sign—one of the signs that begin in each season—but you are also an intuitive water sign, so your own definition of success may shift with your mood. The question is: does it have to do with worldly achievement—perhaps making money or being recognized—or is it about living a happy life in which you're content with what you are doing and the people around you?

Ideally, it will be both, but times change and life changes, and having these all at once can be tricky. This means that defining success for you also has to do with how you feel about yourself and what you're doing—and the joy that you have every day when you wake up.

Compare yourself to others, and it's difficult to have that joy. On the other hand, if you simply feel the best you can each day, then reach out and share that feeling with others, whatever the day holds, you'll feel better, and might even find that those good feelings are contagious.

Even more than that, as someone who is a cardinal sign, it is important that you be bold and take chances at least every once in a while. It is an important muscle for you to exercise, and the more you do, the more you will enjoy what, ultimately, you achieve.

You and others

We often get into rituals—with friends, or often with family at certain holidays or times of the year. While that's nice, it can also be dull or restrictive, so alter the place or activity or even the people involved a little and get others to agree with this approach, you fill find a whole new way of doing something, which, while a familiar ritual, won't become a trap.

Health and well-being

Others may have told you certain activities were good for you, so you are trying them out instead of doing something you really enjoy. This has to do with how you eat and with how you move. But even more than that, it's about doing things to give your spirit a lift. As a water sign, that latter is far more important and can actually be the foundation of your well-being.

Goals and challenges

Everyone has a list of things they want to do. Yours may have been done some time ago. But the fact is, every once in a while, it is not only vital to review that, it's important to take that metaphorical piece of paper that list is written on, and write a new one. There is no better time to do this than the present.

On several occasions over the past few weeks, when discussing certain tricky situations, you sidestepped the full facts. While, at the time, it was about sidestepping pointless discussions, you're urged to inform those involve of the details you left out. And do it now, before they discover these for themselves.

Remedying problems only repositions them. The solution? Rise above them

JULY

16

C
/
A
\
N
/
C
\
E
/
R

You

Many Cancers are easygoing by nature, but most, deep within, have standards that come from their childhood. These shape what they want to do or become in life. There is a part of your Cancerian nature that is just plain driven. And in certain areas, you have very clear ideas about how things should work.

However, being ruled by the Moon, you're also sensitive. Your mood changes. It changes depending on what you are doing, what you have experienced, and is even altered by the people you're around. In some cases, certain individuals undermine your feelings, and you have to be cautious of them. It's the same with joy—certain individuals lift your spirits.

The trick, of course, is to create your own mental and emotional climate. Ideally, you will do that, not based on who you are hanging out with, but on how you actually manage both your mood and your time. There is a challenge here—to break a habit a day, to find something that you do simply because you do it well and wisely and just stop it as an exercise.

But even more than that, the other trick is to find a joy a day. That may be more difficult, simply because it is easier to find things that you are unhappy about, and that is the whole point. In finding that joy a day, you will lift your spirits permanently.

You and others

You don't really think of it when you're with certain people, especially if you know them well, but there are rules about what you do, what you enjoy, and what you don't do. In some cases, that's fun. It's the joy of being with somebody you know. But it can also be restrictive. Consider breaking away from those with too many rules and you will not only find you're able to relax, you're able to have fun in ways you'd forgotten were possible.

Health and well-being

Many people think of the regimen that comes with being well as a strict one, that if you stray, then you are in some way doing yourself a disservice. But actually this is all about what's in your best interest, doing something wild and crazy and relaxing and enjoying life and, in doing so, choosing activities and ways of eating that are in your best interest. Think of that. It will be a lot easier and a lot more fun.

Goals and challenges

It is often useful to choose little challenges, to list those and overcome those, to discover an easy way to surmount what seemed like huge mountains. Achieving certain goals that seem a long way away demands only that first step. The payoff? The joy that comes with doing so.

THIS DAY FOR EVERYONE

After weeks of battling seemingly insurmountable obstacles, you've discovered a fundamental misunderstanding over what you were dealing with. As aggravating as going back to the beginning seems, what you learn will explain what went wrong, and in the process, eliminate that confusion.

Joy can appear in the most unexpected settings, some so extraordinary you're taken by surprise

JULY

17

C
/
A
\
N
/
C
\
E
/
R

You

As a Cancerian, you are on one hand sensitive, but also you're driven. You have a clear sense of what needs to be done—or you do until you talk to other people who have an entirely different agenda. The trick to dealing with this is to acknowledge that they want things done their way, and then very quietly go on and do what you think is most important first.

This doesn't only have to do with tasks. It also has to do with life's joys and, to be honest, who is better at assessing the joys that you will experience than you? There are those around you who are quite sure they know what's in your best interest. If so, listen to them politely, then change the subject and go back to doing what you want to do. With certain individuals, this is easy, but with others, it may seem as if you're almost being secretive or challenging them. If so, those are the ones you want to be particularly aware of, and you also want to be especially conscious of putting you and your own interests and your own goals first.

Do that and the happiness you have won't be their happiness, but will be the happiness you've created from your own goals and happiness, which grows with each passing day, knowing that as you add one achievement to the next, you're able to enjoy what you do and who you are all the more.

You and others

Your message has to do with being aware of and being cautious about complainers, those who need things done a certain way, those who regard those who don't do things their way to be somehow inferior. This isn't about you. However, they will be superb at making you feel guilty. The trick is to ignore them politely and do exactly what you want to do.

Health and well-being

If there is a secret to feeling well, it isn't following someone's regimen or eating the way someone says you should. It's simply to get moving. That may mean getting out and about, or eating in a different way. And it needn't be a tough road. It's about just being sure you enjoy what each day offers.

Goals and challenges

As a Cancerian, you like things that are familiar. You know what you're doing. But there is a part of you that gets bored and needs new things to do. Be conscious of the fact that, occasionally, you'll let something that you're already doing slip so you have an opportunity to fix it. Here's an idea. You might enjoy life more if you embrace a new activity or pursuit—something you can learn about—and a new joy to your life.

THIS DAY FOR EVERYONE

There is little point in arguing with somebody who has already made, and committed to, a decision. Although you don't realize it, that's exactly what you've done, and in a range of situations. Review existing plans, especially those you regard as unchanging. They could be holding you back.

Can you dance with love? Yes, and especially when you're alone, your feelings are free

JULY

18

C
/
A
\
N
/
C
\
E
/
R

You

As an industrious Cancerian, you're always aware of what you want to do and what your goals are that lay ahead, but it's hard not to be aware of setbacks of certain types, situations that you didn't expect or perhaps those that involve others who either aren't happy to get involved in changes and throw obstacles in your road, or who complain with every step.

Instead of waiting for them to catch on to what you're doing, simply proceed. If they discuss what you are doing, and even complain, then change the subject. Gradually, they will realize that you won't get involved in their game of complaining and they will turn their attention to other individuals.

In your case, the task ahead is not a difficult one. It is to find new joys: joys that can be achieved easily, joys that don't require the cooperation of those individuals who seem to have fun triggering obstacles or making problems.

This is one of your biggest lessons and challenges. Choose your own approach to what you're doing, and in doing so, program how it will proceed and the ways you will avoid those complainers.

Do that and everything else will flow with an ease that may be so thrilling that you regard it as sheer magic.

You and others

There are two approaches to any situation. The first is to define your objective, and take that first step. The other has to do with trying to predict the way those around you respond. If you start worrying about others, you might find future steps complicated. If, on the other hand, you make each step your own, you will not only achieve more, you'll enjoy it as well.

Health and well-being

The theme for this is choosing to take care of yourself, to move in a way that is actually fun, that you want to do, maybe with those around you. This suggests that you do something that is uninteresting, but they're enthusiastic. Give it a try. The secret is the word "no," or perhaps "no, thank you"—but definitely "no."

Goals and challenges

Every once in a while, something happens. You begin something, and everything falls into place as if by magic. Then you tell somebody about it and they begin to ask questions: questions that trigger worries. Suddenly that magic is gone. There's a solution, and it's not doing things in a new way. It's deciding who you'll discuss your activities and plans with and who you won't, and then sticking to that decision.

THIS DAY FOR EVERYONE

Having to deal with tedious problems is bad enough. But having to discuss them at length with those who will insist on going into these matters in detail is the last thing you're in the mood for. Despite that, these need attention. And the longer you wait, the more troublesome they will become.

Faced with a complainer? Just listen. Often that is all they need—somebody to embrace their pain

You

Now and again, when you're feeling restless or bored or just want to chat with somebody, you'll talk about what you're doing. In some cases, those you're talking to will encourage you. In fact, they'll even seem excited. But from time to time, you will also encounter somebody who's a critic. They don't even realize it. They think they're being constructive and helpful. Yet you end the conversation feeling worried and perhaps even concerned that you need to rethink everything top to bottom. The most important thing to think about is who you're trusting.

This is a big lesson for you. Refuse to allow what might be regarded as toxic thoughts to influence your thinking. Strengthen the voice in your own head, what might be called your well-being mantra, your chant, and ensure that what you're thinking about boosts your spirits and also gives you the confidence to pursue what you have in mind—and, equally, to recognize that there are certain individuals who think in a very different way and who you must be careful about, especially when you are fostering a new plan.

It's not that there is anything wrong with them or you, but what it is all about is making choices that give you the best possible beginning to each day of your life and to each plan you're unfolding.

You and others

Every once in a while, it is important to consider who you trust, who you would ask for support, as well as those individuals who are interesting to know but who don't have your best interest at heart. Recognizing that is important. But so is choosing who you spend time with, especially during those precious periods where growth is your priority.

Health and well-being

There's a lot of discussion about what to do to be your best, how to eat, the activities you should undertake. But there's another secret, and it's an important one for you. It's what not to do—that is, how to relax. There's a much greater art to that than there is to getting out and exercising. Give it a try. With experience, the odds are good that you'll become an expert.

Goals and challenges

There is a lot said about persistence and about how important it is to stick with what you want to achieve. However, it's more important to pause and consider first whether what you want to achieve is still important to you and whether there's something else you'd rather put first. Think about that. It may answer all your questions about how to achieve your current and future goals.

THIS DAY FOR EVERYONE

The last thing you want to do is upset anybody. Yet if you don't raise and discuss a particular minor misunderstanding, it could swiftly turn into a major issue. True, the simple mention of this is likely to ruffle some feathers. Say nothing and the odds are good you'll face serious dramas anyway.

Want a magic wand to remove every obstacle? It's simple: don't care about those problems

You

You have phases of wanting to keep track of things to save elements of your life that bring memories that you've collected, things you have picked up here and there. Then, every once in a while, there is a feeling that you need to get rid of it all.

The trick, of course, is to do a little of each. But every so often it is about clearing the way, not just stuff but also feelings, feelings about those possessions. Even more, you sometimes tend to save up feelings about experiences with others and, on occasion, those feelings will prevent you spending time with those individuals or even pursuing certain activities. This is key to your awareness of what drives you.

As a Cancerian, you love achieving things. But you're also sensitive enough that you'll tend to avoid situations that have, in the past, been unsettling or even worrying. Notice whether they are associated with a particular experience or an individual who seemed to undermine you.

If so, decide that by no means should you allow that to stop you. Even more, recognize the joy in pushing past doubts and achieving what you want to. Tackle a small thing every day and a bigger thing once a week, and soon you'll have restored that self-confidence that is so essential.

You and others

There's what might be termed a push-pull between you and certain individuals, often after a conversation with some of them, you feel less enthusiastic about life. Not everybody is positive. If you're eager to get going and need support, think about who you want to spend time with. While not everybody is upbeat by nature, you can pick and choose the moments you spend with certain individuals.

Health and well-being

For you, the balance between a strict regimen and excess is a tricky one. What's important is that you enjoy how you take care of yourself, whether it has to do with movement, how you eat, or simply how you think. In every case, the priority is making sure that whatever it is you're doing, you feel better when you pause than when you began. Make that your priority.

Goals and challenges

There are those who set a goal and talk about it constantly. But actually, both goals and challenges change. They change over time and they change with what you accomplish. Also, they change as your focus shifts. Check it out. Make sure you're not talking about goals that once meant a lot to you when actually what is important to you is now very different.

THIS DAY FOR EVERYONE

There are many ways to say the single word "No." While you tend to assume others are aware when things aren't going well, and that a request is unlikely to be agreed to, not everybody picks up on such things. That being the case, you may need to be very clear, if not blunt, about your views.

Joy. A short word, yet seemingly beyond reach. Until you embrace it with your heart

You

As someone who is very much a Cancerian but also part Leo, you're juggling two very strong elements of your nature. The Cancerian part is nurturing and reflective and sensitive, yet also highly creative and often highly enterprising. But the Leo enthusiasm and zest for life are important.

However, you can sometimes get so involved in what's fun that you forget about those goals. The trick is to honor both sides. That may seem complicated, and sometimes it will be, but on the other hand you have double the opportunity to enjoy what life offers and double the opportunity to share those joys with others. Even more than that, it gives you the opportunity to be creative in a way that very few benefit from.

By being a sensitive and nurturing Cancerian, you bring that awareness to any relationship in any situation—from family to career.

Yet the Leo side of you enjoys doing something new, and possibly in a slightly theatrical way. Combine those two and your life will be full—full of changes and full of excitement.

But most of all, it will be full of the kind of satisfaction that comes with being both emotionally kind and generous—and creative as well.

You and others

Rather than getting things organized the way some people like to do, it is important that you be spontaneous, that you do something suddenly, that you just head out perhaps for a run or do something that lifts your spirits, and at times you get others to join you, too. While there may be those around you who think a routine is best, for you, spontaneity is the name of the game.

Health and well-being

Tempting as it is to get involved in some kind of routine, here, again, the trick is to do what you enjoy, although that itself may change over time. But the more it changes, the more you'll discover and the more you'll enjoy.

Goals and challenges

Setting goals is natural. You don't really think of them that way, especially if it's something you want to do anyway, and that is the point of this. There may be those around you who make the idea of setting goals so complicated that even thinking about it seems boring. Yet with your energy, you're always setting goals; it's just that you move swiftly from thinking about it to action and don't realize that you set those goals—and often don't realize what you have achieved, either.

THIS DAY FOR EVERYONE

Unsettling as recent events seemed, you recognize that instead of being reason for concern, they were breakthroughs. True, these weren't in the form you'd anticipated and could take things in an unexpected direction. Be patient. The more you explore, and learn, the more optimistic you'll be.

Leo

Ruler The Sun   **Symbol** The Lion

Element Fire   **Flower** Marigold

July 22–
August 21

Leo Whatever you're doing,
you Leos have style. Being ruled
by the Sun, your magnetism
comes naturally, and being fire
signs, you're usually juggling your
busy calendar while charming
others. However, when you're
relaxing, you'll do it with the
conviction of your symbol, the
lion. Your flower is marigold; your
spice, golden saffron; and your
trees are the heady, scented bay
and the olive. Your stone is gold
topaz, or simply wearing gold.

L
/
E
\
O

GIFTS Entertaining, Generous, Creative

CHALLENGES Willful, Proud, Impatient

NUMBER 2

$(2+2) + (7) = 11 = (1+1) = 2$

I know I have a talent for brightening others' day, and enjoy doing it

JULY

22

L
/
E
\
O

You

As a Leo born close to the sign of Cancer, you share the qualities of both signs. On the one hand, you have the fiery enthusiasm of a Leo, yet on the other, you also benefit from the sensitive awareness that comes from Cancer, which is one of the three water signs.

This balance threads through your life. It means you have the theatrical side that is so much part of Leo, but you can also be tender, loving, and kind, and aware of what people are struggling with. Sometimes, in fact, your own pride will lift the spirits of others, but it also shapes your decisions, and sometimes, when you realize it is time to do something new, you'll hit the wall hard to make that happen, whether it's learning about something, getting in shape, or perhaps pursuing the joy of doing something new.

Yet the vulnerability that comes with the water sign side of your nature is so important. While you can be sensitive to the criticism of others, you can also support those who might be struggling with their own doubts and unsettling feelings. In fact, that balance between the two is one of your most beneficial characteristics as a Leo who lives with a touch of the gentle sign Cancer. That shining light, yet that sensitivity, are your unique gifts: gifts you give to others and those on which you thrive personally.

You and others

The generosity that is your signature is something that touches almost every situation involving those around you. However, that fire sign part of you sometimes dominates as well, and you can be impatient, forgetting that not everybody thinks or moves as swiftly as you do.

Health and well-being

You are a bit vain. In fact, most Leos are, and it is the reason that those born under your sign tend to look fabulous and be so glamorous. However, you can suffer for your looks. The trick to avoiding this is to turn what you need to do—whether it is how you eat or how you exercise—into something that brings you joy as well.

Goals and challenges

Achieving a goal is one thing, but recognizing that you've achieved it and moving onto the next can be rather difficult for you. The solution to this is, when you set out to do something new, begin thinking about what's next. Then tell yourself when you will feel that you've achieved it, and you can congratulate yourself and know that you're moving on.

THIS DAY FOR EVERYONE

The difference between an opinion and a fact may seem clear, but certain matters are so complex, the difference is unclear. Knowing this, for now, focus on delving into the details of the situations in question, then consider what you regard as solid facts versus mere opinion. Your conclusions will surprise you.

GIFTS Openhearted, Chic, Enthusiastic

CHALLENGES Excessive, Inflexible, Petulant

NUMBER 3

(2+3) + (7) = 12 = (1+2) = 3

I have a talent for giving the kind of compliments that lift others' spirits

You

As a Leo, you have a fiery nature. Not only do you think and move swiftly, living an active life is vital for you—for your sense of health and well-being. But, equally, expressing the theatrical side of your Leo nature is vital.

This isn't just about how you move. What you wear—what might be termed your costume—can be remarkably important to you. That may be reflected in what you wear every day, your somewhat dramatic look, and could even lead to collecting beautiful clothing, which then becomes a passion.

Often it can also broaden into an interest in beautiful objects—not merely things to wear but for your home, too. This can lead you to becoming a connoisseur of a particular item, such as watches, ceramics, or even orchids.

It's the same with people. You're drawn to intriguing individuals, then find some a bit boring. The trick to all this, from possessions to people, is to embrace your fire-sign self, the part that needs to feel deeply.

Core to this is deepening the love between you and those closest to you, whether that's your family, loved ones, offspring, or friends. Achieve a balance, then those possessions will have a place in your life, while the love of others, which is central to your being as a Leo—and somebody who is ruled by the heart—will take its place at the center in your life.

You and others

For you, caring about others can turn into a bit of a dance, with you trying to do so much for them that you feel you've done enough, and then being embarrassed by what they do. The trick to all of this is to simply share how much you care, perhaps with words, perhaps with gestures, or perhaps through stillness.

Health and well-being

For you, joy comes in moving. You may think you found the perfect thing to do. It may be exercise, it may be dancing. It doesn't matter what it is; what's important is that you move your muscles in a way that is joyous, that you feel more alive simply because you've done it.

Goals and challenges

It is vital that you remember you always need to have something to aim for. Before you have achieved one goal, you need to line up that next one. Also remember: not everyone is like that, so not everyone will understand how important this is to you.

JULY

23

L
/
E
\
O

True, there are times when a careful assessment of plans and their potential outcome isn't just wise, it is vital, but at the moment, you can afford to be more easygoing. In fact, what is best about these arrangement may also be what is least expected. Knowing that, you'll want to explore everything.

GIFTS Charming, Lavish, Artistic

NUMBER 4

CHALLENGES Stubborn, Haughty, Demanding

$(2+4) + (7) = 13 = (1+3) = 4$

My fire-sign enthusiasm gives me the energy to turn ideas into reality

You

While you are a fire sign, your theme is renewal. True, the fire-sign side of your nature thrives on taking action and, just as much, getting plans and projects going with others. This involves teamwork. Devising a plan, then turning it into action, is very satisfying for you.

Even more, seeing the enthusiasm and excitement others are experiencing lifts your spirits. This is especially because it's unlikely they'd have come up with these plans, or put them into action, on their own.

Yet, also, once in a while, you need to pause, create some "alone time," and reflect on the influence of those activities on the world around you, but just as much, on your own mood—how they lift your spirits. This variety of reflection may be out of character for you, as a fiery Leo, but it is essential for your own well-being and adds to your sense of self.

If you don't do this every so often, you will just keep on going and, in fact, will often end up doing the same thing over and over again, just different versions of it.

However, pause to reflect, and ask yourself whether once-exciting activities, challenges, or even alliances are still interesting to you or whether you should move on. While the joy that comes with being a Leo is yours for good, renew that joy regularly—and you will also renew your zest for life.

You and others

Being close is wonderful, and for you as a fire sign, that warmth is incredibly important. However, you tend to forget that those around you aren't always as intense as you are. When they back off, it simply means they're backing off, not that they don't care.

Health and well-being

The theatrical side of your nature will like to do some kind of fitness routine that is itself theatrical. That may have to do with dancing or doing a super climb up a big mountain. However, it is also worth simply taking a walk, ideally with somebody you care about.

Goals and challenges

While it's natural for you to aim high, that's fine. However, the secret is not to rush. Deep down, you know that time and effort pay off, but in certain of your goals, the capacity to be patient, to persist, isn't just important, it is vital. Understanding that is not only essential, it is a fundamental truth.

THIS DAY FOR EVERYONE

You have been battling to turn one particular plan or project into reality, or perhaps it has been the reverse: you've been fighting to see something undone. Whatever the case, sudden insights will raise questions about these matters. Giving serious thought to these insights is essential.

I only notice how joyful I am when I spot others who need a boost

You

As a Leo, you feel responsible for others at an early age. It comes naturally with being ruled by the Sun. You feel your role is to encourage and inspire others. While this is a wonderful characteristic, and can become part of your life later, if you're working with family, it also is important for you to have time for you alone. Not only that, it is just as important for you, from time to time, to allow others to support you.

Initially, you might be too proud to do it. Leos do have pride and you could brush away others' efforts. The trick to this is not only to recognize those who can and would like to help you, but to add adventure to your life by learning something new regularly. This may be difficult initially, and you may feel embarrassed that you don't already know it—that Leo ego can sometimes feel that way.

Yet, if you make a commitment to yourself to learn something new, perhaps every year, a new skill, a new language, something that excites you, not only will you enjoy life all the more, and quite possibly draw others into your life, you will also discover a new and enthusiastic student who is part of your life every day—someone who enjoys learning something with every dawn and who, when you go to bed at night, feels a tremendous sense of accomplishment.

You and others

The support you give to others is wonderful and they benefit from it, however, you can get stuck, giving but not receiving. The trick, of course, is for you to learn to say yes, and to do it nearly every day.

Health and well-being

While it's true it is important for you to get out and about, and to feel your muscles moving, at the same time, it is vital that you socialize. The best idea for you is to combine the two. Once you're out, doing what you enjoy with those whose company you enjoy, you'll not only do it more often, you'll adore it.

Goals and challenges

While it's healthy for you always to have several challenges that you're chasing, it is also a good idea to edit them from time to time; otherwise you risk never getting any of them done. Saying farewell to some of them, some of which you no longer care about, isn't just wise, you'll be glad you did, and it makes space for the rest.

JULY

25

L
/
E
\
O

THIS DAY FOR EVERYONE

Although you've been referred to as headstrong in the past, you have never really understood why. From your perspective, you were doing no more than making the necessary decisions. Bizarre as it seems to you, often others ask permission, and only once it is given will they make the decisions in question.

GIFTS Direct, Sharing, Magnanimous

CHALLENGES Huffy, Uncompromising, Willful

NUMBER 6

(2+6) + (7) = 15 = (1+5) = 6

Asking for help doesn't come naturally to me, but when others offer, I accept instantly

JULY

26

L
/
E
\
O

You

You are a fire sign, and therefore, very active, but also, your mind works overtime. It is a bit fiery, too. So while you have a busy body, you also have a busy head, all of which raises questions about when to stop, when to pause and reward yourself, when to rest and relax, and when to stop entirely.

Those questions are important ones, because often, you live life at such a pace you don't even think of stopping. This isn't just about rewarding yourself or letting others share their pride in you or admire what you've done, but it's also about reviewing what you're doing. The ironic thing is, while you, as a Leo, are probably a high achiever, you are also anxious about looking around you and considering whether somebody else may be doing something more interesting than you are.

Rather than envying them, talk to them about it. This is the real challenge for you: to recognize that the world is full of people who are doing different things. And while it is important for you to be proud of what you're pursuing and achieving, and of your life with others, it is also vital that you share that with others and you hear what they have to say. Allow those around you—friends, family, and loved ones—to be your greatest teachers, and it will deepen the relationship for all of you.

You and others

You wouldn't think that you'd have to learn to enjoy life with those you care about, but as a Leo and somebody who tends to be out there doing things, it actually is important for you to pause and appreciate how dear certain individuals are to you. This may be family, this may be friends, this may even be colleagues whose company you enjoy. Whoever it is, appreciate them deeply, and let them know you do.

Health and well-being

For you, feeling well and taking care of yourself may have begun with simply being fit. But your particular variety of Leo nature needs to achieve a balance. This has to do with exercising your mind as much as your activities, which in turn may take you into areas such as martial arts or even yoga.

Goals and challenges

Every once in a while, you need to review your goals. You don't think of this because you are so busy achieving them. However, if it seems to be the same goals again and again, it may be because it is time to say farewell to those and explore, then select and embrace a new set. You will be glad you did.

THIS DAY FOR EVERYONE

It isn't until you encounter somebody who has no interest in being diplomatic that you realize how important diplomacy is. Yet the individual in question responds to forthright situations by nature, and consequently, needs to be spoken to in that manner. Adopt that approach, and everything else will be easy.

Gifts of flowers and candy are exciting; the gift of Leo love can be life-changing

You

Every sign has its style, but as a Leo, your style is distinct. Your pride is important and sometimes you have a classic style and approach to life, but also, being a fire sign, there is a certain amount of flash that comes with your way of doing things, even if you're very conservative.

But this isn't just about how you come across. This has to do with what might be termed your inner world—your thoughts and your feelings.

You are generous by nature, you're caring, you are creative, and you love to help others—family and friends. While this is wonderful and important, there is another part of your nature that needs help.

It isn't that you need help in any worrying way, it's just simply that, sometimes, you don't pay enough attention to that inner self, and it becomes restless and temperamental. And for that reason, it is vital that you give as much passion and attention to you, and to what brings you joy, as you do to others.

That will change over time, but that also will turn into one of your greatest passions. In fact, the passion you bring to exploring those inner feelings, the excitement of new ideas and doing things that lift your spirits, won't just benefit you. It will feed back into those who are closest in your life as well.

You and others

As a Leo, you are intense by nature, so your relationships with others, with family and friends, tend to be intense and passionate, too. This isn't necessarily to do with romances, it's just you care deeply. The challenge? Finding that balance between caring and giving others space is an essential one.

Health and well-being

You have an instinctive sense of the need to keep moving—that's part of being an energetic fire sign. You also have an instinctive sense of fun. But what's amazing is, you don't always connect the two. You need to make the moving, the fitness, the health, and the well-being fun. That is the secret.

Goals and challenges

Those around you question why you always seem to be seeking a new challenge when you could just relax. They don't realize that, for you as a fire sign, you thrive on those challenges. If they offer you an easier way to do things, thank them, and then pursue your latest challenge your way, with enthusiasm.

JULY

27

L
/
E
\
O

Only now are you noticing that, in the midst of recent twists and turns, you made all sorts of decisions, but you didn't inform those involved. This wasn't your intention, but rather, things were moving so swiftly that you forgot, which is fine. Still, you have a lot of talking to do, beginning right now.

I know when I'm right, especially when I believe in somebody

JULY

28

L
/
E
\
O

You

As a Leo and a fire sign, you are aware of your reputation for being somewhat flamboyant, yet, at the same time, you rather enjoy a slow pace of living and thinking that seems very un-fire-sign. The reason? It's because you also enjoy spotting the little things in life that are such a pleasure.

In fact, this reflects another of your Leo characteristics, which is the fact that Leo is one of the four fixed signs—the sign in the middle of each season—and so, enjoys stability and can get into a habit.

You work very hard to make elements of your life look and be the way you want, yet every once in a while, that, too, can become boring for the fire-sign part of your nature. It is about finding a balance between these two—between the things that you enjoy and the elements of your life you have carefully created and crafted versus those changes that bring new and important challenges to you. This is a priority for you.

If you review these matters every once in a while—perhaps every six months or so— then you will give yourself the space for those new discoveries. This may be new activities, it may be studying something, it may be getting to know somebody. And in doing that, you'll enrich that wonderful Leo life even beyond the joys you're presently experiencing.

You and others

You like being very close to people and you also like knowing they care about you. However, certain individuals have a tendency to push you to do things that you have no interest in or intention of doing. Tell them you appreciate that, then very firmly thank them and say no.

Health and well-being

As you're well aware, you particularly enjoy ritual. That ritual may be how you eat, how you work out, how you take care of yourself— whatever it is, you really love it. However, every once in a while, you need to review and change that ritual; otherwise, on one hand, you lose the joy in it, and on the other, you may become a teeny bit lazy.

Goals and challenges

You know what you want to do and you know what you want to achieve—and what you don't want to do. However, what you don't know is when to pause and consider whether you need to rethink those things. The trick is to make a date with yourself, perhaps every six months, or even every year, to conduct exactly that variety of review.

THIS DAY FOR EVERYONE

It may seem that certain individuals, or possibly destiny itself, are trying to take over. Certainly, your plans have been disrupted more than once. It may seem you are alone in these struggles, but look around you and you'll soon realize that is not true. Everybody is facing similar difficulties.

Leo confidence gives me a boost, but I often use it to give others a lift, too

You

Like your ruler, the Sun, you shine with a certain generosity. This comes naturally, and for this reason, you rarely pause and consider how much you are giving or receiving from others. Yet every once in a while, it is important to consider that; not because someone is giving too little or too much, but because it's vital that you find a balance in your own life.

While you're a fire sign, you're also one of the fixed signs of the zodiac, which means you get into habits: habits of what you do, but also, you get into habits involving the people you hang out with. While family is one thing, and learning to live with and love them is important, those that you get to know—friends or even colleagues—are also important.

Occasionally, though, it is essential for you to review the nature of those relationships and consider whether they still enrich you. It may be that you simply need to have a heart-to-heart discussion, and that discussion may also be part of your own review about what's working for you and what isn't.

As a Leo and a fire sign, this kind of review may not come naturally. Still, once you begin doing it, you'll realize what a good idea it is and probably decide to make it a regular part of your regimen in every area of your life.

You and others

Being the fixed sign that you are, you enjoy settling into things. However, often a certain individual will do you a favor. They will shake things up for you, encourage you to do something new, to explore—and in doing so, they may trigger a far-reaching and valuable change in your life.

Health and well-being

While you're quite rightly proud of yourself, you also get bored with certain disciplines: disciplines that are supposed to keep you healthy and well. Yet you're unsure of what's next. The trick is to have someone who gets you to try new things. Sometimes, trying them can be more fun than sticking with them, but you'll find the best approach for you.

Goals and challenges

It is easy for you, as a fire sign, to talk about things you could do. Actually undertaking new challenges, however, can be difficult, especially because you're such a perfectionist. The secret is to become an expert at failure. That way, it doesn't matter whether you do things perfectly or not; you'll learn from absolutely everything.

JULY

29

L
/
E
\
O

Deep down, you know that giving in to those who insist they need your help usually leads to problems. Still, ignoring those who are struggling isn't easy. If you must do something, set clear limits and stick to them. That allows you to relieve your sense of guilt, yet avoid major dramas.

I have an instinctive knowledge of the way to enjoy life and to love others

JULY

30

L
/
E
**
O

You

Many of those born under Leo thrive on style and drama. However, there are as many, and you may be one of them, who are, in fact, more focused on their creative side and whose imagination is broad, but who also prefer a low profile. These Leos are most comfortable being around those closest.

If you are one of these, then the art, the joy, and the beauty that comes with being a Leo are important, but equally, so are the kindness, the generosity, and the quiet. The quiet comes with those who are closest, be it friends or family, or even, occasionally, colleagues with whom you share a vision.

Whatever it is, if you are this variety of Leo, you tend to avoid dramas, but every now and then it is important for you to do exactly that. Embrace a certain situation, or perhaps a certain individual, or possibly even a certain goal, with passion.

You may do it quietly, or you may do it so theatrically that you surprise yourself. If so, remember, that you were born under the rulership of the Sun, the brightest object in the sky, it brightens everybody's life, and if you are feeling a bit theatrical, not only is it wise, it will also come very naturally to you.

Enjoy it. Who knows? It may become your way of being for the rest of your life.

You and others

If you enjoy being in the shadow of those who are dramatic types, because it is no effort, then it may help you discover that theatrical side of yourself. True, you may not take to the stage, but it could be that you inspire those around you, from friends to children to be exactly that.

Health and well-being

You can be manically fit—that is, you can do what's in your best interest every day—but be so quiet about it that no one has any idea how much you care about that, how much you enjoy what you're doing. If you begin to talk about it, you might even find you are able to persuade others to join you in those pursuits.

Goals and challenges

For you, some of the best goals are the ones that are adopted discreetly, things you do in the background, things that others are unaware that you've done. Yet, every once in a while, it is important for you to share those, not so much because others will admire you, but they might well learn from them.

THIS DAY FOR EVERYONE

It's not that you're overcautious, but in the past, you have ignored seemingly unimportant details only to discover later that they were significant. Now, such information is unreliable, or worse, unavailable. This means trusting your intuition, which is far better than you acknowledge, even to yourself.

GIFTS Forthright, Generous, Eager

CHALLENGES Impatient, Uncompromising, Proud

NUMBER 2

$(3+1) + (7) = 11 = (1+1) = 2$

Some say I'm stubborn. When I allow others to distract me, I am reminded why

You

It is important that you experiment with your Leo identity, that you view it as a game you're playing. This is because as a Leo and a fire sign, you can take yourself too seriously and be "grand." You don't think of it this way, but when you compare yourself to others, you do.

Yet you also have a very simple nature, in the sense that you are uncomplicated. You want a good life, and it is also important for you that others around you are happy. And when changes are essential, of course, you hope they'll go smoothly.

However, you also have a stubborn streak, and when you have things organized, you want them to stay that way. Similarly, you hope that those closest will accept that and not try to change you in the way that some do.

One of your biggest lessons is to recognize that, sometimes, those changes aren't just worthwhile, they're an opportunity to enjoy elements of your life you simply wouldn't have known about were it not for those individuals coming into your life and making the effort to get you to make those changes—which, as you will be aware, isn't always easy.

At the same time, if you practice a new exercise, which is a simple exercise of saying "yes" first and then trying things out, not only will life be a lot more interesting, you will have a lot more fun as well.

You and others

As much as you enjoy those who are already close to you, life is also about broadening your horizons, and that means bringing new individuals into that circle, and occasionally, letting some go as well. It's like having a garden each year that you need to replant.

Health and well-being

As you are well aware, you do have a lazy streak, and once things are organized with your health, you tend to stick to the same way of eating and the same fitness regimen, except it gets boring and then you begin to slip. Of course, the trick is to find somebody or something that inspires you.

Goals and challenges

On occasion, you complain that life has become a little too predictable, but at the same time, you will often sidestep challenges that appear, because they are too much trouble. It is important you face the fact that you can't do that and then complain about life being too predictable.

JULY

31

L
/
E
\
O

Every once in a while, differences of opinion turn into a more serious and complex conflict. You're on the verge of that happening. Before it does, retreat and examine your priorities. There may be some that aren't so important you'd be willing to provoke a battle. Give this serious thought.

GIFTS Noble, Protective, Arty

NUMBER 9

CHALLENGES Unbending, Agitated, Haughty

(0+1) + (8) = 9

My instincts are so strong, I trust them—and am always glad I did

AUGUST

01

L
/
E
\
O

You

Life is full of questions. That is something you can't argue with, but the tricky thing is that, as a Leo, and one of the fixed signs of the zodiac, the signs born in the middle of each season, you thrive on stability. You like to know what you're going to eat during the day, you like to know what you're going to wear. You like to go to the same restaurants—and possibly you even go on vacation to the same place.

While that's comforting, every once in a while, it is vital that you have a shake-up, and it may well be that those around you are the ones who encourage you to do that. But that may end up with a power struggle, which you, as a Leo, always try to win. The secret is to realize that in allowing them to win—if you go along with what others want you to do—it is you who's actually winning, because you are the one who will be benefiting.

The trick is to embrace the unknown and the unfamiliar and change. Do this in a way that doesn't come naturally to you, but that, with a little effort and experimentation, you might not only develop a taste for, and you might realize just how much you benefit.

This could aide you in every aspect of your life—from the way you feel about yourself to the way you feel about others, and even to the way you feel about getting up in the morning.

You and others

Being one of the more fixed varieties of Leo, sometimes those around you seem to be determined to disrupt you and your life. They may come across as a bit of a bully. Yet deep down, you know they have your best interest at heart. Recognize that and let them win.

Health and well-being

As a luxury-loving Leo, when it comes to taking care of yourself, that is, eating well and being fit, you like to be cared for properly. However, you also tend to develop a routine. The secret to this is to make that routine exotic, which means going far away to places that offer you proper Leo luxury.

Goals and challenges

Signing yourself up for a new goal regularly may seem like a crazy idea. But if you put it in your calendar, then instead of being worried about what you're doing—and wondering what you could do that's new—you will look at your calendar and realize it's time for you to discover and embrace a new goal.

GIFTS Eager, Natural, Forthright

CHALLENGES Fixed, Anxious, Headstrong

For me as a Leo, my job is bringing joy to others, whatever the time or setting

You

From your point of view, the ideal life is one in which you have things organized and you're able to enjoy what you do—that is, the routine of your day, your activities, those around you, how you dress. All of these things are important to you as a Leo.

Yet at the same time, every once in a while, you become aware that things are a bit too predictable. The fixed sign part of you, the Leo that likes things to remain the same, will think this is how events should be. Then, possibly an individual or circumstances will force you to make changes.

This is where the test is for the fixed-sign side of your life. If you do the minimum, then you probably won't enjoy it and will turn those changes into a battle. If, however, you recognize this as a new way of thinking, living, and possibly loving, you will realize that actually this is a breakthrough.

It is a breakthrough from which you will benefit. And even more than that, you'll realize that, as a fire sign, you need to change things every once in a while, and that the changes you are making now are less than the changes you might want to make regularly, as you live out the days of your life. This is simply because you'll discover that in doing so, you not only make life a lot more interesting, you love life itself all the more.

You and others

The changes that seem to be being forced on you aren't just in your best interest, they are encouraging you to alter your pace with those around you. In doing so, you will discover new joys with each other, in the present and in the future as well.

Health and well-being

Over the years, you have struggled to find the perfect routine, the perfect way of eating—those activities that will make you feel wonderful. The problem is, what has not been wonderful is the lack of variety, and now, you have an opportunity to change things.

Goals and challenges

If there is a single concept that is important for you to keep in mind when it comes to the goals you set—and how you deal with the challenges—it's aiming higher. Often, you will try to minimize changes because you find them unappealing, when actually, embracing them makes them far more exciting.

AUGUST

02

L
/
E
\
O

GIFTS Honest, Spontaneous, Lavish

CHALLENGES Demanding, Isolated, Self-indulgent

NUMBER 2

$(0+3) + (8) = 11 = (1+1) = 2$

Others view obstacles as problems; I regard them as reasons to get seriously creative

AUGUST

03

L
/
E
\
O

You

As a fire sign, you hate wasting time, and so you streamline elements of your day. But then, you get stuck in habits that are dull and you find that you want to do, not just something new, but something that's exciting. Of course, being ruled by the Sun, that is second nature to you. You aren't about a low-profile approach to anything. However, the trick is to escape planning and to act with spontaneity, and even more, to act from the heart. This is what others love about you and, when you allow yourself to be truly loving in the way that comes naturally to you, you're not just lovely to be around, you are absolutely magical.

The trick to dealing with all of this is not so much to take chances, but to be totally who you are. As you move into that state of mind and that state of being, you will regularly find yourself doing things that you didn't expect to do.

Even more, you will find a new joy, even when you're dealing with what once seemed like burdens, and they will be resolved by what can best be described as your loving Leo nature: a nature that isn't just generous, but is so creative that you can come up with solutions for issues you just thought you'd have to live with. Even more, you are able to heal once-difficult relationships and bring love to every element of your life.

You and others

If there is any element of your life that is about joint efforts and about pioneering with others, it has to do with maximizing the love in your life and, as it happens, the love and lives of others. You have a magic touch. Use it to inspire others. This is one of those contagious conditions that you want to encourage.

Health and well-being

Fitness alone is boring, but allowing energy to flow through you is positive. And once you're doing that, then you will find the kinds of things you need to do: not only to feel fit, but to radiate the kind of energy that comes naturally to you as a Leo.

Goals and challenges

Embracing certain offers may seem unwise. Still, take a chance—explore. For you as a Leo, this not only comes naturally, it will also allow you to spread the excitement that comes with those offers to the people around you.

THIS DAY FOR EVERYONE

By no means are you secretive. However, you have kept certain complex issues to yourself, mostly because explaining the background would take valuable time. While that is true, certain changes demand this variety of frank discussion. Since you've no choice, tell others everything and right away.

There's no denying Leos are stubborn; that's because I must accomplish my goals

You

Born as a fire sign and as a Leo lion, you are powerful. Yet you have fixed habits and beliefs, beliefs that can actually end up becoming your own lion's cage, with habits that you feel uncomfortable letting go of. These are habits you complain about, but regard yourself as weak for relinquishing.

Still, you're bored, and that boredom is a recognition of the need to break free— something that may seem strange until you actually do it. The secret is to begin that process of breaking free in little ways.

Once you start to let go and discover how to take those steps, then it will be like an explosion, but the wonderful type that comes with fireworks. Suddenly, you'll see your life working in a completely different way, and with each step, you will feel freer and more inspired to walk away from the old way of doing things and to take chances.

This isn't just about making changes in how you lead your life day to day. It's about changes in how you love, how you take care of yourself and what you are doing. Nor is it about a single day or a single period; it is about a shift in your point of view about your own life.

It is about leaving elements of the past behind and embracing a future that is, itself, constantly new, fresh, and inspiring.

You and others

While usually you are the inspiration for those around you, when it comes to making big changes, sometimes, it's important to let others take the lead. They have a different nature, and although they aren't Leos, they may be able to teach you a new approach to the changes you are embracing.

Health and well-being

With good reason, you are proud to be a Leo, yet it's also vital that you recognize how important it is that you be flexible. This is not merely about your body, from exercise, but you need to be flexible in your mind, in a way that allows you to reinvent yourself.

Goals and challenges

One of your greatest characteristics is that you never give up. However, it can also mean that you get stuck in certain strategies when actually the best thing you could do is let go of all your goals and begin again. The result will be magical.

AUGUST

04

L
/
E
\
O

THIS DAY FOR EVERYONE

Last-minute changes in plans are always a problem, but that is especially the case now, because this means discussing, then rethinking, everything. On the other hand, this will indeed get you thinking a lot. What you learn and the improvements you make will almost justify the stress you're currently facing.

GIFTS Trendy, Benevolent, Enthusiastic

CHALLENGES Uncompromising, Self-centered, Anxious

NUMBER 4

$(0+5) + (8) = 13 = (1+3) = 4$

My creative side is always coming up with ideas. Some are simple, others life-changing

AUGUST

05

L
/
E
\
O

You

Every Leo has a certain pride, and you love looking good. However, you are also getting bored with having to look like what you think other people think is good.

This is because it is vital that you get in touch with an important part of your Leo nature, which is the child within. In fact, it's said that the sign Leo actually rules childhood, with that spontaneity children have, that joy at simply being alive and that freedom to play.

You can have that, too. All it requires is for you to abandon your ideas about what you think others would appreciate or be impressed by, and instead, come closer to that joy.

Ironically, in doing that, then what you do, the way you live, and what you wear will be a reflection of a person who is much more comfortable in their skin and much happier with themselves. Soon, you will find that by simply being you, you will begin to inspire others. They will ask you how you discovered this new way to be, and the fact is, it's not just that you'll look better, you'll feel free to do what might be termed play.

That is, in fact, to play in a way that you never have before and to feel free, along with those around you, inspiring them to discover a whole new way of being. Could there be any better way to live life than that?

You and others

The secret for you is to organize less. That is, have an idea to get together, but don't actually plan. This is part of your new course in joy, in simply allowing things to be—and relaxing and watching what destiny brings your way.

Health and well-being

The most important question for you, at any moment is: are you happy? If you're not happy, then, why not? True, many things in life are challenging, but there is a difference between being challenged and responding to that, and being unhappy, which may mean you are actually ignoring that challenge.

Goals and challenges

There is a tendency as a Leo to think that you absolutely have to win. You have to do what you are doing perfectly. However, here's another option. Whatever you are doing, decide that what you are really committed to is giving things a try and taking your chances. That is what makes life fun.

THIS DAY FOR EVERYONE

When discussing changes, you thought you could stick with existing arrangements and gradually incorporate the two. Now you're in the midst of making those changes, you realize this isn't possible. Don't panic. Just consider whether it's time to say farewell to past arrangements, or to the new ones.

GIFTS Heartfelt, Honest, Delightful

CHALLENGES Proud, Unyielding, Willful

NUMBER 5

(0+6) + (8) = 14 = (1+4) = 5

When others are bored, they do puzzles; when I am, I come up with an amazing plan

You

There is a part of you as a Leo that is all about seeking perfection in life. It is a part of you that wants beauty, that wants a certain glossy presence in your life. But there is another, more playful part of you that wants to try things out, and is just as happy to flop, to fail, and then to do it all again—in life, in work, and in love.

This is an example for others as well, and the more you do this, and the more you make changes in this way, the more joy will show on your face and in your body. You'll be relaxed, you'll be healthier, and not only that, you will be the you who takes part in those activities and so will inspire others.

That easygoing attitude will mean that you'll probably enjoy what you are doing far more, but gradually, you'll shift from simply looking good to radiating the kind of joy that comes with being ruled by the most powerful body in the heavens, the Sun.

Having been born a Leo, this is your birthright. But it is strange how few of those born under your sign actually embrace the potential to be a true Leo: not living a glamorous life according to some else's values, but actually radiating the joy of the Sun within your being every day, and becoming closer to that as every day passes as well.

You and others

As you become more easygoing and free and loving, you'll find that it's easier to be more free and loving with others, too. You won't complain in your head so much about them, but instead, you'll simply accept them. Better yet, the radiance in your mood will add to both your lives.

Health and well-being

The question isn't what you should do to feel better, but what you truly enjoy doing. The closer you come to that inner sunny core, that being of love, the easier it will be for you to decide what's best to do without even having to think about it.

Goals and challenges

You're determined, you always will be—that's part of being a Leo. But the big question is, will you still want the goal you're going after once you achieve it? This is a question that you will find yourself asking increasingly and one that, eventually, having recognized the answer, you will no longer need to ask.

AUGUST

06

L
/
E
\
O

THIS DAY FOR EVERYONE

Nobody would blame you for taking the rather abrupt manner of certain individuals the wrong way. While you'd be justified in thinking they've been rude, the fact is, they have had too much to do and not enough time to do it. For now, say nothing. Within days, they will make it up to you.

GIFTS Entertaining, Captivating, Protective

CHALLENGES Headstrong, Impatient, Extreme

NUMBER 6

$(0+7) + (8) = 15 = (1+5) = 6$

Doubts rarely trouble me, and my confidence enables me to overcome others' doubts

AUGUST

07

L
/
E
\
O

You

You have a natural style and also a determination to do and have everything that you can. However, increasingly you have questions about your goals. On one hand, you've been seduced by what others do and seeing what they have, yet at the same time, you are increasingly aware that the deeper you go within, the less you care about them, and the more you want to learn to laugh and to play and to enjoy who you are.

This is the journey of being born a Leo. While on one hand, there is a theatrical side to your nature, and a part that really enjoys being admired. Your style comes naturally with that. However, if you were only your style and nothing more, then it becomes very empty and very hollow.

If, on the other hand, you begin to use the energy of the Sun, which is connected with your deep inner being, and begin to explore it in different ways, you'll discover ways to laugh, play, and have fun in whatever you're doing—whether you are in a job, at home, climbing a mountain, or simply relaxing.

The key? It's to move increasingly closer to the essence of your nature, that sunny being within you. And if you are guided by that, then the choices you make will always be ones that don't just suit you, they will add new sunshine to your life.

You and others

If you're still living with a book in your head that tells you what success looks like, then you may not be having a very good time dealing with others. But if, on the other hand, you're easygoing about things and simply do what makes you happy, you'll be amazed how others are happy as well.

Health and well-being

There are enough books on health and well-being to fill a large library, but that doesn't seem to make people more joyous. The secret? Take advantage of your inner Leo child and the joy that comes with that individual. Do that, and you'll choose naturally to move in a way that makes you feel terrific, and to eat in a way that is good for you. Then there will be absolutely no problem with anything else.

Goals and challenges

There is an odd belief that achievement requires suffering. However, as you live your life as a Leo, and somebody whose inner light is powerful, you'll realize that those challenges simply complicate matters. Instead, you will approach things with joy, and both achieve them and love them as well.

THIS DAY FOR EVERYONE

The last thing you're in the mood for is a discussion about the tendency of one individual to be careless in certain matters. Ordinarily, it wouldn't be important, but increasingly, you end up dealing with the details they ignore. If you can disentangle yourself, take over entirely—that's really the only option.

Feeling inspired is great. Spreading that feeling to everybody I meet is even better

You

You have a tendency to get involved in a lot of things with a lot of people. Of course, this comes with being a Leo. Yet at the same time, that energy tends to be focused on what they want and what excites them. And one of your journeys as Leo is first to discover what excites you, what brings light to your life.

In a world and in a society where there are all kinds of trends about what excites people, being a Leo can be a challenge, because simply discovering what is most important to you as an individual can actually be very difficult—mostly because there are plenty of other people, and forms of media, ready to tell you what you should be enjoying.

This doesn't just have to do with what you do; it has to do with how you live and your priorities. Yet at the same time, being a Leo you have what might be termed a big energy, and once you embrace that in a way not everyone will fully understand, you will also begin to realize just how much joy you can live with—even more than that, the kind of joy you can bring into the life and experience of others.

In doing that, you will discover your true purpose as a Leo, which is not to follow anyone else's plan or anyone else's routine, but instead, to be completely and utterly true to yourself.

You and others

Many of those close to you look up to you. You don't really think that until you realize that often, people will imitate what you're doing. This is all the more important as you move closer to that amazing inner you that is the true Leo within.

Health and well-being

There are many complicated routines for being healthy. However, in your particular case, that routine has to do with one simple thing, a variety of love: for earth, for water, for the Sun, for grass, for laughter, for resting. The rest of it is secondary. Once you realize that, you will also realize the being deep within you is the one who experiences joy, the joy from which all forms of health will come.

Goals and challenges

There are all sorts of formulas for achievement that people will discuss with you, as well as plans to make those achievements. However, the more you realize your nature as a Leo and somebody ruled by the Sun, the more you will realize how hollow those objectives are and how much can be achieved by being motivated from within.

AUGUST

08

L
/
E
\
O

Problems are an invitation to pause and plot a more creative approach to plans

AUGUST

09

L
/
E
\
O

You

As a Leo, somebody ruled by the Sun, and a fire sign, you may feel a burden to inspire. This is probably something you've felt your entire life, but weren't aware of until firstly, you were grown up, and secondly, you were aware that not everybody else particularly cared if they inspired those around them.

And then, as you've learned more, you have realized that inspiration isn't about outer achievement alone, although you are very happy to encourage others to do what they want and to achieve a lot. But it is also about a deep link to an inner power. This is something that comes naturally to you as a Leo and somebody ruled by the Sun, but one that you're only getting to know yourself as the years pass. And as you become more familiar with it, you are in a better position to share it with others.

At one point, you thought it was just about being a little bit different, but now, as you live out the days of your life, you realize that, while achieving what you have in mind is important and very gratifying, achieving what is possible for your inner self—that magical being that is who you are—is even more important.

And those achievements will grow each day and add to the joy in your life, when you wake up in the morning and when you go to bed at night.

You and others

There are all sorts of ways of relating to those around you—talking about things you have done and will be doing—but for you, as a Leo, and someone who carries joy within you, sharing that joy is the most important thing. You can't really plan it, but when you are able to do it, there's nothing better.

Health and well-being

Often, when certain individuals are encouraging those around them to take care of themselves, to eat well and to work out, they will encourage good habits. While that is appealing to you as a fire sign, it can also be incredibly dull. The best possible approach for you is to be spontaneous—joyously spontaneous.

Goals and challenges

Planning ahead is wise, and setting goals is great. However, for you as a fire sign, what is even better is acting spontaneously. When you do that, you may need to alter those goals, but what you'll be doing is taking advantage of the moment.

THIS DAY FOR EVERYONE

You are on the verge of upsetting somebody—and the problem is, you were worried about their seemingly underhand behavior. Once, you trusted them, but now you're not so sure, and this is the problem. Watch them too closely and they will feel guilty, which will only make things worse.

When challenged by others, I can be fiery. At the same time, I'm devising solutions

You

As a Leo you are loving, and not only that, you watch out for others as much as you do for yourself. So if they're up to something worrying, you'll do your best to lift their spirits or encourage them to go in the right direction.

However, it is important for you to recognize that while you can encourage them, they are not necessarily a Leo. What you can do, however, is share with them a condition that's called optimism. That is, it is an infectious condition that means they don't want to be you, but rather, they are determined to become the best them they can be.

This seems strange to you because, as a Leo, this characteristic is built in to your being. But many others don't have the courage, the conviction, or the enthusiasm that you do. If you are able to help others see that, then you can withdraw and busy yourself with your own activities, and watch them thrive, rather as if you were watching a plant grow.

But also, this will allow you freedom to nurture yourself in the same way. Rather than overplanning what you're doing, you'll be spontaneous. Embrace that approach in relationships with others and in your own life, and you'll remember what it is to wake up in the morning full of joy and go to sleep at night delighted with what you have experienced.

You and others

If there's a single phrase that should define your relationship with others, it's "Let them take the lead." Once they are doing that, encourage them. If things don't work out, encourage them to find a solution. Most of all, shine your enthusiasm on them. It is the best thing you can do.

Health and well-being

While there is a great deal to be said for keeping fit, some of those people who do keep in shape aren't very happy when they're doing it. There is another component that is important for you to recognize as well, which is to keep calm. If you do that, along with keeping fit, then you will have perfect health.

Goals and challenges

If there is anything tricky, it's that once you line up a challenge, you'll stick with it. However, the gift for you is to learn to recognize when you don't care about that challenge any more, and when the world has moved on, and to embrace something new.

AUGUST

10

L
/
E
\
O

Only days ago, you wouldn't just have objected to last-minute changes in plans, you'd have been irritated that others didn't keep an eye on things. However, recent events have taught you that if you adopt a mellow approach to such matters, you'll easily ignore minor issues that would ordinarily upset you.

GIFTS Chic, Entertaining, Altruistic

CHALLENGES Fixed, Domineering, Obstinate

NUMBER 1

$(1+1) + (8) = 10 = (1+0) = 1$

Others questioning my plans is irritating. However, their concerns can be informative

AUGUST

11

L
/
E
\
O

You

One of your most attractive characteristics is the joy you find in watching others thrive. In fact, it always surprises you when others don't feel that way. While this may apply to family or friends, it can also apply to anyone you know, to colleagues, to neighbors. And while this is important, it's also essential that you're aware your spontaneity and enthusiasm for others needs to be reflected in your own life.

True, you aren't always as much of a cheerleader for yourself, and, in fact, you can settle into habits that once worked for you, but which no longer do. The trick is to pay as much attention to the joy in your own life as you do to that in others, and to track down any of those habits that are no longer appropriate and change them.

As you may be aware, as a Leo, you are a fire sign, but you are also a fixed sign. You get into habits and don't even realize that they are holding you back. Sometimes, events in the form of circumstances, and possibly situations involving others, will jolt you out of those habits and, bizarrely, you will fight them.

The lesson? It's to let go completely— and to plunge into something new. As wary as you are of those changes initially, once you make them, you will wonder why you hesitated even for a moment.

You and others

Certain individuals around you have a habit of asking questions about what you are doing and where you are going. And even worse, they ask why. That may annoy you. However, these individuals are true friends, because they're actually asking you to think about whether you care about what you're doing.

Health and well-being

As a Leo, you were probably born with an interest in looking good. It's part of being a Leo, so it is likely to do what is necessary to ensure the outside is in good shape. The trick, however, is to make sure the inside is also thriving, and that doesn't just have to do with your muscles. It has to do with your heart.

Goals and challenges

The idea of regularly changing your plans is unappealing to you as someone who likes to know what you're doing. Yet the fire sign part of your nature needs regular new challenges, small and large. The irony is, if you make those new challenges part of your routine, then you'll benefit doubly.

THIS DAY FOR EVERYONE

When you learn breakthroughs are coming, of course you're delighted. Yet the form and direction they take may not seem remotely welcome. Still, explore it. You'll soon realize this isn't about reorganizing existing arrangements, but about creating something new and exciting.

GIFTS Protective, Lavish, Creative

CHALLENGES Inert, Petulant, Anxious

NUMBER 2

(1+2) + (8) = 11 = (1+1) = 2

When I say "Yes" to a plan or idea, that releases powers that can make magic happen

You

As a Leo and a fire sign, you have a wonderful ability to care for others. In fact, you feel responsible for ensuring that they're happy and for providing for their well-being.

While this is fantastic, it also means that, sometimes, you can take over, and they don't get a chance to develop their own instinct for making their own choices.

Finding that balance is difficult, because of course, you hate to see them fail. However, you learned a lot from things not working out—and they will, too.

This is one of the greatest lessons for you, to recognize those moments when it is important for you to encourage others and be there, yet recognize when it is important for you to be on the sidelines.

But this doesn't just have to do with others. It has to do with you as well, and with making changes in your own habits, your own way of thinking, your own activities.

There are things you have intended to do differently for a long time but have never got around to, simply because the part that needs a boost you always seems to be taking a break at the moment when you need encouragement the most.

And that is the secret for you—to encourage yourself when necessary, as much as you encourage others.

You and others

The trick when dealing with others is to know that moment when it is time to hand over the reins to them and let them go on their way. Then you can celebrate with them as they succeed, inspired by you.

Health and well-being

The formula for health and well-being for you challenges a part of your nature that settles into a plan. And that is the part that's associated not so much with being a Leo but with being a fixed sign. Despite that, if you make a point of changing what you do and how you take care of yourself regularly, you will not only be more enthusiastic, you will feel better, too.

Goals and challenges

While you, as a Leo, love to succeed—and every Leo thrives on that—there's another part of you that actually enjoys a bit of drama. Allow yourself that. Create challenges for yourself so you'll feel that success is well-earned—then you'll enjoy it all the more.

AUGUST

12

L
/
E
\
O

THIS DAY FOR EVERYONE

You knew you'd have to draw the line with one particularly uptight individual, but you've put off saying anything, mostly because you dreaded any confrontation. At this point, however, you'd rather deal with that than face even one more day of their negative attitude and unruly behavior.

Helping others is a joy. While usually they know about it, just as often they don't

AUGUST

13

L
/
E
\
O

You

As a Leo and being ruled by the Sun, you almost have your own inner energy and light. You don't think about this until you encounter situations where others seem so needy. You have spent time with them, and after you leave them, you feel you're being drained.

Still, you kind of believe you're superhuman, and in a way you are, but balancing this is important. Giving to others is essential, yet at the same time, it is also essential that you teach them to create their own light and life.

That may sound unkind, and many Leos dislike the idea of not being generous. It is natural to you. Yet sometimes, in holding back you force those who are possibly just lazy to get their own act together, and that's the greatest gift you can give to them.

While as a Leo, you are naturally full of enthusiasm, not everybody is, and occasionally they need a serious kick to get them going. Do that; instead of shining that light on them you'll teach them to create their own. Perhaps it's not quite as bright as yours, but it's bright enough to add to the world.

It will enable you to stand side by side and enjoy each other's company, and the company of those around you. From friends and family to loved ones, know you're all contributing to the world.

You and others

You enjoy your gang, that is, those people whose company you thrive on. But at the same time, they can be dull and demanding. The trick is to find a new group, a group that doesn't just enjoy your company but will also challenge and encourage you.

Health and well-being

There is a bit of you that has the feeling of taking care of your well-being as a chore. One of the greatest gifts you can give yourself is to turn it into something that is not only beneficial, social, and fun. In fact, maybe you'll get a group together that turns life into a joy.

Goals and challenges

It's easy to get caught up in being successful, according to others' values. For you as a proud Leo, success is complicated. It includes many things, and this, in part, is sharing what you achieve with others. Do that and the rest will come naturally.

THIS DAY FOR EVERYONE

You recently agreed to last-minute changes in long-standing plans. While it was annoying and upsetting, circumstances shifted and there was nobody to blame. Actually, with so much in transition, you're urged to adopt a flexible attitude toward sudden changes. It will make your life a lot easier.

GIFTS Charming, Openhearted, Charitable

CHALLENGES Self-centered, Excessive, Proud

NUMBER 4

(1+4) + (8) = 13 = (1+3) = 4

I'm strong but also easily hurt. Fortunately those closest spot it, because I never admit it

You

Once of the greatest benefits of being a Leo is what could be called your lustrous nature. There is a beauty that comes with your energy. It's not just glamorous—although most Leos are—but actually, it is a side of your nature that inspires others without actually realizing that you're doing it. A smile from you—some encouragement to do something—will set others off, going after things that wouldn't previously have crossed their minds.

This variety of generosity is wonderful and, occasionally, people will ask why you do so much for others. The fact is, you don't even think about it, but actually, if you do, you realize that, by nature, this feeds back to you. If you do something for someone else, it always comes back in some way. It is a contagious situation called joy, in which what you do adds to the lives of others—and they, in turn, then add to the lives of yet others still.

But even more than that, it means that those around you, whether it's family or friends, colleagues, or even neighbors, all simply feel better about themselves and about their lives. Which means that the time you spend with them isn't about helping to lift them up, but about all of you enjoying who you are all the more, every day.

You and others

Talk is important—getting others to talk about things, but also you talking about what you intend to do. However, as fire sign, you will understand that doing—taking action—is best. And if that means you need to go off and do what you need to do first, leaving others behind, not only is it essential, you will also teach them the importance of taking action themselves.

Health and well-being

While a workout is okay, being a Leo and somebody who has joy in your life, playing a game, getting out and about and having fun is even better. Why? Because you'll not only get moving but you'll move the most important part of your being, which is your heart.

Goals and challenges

There are two kinds of goals. There are material goals—goals in the world, the kind of goals recognized by people in business. And then there are goals that have to do with climbing mountains: metaphorical mountains or very real mountains as well. And those are the goals, which, when achieved, mean the most of all.

AUGUST

14

L
/
E
\
O

GIFTS Spontaneous, Natural, Generous

CHALLENGES Uncompromising, Static, Agitated

NUMBER 5

(1+5) + (8) = 14 = (1+4) = 5

My capacity to love others unconditionally is one of my superpowers

AUGUST

15

L
/
E
\
O

You

You may be a fire sign, but every once in a while, you run into individuals who draw you into debates that have to do with yes or no, right or wrong, more or less, all of which drive you crazy. But because they seem so determined to talk about things in that way, you get involved.

Of course, the trick is to stop and do something that is quite natural for you as a fire sign—simply plunge in and see what works. That may upset others, but by that point, you'll actually begin the process of teaching them something.

It is something that is also important for every Leo to do, because your enthusiasm for life involves exactly this kind of what might be termed "daredevil behavior"— that is, taking chances.

This will enable you also to break the habit of trying to please others, which you sometimes do, and instead be the best you that you can be—someone who is full of life and who brings that vitality to any setting or situation. Once you've done that, then you will wonder why you allowed those individuals and their very narrow ideas about how things could work to distract you. And that may be the biggest lesson of all, one you will learn again and again, and one that you will benefit from every time you learn it.

You and others

The trick is to notice how those closest to you, whether it's family or colleagues or friends, live life but also to make it clear that, while you are delighted for them to live life the way they want to, you approach life in a very different way, one that is as spontaneous as it is joyous.

Health and well-being

There are many ideas about what looks good: a sleek body, glowing skin. But actually, what looks best on anybody is being relaxed and moving in a way that shows you are at one with yourself and with your body, that you're glowing with vitality. There is nothing better than that.

Goals and challenges

Every Leo has their goals. You don't really think about it, you simply have them and act on them. However, those around you may be challenging you to explain those goals. If so, simply change the subject. It is by far the best solution.

THIS DAY FOR EVERYONE

Few things are as annoying as facing last-minute changes in plans you struggled to organize in the first place. But the more you learn, the more you will realize these changes aren't just wise, but could eliminate problems that have been a source of concern for you and others. Now, you needn't worry.

GIFTS Benevolent, Charismatic, Eager

CHALLENGES Obstinate, Extreme, Demanding

NUMBER 6

_(1+6) + (8) = 15 = (1+5) = 6_

Often, disagreeing with others is pointless, but when it matters, it's crucial

You

The Leo energy, the Sun energy that is naturally within you, is powerful. However, sometimes you can get so involved in what you're doing and so determined to achieve what you have in mind that you actually lose yourself in those pursuits.

The trick is to catch that compulsive drive and stop it before it takes over. and in fact, exhausts you.

There is also another side of your nature, one that you visit less frequently, because it's not as dramatic, but one that is important for you, simply because it is that side of you that helps you understand why you truly want to do what you do. It is what might be termed the quiet, reflective side of your nature.

It is warm and quiet and most of all, when you're there, you know instinctively what and who is important to you, what you want to embrace next—and equally, what you want to leave behind.

Even more than that, it's in these still moments that you gain joy from life itself and from being who you are. And while, as a Leo, you will always have that expansive side—that very special kind of Leo luster that is part of your nature—the quiet side is what makes life worth living, and the more you are aligned with that, the more wonderful your life will be, each and every day.

You and others

While you can pursue your own goals solo, there are certain instances when you'll need a team, when you will need those with you. You may need their knowledge or their ideas or enthusiasm. Whatever the case, the trick is to do exactly that. Create that balance so you support them and they support you.

Health and well-being

Usually this is described in terms of how well you look, and the success of a new regimen has to do with that. Are you healthy and glowing? Actually, this has as much to do with your inner world and feeling wonderful within.

Goals and challenges

There are all sorts of achievements you can make and, in fact, as a Leo, you are likely to do whatever you choose. However, there is one achievement that is often unreachable for most and that is important for you: inner peace.

AUGUST

16

L
/
E
\
O

Sometimes, minor disagreements are no more than that. However, those you have now could expose long-standing and unresolved issues. You've been ignoring these because you had no idea how to deal with them. Now, suddenly, there's a way. While this is inconvenient, you must still take advantage of it.

GIFTS *Altruistic, Entertaining, Lavish*

NUMBER 7

CHALLENGES *Anxious, Headstrong, Haughty*

$(1+7) + (8) = 16 = (1+6) = 7$

I never listen to those who tell me their way of doing things. It won't work. I'm not them

AUGUST

17

L
/
E
\
O

You

There are two sides to your nature as a Leo: a fire sign, and someone who is born with the Sun as your ruler. One part of your nature is driven—the one who gets up in the morning and can't wait to do something, and thinks, having done that, "What's next?"

And the other can be exquisitely lazy and will kick back and really enjoy doing nothing. But there is a part in the middle that needs to come out, too. And it is a part that has to do with a childlike joy in discovering.

There is a certain fear that if you don't keep doing what you're good at, then you'll descend into boredom. But the fact is, that intuitive part of you enjoys doing things in new ways.

True, this would mean breaking certain habits and doing things differently. However, the compensation for that is a single thing: joy.

It's about moving into new territory and doing things in new ways—and it is rewarding simply because you are doing it, not because of your own success or the success that others recognize.

Not only that, once you get good at this, that variety of joy can become a habit, and it will be something that you not only love to have as part of each day; it will be something you are able to create every day as well.

You and others

If you are a typical Leo, you probably have a gang, a gang of friends, some of whom you have been around for a long time, and possibly even family. But it is time for you to add new people to this gang—those who don't encourage you to do the same thing because they like it, but who encourage you to break patterns and do new things.

Health and well-being

As you know well, your habits are very strong, and once you get into one, it's hard to break. The trick is to create a habit that makes space for you to feel well, no matter what you do, to eat well, and most of all, to think and rest well.

Goals and challenges

If you are ready to break through, to leave certain elements of the past behind, it is time for you to get what might be called a good coach. This may be an individual, but could also be embracing a side of your nature that often inspires other people. Now, it's time to inspire you.

THIS DAY FOR EVERYONE

There is a fine line between a sudden breakthrough and an exciting but unwelcome surprise. And in one particular situation, you're experiencing both. The trick to all of this is to forget about planning ahead and instead, take each day and each hour as they come. It will make life a lot easier.

GIFTS Creative, Charismatic, Commanding

CHALLENGES Impatient, Irascible, Rigid

NUMBER 8

(1+8) + (8) = 17 = (1+7) = 8

Fun can be planned, but the best moments are as unexpected as they are thrilling

You

As a Leo and a fire sign, for you action is like breathing. However, every once in a while, you need to stop and take a different kind of breath, the kind of breath that stimulates you and also that helps you break patterns.

As a Leo, you can get so involved in doing—doing what you're good at and doing more of it—that you don't stop to consider whether it's just repetitious and if it's time for you to break patterns, to do things in a new way, to develop new habits.

If there is any difficulty with this, it's that being what's termed a fixed sign, one of the fixed signs of the zodiac, you occasionally have trouble coming up with that new pattern, and this will actually encourage you to do something else, which is seek guidance or help from another.

Normally, you're the one who is advising and supporting those around you, but in this particular case and, in fact, every once in a while in your life, it is essential that you recognize that you need that little boost from somebody. Perhaps it's a sharper kick that is important, to break those habits and to discover the new world that is ready to open up before you. This world will open up only if you begin to do things differently, and, more than that, see possibilities in different ways and in looking at life from a different angle.

You and others

In this particular case, the trick is to learn the degree to which you tend to lead the way. Even more it is about the importance of letting go of that. Why? So you can allow others not only to shine their light, but to shine their light for you.

Health and well-being

The standard combination of eating well and living well is an important one. However, for you to feel truly well, another component is essential. In fact, it is even more important, and that is joy. Joy in life, joy when you wake up in the morning, and joy when you go to sleep at night.

Goals and challenges

Oddly, your biggest challenge isn't facing challenges; it is knowing who you can rely on when you need guidance. Being the one who others come to, you are not always aware who you need to go to. This may be one of your biggest challenges of all.

AUGUST

18

L
/
E
\
O

THIS DAY FOR EVERYONE

One of those difficult periods, during which single problems seem to have no solution, is what you're facing. The trick to dealing with these is to walk away, possibly for a few days. Once you have some distance, you'll recognize there is an entirely different approach, one that works perfectly.

GIFS *Honest, Charming, Compelling*

NUMBER *9*

CHALLENGES *Willful, Self-indulgent, Demanding*

$(1+9) + (8) = 18 = (1+8) = 9$

Last-minute ideas, plans, and passions can turn an ordinary day into a glittering event

AUGUST

19

L
/
E
\
O

You

As a Leo and a fire sign, you have a talent for living life well—and not only do you manage to look great and live abundantly, you also manage to accumulate the good things that come from a life well lived, from memories to, often, gifts from others.

While this collection of both experiences and objects can be rewarding, at the same time, there is a sense that you're carrying baggage around.

That isn't the most important thing in life, except you can't quite define what it is. That is partly because you're living in a period during which people think so much about possessions and objects and clothes that they forget about the core meaning to life—which, of course, is your inner world, your feelings. This could be your feelings for others, but even more, it's about your feelings for yourself, and that part of your nature that also reaches for something higher and more compelling.

And this is part of your challenge as a Leo, who on one hand,has lived, and is living an exciting life, but who also recognizes that there must be something deeper, perhaps something that is less easily defined.

Make that your goal, make that awareness your journey, and not only will you learn a lot each day, you will enrich your life in a way objects never could.

You and others

As you begin carefully to choose those with whom you spend time, you will also begin to realize that, while some people are merely a distraction, others add to your life in ways you are only beginning to understand. And that may make them some of the most important people in your life.

Health and well-being

While you can focus on life's celebrations, you can also do something different. You can take another approach to your well-being and make every day a party, a well-being party— one during which you do things that will make you feel better at the end of the day than you did at the beginning of it.

Goals and challenges

Tempting as it is to stick to certain personal goals and achievements that are important, the trick is to find a balance between those and the individuals with whom you are pursuing those goals, or possibly even who are challenging you. In every case, recognize how much you are benefiting from them.

THIS DAY FOR EVERYONE

If ever there were a time when it was essential to be cautious of those who are manipulative or who never think of others, it's now. True, they aren't always easy to spot. Still, if you think back to other individuals who had those traits, you'll find it easier to recognize those who are similar in the here and now.

Letting others take the lead isn't easy; however, certain individuals' ideas are magic

You

As a Leo, you are creative by nature, and as a fire sign, you enjoy making things happen. It's just, as you've learned, that if you do too much, you don't just exhaust yourself; often those around you benefit more than you do from your generosity of spirit and creativity.

From your perspective, life is very much about using that enthusiasm, and in all sorts of ways. This isn't just about creating a happy life for yourself and others. Nor is it about creating success in your work, although this can be a vital expression of your zest for life.

However, there is another variety of success that is essential, and this is the variety that lives within you and is lasting. While on one hand, it has to do with being able to enjoy each day, to feel thrilled when you get up in the morning, on the other, it is also about feeling contented when you go to bed at night.

As a Leo, you were born with a generous spirit—one that is so generous, you sometimes neglect your own interests. The trick is to think a little less about the happiness of others. You may thrive on your ability to create that joy for those around you, and the more of it the better. Yet as you go through the day, it is essential you feel joy simply for being alive.

That is one of your greatest gifts as a Leo. When you achieve that, the rest of those joys will be a bonus.

You and others

The trick to enjoying the world around you is to go from finding friends who are all about having a good time to finding the friends who recognize how important it is to enjoy life's precious moments—and to ensure that they happen every day.

Health and well-being

Tempting as it is to find exercises you can do quickly, you are urged to become obsessed with something that makes you feel excited, whether it is a sport, whether it's yoga, or even if it's fishing. Whatever it is, if it brings you joy, make that your priority.

Goals and challenges

The message for you is a simple one: "Are you bored?" Well, if you are, then the fact is that it's time for you to rethink things completely. That may seem odd, but if you aren't making the best of events, it is time to change them.

AUGUST

20

L
/
E
\
O

THIS DAY FOR EVERYONE

Only days ago, you were battling with certain individuals about details that seemed important then. Now, looking back, you are beginning to realize you were sidestepping the real issue. Deep down, you know what it is. The challenge is raising it. Once you do, everything else will be easy.

GIFTS Creative, Noble, Enthusiastic

NUMBER 2

CHALLENGES Headstrong, Exacting, Unbending

$(2+1) + (8) = 11 = (1+1) = 2$

True joy is about the right moment, the right people, and, most of all, love

AUGUST

21

L
/
E
\
O

You

For you, the idea of getting into good habits is wonderful, and once you know what you're meant to be doing to take care of yourself—to live well, and to manage your life well—then you know that you're doing the best you can. Or so it seems, because there will be a part of your nature that feels that there's something better.

To a certain extent, this is also an influence of your neighboring sign, Virgo, which is a little bit of your own being and has some influence on your character. But mostly, it is about departing from that belief that if you can get your habits fixed perfectly, you'll be happy. Then you'll realize that, actually, the thing that will bring you the greatest joy is living a life that is about discovery—about little discoveries every day, and also about major discoveries every now and then.

While it is true that sometimes these can be disruptive, each of them adds to your life in a wonderful way. They're like a variety of intellectual or even spiritual vitamins.

Whatever the direction that you take, the minute you begin to program that variety of exploration and the resulting discoveries into your life, life itself will take on a new luster. And every day, you'll wake up with a new enthusiasm about what will be coming your way over the next 24 hours.

You and others

If you view life as something to get on with in an orderly fashion, then you might not like this idea, but if, on the other hand, you view it as a celebration, a party, then you'll know exactly what to do next.

Health and well-being

There are two approaches to your health and well-being, listening to what others say you should be doing and eating. Then there is actually feeling your own body, feeling your own muscles, and feeling whether you are on top of the world. Pay attention to that and you will know exactly what's in your bets interest.

Goals and challenges

While it is simple to set goals and stick with them, the most important thing is to keep those goals growing and changing. It's as if you have a very enthusiastic plant growing and you have to send it in the right direction. Live a life that is as full of enthusiasm and you will enjoy every minute of it.

THIS DAY FOR EVERYONE

You're beginning to recognize that instead of being reason for concern, recent unsettling events were actually breakthroughs. True, these weren't in the form you anticipated, and it could take things in a worryingly unexpectedly direction. Be patient. The more you explore and learn, the more optimistic you'll be.

Ruler Mercury
Element Earth

Symbol The Maiden
Flower Buttercup

Virgo

August 22–
September 21

Virgo   As a Virgo, you combine
an earthy sensuality with the sharp
cleverness of your ruler, Mercury.
The pleasure you derive in beauty,
nature, living, and eating well is
genuine, yet being the sign of
early fall, you have an instinctive
awareness of the wise use of
resources. Your flower is forget-
me-not; your spice, redolent
cardamom; and the mighty oak
and the hazel are your trees. Your
jewels have earthy colors, from
topaz to sardonyx.

V
/
I
\
R
/
G
\
O

There is a joy to having the facts, acting on them, and being confident of the result

You

As a clear-minded Virgo, you know exactly what you want to do. However, because you were born right next to the rather fiery sign of Leo, which is ruled by the Sun, there is a part of you that doesn't mind a little flurry of energy, a little excitement when you walk into the room.

This can be confusing, but on the other hand, it allows you to have a much more exciting life than other Virgos. And in fact, the secret to this is to note the part of you that likes to figure out the correct way to do things. Then, you also need to recognize times when you not only want to ignore it, but actually would benefit from doing that, and allowing your Leo side to take over a bit.

And eventually, you will find a balance between the two. The Leo side is always about fun and joy, and isn't nearly as responsible as the Virgo side. Yet, when you combine the two, you will not only enjoy life more, you'll also share that joy—a very logical and ordered joy—with those around you, and it becomes a kind of infectious variety of fun.

Not only that, you will also bring a sense of joy to some of the more orderly, Virgo elements of your day and your life. You might even find yourself taking chances that previously, you never would have thought of.

You and others

Your instinct is to help people at any time. If there's something they need to learn to do, or just simply learn something new, you'll be there. However, the trick is often to stand back and let them learn for themselves, and then congratulate them when they do it.

Health and well-being

As a Virgo, you can come up with a plan and obsess about it, and do it precisely every day. However, the secret is to borrow a little energy from your Leo side and to turn that plan into something thrilling.

Goals and challenges

One of your skills is your ability to set very clear goals, except there is one important goal you need to include, and that is one that involves getting things wrong. While there are many things you can learn perfectly right away, the things you get wrong several times turn out to be the most instructive.

AUGUST

22

V
/
I
\
R
/
G
\
O

Beauty appears in many forms. However, acts of kindness have their own unique beauty

AUGUST

23

V
/
I
\
R
/
G
\
O

You

You have a strong instinct, an instinct that tells you what is in your best interest that you should do. But then you'll make a list, and turn that instinct into a list that is very much in order, yet it seems to ignore what's actually most important.

The secret? Be spontaneous. Make that list, and know that everything is there, but at the same time, if something comes to mind, do it. Plunge in, take a chance, and even more than that, take joy in the outcome, even if it isn't what you'd expected.

Begin to walk away from the idea of things being good or bad or right or wrong, and rather, simply view them as a life experience. As a Virgo, once you learn to do that instead of worrying about getting things right, you will live in the moment on your own or around others, and whatever the outcome, you won't look back because you'll be anticipating yet more adventures. These adventures arise in part from plans you've made, but there are other adventures that also appear as a result of an unexpected discussion, something you spotted, or an encounter with somebody else.

They are the kinds of things that will increasingly become part of your everyday life and your everyday thinking, and the kinds of activities that will add to your life in ways you wouldn't have dreamed possible.

You and others

Tempting as it is to talk about how things went last week, yesterday, or even a short while ago, avoid it. Reviewing such matters with those around you means you are living in the past, and the only time you can really have a good time is in the here and now.

Health and well-being

As a Virgo, you have a strong instinct for taking care of your body, but the trick—not only to taking care of it but to enjoy every day—is to glory in the miracle that is your body, that it breathes, that it grows, and most of all, that it's you.

Goals and challenges

We're all taught to set goals. However, perhaps the most important one you can set is a list of goals to have fun. Once you've done that, then you turn your attention to all those practical necessities. They may look very different.

THIS DAY FOR EVERYONE

By no means are you overly sentimental, yet you seem determined to hang onto certain arrangements. You may hope they'll spring back to life. Not only is that unlikely, the more time, effort and thought you invest in them, the less you'll have for the new developments currently coming your way.

Doing things right initially isn't just wise, it sets the tone for a plan, project—or romance

You

As a Virgo and an earth sign, you sense quality in the world around you—in food, but especially in objects. Not just objects of value, but from the simple beauty of a flower to something on a table in a home.

Not only that, you are interested in their stories and their backgrounds and will discuss them with others, and you enjoy learning about them as well.

This is one of the wonderful things about being a Virgo. You can appreciate what you encounter while not necessarily wanting it to be part of your life. But, there are times when something—perhaps an object or even an activity—wakes you up and you feel delighted. You want to learn more.

This is when it is important for you to take action. Don't waste any time thinking about whether it's in your best interest. Simply plunge into it in a way that you, as a Virgo, might not ordinarily do.

This act of responding to what you care about is itself important. While you may stay involved in that particular study or activity for the rest of your life, it may also only last a month, but whatever the case, you'll have learned something important.

And that is how to overcome your often very sensible mind and instead follow your rather spectacular passions.

You and others

Acknowledging that while you may like people, and even be related to them, you won't always agree with them is difficult. But the minute you recognize that, instead of trying to figure out a way you can share a common value, realize it's okay that you don't agree at all.

Health and well-being

At some point, somebody must have told you that you're always supposed to maintain an even mood. It is something that is very common with Virgos, and here's the news flash: you don't need to feel the same. In fact, you will have ups and downs, and that's not only normal, you'll learn a lot from them.

Goals and challenges

Being a Virgo, you probably have a list of goals, and you may even have a list of challenges that you want to overcome. However, make sure that list is in pencil, maybe literally, or possibly, metaphorically, in the sense that those goals and those challenges will change every day.

AUGUST

24

V
/
I
\
R
/
G
\
O

Tempting as it is to offer advice to certain individuals who are complaining, it would be unwise. Saying nothing may seem uncaring, but the fact is, they actually enjoy all the drama, so have no intention of making an effort to improve on things. That would end the pleasure they get complaining.

GIFTS Caring, Coherent, Perfectionist

CHALLENGES Exacting, Doubting, Fussy

NUMBER 6

(2+5) + (8) = 15 = (1+5) = 6

AUGUST

25

V
/
I
\
R
/
G
\
O

Simple joys can bring the greatest pleasures, from a quiet chat to a joyous event

You

Most young Virgos, even those who haven't yet gone to school, have an instinct to analyze things. They make lists, possibly in their heads, or they will organize their toys. This analysis is as natural to you as breathing, and next comes making plans. That is the point at which you can write things down, then turn plans into action.

All of that works well. However, there is another part that's important, and it's allowing the unexpected event, the surprising idea, even an invitation that takes you into new territory, to become part of your life. If you're to learn from experience, you need to allow the uninvited into your life. This may seem worrying, because of course, you like things organized, but you will learn from it.

First, it will teach you to become more inquisitive if something you don't know about appears. Then, you will begin to explore it, and either you will discover that actually you find it quite boring, or—and this is more likely—it will become part of that process of broadening your horizons.

Equally, it will have to do with meeting people you wouldn't otherwise have met, or having experiences that you wouldn't have encountered. But most of all, and this may be what is most important, is that it will teach you to experience life's joys in many ways.

You and others

There is a trick to listening to others when they speak, and that is to listen with interest, not with the part of your brain that's so good at analyzing what they're saying switched on. Turn that off and simply listen, and enjoy what they say for exactly that: their words.

Health and well-being

As a Virgo, you don't always love paradoxes, but here's an important one for you. You want a perfect routine for taking care of yourself and the way you eat, but the fact is, that perfect routine needs to change and to change regularly. The more often you change it, the more perfect it will be.

Goals and challenges

This is a very old saying, but it is one that is particularly appropriate for you, and that is that failure is a far better teacher than success. For you, as a Virgo, you try very hard to organize things and get them right, yet recognizing that you might fail actually could be a treat.

THIS DAY FOR EVERYONE

There are minor disagreements that occur in all sorts of settings which come and go swiftly. But what's arisen recently— and will continue to be a topic of serious discussion over the coming days—may seem overwhelming, at least initially. Still, talk these over; the more you do, the more you'll learn.

Living with others' mistakes is annoying, as they'll do it again. Explain the changes needed

You

As a Virgo, your instinct is to work hard to figure out your day and the order in which you'll do things—and, equally, with the week, and the month, and the year, and even several years ahead. This comes naturally to you, so much so you don't even think about doing it.

Yet, at the same time, life often dishes out unexpected events, which means that you need to rethink those plans. Again, this is something you have become accustomed to, and when you're doing that, you try to get it just right as well. In fact, you try to plan ahead simply because you're adjusting plans that change, and that's the key for you. Recognize that even the most carefully made plans will change, because life itself changes. Instead of working so hard to get everything organized in detail, which you tend to do, you will give yourself a wonderful gift and that is the gift of spontaneity. To be willing to do things suddenly—in fact, you might even start doing things suddenly without being prompted by others.

You might just change your mind and call someone and suggest you go some place you've never been to. Whatever it is, whatever you do, and whoever it is with, make that gift of spontaneity to yourself and your life will go from one that is organized to one that is full of joy.

You and others

While harmony is nice, and being able to work together with even difficult individuals is also nice. There's an important secret to making the best of others, and that is to support each other: for you to support others, and for them to support you. Then you'll know that in doing so, you're helping each other be the best you can be.

Health and well-being

As an earth sign, you tend to think the condition of your body has to do with what you eat and how you move and how you take care of it. And while that is important, it's also vital to recognize how much your mood has to do with how you feel. Sometimes, if you can lift your mood, you'll feel a whole lot better.

Goals and challenges

Planning ahead is a virtue, it's true, but there's one of the most important plans that you can make, which is to plan ahead to fail. That may sound strange, but the thing is, if you give yourself the space to take chances where you might fail, the odds are good that your successes will be far more spectacular.

AUGUST

26

V
/
I
\
R
/
G
\
O

Teamwork is essential, in both your personal life and activities out in the world. Yet one or two individuals are driving you crazy. Ignoring their antics won't be easy, but it's better than trying to get them in line. Besides, those individuals will soon calm down, actually before you'd have expected it.

GIFTS Articulate, Analytical, Neat

CHALLENGES Worrying, Challenging, Critical

NUMBER 8

(2+7) + (8) = 17 = (1+7) = 8

It is better to do something right once than plunge in while short of facts

AUGUST

27

V
/
I
\
R
/
G
\
O

You

There is a difference between a drive to have things well done—to have what you might call Virgo perfection, which is something you will always have on your mind—and living a real life.

And in that life, the line between things being done adequately and perfection is unclear, and in fact, not only that, it allows you to view yourself and your life as what might be termed a work in progress.

That is, rather like a plant growing, it, too, can shift. If you move it into the light, it will shift; if you trim it, it will grow differently. In your case, it is also about where you shine the light on your own life, and the direction in which you are growing.

Tempting as it is to stick with what worked before, you—just like that plant—will grow better if you put yourself in a different setting and in a different light.

And yet you are in a position where you can also do something that the plant can't do, and that is try out new things regularly, and throw caution to the wind.

Take chances in a way that you, as a cautious Virgo, might not ordinarily do, and not only will you grow as well as a plant that has been given a lot of fertilizer, you will enjoy every day of that process of discovery as well.

You and others

There is a secret to having a good time, and that isn't figuring out what would be fun, but seeking out those individuals who are what might be termed renegades—the ones who do something unexpected and have a great time doing it. You will learn a lot from them.

Health and well-being

There is a secret to feeling really good, also, and that is to learn to actually feel your vitality. If it's low or isn't there, don't think that the answer is to take more vitamins. It's about restoring your energy and actually pausing and resting in a way that you don't often do.

Goals and challenges

Many Virgos have a very, very long list of goals. Here's a suggestion. Make a very short list of goals, like maybe three, then deal with those and take on the next ones. You will be amazed how easy and how much fun it is.

THIS DAY FOR EVERYONE

Nobody would blame you for worrying when somebody close is keeping pivotal facts to themselves. However, it would be unwise to judge, no matter how convincing what you've learned appears to be. There are other facts of which you're unaware. When these surface, it will change everything.

GIFTS Meticulous, Diligent, Natural Carer

CHALLENGES Distrustful, Self-pitying, Fussy

NUMBER 9

(2+8) + (8) = 18 = (1+8) = 9

Sometimes a kind word or gentle touch isn't just helpful, it can change another's life

You

As a Virgo, you like to make plans, and you prefer those plans to be well thought out. In fact, you are perfect at planning.

However, when it actually comes to living life, those plans don't always work, and that is because life itself is unruly.

Your big lesson is to learn to make those plans more like life, and in a way, that means not to be quite so detailed, but leaving yourself room to grow.

If you make plans that are too detailed, and then try to stick to them, first, things won't go as you expect, and second, you'll see something else going on that has nothing to do with those plans. You will feel like if you pursue that instead, then you are not following the plans you should be.

There is joy in imperfection, including plans that don't work, and there is joy in new beginnings and discovery, and that's what this is all about. There is even joy in getting things wrong—and that is something that you as a Virgo find very difficult to accept. Yet as you'll discover in love and life, the more you experiment, the more you will come to understand this truth.

Yes, you may hit a few hard walls in the process, but what you learn will teach you to enjoy that, and to enjoy what each day brings you, whether it's what you planned or not.

You and others

There is a single rule that will make it much easier to get along with others, and that is to ban two words: right and wrong, when, talking about what you've done, and talking about what they've done. It is amazing how much more pleasant conversations will be when you make that single, simple change.

Health and well-being

While it is important that you eat well and that you get enough sleep, there is another issue that it is also vital to be aware of, and that is how exhausting feeling guilty can be. As a Virgo, it is something you often experience, and it is a feeling that does you absolutely no good.

Goals and challenges

The idea of getting things organized is appealing, and that has to do with listing your goals. However, what's most important is to do what might be termed write them in pencil. The more frequently you review and change them, the more fun life will be.

AUGUST

28

V
/
I
\
R
/
G
\
O

The capacity to forgive is a virtue, one you usually manage to achieve. Yet in several situations, you simply let go of these feelings. Don't. Instead, return to the setting or the individual in question and acknowledge the problems that happened. While this won't be easy, it could achieve miracles.

Debating versus arguing is rarely clear. The objective, getting things right, always is

AUGUST

29

V
/
I
\
R
/
G
\
O

You

The line between things being just okay and them being perfect is very clear to you, and it always puzzles you, as an organized Virgo who pays attention to the smallest detail, that others don't notice.

The fact is, they may well want the best, but they don't discriminate as clearly as you do about an ideal you will figure out in your mind. And often, you'll do the necessary footwork to make things happen.

Yet, every once in a while, it is vital for you to recognize that compromise isn't just necessary—it's actually by far the best approach to making things happen.

On the one hand, this means you have to be willing to listen to what others have to say, and in fact, to go along with their ideas—even when you don't necessarily think they are wise. But it also means taking chances on either new or untried activities, or even taking what may seem like unprecedented risks.

Initially, you may worry about this, but gradually, you'll discover the good fun that comes with venturing into new and potentially risky territory, and the success that comes with it. Enough that you'll wonder why you waited so long before plunging into activities that are as exciting as they are risky. Make a habit of it, and life will be a lot more fun.

You and others

While it is wonderful to hang out with people who think like you do, ensure that there is always at least one individual who could be regarded as a troublemaker in your circle. That's the person who's going to take you new places, and even more importantly, come up with inspiring and exciting ideas.

Health and well-being

Everybody loves feeling great. However, it is important that you enjoy both the ups and the downs in your life, physically, and even when you're a bit low emotionally. Why? Because every time you have a down, you will appreciate the ups all the more.

Goals and challenges

People admire those who aim high, and you have a habit of doing that. However, if you aim too high, then you will be so focused on that distant goal that you may not notice ones that are closer, and actually far more exciting.

 THIS DAY FOR EVERYONE

It's worth considering the fact that while some decisions can be made once and will last forever, others must be regarded as tentative. This means that, for now, things are settled. Yet at the same time, you'll have the freedom to explore the rather intriguing ideas and offers coming your way.

GIFTS Tidy, Painstaking, Caring

CHALLENGES Doubting, Critical, Easily Petrified

NUMBER 2

$(3+0) + (8) = 11 = (1+1) = 2$

Experience proves the high cost of compromise, while caution always pays off

You

You are probably aware that, as a Virgo, you're a bit of a perfectionist, and can also be impatient, which means that you line up very specific goals, and then want things to happen right away.

The funny thing is, often they do, which proves that if you are demanding enough of yourself and of the world, then that will occur. But it also means that, first, you don't have much fun, and second, you can miss out on the things you will learn about, the people you'll encounter, and in fact the exciting developments that come because of mistakes, because you've gone in entirely the wrong direction. And, at the same time, you'll have learned a lot and maybe met some very interesting people.

In fact, it is those adventures that a very precise Virgo often misses simply because you're so busy getting things right. This isn't just about life or places you go; it has to do with the people you hang out with and who you care about. It may well be that if you're a little more laid-back, you'll find it easier to get along with family members, and equally, you'll find you have more fun with those closest.

In fact, if you are a little more easygoing, you might even get a lot more pleasure from what the days in your life, and the companions in your life, have to offer.

You and others

Simply deciding that life is going to have joy in it, wherever you are and whatever you're doing, may seem pretty radical. But if you begin talking about it with those closest to you, they might join in and, in fact, you might find yourselves all having a wonderful time.

Health and well-being

The idea of seeking fun when you're having a workout, whether it is running or being at the gym, may seem strange, but it is possible to do. It is possible, in fact, to turn taking care of yourself into a party. That's the secret.

Goals and challenges

You are an idealist, and often, you will set yourself goals that are what might be termed astronomically high. While that's inspiring, it is also overwhelming. There is something to be said for setting your goals very low and achieving a lot of them.

AUGUST

30

V
/
I
\
R
/
G
\
O

There is a difference between things going wonderfully, which they will be over the coming weeks, and events being what you'd planned. Ironically, what is least expected could turn out best in the long run. Knowing that, explore absolutely every idea and offer that comes your way. You won't regret it.

GIFTS Systematic, Conscientious, Exact

NUMBER 3

CHALLENGES Unconvinced, Difficult, Judgmental

$(3+1) + (8) = 12 = (1+2) = 3$

The instinct for kindness is natural to all Virgos. Bizarrely, many are taught it's weak

AUGUST

31

V
/
I
\
R
/
G
\
O

You

You are very clear about your own style, your own objectives, and your priorities, and often, you simply do what you do.

Yet there are situations where you find you have to explain a lot in detail to others. If that process of explanation goes into justifying them or even seeking their approval, then it's important that you stop and think about whether it matters.

If you need the cooperation of certain individuals, fine, but if you are in a position where suddenly you find that you're trying to get their approval, then it is important to take a deep breath and change the subject.

It might even be a good time to find something else pressing that you need to go and attend to. Then you can choose to spend time with that individual later.

This process of not just embracing new challenges and adventures but also celebrating them—and celebrating the chance you're taking—is a vital one for you as a Virgo.

It is very important for you to achieve what you want in whatever area of life, whether it's your job if you go to one, your physical well-being, your creativity, or just the quality of life. But in every case, the most important individual you can please is you, and that is something that you and you alone can make decisions about.

You and others

It is important to recognize that those around you, whether friends or family or colleagues, are all very, very different. And while you are close to some emotionally, others you aren't, and with some, you may have fun doing things but you can't really chat. Recognize that, and you will be much less aggravated.

Health and well-being

As a Virgo, you can very easily analyze something and divide it into pieces, and it is true: feeling well can have to do with your body, with your mood, with your spirit. But actually, each of them is the same, because they all influence each other.

Goals and challenges

Make a list of what you want to do, but when you make that list, make sure to leave spaces on it for new ideas. What arises unexpectedly, and on occasion out of the blue, may be far more important than those goals you'd spent a lot more time thinking about.

THIS DAY FOR EVERYONE

Some disappointments are a mere nuisance. However, one you're about to face could seem disastrous. While ordinarily, you'd respond swiftly to a situation of this nature, do some serious investigation first. Once you discover just how timely those changes are, you'll exchange feelings of panic for relief.

GIFTS Well-being Oriented, Precise, Virtuous

CHALLENGES Self-critical, Fussy, Demanding

NUMBER 1

(0+1) + (9) = 10 = (1+0) = 1

Often, what is best varies with the time and place. Rarely is there only one right moment

You

When you're busy making plans—whether it is in your own life, whether it involves how you live or your life out in the world, and even whether it's around you—you will consider everything, and you'll do your best to ensure that those plans unfold as you intend.

However, it is important to recognize that plans are rather like breathing: they change as your circumstances change. If you're sitting in a chair, you breathe slowly, whereas if you are walking or running up a steep hill, your breath becomes quite different.

In the same way, it's vital that you recognize those plans will be easy at times, then difficult, then challenging, and then perhaps they will change entirely. When you expect that, you'll see them as a bit of an adventure, instead of something that is supposed to be perfectly organized. And equally, you'll feel more comfortable about sharing them with others, and perhaps allowing others to get involved, where ordinarily, you might be hesitant, because you have no idea what they'll do.

While that's true, certain individuals can be tricky, and others come up with ideas you would never pursue. That may be the point of it. The more you explore because of the people in your life, the more fun you will have simply being alive—whether it has to do with plans, or every day.

You and others

One of the things that surprises you as a Virgo, and somebody who tries to be true to yourself all the time, is how different certain people can be at different times: almost as if they were different individuals. Not only is this interesting, you may have more sides to you than you realize as well.

Health and well-being

There is a great deal of talk about the importance of sleeping well, if you are sleeping in the right kind of bed, and whether or not you're having dreams. But there is another part of you that also needs to rest, and that's your mind. You don't need to go to bed to rest your mind, you simply need to prevent it from running around and stirring things up.

Goals and challenges

When you're setting goals, it is important to think about what you want to do. But probably what is even more important is that you write those goals down in pencil. What you learn in the process of trying to achieve them is far more important than what you'll think about when you're beginning that list.

SEPTEMBER

01

V
/
I
\
R
/
G
\
O

THIS DAY FOR EVERYONE

Breakthroughs won't just be a relief, they will enable you to turn your attention to certain less pressing matters involving loved ones. While they've understood just how demanding what you have been dealing with has been, make a point of ensuring you know how grateful you are for their patience.

GIFTS Good Planner, Lucid, Precise

CHALLENGES Particular, Skeptical, Wary

NUMBER 2

(0+2) + (9) = 11 = (1+1) = 2

Those who are complaining need instructions. Those who are suffering need kindness

SEPTEMBER

02

V
/
I
\
R
/
G
\
O

You

As a Virgo, you learn in a lot of ways. You learn by research, you learn by talking to people, you learn by being observant. But most of all, we all learn by discussing things. The reason is that those around you, people you know, or experts, will have had experience in what you are doing. This is particularly important for you to bear in mind, because you always have a lot of projects going on. While you can do your own research, by talking to others, you will not only add information, you will also develop a fresh perspective.

But, ironically, when planning gets dull, when it's boring, or when it is just taking too long, it may be that others can help you on your way. And there's another kind of information they can offer, and that is when it's time simply to stop and abandon that plan, because things simply aren't working.

You might not be willing to do that on your own, but allowing those around you to both inspire you and guide you is one of the most important lessons for you.

As a Virgo, you can often be very determined. So determined, in fact, that you refuse to acknowledge when clearly something won't work, and instead turn your attention to something that might work a lot better.

You and others

The most important thing for you to remember about relationships, whether it's family, your friends, colleagues, or even neighbors, is that everyone is there to teach everybody else. You are teaching others things, but they are also teaching you things. Many of which are very important indeed.

Health and well-being

There is a tremendous emphasis on figuring out the right kind of physical activity to pursue, and the right kind of diet to follow. However, perhaps the most important message for you is to learn when to stop—simply to stop—stop thinking, stop doing, and rest.

Goals and challenges

Aiming high comes naturally to you. You don't think of it that way until you compare notes with other people. However, what is even more important is for you to pause and review what you're doing often—too often. It may be that it would be time for you to change those goals.

THIS DAY FOR EVERYONE

It would seem that while problems cause dissension, everybody would agree that there are golden opportunities to be taken advantage of. Unfortunately, that's not the case. In fact, if you are to make the best of what comes your way, you may need to compromise, at least in the short term.

Beware of those who insist their advice is vital. Their guidance may be more ego than fact

You

As an earth sign, you are practical, and your ideas are very clear, but as you well know, not everybody around you is quite as practical. And, in fact, they'll often come up with ideas that are so wild, you can't even believe they've thought of them.

Yet at the same time, the more you talk with them and the more you explore their ideas, you realize that although some of what they have in mind is pretty far out, on the other hand, some of the ideas that they have to share are fascinating, if not a very real gift—simply because it is something you never would have thought of yourself. And this is the important point about expanding your activities. Not figuring it out yourself, but allowing space for those around you—family, friends, colleagues, or neighbors—to add something exciting to your life. Allow them to bring something new.

This process of exchanging ideas is something people talk about a lot. But for you as a Virgo, often you will allow others' ideas to influence your own. In this particular case, the lesson for you is actually to learn to accept others' ideas, to embrace them, and in some cases, to embrace their point of view with enthusiasm as well. It will add to your life, whatever you are doing, and it will add to your life for the rest of your days.

You and others

As a Virgo, and somebody who has a clear sense of what works and what doesn't, you will often be in the role of teaching—that is, adding information to others. Yet at the same time, often they will have things to show you. The most important thing you can do? It's to listen.

Health and well-being

There are lots of way to feel good, and in fact sometimes when you don't feel so great, you will find that you're suddenly healed, not by having the right thing to eat, or the right medication, but by great company. That is one of the most important ways to take care of yourself.

Goals and challenges

Every once in a while, you need new goals. You need a new hill to climb. However, finding that hill is a skill, and it may involve asking the guidance of others in a way you wouldn't usually do possibly, so the guidance and the new skill may come together.

SEPTEMBER

03

V
/
I
\
R
/
G
\
O

Sooner or later, you'll need to disentangle yourself from an arrangement that once made sense, but no longer does. The problem is, the actual process will involve facts, figures, or the kinds of formalities you loathe. Tempting as it is, putting it off achieves nothing. The sooner you tackle this, the better.

GIFTS Accurate, Selective, Organized

CHALLENGES Critical, Arduous, Hypercritical

NUMBER 4

$(0+4) + (9) = 13 = (1+3) = 4$

Being disappointed by others is no surprise; disappointing myself is a worrying shock

SEPTEMBER

04

V
/
I
\
R
/
G
\
O

You

There is little more challenging to you than imposing order on chaos. You run into this frequently, and as a Virgo, you often wonder how others can cope with being in such unruly, unsettling situations.

However, as you'll often discover, what seems unruly actually is a setting that allows people to think in a new way, and in a way that sometimes you don't allow for yourself.

It is so random and so chaotic that sheer chance, unexpected developments, or an idea that comes out of the blue, opens everybody's mind, including yours, to a new way of doing things, . In fact, you might find this so inspiring that you'll alter the way you organize your life, or how you live at home, so that you can be more easygoing.

There have been times when your high standards have overshadowed life's joys, or even prevented you from taking chances. If you can embrace a little of that chaos, then you'll take chances—not only in what you're doing, but perhaps in certain relationships, or even in life's joys.

Each step that you take in this direction clarifies in your mind the fact that you have the capacity to have a good time. And it points the way to taking more chances. Not the kind that are risky, but the kind that will lead to the sort of joys you are developing a taste for.

You and others

It is only on occasion that you realize the people around you don't share your drive, whether it is to get things done, or to achieve a certain quality. And then there is the fact that even if you talk to them about it, they won't care. Let them be who they are, and enjoy who you are.

Health and well-being

There are a number of ways to improve on a difficult situation. One is analyzing it, another is talking things through. But perhaps the most important one, and the one that occurs to you least frequently, is simply to get away, to create a little space between you and the issue in question.

Goals and challenges

The thing that is most challenging for you is to recognize that, sometimes, the best thing to do with a problem is either to back off from it, or to give it up entirely. At the very least, take a break. It will change everything.

THIS DAY FOR EVERYONE

Recently, you were upset by sudden developments. Since then, you've learned a lot, much of which has both surprised and delighted you. Remember this when other dramatic developments arise over the coming weeks, and instead of battling them, you'll focus on exploring what they offer.

Kindness takes minutes and, usually, no money. Yet others treat it as if it were gold

You

As a Virgo, you tend to want a single plan, and to focus on one thing at a time. Yet, as you've discovered, because you are inquisitive by nature and you enjoy learning about what other people are doing, you tend to turn that single plan you had in mind into a variety of activities, some of which involve others, some of which you're sharing with them, and a few that are merely about you giving advice.

However, what happens is, it fills your day, and your mind, and can sometimes be overwhelming—unless you do something which is very difficult for you as a Virgo, and that is, care very little about the outcome.

To you, things being done perfectly is a passion. Yet in some cases, it actually isn't yours to deal with, while in others, if you stop worrying about the outcome being perfect, then you'll simply do what you can each day. And what will happen as a result of that is you'll enjoy what you accomplish on that day.

Then, when the day is over, you will be able to relax, instead of worrying about what will happen next. This is one of the greatest skills for you, as a Virgo, and someone who hurls yourself into life, to learn. It is not just to take a deep breath, but it's to truly relax. And to find the right people with whom you can enjoy downtime as well—individuals you might regard as your relaxation gurus.

You and others

In certain situations, you have to tolerate people, whoever they are. But in others, you have a choice, and one of the most important choices you can make is to get away from those who complain, and complain as regularly as possible. They don't belong in your life.

Health and well-being

Every once in a while, you think it is a good idea to ramp up your physical activities, to eat strictly, to get out and perhaps go for a run, or to work out a lot. Actually, often what's best is to adopt something a bit gentler, and that is, be kind to yourself.

Goals and challenges

For you, setting half-goals may seem a real compromise. However, if you do that, you will soon realize it gives you the option to alter those goals, and to include new ones. And, even more than that, to explore in a way that is as helpful as it is delightful.

SEPTEMBER

05

V
/
I
\
R
/
G
\
O

Life often brings surprises, yet those you remember best are the ones that were challenging. The surprises coming your way now will be memorable for other reasons. While you may be short of reassuring facts to begin with, once you get involved, you will recognize just how promising they are.

GIFTS Logical, Sensible, Nutrition-aware

NUMBER 6

CHALLENGES Obsessive, Judgmental, Cynical

$(0+6) + (9) = 15 = (1+5) = 6$

To a Virgo, indulgence must be earned. Once it is, those luxuries will be the finest

SEPTEMBER

06

V
/
I
\
R
/
G
\
O

You

As a Virgo, you were born knowing what is best in any setting. That may sound like an extreme statement, but it is true. Even from your youngest days, you had an instinct about what was appropriate, what was wise to do. About how a room should look. About who was trustworthy, and who wasn't. About who was fun, and who might not be.

And you still have that, but what's tricky for you is being in situations where other people not only are unaware of such matters, but actually don't care. Tempting as it is to give them advice, the trick is actually not to offer it.

This may seem unwise and uncaring, because if you suggest something, they could avoid having problems. But the fact is, they might enjoy the idea of running into difficulties and then having to solve them, because they aren't Virgos. And in your case, it is also important that you have a few things you can devote yourself to that satisfy your need for beauty and perfection in life.

This may have to do with activities on your own, or involving others. It may have to do with something new, or it may even have to do with keeping an eye open for an encounter: a place, or an individual, that will give you an opportunity to exercise that muscle of perfection in a way that gratifies you, which is so important.

You and others

There have been times when you have been critical of others, and it seemed natural. It seemed important that they also know about that, but as years have passed, you have begun to understand that not only was it unimportant for you to say anything about it, actually the individuals in question would have no intention of making any changes.

Health and well-being

Tempting as it is to get a routine going that you know is in your best interest, it is more important to take chances—and even more than that, to find something that isn't as good for you, but that you adore, that makes you feel like a million.

Goals and challenges

It's important that you set your own goals. It may seem obvious, but sometimes you allow those around you to influence your thinking. You then set goals that you think will impress them. Make sure those goals are a part of your heart and your mind, and then everything else will go well.

THIS DAY FOR EVERYONE

As the saying goes, never say never, and rarely was such advice more apt than now. In the past, you may have said there were certain things you wouldn't consider, or even certain individuals you'd do anything to avoid. But that was then, and times have changed—and so have you.

There is no more powerful passion than one that has been tested by time and reflection

You

If you could live life on your own, if you had your own little planet, or your own island you lived on, it would be a lot easier. Because then you could make the plans you needed to make without having to deal with others.

But as you have learned, not everybody is a Virgo, and you do have to deal with others, which means that you face questions that are unsettling, shake-ups in plans you've made, and individuals whose priorities are very different from yours.

All of which means that turning a plan into action can be difficult. Yet at the same time, you're aware that those individuals have an amazing touch when it comes to making things happen, and to life itself, and it is something that you rather envy.

That touch has to do with spontaneity, that you as a Virgo don't always allow to emerge from your character. And this is a big lesson for you: to let those unexpected events, surprise invitations, or developments you didn't foresee to become a part of your life.

They will broaden your horizons and bring a kind of joy that you might not know how to do, at least initially, but it is something that you, being a clever Virgo, and someone who's very good at learning what you need to learn, can pick up on. You will have to allow those who are very good at doing joy teach you.

You and others

Not surprisingly, when you are organizing things with others, you are tempted to take the lead. However, the fact is not everybody around you is interested in the same things as you, or in the same depth. The trick is to compromise. Take turns.

Health and well-being

There is a tendency to think that health and well-being have entirely to do with how you eat and how you take care of yourself. But they are also about learning different skills—about adding new activities to your thinking, and even more, exercising your mind as well.

Goals and challenges

The trick to making the best of the twists and turns that occur frequently in your life is to recognize that each is an opportunity—not simply to learn something, but to thrive on the process of making your brain cells work harder.

SEPTEMBER

07

V
/
I
\
R
/
G
\
O

Being interested in others is one thing, but there are one or two individuals who seem to think that you will be there for them, whatever your other commitments. Thus, saying a firm no can be very difficult indeed. That is, however, exactly what you'll have to do, or face yet more unrealistic demands.

GIFTS Natural Carer, Virtuous, Diligent

NUMBER 8

CHALLENGES Skeptical, Demanding, Overconcerned

(0+8) + (9) = 17 = (1+7) = 8

Accepting that somebody doesn't care they cause problems isn't easy, but brings peace

SEPTEMBER

08

V
/
I
\
R
/
G
\
O

You

You don't normally think of it, but when you are making plans—whether they are entirely social plans, something that has to do with your job, if you go to one, or family matters, or when you're organizing things—you will focus on practicalities. In fact, it is a pleasure for you, and you are good at it.

However, as you discover, the more people who are involved in those plans, the more ideas there are, and the more your vision of what's possible—and even more, what is best—can be watered down by their ideas. Tempting as it is to encourage others to do what you know is best, instead do something that is very difficult for you—stand back and listen to what they have to say, perhaps even go along with it.

This is something you'll have experienced in the past, and will again in the future. Except when you're ready to embrace the fact that it is not so much that others know better, but they may have an idea that works better in that situation, then you will be more relaxed about letting them take over.

This also means that perhaps you will have free time to pursue what is more important for you on your own, or with those whose approach is more suited to you, and that is the big lesson in this: to allow others to take over, and then to go off and do what you enjoy.

You and others

Frequently you inspire others, but sometimes they also inspire you, which can be a bit of a surprise for you, because often you know your thinking is clearer. However, the special thing that others have is a variety of hope that you occasionally find hard to achieve.

Health and well-being

While your well-being has a lot to do with your physical body, and even your mood, another thing that is important is your sense of hope about the future, and that is something that can't be rushed. It needs to be developed slowly, kind of like doing exercise. The more you dwell on it, the more you'll benefit from it.

Goals and challenges

Setting small goals may seem to be awfully modest, but as you do, and as you achieve them, you will realize how wise it is. Because then you will have much more to celebrate, and each goal you achieve will help you shape the next ones.

THIS DAY FOR EVERYONE

Sudden changes are unsettling, and could upset others. Still, there is no question these are in everybody's best interest. Knowing that, discuss recent developments, not with the objective of keeping everybody happy, but rather with the intention of defusing issues before they turn into problems.

GIFTS Detailed, Perfectionist, Eloquent

NUMBER 9

CHALLENGES Overworking, Picky, Worrying

(0+9) + (9) = 18 = (1+8) = 9

It's tempting to speak frankly. But I learned others are not ready for the truth at once

You

One of the most important skills for you as a Virgo is learning to let go. As you well know, you work hard at getting things organized, and coming up with a perfect vision of what's possible. The perfect plan. The perfect solution for a problem. And often, you will be involved with rescuing individuals who are struggling, helping them sort out their lives.

All of this is important, and, in some cases, it may be your job as well. There is a skill that needs to be used to deal with all of them, and that is the skill that comes with saying, "That's enough."

It may mean that you've done everything you can, or it may mean that you need to hand over those tasks to somebody else. Yet there's a part of you that finds it very difficult to let go. You have a certain pride in finishing things, and that's your big lesson: to let go.

However, there is also another reason—and that is when you let go of one thing, quite naturally, the next thing will appear. And that thing that appears will fit in with the skills you've learned recently.

Adopt that approach, and instead of clinging to what you want to finish you will say farewell to it, knowing that something wonderful, and something that is perfectly suited to you, is coming your way, and probably within the blink of an eye.

You and others

Sometimes you are modest—too modest. It is important that you learn how powerful you can be when you need to be. This isn't about explaining what you have in mind, or getting others to do what you think. It is simply a matter of stating the truth.

Health and well-being

It's very possible for you to feel guilty, even when you're taking care of yourself. Why? Probably because the regimen you have in mind is almost impossible to attain. The trick is to be a little more easygoing, and a little more forgiving with yourself.

Goals and challenges

As a Virgo, and somebody who likes to organize things, you know very well how much you like a list. Yet it is vital that you recognize that the goals in your life will change: every year, every month, every week, and, in fact, every day.

SEPTEMBER

09

V
/
I
\
R
/
G
\
O

THIS DAY FOR EVERYONE

Although you are likely to be short on facts about recent developments, that shouldn't keep you from taking action on what you do know. If others say you will need to organize plans beforehand, thank them politely, but ignore them. With things moving swiftly, you'll need to think and act fast.

The joy of anything perfectly done is rare and wonderful. The mystery? So few recognize it

SEPTEMBER

10

V
/
I
\
R
/
G
\
O

You

This may seem an obvious statement, but you've been you for your whole life, which means that clear and crisp mind of yours, that observant nature, has been looking at things from the time you were very tiny.

In fact, many Virgo children are amazing at being able to sort out elements of the world around them, long before others. So you have grown up watching the world around you. The trouble is, sometimes nowadays those observations turn into a concern that things aren't being done right.

And this is where it is vital to recognize that, at times, others will want your guidance. But there are other times when they won't, so it is important to ask. And if others don't realize you could help them, then quietly back off and do something else.

This is very difficult for you, because you really care. But in doing so, you're also using a different portion of your nature that is actually looking after your own interests, and ensuring that what you're dwelling on is something that is rewarding for you and is appreciated by those around you. That is one of the most important lessons for you. Often, you've helped those who are ungrateful. Now is the time, not only to share your thoughts and gifts with those who are grateful, but to recognize how valuable your company is.

You and others

Often you are the one who's a guide for others. However, there is a big lesson here: to recognize that those around you have ideas and advice to offer you that isn't just good, it could be valuable, if not life-changing.

Health and well-being

Of all the difficulties you may face in life, boredom is, for you, the worst. This means it's vital for you to have fascinating activities and challenges around you. At home, that means people you can spend time with, but most of all, that you ensure you have adventures of your own.

Goals and challenges

If you don't have any challenges around at the moment, it is important for you to create a few. In fact, you might always want to have some handy. Things you'd like to do, physical challenges, puzzles you want to solve, or perhaps even something you want to paint … whatever it is, make sure you have it handy.

THIS DAY FOR EVERYONE

As much as you enjoy learning about changes in the world around you and those reshaping the lives of others, you're less enthusiastic about changes in your own life. Yet judging by recent planetary activity, they're unavoidable. Explore what's arisen. You need only learn a bit more, and you'll be thrilled.

GIFTS Reliable, Worker, Fitness-aware

NUMBER 2

CHALLENGES Fussy, Unconvinced, Insistent

(1+1) + (9) = 11 = (1+1) = 2

To you, a minor but vital correction is just that. Others neither understand why, nor care

You

As a Virgo, you love it when life is in order. It makes you feel like everything is balanced. However, you have also learned that if things are too organized, and events are too predictable, then even you get bored. In fact, occasionally, you'll let something go or change something, just so you'll have a new challenge.

However, on occasion, it is important for you to begin to broaden your horizons—that is, to take yourself into new territory, where you're dealing with situations or people about which you know little. You don't even know whether you're getting it right or wrong. But that's the whole point of learning in this way.

Also, it is about using a different muscle in your character, which is inquisitiveness.

While you have always been interested in what's going on around you, this variety of learning has to do with an entirely different part of your mind and your spirit: the part that is totally about discovery.

Ironically, many Virgos avoid this because they are anxious about the fear that they won't be able to learn.

On the contrary. Not only will you learn a lot, each day you will discover new facts. But even more you'll discover a new passion in your life—about living, about learning, and about how exciting it is to discover something new each and every day.

You and others

Teamwork is an interesting word, because often it is useful, if not vital. But it can also be a problem, and hold you back. The issue? Trusting others. Discovering that alone is tone of life's most important insights.

Health and well-being

Learning to notice when you are feeling overwhelmed is difficult, because often you're so busy figuring things out, you don't even realize if you're stressed or tired. The trick? Take a deep breath every once in a while. And if that feels like an effort, maybe it's time to take a break.

Goals and challenges

It seems natural for you to want to seek the perfect plan or the perfect goal. However, in certain situations, not only is that difficult, it simply doesn't exist. Acknowledging that is the greatest gift you can give yourself, because it turns the situation in question into one of life's most important adventures.

SEPTEMBER

11

V
/
I
\
R
/
G
\
O

Those simple moments when the food is good and the company better are sheer joy

SEPTEMBER

12

V
/
I
\
R
/
G
\
O

You

Every once in a while, you find yourself in a situation where things are so complicated that you know you need to do something, and you are seeking the perfect plan. But then you realize that probably nothing will work unless you simply allow things as they are to fall apart, then deal with the complaints.

This runs counter to your nature as a Virgo. Yet what it does is take you to the deepest core strength, the strongest part of your nature and allows you to let go of something that isn't working and make space for new ideas. And to experiment and possibly to have to learn something new.

All of this is wonderful. The minute you decide it is the best option, you will feel better. And this is the hard part for you, as a Virgo. This doesn't just have to do with activities; it may have to do with close alliances—with taking care of yourself, with a personal crisis.

Whatever the case, this process of discovering what's new isn't just important. It will take you on a journey of exploration beyond anything you've done before. Because previously, you have been in control of situations, and this is about tangling with destiny. It is about allowing destiny to become your teacher in ways that you wouldn't have considered possible, but that you will find amazingly informative.

You and others

Normally those around you look to you to organize things. So when they see you letting things fall apart, they wonder. Actually, you may have the kind of discussion you've never had before with others, in which you learn how to cope with what looks like disaster, but is actually an opportunity in disguise.

Health and well-being

There are some situations for which there is a particular remedy. In the situations you will face, the remedy has to do with a single thing: deep breaths. There is nothing more powerful when it comes to well-being.

Goals and challenges

There's nothing better, when you're dealing with goals and challenges, than simply to allow things to unfold, to stand back and let destiny take over. This is more of an art than figuring out a plan. The art is to know when to step in. That may not be when you expect—and this is the greatest skill of all.

THIS DAY FOR EVERYONE

If you were told you were a creature of habit, you'd probably disagree. Yet you're battling necessary changes in elements of your daily routines. What's more, you are aware how much of a benefit these could be. Consider the possibility that those habits are more dominant than you care to admit.

The greatest Virgo lesson? Spotting those who don't care about getting things right

You

Being an earth sign and ruled by the clever planet Mercury, you're well aware of what works and what doesn't. But those around you aren't—and that's really part of the problem.

When things are going wrong, you're usually the one who points out not only that things need to be done, but also what the solution is. However, as clever as you are, there are certain situations where, first, things may actually need to fall apart, and second, the solution may be you dealing with something else entirely.

It may well be that there's some other area of your life that needs attention, but you've always been so busy with other things, you haven't dealt with that.

This, therefore, is your lesson. It is why you're very good at dealing with certain kinds of crises, yet you're not quite as good at spotting unworkable situations in your own life. Every once in a while, you get a handwritten invitation to deal with it.

If you learn to spot those, then you'll also add a skill, which is being able to learn from them and deal with them. The trick is to ask others' advice willingly, even if it's uncomfortable. That, too, will change your relationship with those individuals from what was tension to a closeness you would never have thought possible.

You and others

Often you take on the role of advisor, which comes naturally with being a Virgo. Yet every once in a while, it is essential that you not only listen to others' advice, but you seek it. It is an important lesson and one that will prove incredibly valuable.

Health and well-being

Typically, you rather like going for a rigid regimen. It's because it's well defined and you know where you stand. Except every now and then it is important that you relax—not so much spoil yourself, as simply live day by day, free of duties and obligations.

Goals and challenges

The single message for you is to set flexible goals. As a Virgo, you like to know where you stand, so you tend to measure your goals by both achievement and the time they will take. Except sometimes you need to give yourself a break, and simply have an idea of what you would like to achieve—nothing more.

SEPTEMBER

13

V
/
I
\
R
/
G
\
O

THIS DAY FOR EVERYONE

Every once in a while, life is good. So much so, there is no need to query ideas or offers, and all that is necessary is that you respond to events as they arise. Yet certain well-meaning individuals are warning you that things are just too easy. At other times that might well be true, but not now.

GIFTS Orderly, Sensible, Lucid

CHALLENGES Judgmental, Exacting, Finicky

NUMBER 5

$(1+4) + (9) = 14 = (1+4) = 5$

Doing things right seems simple. But you've learned others' views differ greatly from yours

SEPTEMBER

14

V
/
I
\
R
/
G
\
O

You

Every once in a while, others come to you for insights about the circumstances they're dealing with, or for advice. This is so natural to you, you don't really think about it. Being a Virgo, you have an instinctive ability to analyze situations, and to view the issues others need to deal with, in a way that they don't. However, every so often, you, too, need to pause, take a breath, and consider what is going on.

And that is exactly the case now. Just as you would encourage others to look at things from a different angle, it's essential that you stop. It may not be that you want to ask others for help, but rather that you simply want to pause for long enough that you begin to realize what it is you don't know, what you need to learn or what you need to explore, in your own way.

And in doing that you need to alter your habits, your way of looking at life and even your way of thinking.

Others may tell you about that, but as a Virgo you need to figure it out for yourself. And when you do that, you will have broken a habit of self-sufficiency that has served you but also restricted you. It will also open your mind, and quite possibly your heart, to experiences beyond anything you would have imagined possible only a short while ago.

You and others

You have a tendency to expect others around you to stay as they are, partly they can be rather stubborn. Yet you may notice that they're changing, they're evolving, possibly along with you. In fact, you can share the experience together.

Health and well-being

You don't think of yourself as being extreme. However, when it comes to your health, you can be extremely good to yourself, in the sense that you can be very rigorous about what you will allow yourself to eat and the fitness you're doing. Try relaxing instead.

Goals and challenges

Once you make a commitment, it's a steady one—and you keep your word. That's also the case with the personal goals you set. It is worth reminding yourself, however, that the world around you changes, you change—and you can revise those goals as well.

THIS DAY FOR EVERYONE

Sometimes, even the simplest of plans takes a long time to organize. While that has been the case recently, now and over the coming days, things will move with astonishing swiftness. Bear in mind, however, that you'd best have all the details beforehand—because you'll have no opportunity afterward.

GIFTS Diligent, Precise, Purist

CHALLENGES Harsh, Disapproving, Picky

NUMBER 6

$(1+5) + (9) = 15 = (1+5) = 6$

The sheer joy of well-organized luxury may not be lasting, but the memory will be

You

As an earth sign, you're logical—you know that. However, you sometimes forget that others aren't just not particularly logical, but more than that, they also don't have your appreciation for style, for doing things well, for quality, and for beauty.

And the fact is, much as you may try to explain this to them, it seems they don't care, they actually aren't interested.

They may be interested in other things, they may be interested in sports or music, but the quality that's important to you simply isn't to them. This also means, therefore, that if there are certain tasks you may undertake together, it's important that you make space.

It's also important that you leave certain things to them—allow them to get on with their good ideas, and focus on what it is you want to do. That seems obvious, but often you feel that it's important you share those tasks.

The trick is simply to do what you need to do and leave them to their own ideas or pursuits, without even discussing it. That again, for you as a Virgo, may seem difficult, but simply allowing people to do what they do naturally will make life a lot easier.

The more skilled you become at that, the easier it will be to live with those individuals with whom there used to be constant tension, if not arguments.

You and others

Tempting as it is to discuss certain situations, there is a secret to making changes and avoiding difficulties, and that is: don't explain. Simply make those changes quietly. The odds are good that others won't even notice.

Health and well-being

There are times when we all like to work up a sweat, but there are other ways to feel well, too, and in your particular case a little crazy wildness is a good idea. That could mean doing something like dancing off all those excess calories, and having a lot of fun at the same time.

Goals and challenges

Every once in a while, you feel it's important to explain to others what your priorities are and what you have on your mind. The fact is, they don't understand, and they don't care, either. This may sound cruel, but they live in a very different world from yours. Accept that, and the rest will be easy.

SEPTEMBER

15

V
/
I
\
R
/
G
\
O

GIFTS Tasteful, Stickler, Natural Carer

CHALLENGES Obsessive, Condemning, Fussy

NUMBER 7

$(1+6) + (9) = 16 = (1+6) = 7$

The minute you discover a mistake, you'll remedy it. Puzzlingly, others don't even care

SEPTEMBER

16

V
/
I
\
R
/
G
\
O

You

Some Virgos decide from a very young age what works in life for them. Whether it's about what works at home, what works out in the world, what works in love—they stick with that philosophy their whole life.

But other Virgos, you included, are inquisitive by nature and regularly change your approach to such matters.

You change your rules simply because every time you do this, you learn something new. And what you learn will then go on to enrich your life.

While you understand this, others don't, and if you're asked by somebody to explain, you're urged not to. Just say that the changes you are making were an idea you had and you will probably have many more.

And then quietly go off and think more. Because for you, this process of exploring options is like taking a kind of vitamin, it is very special. It allows you to be more like yourself than others.

While all Virgos share some characteristics, certain particular Virgos (you included) have a talent for examining life—making the best from it and making every twist and turn count.

Enjoy that, even though sometimes others won't understand why. Yet it doesn't matter. Because you're the one who is making the best of every one of those twists and turns.

You and others

Ordinarily, as a Virgo and somebody ruled by Mercury, you'd happily talk things over with others. It's natural. However, there are moments, and you'll recognize them, when it is best to say less and in fact simply to stick with looking a bit vague about the reasons you made certain decisions.

Health and well-being

What is important for you is to recognize that while there are lots of things you can do that are good for you, such as eating certain ways and doing certain types of activity, what brings you joy is quite another matter. Make sure that this shapes what you do. Good health will result.

Goals and challenges

Being told you need to be wary of other people's thinking may seem strange, but the fact is others' standards are very strict and suit them. If they start giving advice, thank them and ignore them. That is the only solution.

 THIS DAY FOR EVERYONE

Urgent as certain decisions seem, don't let anyone corner you into committing to something you're not sure about. The problem isn't a lack of options but rather, too many. Explore and experiment. Just ensure others know that that's the approach you're taking and that you'll finalize plans later.

Joy is those golden moments when everybody seems to understand what's needed

You

As a practical earth sign and as a Virgo, you always know what needs to be done. And when you know there are things that need to be dealt with, you will also take action—often without discussing things with others.

Yet there are certain situations where you have no choice. And this is where it can get tricky, unless you recognize something. And that is the fact that, while you know what needs to be done, those around you don't necessarily need to hear the details.

In fact, if there is any secret to dealing with this, it is to avoid pointless discussions and debates. Begin to explain and others will quite naturally ask questions. They may even challenge you, even though they don't know what they are talking about.

The trick, therefore, as with so many of these things, is to do what needs to be done and do it all at once, and to keep very quiet about it. If you need support of any kind, find an expert; don't ask someone who is around who is part of your life, your work, or your family. Once you become accustomed to taking this approach, life will be much easier.

In fact, you will find that you're able to relax and enjoy life with those whose company you take greatest pleasure in because they, too, are able to deal with things swiftly, easily—and without drama.

You and others

You may not be aware of this, but you can seem on top of everything, gliding through. Yet, every once in a while, you have a crisis. Ask others for help, but only ask those who are knowledgeable and you know are capable of giving you a hand.

Health and well-being

Shouldering everybody's burdens is typical of you—and it is completely unrealistic as well. The trick is to have a joint effort. This doesn't come naturally, and of course, the most important thing is to ensure that those who are by your side are as capable and as experienced as you are.

Goals and challenges

When you are planning ahead, it is important to anticipate challenges. That may sound a bit negative. But you'll realize that if you line up those who can help you, they will be there for you all the time—and that could even be when things are going well.

SEPTEMBER

17

V
/
I
\
R
/
G
\
O

GIFTS Hardworking, Analytical, Fastidious

CHALLENGES Disdainful, Worrying, Particular

NUMBER 9

$(1+8) + (9) = 18 = (1+8) = 9$

Trust seems simple, so universal. Yet what you expect is entirely different from others

SEPTEMBER

18

V
/
I
\
R
/
G
\
O

You

Ever since you were a very young Virgo, you have been aware of endings and beginnings—that is, endings and beginning in the world around you from the time you could be aware of seasons, but also the endings and beginnings of tasks. First with the grown-ups around you, and then, as you began to do things on your own, you realized that everything starts and then comes to an end.

This is wonderful for you because, as a Virgo, and somebody who appreciates order in life, this knowledge is crucial.

In fact, being able to observe this in nature has allowed you to develop the kind of relationship that is so important for you as an earth sign with events such as this.

Another side of this has to do with developing what might be termed another muscle of your character, and it has to do with being loving and creative. It also has to do with allowing yourself to express those feelings. Whether it is perhaps through cooking for others, whether it's doing things for others, whether it's doing something on your own: in every case those activities nourish your spirits and are a variety of vitamin that is far better than anything you can get out of a bottle. Most of all, enjoy this quality. It is a very special one, and one that comes with being a Virgo.

You and others

You would like to straighten things up with others but there are times when it is important to leave arrangements open-ended, not to say much, not to do much but simply to watch what happens. In waiting and watching, you will learn a great deal.

Health and well-being

When you're feeling stressed, you tend to seek a regimen that you follow. It may have to do with something you eat, or something that you do, exercise or even something like yoga. While that's good, the most important thing that you can do as someone who understands nature, is spend time in it, even if it is simply watching a sunset.

Goals and challenges

It is important that you set clear goals for yourself, which are very specific for you as a Virgo. Yet at the same time, it is important to keep your heart and mind open for the unexpected, because what's least expected could be exciting—and life-changing.

THIS DAY FOR EVERYONE

Exciting as recent ideas or offers were, they're taking you into unfamiliar territory. As much as you enjoy new experiences, you prefer to undertake them when it's convenient. Now, however, events have made the decision about timing for you, so simply go with the flow. You'll be glad you did.

GIFTS Precise, Organized, Nutrition-aware

CHALLENGES Suspicious, Picky, Hypervigilant

NUMBER 1

$(1+9) + (9) = 19 = (1+9) = 10$
$= (1+0) = 1$

Sharing life with others is an adventure. Nature's joys are both simpler and more reliable

You

The Virgo earth sign-side of your nature enjoys analyzing things. It is something you're good at, but it's also something that makes you feel that you understand what's going on. And to a certain degree that you're in control.

However, it is also vital that you do two things. The first is that you learn from experience and the second is that you borrow a little of the energy you get from Gemini, the sign that shares the rulership of Mercury with you. Geminis can come up with a dozen ideas before noon.

It isn't that you're going to take advantage of those ideas; it's just simply realizing that despite the way you feel, you could do all kinds of things and that there are many options, some of which could be unexpectedly exciting and a few even bizarre.

That, then, will make it easier for you to sit back and relax and let things unfold without you worrying about the outcome, which is the biggest lesson for you.

Because, as you have experienced in the past (although often forget), it is what happens at the last minute that can be most important and least expected.

Take that approach and instead of worrying, you will indeed pause and enjoy what nature has to offer you, knowing that something spectacular is coming your way.

You and others

Your capacity to analyze almost anything is a gift. In fact, others often benefit from it, so they will want you to come along and want your advice. While that's okay when it comes to others, it is also important that you say the minimum about what's on your mind. You know why.

Health and well-being

Someone tells you that when you're stressed, you need to get out and about and do a bit of sweating. While there are times that this is true, there are also times when you, in particular, benefit most from not doing: that is, from sitting, and being quiet and reflective.

Goals and challenges

When you set a goal, you tend to stick with it, simply because it means a lot to you and as a Virgo, you will have thought it through. However, it is important that you realize that not only it is okay to rethink goals, it is actually often a very good idea.

SEPTEMBER

19

V
/
I
\
R
/
G
\
O

GIFTS Fastidious, Methodical, Tidy

NUMBER 2

CHALLENGES Fretting, Finicky, Difficult

$(2+0) + (9) = 11 = (1+1) = 2$

When you explain plans to certain people, they soon forget. Instead, write them down

SEPTEMBER
20

V
/
I
\
R
/
G
\
O

You

As you go through life as a Virgo, you learn a lot. You learn from experience, you learn from what you discuss. But also as you move through life you tend to attract objects—you tend to buy things, collect things, and each one of them adds to your life.

In some cases, a single object turns into a genuine collection. It can be anything from seashells to some variety of ceramics or, indeed, to a sports car—whatever it is that you might be interested in.

However it's also important that, from time to time, you shed both the thoughts that are connected to that collection and maybe that collection itself.

That isn't to say you shouldn't have things around you that you enjoy. Rather, that it is encouraging you to consider whether that time and energy you invested in collecting something is part of the past and perhaps there is a new future waiting for you.

The simple thought of considering that alone frees you. And that, for you, as someone who works so hard to make life perfect, is in itself freeing.

Give yourself the gift of considering the possibility of letting go—that is, of both elements of your past and of physical memories, souvenirs, collections—and you'll find you feel much freer and happier.

You and others

It is useful to recognize that while you may enjoy the company of a lot of people, you actually relax with very few of them. If you need a time to chill, time to enjoy yourself, make sure that those individuals are who you decide to be with.

Health and well-being

There is something to be said about having ambitious plans about taking care of yourself. But there are also times when keeping things simple is more important. That may mean simple movement, simple ways of eating— or even simple rest and relaxation.

Goals and challenges

As you well know, you have in the past been, and may even be at the moment, distracted by certain obsessions, things you want to do, or other desires, ideas, or concerns. The lesson isn't dealing with those obsessions, it's learning how to still your mind. That is one of life's greatest challenges and most rewarding accomplishments.

THIS DAY FOR EVERYONE

As much as you enjoy talking over intriguing ideas, ensure others understand you're doing no more than that, exploring possibilities. Certain individuals will mistake your enthusiasm for serious interest. Explain that as clearly as you can now and you'll avoid misunderstandings, if not hurt feelings, later.

You expect so much from yourself, there is no room for more perfection in your life

You

As an earth sign you are very good at handling practical matters, but being ruled by Mercury, you are also an ideas person and can sometimes get so involved in those ideas, those things that you want to do, that you'll focus on that alone and completely forget about the practical side.

The challenge here is to embrace that practical side as well so you have the time and, when necessary, the money, to pursue those ideas that excite you. This is about juggling in a way that you don't usually have to do, because in many areas of your life you have what might be described as a golden touch.

You are able to do whatever you do and figure it out well. But there are also certain moments when twists and turns in life force you to look at things from a different angle. In doing so, you may struggle at first, but then you will begin to see what can only be described as a golden sunrise.

This may be literal, but probably it is the new way of looking at things that will be the answer to many of those difficulties that you have been struggling with.

Remember that sunrise when similar difficulties arise, and you'll realize that it isn't about analysis but about allowing your intuition to guide you. That is the answer now and it often will be in the future, too.

You and others

You have a gift, a knack for spotting the skills that others have, sometimes ones they're unaware of. Take advantage of their abilities in the most positive way—ask them to help you but encourage them to develop those skills as well.

Health and well-being

You may not be excited about getting involved in any kind of regimen that has to do with eating or fitness, and that's fine. There are wonderful ways to do what you need to do, like walking, getting out and about, taking deep breaths. All of those are perfect.

Goals and challenges

Often you will stop short of polishing off a plan or project because you like the idea of continuing to work on it. There is a secret, and that is to have several such activities at once, each of which is contributing to your life.

SEPTEMBER

21

V
/
I
\
R
/
G
\
O

After a fast-paced and exciting period, things are slowing down enough that you're finally able to focus on the practical side of things. You'll realize that you're just in time, and if you don't act swiftly, certain obligations or financial issues could become troublesome. The sooner you tackle these, the better.

Libra

September 22– October 21

Libra   Being ruled by Venus, the goddess of elegance, beauty, and love, you as a Libra have an instinctive elegance and talent for making others—everybody you meet—feel special. This talent often becomes your career, and those personal links develop into a lifelong passion. Your flower is the rose; your herbs are redolent mint and sorrel; and ash and poplar are your trees. Jade, in its infinite shades, is your stone.

L
\
I
/
B
\
R
\
A

GIFTS Fair, Balanced, Loving

CHALLENGES Indecisive, Unclear, Aloof

NUMBER 4

$(2+2) + (9) = 13 = (1+3) = 4$

It is possible to say "No" so charmingly, others don't realize they've been refused

L
\
I
/
B
\
R
\
A

22

SEPTEMBER

You

Being born on the 22nd, you are the beginning of the sign of Libra. Some would call it the cusp, but actually it is more about the beginning of a cycle and, at the same time, a change in the rhythm of life. Fall begins in the northern hemisphere, and spring in the southern hemisphere. But just as much, it's about embracing an entirely new vibe.

It is about leaving the painstaking, earthy Virgo behind you and embracing Libra's expansive nature. As an air sign, you're all about ideas—about the past, the present, and the future. Beyond that, it's the perspective that comes with having the scales as your symbol. You will always be seeking balance: in life, with others, and in the world around you.

Of course, this brings with it a challenge, and that is the discovery that however close you are to others, they won't necessarily think the same way you do. You're always confident in creating that accord, and always understand others. Yet nobody, even a twin, is the same as you. However, there is a joy in that, too: the unending exploration of what makes another person think—what makes them tick—and most of all, of the differences between you.

Once you learn to enjoy that and become skilled at the process, everything else will make sense. In fact, every day you spend around those closest will be a joy.

You and others

There are many different languages in the world, and many ways of looking at things, but the most important language to discover is that spoken by those closest to you, whatever their role in your life—whether they're family, friends, neighbors, or colleagues. While their words and even ideas may differ from yours, the message from the heart will be similar.

Health and well-being

The formulas for both looking and feeling your best are infinite and seem to grow each day. Equally, there are innumerable diets and routines to hone your shape and well-being. However, being ruled by Venus, the planet of balance, if you follow that Venusian instinct about what is best for you, and especially, what is balanced for you, you will always do exactly the right thing.

Goals and challenges

Your greatest goal isn't achievement in the world, although that matters to you. It's quite a different one, and it has to do with finding the balance of happiness. This is something very few find, but if anybody ever could, it's you, being born on the first day of Libra.

THIS DAY FOR EVERYONE

The last thing you're in the mood to do is discuss troublesome problems again. What you don't realize, however, is that with things moving so swiftly, these are rapidly being transformed from being a nuisance into events as welcome as they are unexpected. The sooner you get involved, the better.

I can stand up for myself without worrying what others think

L
\
I
/
B
\
R
\
A

You

We all go through it, that mission of being on the lookout for a single way of dealing with each day, of dealing with others, and, once that elusive goal has been achieved, trying to maintain it. However, with each breath, life changes, and whether you're dealing with someone close to you—a family member or partner, or possibly a dear friend or colleague—each breath alters that relationship with the individual in question.

Still, as a Libra, you cling to the idea that if you can just figure out that formula, you will be able to achieve that balance symbolized by the scales. Better yet, you hope that you'll be able to maintain it forever—and that is your lesson. You are ruled by Venus, which, on one hand, signifies harmony and balance. But you must also remember that Venus is the ruler of earthy Taurus, the sign that's all about what's practical and what works.

If you borrow a little energy from practical Taurus, you'll stop worrying quite so much about figuring things out and will, instead, focus on the joys of the moment. And, even more than that, you'll allow yourself to enjoy pleasures of many varieties you'd worry about if you were in Libra mode, and will instead embrace them wholeheartedly, as a Taurus would. Learn to combine the two, and you'll benefit from both, now and in the future.

You and others

The idea of taking chances in relationships is unappealing to most Libras. And, even worse, the idea of allowing things to go wrong, then possibly explode, is really unappealing. Yet once you allow that to happen, and get through one or two explosions, you'll realize that often those bring you closer than your efforts at harmony would ever have achieved.

Health and well-being

Most Libras have a luxury-loving streak. Even if you don't, there is a part of you that really doesn't like the idea of austerity. Yet every once in a while, you may embrace a routine, a diet, or some form of health regimen that is tough. The trick, of course, is to be a Libra, and to find the balance between the two.

Goals and challenges

From the time a child is very young, they're asked what they want to be when they grow up—as if any child would know. However, as an adult, you may still wonder what you want to do. The answer is not to wrestle with possibilities, but to reach out, to take chances, to have experiences. There is no better way of learning what you enjoy than by doing it.

SEPTEMBER

THIS DAY FOR EVERYONE

If ever there were a time to do a lot of listening, it's now. While you've plenty to say about plans currently in place and changes others are suggesting, there is a lot going on behind the scenes, and some of those developments could change things overnight. Knowing that, avoid unnecessary discussions.

Often, winning others over requires charm blended with persistence

L
\
I
/
B
\
R
\
A

24

SEPTEMBER

You

As a Libra, you think carefully about most things. Yet this thought process can go through many chapters, each focusing on a different element of that particular plan or passion. This achieved, then the air sign part of you, the part that enjoys exploring options, begins to wonder if you couldn't improve on that perfection. You may think about it yourself or, equally, you may discuss various ideas with others. Or you may begin to worry.

You are actually enjoying this back-and-forth debate. This may have to do with something today, next week, or it may be a different and distant concept. Whatever it is, this process is core to you, as a Libra. It's about the deepest side of your nature. But you also put pressure on yourself, on relationships, and on your activities out in the world, pressure to change and to become more perfect—and solely because of the ideas that are spinning around in your head.

Actually, the most important relationship you have isn't with those around you, it is with those ideas. When, instead of struggling with them, you are able to rein them in—to become their master instead of wrestling with their ups and downs—they will become your servant. Achieve that, and you will be able to enjoy your own life, what you do, and your relationships with those around you all the more.

You and others

There is a secret to being happy with others, and that's to shift from worrying about others and wondering what a smile means to enjoying the moment. But most of all, it is about savoring the preciousness of the time you spend with those closest to you, from friends and family to loved ones. Each one of those minutes is a gift.

Health and well-being

There are many kinds of health and many kinds of well-being, and you can, in fact, whip your body into a perfect shape. But, if there's tension on your face, it is a whole different matter. The solution? Find joy in life. Do that, and that tension from your face will go, and you'll glow—whatever the shape and size of your body.

Goals and challenges

Others will often interfere with your plans and make suggestions, because they want to be involved. But what's most important is to do what you want to, whatever others say. You may worry about finding a balance—that is the nature of your sign—but in the case of achieving your goals, you come first.

THIS DAY FOR EVERYONE

This is one of those rare periods during which the mood is about turning even complex ideas into plans that aren't just practical, but that everybody is happy about. Knowing this, don't just focus on what is most important or pressing, but also think about those that will shape your future.

GIFTS Reasonable, Inquisitive, Harmonious

CHALLENGES Distant, Ambiguous, Manipulative

NUMBER 7

(2+5) + (9) = 16 = (1+6) = 7

If I didn't get what I wanted, it's okay to revisit the issue—and be tougher

L
\
I
/
B
\
R
\
A

25

S
E
P
T
E
M
B
E
R

You

It is easy to lose track of what you're doing, and even to lose track of your objectives. As a Libra, the sign of the balance, and the sign that is powerfully linked to others, it's easy to do this. What's more, it is also easy to be drawn into the behavior of your opposite sign, Aries, which is ruled by Mars, the planet of individuality, ego, and energy, and which can sometimes be so "self-involved" that it forgets about others entirely. While this is something that doesn't come naturally to you, it's worth borrowing that Aries self-absorption from time to time. This is about developing a skill, one that is important for you. It is about recognizing the balance between you and others—whether you're talking about something, whether you're silent, whether you're out playing, or whether you are working at a project.

First, note what you are talking about and, equally, who is in charge of the conversation. Then, think about what you actually want to achieve, discuss, or learn. And finally, recognize that at no time will this exchange of ideas, or any other, ever be perfect.

That is the point of it, and that is part of your journey having being born under the sign of the balance—understanding that things are always changing. Once you embrace those changes, you will enjoy every minute of it.

You and others

As a perfectionist in your relationships, you analyze and often discuss tensions with those closest. While certain individuals tell you not to let things bother you, others advise staging a confrontation. However, this isn't the way you think. You want harmony. And that comes from accepting relationships the way they are.

Health and well-being

You sometimes take others' minor comments too much to heart. While they may be actually asking about you, it is possible they're thinking about themselves. Yet the most important person in the world is you—and how much you are able to love yourself.

Goals and challenges

As a Libra ruled by balance, you have a tendency to shift your goals from day to day, at least in your mind. Yet it's important to be flexible, and willing to rethink those goals when an opportunity appears. There are times when, to your own surprise, you've simply refused to entertain changes because you struggle so much to make plans, but life is like breathing. You must continue to breathe, and you must continue to make plans.

THIS DAY FOR EVERYONE

Offers that come from out of the blue are intriguing, even those that don't really seem to fit in with your interests or lifestyle. In this case, however, while these may seem strange, if not odd, because they are about breakthroughs, that's as it should be. These will considerably broaden your horizons.

GIFTS Diplomat, Amorous, Attractive

NUMBER 8

CHALLENGES Detached, Scheming, Fluctuating

$(2+6) + (9) = 26 = (2+6) = 8$

Sharing others' joys is wonderful, but having different interests is great, too

L
\
I
/
B
\
R
\
A

You

As a Libra, you have a well-earned reputation for being a charmer. Yet, deep down within every Libra lies a troublemaker—a part of your nature you may be aware of, but one that can provoke clashes. Some you battle within yourself, but some are with others, even those with whom you're friendly and comfortable.

There are all sorts of reasons this occurs. Sometimes it is because things are a little dull. However, you'll also use this technique—sometimes unwittingly—to provoke others, to wake them up and get them talking about things they need to discuss, possibly about you and them. But at times, the focus is on them as individuals and their issues: often those they refuse even to acknowledge.

This is a skill, but as a Libra, it's difficult for you to acknowledge this provocative side of your nature. If it is mentioned, you may deny that you ever provoke anybody. Yet the fact is, many Libras are powerful negotiators, and because they know exactly how to throw others off-balance. Whether it's in the realms of law or in government, in counseling—or at home, or even with friends—it's a valuable asset. But it's made all the more worthwhile not only by acknowledging it, but by embracing it as well. Do that, and you will not only understand yourself better, you will appreciate who you are all the more.

You and others

A good debate is always healthy, but actually engaging in one isn't just important; doing so reminds you of the questions you have, of what's most significant to you, and what you admire in others. Most of all, it is about the zest that comes from standing up to those around you.

Health and well-being

There are all kinds of workouts. There is a workout in the gym. There is a brisk walk. But there is another kind of workout, and that has to do with being willing to stand up to others. Not that you'll be boxing with them, but that in standing up to them, you will be using the muscle of the mind, a very powerful muscle in your life and in your world.

Goals and challenges

As somebody who is acutely aware of the need to create balance in your life, putting yourself and your interests first can be difficult. In fact, you may even feel you must explain why you're doing it to others. Actually, those closest know how important that is, and they may even have been encouraging you to do exactly that. Put yourself first, and not only will you enjoy it, they will be delighted as well.

THIS DAY FOR EVERYONE

When you took a tough line with one tricky individual, you feared they'd only become more troublesome, but bizarrely, they're calmer and their attitude is far more cooperative. If you're thinking that all they needed was for somebody to draw the line, that's true. The fact is, you did them a favor.

GIFTS Liberal, Kind, Negotiator

CHALLENGES Fluctuating, Indifferent, Uncertain

NUMBER 9

(2+7) + (9) = 18 = (1+8) = 9

Seeing others happy is heartwarming; being happy with them is better

You

One of the difficulties of being an idealistic Libra is that, from time to time, you can be fooled by what appears to be the sincere friendship of others. Of course this isn't necessarily about a friend—it may be anybody, from a family member to a colleague. Whoever they are, the fact is they seem to be trying very hard to make things easy, and instead of being difficult, as others often are, they're easygoing, and understanding. It may even seem they're seducing you into having a relationship with them that you've always hoped for. They are.

And once that trusting friendship has been achieved, they'll turn the tables. Unsurprisingly, this shocks you. Yet, it is important to remember that while you as a Libra value harmony, not everyone shares those values. And certain individuals regard the ups and downs of relationships as fun, and will trigger excitement and challenges by misbehaving.

How can this be dealt with? Do nothing. Don't respond. Learn from it. And, just as important, recognize them as they are. They'll never change. Instead, busy yourself with those whose company you enjoy, then return to those individuals in question, knowing they, too, will turn around as they always do. Just as the sun rises and sets, certain individuals will behave in different ways. Understand that, and the rest of life will be a lot easier.

You and others

Deep down, you have a conviction that the perfect balance exists in life, and that once it's achieved, you can relax and enjoy relationships with others. But in almost every case, there is a give-and-take that is very much a part of life. If you achieve that balance, enjoy it, but realize that the rest of the world will probably still need to indulge in those ups and downs.

Health and well-being

As a Libra, you tend to swing between not taking care of yourself at all and following a healthy regimen. But for you, balance is the most important thing, as is the pleasure that comes with taking care of yourself. If you can find a way of eating and taking care of yourself that gives you pleasure, the rest will be easy.

Goals and challenges

As a Libra, you will often set goals in relationships—you'll either be influenced by what others are doing, or listen to their advice. This can be risky, because those around you could change, while you'll be stuck with their advice. The solution? Doing what is most challenging yet essential, and that is putting yourself and your own interests first.

L
\
I
/
B
\
R
\
A

27

SEPTEMBER

Even the most difficult individuals will always respond to charm

L
\
I
/
B
\
R
\
A

28
SEPTEMBER

You

As a Libra, you are often seduced by the side of your nature that's ruled by Venus, the planet of balance, charm, and grace. And you believe that if you can manage to organize things in such a way that your own life and the lives of those around you are harmonious, then things will run smoothly and fall into place. While that might actually be the case for a little while, with the world around you changing as it does, and with individuals changing as they do, that balance is unlikely to last for long.

And this takes us to the symbol for your sign: the scales. They are designed to shift, a reflection of the way in which the world shifts. There is day and there is night, and there are the seasons. And, as those shifts take place, they influence the people in the world. And so, quite naturally, you need to shift as well. This means that, instead of the eternal balance that you're always seeking, as a lasting goal, there is a secret. And that is to recognize that contrast is key, in your own life, in relationships, and in the world around you.

When you're able to embrace that, then instead of struggling to ensure things are perfect, you'll enjoy every contrast, from those that occur suddenly to those you expect, between day and night, between winter and summer. Whatever their nature, you will embrace them wholeheartedly.

You and others

There is a secret to living happily with those around you, and it is to discover the joy, not in harmony but in intention, the joy in the dramas between you and others—even the joy in the clashes. Once you embrace those, then instead of worrying when someone is upset, you will treat it as if you were at an opera, where people turn dramas into beautiful music.

Health and well-being

While one side of your nature thrives on a routine, from exercise or eating, there is another side that enjoys change, so much that if you are too strict, you'll rebel. There's a trick to dealing with this: to go for the contrast in each, a week doing one, a week doing another, a day doing one or another, or even one meal changing, and then the next.

Goals and challenges

As important as having a single challenge can be, you also need smaller challenges for each day and week, and a few that are long-term. It may seem strange, but if you come up with a range of challenges that will keep you busy, instead of complaining about life's twists and turns, you will actually learn to savor them.

THIS DAY FOR EVERYONE

For weeks you've sensed you'd soon have to alter or rethink certain unchanging elements of your life. While these once flowed without a hitch, problems are more frequent—so much that you'd rather wrestle with the necessary changes and deal with them now than wonder what will go wrong next.

Don't justify your dreams to others. State them simply, no more

L
\
I
/
B
\
R
\
A

You

Every Libra is familiar with having arguments in their head: a debate about something they might be doing shortly, or did do in the past. This "Yes," "No," "Maybe" discussion is something that is all too familiar to any Libra, and it can be exhausting, especially because very often what you are thinking has absolutely nothing to do with the life you are living or what you will actually be doing that particular day.

It is a variety of distraction for you as an air sign: something that occupies you and prevents you from dwelling too much or thinking about things that are either dull, or perhaps issues you have been sidestepping because you have no idea how to deal with them. The most important thing to learn from this, however, is that it is part of being an air sign, one of the three signs associated with the mind, ideas, and imagination.

The issue is whether you will go into what might be called "air-sign overdrive" and allow your mind to spin out of control. If so, you can miss out on a lot of life's joys. Simply recognizing this is a huge victory. Learning to sideline that chatter is even more important. Do that, and instead of facing the challenge of ignoring that ongoing inner chatter, you will be enjoying each day's golden moments, and the resulting golden twists and turns.

You and others

If you're uptight, if your mind is in overdrive, then put off the discussion you have in mind. Wait until you are calmer. Similarly, if it seems that others are looking for a battle, here, too, back off. You have a choice, and achieving some kind of accord comes more swiftly when both of you are in the right mood.

Health and well-being

There are many kinds of addictions. We hear lots about sugar and caffeine, substances that overstimulate your mind. But as an air sign, be cautious about the unending and pointless mental chatter. The secret? Busy your mind with other, compelling interests. That will change everything.

Goals and challenges

Everybody asks what you're planning, but often, it is important to think about what you are going to do today—to develop what might be called mini-goals. A lot of them might be tiny, personal goals, yet they are still accomplishments. Very rarely have there been more worthwhile goals, and very rarely will you have had a greater sense of achievement in accomplishing them.

29

SEPTEMBER

Somebody has been telling tales, saying things that aren't actually lies but have little to do with the truth. They assume that because these aren't clear-cut falsehoods, they'll get away with it. You're urged to point out you are aware of these, and that you have no intention of putting up with them.

GIFTS Cordial, Sympathetic, Kindhearted

CHALLENGES Interfering, Standoffish, Testy

NUMBER 3

(3+0) + (9) = 12 = (1+2) = 3

Confrontation only fuels battles, while silent strength defeats them

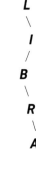

L
\
I
/
B
\
R
\
A

30

SEPTEMBER

You

The phrase "Be true to yourself" is about an ideal—and it is an appealing one. However, for most human beings, it really isn't possible. For you as a Libra, it is actually a challenge. Of course, this is simply because, as a Libra, you are often swayed by others. There's what you have on your mind, yet others could have an entire agenda that is very different from yours. You'll try hard, not only to understand what they want and their demands, but to go more deeply—your hope being to achieve greater insights about their thinking and views.

Your challenge is to acknowledge that they live in an entirely different world, and that as much as you would like to share those feelings, you're unlikely to understand them fully. In some cases, with certain individuals—no matter how much of a Libra you are—their ideas will be as foreign to you as if they were speaking another language.

This is the secret of being born a Libra, and under the rulership of the scales. That balance swings back and forth, but you wouldn't have anything to balance if you weren't dealing with individuals who live in a different world, have a different way of thinking, and a different set of values and ideas. Once you understand them, not only will you not mind being mystified by what makes them tick, you will enjoy the process of coming to terms with that.

You and others

There are many tales—songs, novels, plays—about the swings in close relationships. However, there is a joy in this. For you, as a Libra, discovering that joy is part of the point of dealing with those around you. Once you do that, there may be a little less drama in your life, but there will be a lot more harmony and a lot more sweetness.

Health and well-being

You don't think of yourself as a perfectionist, yet when it comes to eating or working out, you are. While some may appeal for a while, there is another option; to forget about doing it "right," and simply go for what works in the moment. And when it comes time to make changes, you will do so without regrets.

Goals and challenges

You have a tendency to obsess over the perfect goal and how to achieve it. Of course, this isn't unusual. Yet you tend to base your own feelings on the reaction of others. Here is a secret: make what you feel and what you care about the most important. Base those goals on that and that alone.

THIS DAY FOR EVERYONE

Only days ago, others were on edge about changes. You were cautious about both questions you asked and suggestions you made. However, not only has the tide turned, things are falling into place, almost magically. A lot of this is a result of the sudden unsettling yet amazingly productive changes.

GIFTS Considerate, Fair, Curious

NUMBER 2

CHALLENGES Scheming, Inconsistent, Uncertain

$(0+1) + (1+0) = 2$

Ignoring those who are unkind or rude is more powerful than confronting them

L
\
I
/
B
\
R
\
A

01

OCTOBER

You

As an air sign, you benefit from the capacity to be amazingly logical. However, you are also sometimes subject to feeling something that is entirely illogical, and that is guilt. This is often the result of a conflict, a sense that you should be doing something other than what you're currently doing—even if you are being entirely responsible or, quite simply, enjoying life for what it offers you.

So the issue isn't what you are doing, but what your mind insists you should be doing, even if it's not possible or realistic. That is what makes this complex issue tough to spot—you're worrying so much about others, you don't pause to think whether those feelings make sense. And that's what is most important. While, it's true, you are an air sign and therefore incredibly logical, there is a part of your nature, particularly when it comes to alliances with others—with loved ones, with family, and even with partners—where your loyalty to them overrides your logic. Most of all, you feel that if you can make them happy, then everything else will be great.

The lesson now is to recognize those commitments: the sense that you have to deal with your own guilt about others not being happy, and your responsibility to make them happy. In both cases, it is entirely up to them. For you, life's joys are entirely up to you.

You and others

Building on the issue of guilt, here is what's important for you to recognize: you don't need to help those around you to be happy. Let them take care of themselves. Your job is to be true to yourself. The more real you are, the more authentic you are, the more passionate you are about life itself, the closer you will be to those who matter most.

Health and well-being

There are certain individuals who are by nature excessive, and who plunge into things. For you, as an air sign, a balance is essential. If you are hanging out with somebody who overdoes it, the biggest gift you can give to yourself is to stop—even if they carry on. Tell them you'll join them later, then take a deep breath and appreciate who you are.

Goals and challenges

These days, the custom is to talk about what you've done, about what you're happy with and aren't and, equally, plan for the future. Everybody discusses their goals with others. However, be selective about who you talk to. Certain individuals have an ability to undermine the strongest convictions, but you don't realize this. Learn when to stop. You will be glad you did.

Standing my ground with those who are impossible requires persistence

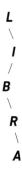

L
\
I
/
B
\
R
\
A

02

OCTOBER

You

The subject of making changes is a tricky one for Librans. Not just changes in your own life, but changes in the lives of others—and the fact that, as a Libra, you think all such things through, and in depth. You will discuss various options in your own life, what others are thinking about and then, often, discuss them further. As an air sign, while logic is important, that won't keep you from having the same discussion several times.

The trick is to recognize that, as important as these ideas are for you as an air sign, ultimately, if you're going to make changes in the world around you and what you do and think, you need to commit to those changes.

The perfectionist side of your nature wants to get things totally organized, so there is no anxiety about this. But of course, with each day, with each hour, changes arise anyway.

When you recognize that, when you embrace the fact that life and your world are constantly changing, not only will such matters no longer worry you, you'll realize this is all about learning something new and important. First, we all came here to experience what life offers, and to grow and change because of that. Also, because it is about what you are learning, you can never get things wrong. If there is a secret, it is to plunge in and learn from those experiences.

You and others

Simply recognize that life is a game of choices: the choices you make, the choices others make, and sometimes the choices you make together. It is difficult because you get so lost in that game. Yet that is the fun of it. However, sometimes it is important to back off, and recognize that you're playing a game. Do that, and instead of worrying about winning, you will enjoy the process.

Health and well-being

Yes, there's eating well, and yes, there is going to the gym. But there is a better way to deal with health problems, and that is to take a deep breath, then take another. As a Libra, you often forget to breathe when you're worried, and then wonder why you're so uptight. Try it. It's an easy way to deal with tension.

Goals and challenges

In most of Western culture, there is a win/lose story—that is, the person who wins gets what they want, and the person who loses doesn't get much of anything. Yet there is a better approach, and that's about tackling things together, as a team. That way, everybody wins and nobody can lose—now or ever.

THIS DAY FOR EVERYONE

The past few days have been demanding, if not just plain exhausting. Still, looking back on what you have faced up to—and have mostly managed to deal with—you should have a sense of accomplishment. Better yet, the decisions you have made will last longer than you imagined possible.

Complaining is satisfying but achieves little, while charm can do wonders

L
\
I
/
B
\
R
\
A

You

The word "commitment" is an important one for you as a Libra, because as an air sign, getting things figured out is vital. It may have to do with life, with love, with goals, with work—or with how you live with a passion. Whatever the case, that commitment requires a lot of thought and a lot of discussion—or at least, so you think.

However, there is an easier way to deal with this, and that is what might be termed very "un-Libra." It is a way that has more to do with ignoring discussions with others—and ignoring gathering the facts—but feeling what goes on deep within when you think about a certain activity, a certain pursuit, or a certain individual. Indeed, it may have to do with what you're going to do for a living if you work. It may have to do with a certain relationship. It may have to do with what brings you joy or love.

The key is to feel what is going on within, and instead of debating what will happen if you take action on it, simply take that first step without turning it into a major plan. Then take the next step, and the step after that, and the one after that, and so on.

Instead of wasting time, effort, and quite a lot of energy on debating, you will learn from life itself.

You and others

There is a solution for tensions with others, and that is to talk. Not about what's on your mind, or about an idea or a solution, but to let that talk wander, let it take on its own life. Do that and you will soon discover why it matters so much that you achieve an accord with the individual in question. Then achieving that accord will be easy.

Health and well-being

We all know what we should and shouldn't eat, and how we should exercise. But there is not much about how to eliminate anxiety. As a Libra this is important, because it influences so much else—when your mind rampages, or focuses on worry. The secret is simple. It is to decide where you will allow your mind to go.

Goals and challenges

The trick here isn't to figure out a formula, but to question whose goals you are following. Are they someone else's, or are they yours? If they are someone else's, of course, the first step is to get rid of them and to figure out actually what you care about most. Do that and everything else will fall into place as if by magic.

03

OCTOBER

After a tricky couple of weeks in which you've had to compromise, not always willingly, suddenly things are coming together. This isn't just an improvement. It is worth revisiting certain of these recent tricky matters and discussing the possibility that arrangements could be reviewed.

GIFTS Elegant, Committed, Agreeable

NUMBER 5

CHALLENGES Irrational, Diffident, Unavailable

$(0+4) + (1+0) = 5$

Those who think they have a right to be rude can be trained to behave

L
\
I
/
B
\
R
\
A

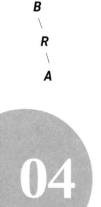

04

OCTOBER

You

The words "Yes," "No," and "Maybe" are unhealthy for you. Of course, you can't stop using them. Yet they come into conversations with others where you're trying to figure something out, and while you're trying to achieve a firm "Yes" or a possible "No," others keep saying "Maybe," which drives you crazy. For some Libras, this kind of debate isn't just important, it's actually a part of your life. It may even be something you do for a living.

At the same time, you often come across those who seem to make a career out of complaining—not a professional career, but who do it very frequently—and when they complain not about you, but about the world around you, it is hard to tell them you just want to back off.

Yet that is what you need to do. You may not say those words, but as a Libra, your obligation to yourself is to be aware of what you are putting into your body and your mind. While you may eat well, if you hang out too much with those who are constantly doing the "Yes," "No," "Maybe" routine, it is like eating a variety of toxic food.

Once you back off, you are doing yourself a favor by putting yourself and your interests first, which for you is always a challenge. Do that. Not only will you feel a lot better, you can pat yourself on the back for having done it.

You and others

Sometimes, it's difficult to acknowledge how others really are, but this is an important point for you. Certain individuals are argumentative while others are actually bullies. Once you know that, you'll also realize how important it is to draw the line with them. The healthiest thing in the world you can do is to say "I've got to be someplace else" politely—and leave.

Health and well-being

Tension can be a problem for a lot of people, but ironically, for you, it can be a hint that you're hanging out in a situation that isn't in your best interest. If you're feeling uptight, if you can't sleep, if you're restless, think not so much about your body, but about your mind. It may well be that you need to go on a diet, but that diet has to do with who you are hanging out with, not with what you're eating.

Goals and challenges

As a Libra, you are a planner by nature. But what if you just plunged into something, not only without a plan, but without any rules at all? What if you simply just see what happens? For some Libras, it is a wild and crazy idea, but for you, it will be incredibly helpful.

THIS DAY FOR EVERYONE

Pivotal decisions are pressing. Although your views may seem clear—mostly because they involve matters you've dealt with in the past, so thought about in depth—there is more. These are more recent events, some of which seemed important at the time, but actually have changed everything.

It is possible to confront somebody without them knowing it

L
\
I
/
B
\
R
\
A

05

OCTOBER

You

Your ruling planet, Venus, is the planet of beauty and of balance, but interestingly, not of joy. So when you're trying to create that perfect life, you won't always naturally assess what can, and will, bring you joy. Also, when you are with others, you won't always think about who lifts your spirits and who leaves you feeling empty. You may notice that certain individuals make you feel uncomfortable, but you can't quite pinpoint why. That is because you focus on keeping things flowing, ensuring everybody is happy with what's taking place and the company of others.

While obviously this is crucial, it is not so much because you need to do something right away. Rather, it's about recognizing that, despite your best efforts, certain situations and individuals will be tricky. You need to ensure you are providing yourself with backup, in the form of people and circumstances that bring you joy.

Whatever it is, ensure it will boost your spirits. This could range from activities you love or things you do in nature, being with animals. These provide a variety of emotional vitamins for you, and they are important for you as a Libra and someone who is sensitive and generous by nature. Make this change and should those joyless situations arise, you will be prepared to deal with them.

You and others

It's easy to fall into a conversation comparing things: comparing your day, your vacation, a meal you had, but also comparing your life. There are those who, no matter what you say, will always top what you have done until you begin to feel that, somehow, you are a bit of a failure. That has nothing to do with you and everything to do with them. By no means is their life joyous. They just enjoy making others feel unhappy.

Health and well-being

There is a trend these days for those who are taking care of themselves to live a fairly austere life. That is, to give up one thing or another because it's "good for you." While that may be the case, less is not more. In certain situations, a little more may be what's needed. For you, ruled by Venus, indulgences aren't just worthwhile, they provide a variety of vitamins.

Goals and challenges

Have you been battling to achieve certain goals but getting nowhere? Don't alter what you're doing. Instead, pause and think whether (a) you really care about them, and (b) there is actually something else you'd rather be doing. There may be other things that are dearer to your heart.

THIS DAY FOR EVERYONE

It is clear that one particular individual is trying to use guilt to corner you into doing something that you would otherwise refuse outright. While you're usually tactful about such matters, you are tempted to confront them. Don't. They will never admit to what they're doing.

I have every right to say a firm "No" to unreasonable demands

L
\
I
/
B
\
R
\
A

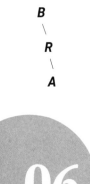

06

OCTOBER

You

As a Libra and somebody ruled by the gracious planet Venus, being in the midst of those who are unhappy—people who are combative or even those who simply can't seem to get on with things—is difficult. This is because you want the best for everybody, and if you see someone struggling, you feel you must help in some way. It is natural for you.

However, it's vital that you recognize there are certain individuals and certain situations where others' problems are theirs, and theirs alone, to deal with. Their difficulties and even their pain aren't your responsibility.

Acknowledging this is a challenge, because you have a need to look after others, to show interest in them and do what you can. So putting your own interests first isn't just out of character, it makes you feel uncomfortable, if not plain selfish. However, there are times when it is crucial that you recognize your values and needs come first. This variety of "Libra balance" can be one of the most challenging for you to spot, and understand.

This is especially the case when you're around individuals who are addicted to their own dramas. You know that about certain individuals, yet you are still drawn to them. The secret to dealing with all of them is to tell them you're sorry they are struggling, and then say you have an appointment elsewhere.

You and others

At times, it seems as if your role in the lives of others, and theirs in yours, is fixed. In some cases, if it's family or somebody you work with, it is. In others, it is negotiable. In fact, in certain relationships that might be termed toxic, it is essential that you negotiate. In many cases, make changes before the day is over.

Health and well-being

There are many ways to recover from life's difficulties, but perhaps the most important one is to have a good time. That may seem unwise, especially if you are around people who are struggling, but the best therapy for you is to duck out of those situations and do something that lifts your spirits and makes you feel glad to be alive. If you have to go back to others' problems, you will return to them in a much more positive mood.

Goals and challenges

It's very easy for those around you to change the past according to what suits them, and they begin to include you in their past. Being able to say, "No, that's not what happened at all," may sound argumentative, but in certain situations, it's not only wise, it is essential.

THIS DAY FOR EVERYONE

Somebody seems to have either decided to do things their way, or alternatively, ignored important facts, yet they intend to proceed with their plans. That would be no problem, but inevitably, what they do will have an impact on you. This means getting involved. You really have no alternative.

GIFTS Devoted, Fair, Understanding

CHALLENGES Ambiguous, Fluctuating, Elusive

NUMBER 8

(0+7) + (1+0) = 8

Facing impossible people? You can help them learn to be agreeable

L
\
I
/
B
\
R
\
A

OCTOBER

07

You

Are you finding that you are diving into the past? It is easy to do, especially when those around you seem determined to remind you of certain experiences. Talking to others about them is one thing, yet those discussions often dwell more on what they're are going through than what you have in common.

And this is often a tricky moment for you, as somebody who truly cares about others, but who wants to ensure those relationships are balanced. That is, you are interested in their concerns, and you want to ensure yours get "equal time." The trick is to listen to what they have to say, but only so much. Then pause, and broaden it from you and them to, possibly, a shared experience.

The point is to draw a line politely. You may even need to break away for a while. This isn't about escaping, but rather, allowing you to shift the power in the situation—and the power over your own mind: what is influencing your thoughts as a result of those conversations. As a Libra, you're sympathetic by nature and you want others to be comfortable. But what is most important, particularly in circumstances of this nature, is that you look out for your own well-being—and not just in terms of your physical well-being. This means making very sure that what you're doing is in your best interest.

You and others

You're urged to listen to what others are thinking about so you can begin to organize your thoughts into a clear vision of what you want. It may seem strange to say, but you can't have a dream come true if you don't know what that dream is. This is about exploring that dream, its nature, its promise, and its power in your life—for now and the future.

Health and well-being

By no means are you rigid in your thinking. Yet every once in a while, you'll discover that you are so caught up in certain activities from practices and ways of eating that it doesn't occur to you to do something different. Yet as an air sign, it is vital that every once in a while you shake things up. Not only will you benefit from it, you will have a good time doing it.

Goals and challenges

The focus is on your dreams. Not plans, but dreams that, as you've become more practical, have vanished. Now is the time to revive them. When asked what you're planning, talk about those dreams. Gradually, what you do, the people you encounter, and sheer luck will conspire to make them a reality.

GIFTS Compromising, Diplomatic, Rational   *NUMBER* 9

CHALLENGES Hesitant, Uncertain, Unapproachable   *(0+8) + (1+0) = 9*

Ongoing calm is the result of dealing with issues when they arise

L
\
I
/
B
\
R
\
A

08

OCTOBER

You

Theoretically, as a Libra you have a capacity for calm, to stand back and observe what is going on in your life, as well as in the lives of those around you and in your world. Yet at the same time, that Libra part of you can get drawn into the dramas of others to such an extent that, before you know it, they become your own. Then you go from being contented with life to dealing with those ups and downs.

Of course, because these dramas are in others' lives, you can't control them. They begin to undermine your well-being. Spotting this isn't easy. And it is tricky, because you think that if you care about others, surely you will care about their feelings. Yet in some cases, that cool reserve you can cultivate as an air sign is crucial. True you can add some pizzazz to discussions by getting enthusiastic. But that doesn't mean you need to be swept up in their dramas.

This then leaves you time to enjoy what is going on in your own life. Of course, it may be that there are certain things you've been trying to avoid, so others' dramas give you an excuse. If so, tackle those things you have been trying to avoid, get them dealt with, boost your spirits with that sense of accomplishment, and then when you returned to others' dramas, it's amazing. They might not seem quite as important after all.

You and others

On occasion, you realize certain individuals aren't good company, but, rather, they are a "duty." They're family, business, or an obligation. You have no choice. But that doesn't mean it can't be interesting. You just need to ensure they contribute as much as you do to the proceedings.

Health and well-being

There is a lot of talk these days about what you eat, the nature of your diet, and how you move. However, your emotional diet is mentioned far less frequently. For you as an air sign, what you put into your mind is just as important as what you put into your body. If you're feeling upset, tired, or unwell, maybe it's time for you to look at your emotional diet, particularly when it comes to who you're hanging out with and who you are letting undermine your spirits.

Goals and challenges

There are lots of good causes in the world. Often it is important to give them a hand, but it's equally important to consider the nature of those causes and how involved you'll get in them. If it isn't your passion, and if it isn't your job, then it also isn't your top priority.

THIS DAY FOR EVERYONE

If ever there were a time to believe in yourself and what you wanted to do, have, or achieve, it's now. Similarly, the tide has turned in your favor, which means sudden and possibly totally unexpected events could turn what are promising ideas into an arrangement far better than you'd imagined possible.

Don't allow those who are negative about life to influence your expectations

You

It is difficult for you to admit, but certain individuals aren't just tricky, they're actually deceptive and will happily take advantage of you. Of course, the problem is, you don't always recognize that. This has happened in the past and it could well happen again. In fact, it happens frequently enough that it is important that you recognize these individuals, and once you do, distance yourself from them.

This is the tricky part, because as a Libra, you prefer to believe the best in others. While that is admirable, it is worth taking a hint from the sign next to yours, Scorpio, which can be somewhat suspicious, and recognize that if somebody seems not to be trustworthy, this may be because that is actually the case.

This will teach you not only about those you can trust, but will also allow you to enjoy the company of those you care about and with whom trust has been built over a long period of time—which for you as a Libra is one of the most valuable varieties of relationships there are.

Tempting as it is to invest time in dealing with those tricky individuals who are actually manipulative, if not just plain challenging, if you enjoy it, ensure they are just a sideline and make those who you can trust and who care about you the main course for your day, for your week, and for your life.

You and others

As you begin to study certain individuals and notice their rather tricky nature, you will also notice how they're adept at changing the rules; how it's absolutely okay if they cut things off at the last minute, or even if they lie to you. Is this what you would do with someone else? And if you permit it from others, then think about why you spent any time with them at all.

Health and well-being

There are many ways to feed yourself. Obviously there is food you eat and the air you breathe. But, the emotions around you also feed and influence you. This is especially important for you as somebody who's often very tolerant of tricky individuals. They can be exciting but, as you know, they can be toxic, and undermine your well-being. The solution? Be alert, and put your interests first.

Goals and challenges

You are very accommodating with others, but once in a while you need to draw a clear line in situations or relationships. It may have to do with activities in your working life, and that clear line is to say what you are willing to accept and what you aren't. If you can make changes, do. If you can't, then get yourself out of the situation in question.

L
\
I
/
B
\
R
\
A

09

OCTOBER

I can simply ignore those who are being moody or temperamental

L
\
I
/
B
\
R
\
A

10

OCTOBER

You

Every Libra has experienced somebody—a friend or family member—expressing concerns about a particular situation or individual in your life. And worse, saying they think the individual may be taking advantage of you, or that the situation is risky. As a Libra, you will probably say, "Thanks for telling me," and brush it off. Yet deep down, you've sensed thing weren't right, but hoped you were wrong. However, there is a part of your Libra nature that enjoys imbalance and taking a risk. It is perhaps because, being ruled by the scales, if life is too balanced, then it is a bit too predictable, if not just plain dull. This is why you are drawn to dramatic individuals.

However, there is a difference between those who are experiencing dramas and those who have their own interest at heart and enjoy undermining the circumstances of others. That could well be the case. It has been in the past and it could be again.

The trick now is to think carefully about whether they remind you of ones in the past, when in some way the influence of that person harmed you. That may sound extreme and you got over it, yet would you want it to happen again? If so, is the answer is very simple: very quietly walk away from that situation and spend time with those you know you can trust, at least for a while.

You and others

As an air sign, you have a quick mind and you're brilliant at analyzing situations, but there are those where overanalysis confuses things. The answer? To trust your instincts. They will tell you whether what you are doing, or who you are hanging out with, are in your best interest.

Health and well-being

There are all sorts of solutions for not feeling well. Some say you should take vitamins, some say have a drink, but actually for you as an air sign, one of the best remedies is to take a walk. It doesn't need to be a long walk, and it doesn't need to be in the country. What it needs to be is a walk. It's goal? To allow you to breathe fresh air. The fact is, it isn't just the air; it's being away from all those things that are a source of concern.

Goals and challenges

Everybody is told to make a list of what they want to do and that's not a bad idea. However, sometimes goals stay on that list for so long that you end up being discouraged. The secret? Make the list in pencil so you can erase those goals that no longer mean anything to you and put new ones in and without even caring about saying farewell to them.

THIS DAY FOR EVERYONE

You're by no means fixed in your thinking. On the contrary, you are inquisitive about others and the world around you. Yet you assume certain elements of the past are unchanging, and that's not the case. These aren't just in transition. The outcome of those changes could lead to a timely rethink.

GIFTS Friendly, Uniting, Dedicated

CHALLENGES Testy, Uninterested, Fluctuating

NUMBER 3

$(1+1) + (1+0) = 3$

Just as others have a right to demand what they want, I have a right to ignore them

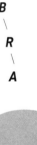

L
\
I
/
B
\
R
\
A

11

OCTOBER

You

If you're into astrology, as a Libra you will be aware that Venus is your ruling planet, and its influence means you value harmony in both yourself and your relationships. You may be aware that it is also said to rule the earth sign Taurus, the second sign of the zodiac, which accents what you earn, what you own, and, in fact, the practical side of life.

Actually, many Libras benefit from a great sense of practicality and manage to live a life that is both profitable and beautiful.

However, the earthy side of your nature can sometimes take over, and that Taurean stubborn streak—as opposed to the usual kind of negotiation that comes naturally to you as a Libra—means you will get stuck into a particular ideal, objective, or point of view. It means that relationships can turn from easygoing exchanges into challenges.

Think about this. If there is a situation of this nature, it may seem that sidestepping clashes is a compromise, but actually it is an important lesson for you.

And that is one that is about discovering why you were born as a Libra and what there is to learn from the skills that come with being a clever air sign—not to mention an air sign whose symbol is the scales, which have to do with balancing things wisely and fairly.

You and others

As a Libra, you love a peaceable situation, but when you need to, you're good at standing up for yourself. Except there are moments when it is wise to back off. Remember that compromise. You use the art of the compromise to gain a powerful advantage.

Health and well-being

Being ruled by Venus, you have an indulgent side. The Libra side of your nature knows that sometimes that is appropriate. You also have an instinct about when enough is enough, but there are moments when you cross that line and too much seems a very good idea.

Goals and challenges

There is an old saying about choosing your battles, and it's an important one, especially for you as a Libra, because very often your battles will be behind the scenes. It will be almost as if they were a fencing match as elegant as it is brutal. Every once in a while, however, it is important to create another kind of battle, and that is simply saying "No." That may be even more powerful.

GIFTS Amorous, Supportive, Reasonable

CHALLENGES Inconsistent, Unclear, Interfering

NUMBER 4

(1+2) + (1+0) = 4

While charm wins over almost everybody, certain individuals need a firmer approach

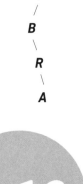

L
\
I
/
B
\
R
\
A

12

OCTOBER

You

The question is, have you ever regretted going along with others' ideas or demands? This is always a bit of a push-pull for those born under the sign of Libra, because on one hand, you know very much what you think, but on the other hand, you are a team player.

It's like a game for you—sort of like tennis, or even politics, where you have to work with others. It is interesting to note that many Libra politicians use this ploy. They will get involved, but then they will do something that you may do naturally, that is, say the minimum and watch what is going on.

This is something you can do, and in certain situations, it is something you're encouraged to do—to watch, to learn about the actual situation and the individuals involved before you even begin to commit.

True, you may be under pressure from others to speak up. This has happened in the past, and it is likely to happen again. The skill is in figuring out the right thing to say—being able to stand back long enough from the situation, first to decide what your own priorities are, and then to ensure that you know enough about the situation and the people involved to decide what's in your best interest. Do that and not only will you be making a wise move, you will be making the most of the situation in question.

You and others

There is an old phrase that says to keep those close, close to you, to trust them and them alone. However, every once in a while, you venture into new territory, getting acquainted with individuals who have some kind of exotic charm and they become your fascination, your priority. Think carefully, because at times, that charm can be somewhat undermining.

Health and well-being

The message for you is to relax. That may seem easy to do, but as an air sign, while you may appear to be relaxing—that is, not moving around much—at the same time your mind is going overtime. Being able to slow down mentally is quite a challenge, but it is an important one and one that, for you as a Libra, can be a source of discovery and joy.

Goals and challenges

In standing up for others, you're standing up for something you believe in. It may be that those closest need help, or it may simply be that you're standing up for something you believe in. You needn't make an issue of it. Just quietly express your views, knowing that you're speaking not only for others, but for yourself.

THIS DAY FOR EVERYONE

It's tempting to stand your ground against somebody who has been pushy and in ways that make you uncomfortable. While their manner may make you uncomfortable, their intentions are good, and once you overcome that irritation, you'll realize that, actually, they are very good company.

GIFTS Steady, Understanding, Doting

CHALLENGES Scheming, Obscure, Standoffish

NUMBER 5

(1+3) + (1+0) = 5

I refuse to listen when others complain that I am not making them happy

L
\
I
/
B
\
R
\
A

13

OCTOBER

You

As a Libra, you were born under the sign that symbolizes harmony. That's true, but at the same time, you can get so caught up in disharmony, if not clashes, that you forget about that harmony—and those clashes, those difficulties, those facts that just don't fit together, can become almost an obsession.

Even more, there are certain individuals who thrive on that and they may draw you into a kind of relationship that is powerful for you, for the Libra side of your nature, yet is ultimately undermining.

You like the passion. However, the more you learn, the more you will realize that that variety of passion actually serves others, not you. More than that, it throws you off balance. Yet disentangling yourself can be difficult, simply because you will worry that you'll upset others, which is a very Libra concern.

The trick to this, whether it's a minor issue or something more major—or even something that you've committed to—is simply to walk away.

You can give an explanation if you want—or not. Those who you're walking away from will fully understand why you are doing that. And even more than that, they'll respect you for looking after your interests. That, alone, is the most important thing—deciding what is good for you and acting in that manner.

You and others

As a rational Libra, there is a part of you that can be sensible, but you can also be so swept away by feelings about a situation or an individual that you take things too much to heart and don't even pause to think about the rational side of that commitment. The lesson is to think first, and commit later.

Health and well-being

If you are being advised to eat differently, to exercise differently, to sleep differently, that's probably good, but actually there is one thing that you can do, particularly if you're stressed. That is to breathe—and to breathe deeply. Do that and you'll be amazed how much better you feel about what's going on in your life.

Goals and challenges

Every now and again it is important to pause and consider whether what you're putting first is actually your own interest, or others'. While there is nothing wrong with supporting those around you in their pursuits, consider whether their dramas are truly worthwhile or actually are pointless. This may seem cruel, but acknowledging that will then free you to focus on something that is worth your while.

THIS DAY FOR EVERYONE

On rare occasions, an idea or offer appears almost magically. While there's no question that it's worth pursuing, it would involve a serious change, not only in some element of your life, but also in your attitude about one particular activity or pursuit. Still, it is worth overcoming those objections.

GIFTS Reliable, Adoring, Cordial

NUMBER 6

CHALLENGES Indecisive, Uncooperative, Ambiguous

$(1+4) + (1+0) = 6$

There are many ways to raise contentious issues. Some seem like a compliment

L
\
I
/
B
\
R
\
A

14

OCTOBER

You

When those around you ask for your help or assistance, you will usually extend it right away, then pause and think about whether there's something you can really do that is helpful. Ironically, certain individuals are so good at drawing you in that, before you even know it, you are part of what might be termed their mission, when actually what they are doing is entirely for their own interest and not only won't help others, it may even be undermining them.

The trick for you as a Libra is to stop and question this. And this is a difficult part: to walk away from the situation without discussing it with the individuals in question. That may seem dishonest, but it is actually the only way to deal with this. Once you have learned it, it is an vital skill to make part of your life.

While relationships are important, individuals who are manipulative in that way must be recognized—and dealt with in precisely that manner. This, then, is about doing something that is essential for you, which is putting yourself first.

It sounds very "new age" to say it is about loving yourself, but it is about exactly that. It may take a while for you to recognize walking away from situations is about loving yourself, but if ever that were the case, it is now.

You and others

The message for you is to choose your friends carefully. That may sound silly, but as you know, in the past, you have aligned with certain individuals who seem friendly or who you feel you are able to help, only to discover that they are in some way devouring your time, your money, or even endangering your heart. Recognizing that can be challenging, but it is one of the most important gifts of all.

Health and well-being

It is very chic these days to follow a rather strict regimen. However, for you as a Libra and somebody ruled by Venus, the planet of beauty, the message is to eat wisely and well. You need treats, and your Libra nature that craves balance will tell you exactly how much of those treats you need and when.

Goals and challenges

For some people, no matter how much you do, for them it isn't enough. Help them, give them money or support or make introductions, and they'll want more but show no gratitude. The trick? Do nothing, say a silent "Thank you" to them for teaching you an important lesson, then quietly but firmly walk away.

THIS DAY FOR EVERYONE

Facts may be facts, but this is one of those times during which twists and turns and circumstances will raise questions about both existing arrangements and the plans you're making. Bear in mind that the changes you're facing are ongoing, which means that any decisions must be flexible.

GIFTS Amiable, Diplomatic, Dedicated

CHALLENGES Unavailable, Manipulative, Touchy

NUMBER 7

(1+5) + (1+0) = 7

Certain individuals are intimidating, but you can outwit them with kindness

L
\
I
/
B
\
R
\
A

You

Certain individuals live their lives in their own self-created castle and they think that you should feel honored if they decide to share their fantasy existence with you. Be wary of this, though, because this fantasy, this game, is very seductive. For you as a Libra, as an air sign and somebody who is imaginative, you can be drawn into their fantasy world while gradually they make it a real world, and they even begin to exercise some control over you.

This variety of seduction is appealing to your Libra nature, partly because perhaps it allows you to escape from certain rather dull and more mundane situations you are facing in your everyday life.

Yet, if you can manage to take a look at this castle of theirs and say, "That's a romantic vision, but my everyday life offers me rewards of a more lasting nature," then you will be able to look at that castle and say, "Thank you for those insights. However, I am going over here to my everyday dilemmas and my everyday joys and my everyday friends. And I'm going to appreciate them all the more because of the rather toxic fantasies you have just exposed me to."

Then, as you live out your days and your weeks, you will be very thankful for having had that brief but illuminating adventure.

You and others

The theme for you is to learn who is fortunate and who is trustworthy. That may seem strange, but actually those individuals who are trustworthy and fortunate don't always advertise it; they just live a life that may be very simple, but it's happy. Notice that and spend time with those individuals. This is a variety of contagion that is a welcome one.

Health and well-being

Doubt is an important emotion. Sometimes people are criticized for it because they are hesitant, but often that hesitation is an invitation to explore, to gather information, and sometimes if you do, then you will proceed. But in other situations, that doubt is telling you that you need to learn something. It may be that it is either time to back off or possibly even time to say a firm "No."

Goals and challenges

We all have to deal with challenges, to face what is often an uphill climb, but in every case, doing it is an achievement. The important thing for you is to recognize that and not allow others to pretend that what you achieve is in any way due to their inspiration. What you've done is 100 percent yours.

15

OCTOBER

The last thing you are inclined to do is explain why you're so cautious about certain matters and protective of certain individuals. You tend to think that if others are unable to see what's obvious to you, they will never understand. Actually, you've been so discreet, you've left everybody mystified.

GIFTS Constant, Rational, Agreeable

CHALLENGES Ambivalent, Distant, Wishy-washy

NUMBER 8

$(1+6) + (1+0) = 8$

While joy comes in many forms, being happy with my own company is best

L
\
I
/
B
\
R
\
A

16

OCTOBER

You

As a Libra, as you well know, you are ruled by balance, the symbol of the scales, and while it looks static when you see a picture, by nature it swings; that is, the balance is never stable.

Yet at the same time, you tend to feel that if you can just get things organized, it will indeed be unchanging. Not only is that impossible, it actually means that you struggle with something that is preventing you from venturing into new territory and from taking chances in a way that won't just be interesting, it will add to your life.

It is preventing you from taking advantage of the swings that are part of being a Libra. It is preventing you from taking advantage of meeting new people and doing things that may be a little bit risky, but will always benefit you. And as you do that, it means you will be meeting new people and adding to your experience.

As an air sign, sometimes you figure things out in your head, but you don't always connect the experiences you've had with what you have envisioned.

This process of plunging into things carefully but still taking chances, will lead to experiences that in every case will not only add to your life, they will add to perhaps your passions, your joy, and possibly even your pocketbook.

You and others

One of the most important lessons for you is to note those around you who seem to enjoy life's shifts. While many will complain about even a minor change, others will detail the twists and turns in their own lives and how they're benefiting from them with enthusiasm. Make these individuals your best friends, if not your colleagues or your partners.

Health and well-being

Tempting as it is to search for a regimen you will follow, it can be difficult for you as an easily distracted air sign. The actual point of taking care of yourself is to be flexible. In fact, it could be said that any regimen is unhealthy, because it means you're not aware of what you're doing. If you're learning something new, then not only will it be interesting, you will be broadening your horizons in every way.

Goals and challenges

For you, it is good to rethink things regularly, because it may be that you could do something better. You could add something to it, or it may be there is actually something else you should be doing. Those rethinks aren't just a good idea, they add a new vitality to your life, to your plans, and to your future.

THIS DAY FOR EVERYONE

Some disagreements blow in like a fierce storm but are resolved swiftly and then forgotten. Those you are currently facing, and there could be several, will seem unimportant, but as the time passes and you learn more, you will realize just how vital it is you deal with them soon and in depth.

GIFTS Uniting, Thoughtful, Congenial

CHALLENGES Detached, Hesitant, Meddling

NUMBER 9

(1+7) + (1+0) = 9

Others don't have to agree with my feelings

L
\
I
/
B
\
R
\
A

17

OCTOBER

You

One of your lessons in life needs to be borrowed from the sign next to yours, Virgo, which is all about practicality and being down to earth. Of course, some of this is a bit dull for you as a Libra, because, as an air sign, you're very thoughtful and in fact, a bit of a visionary. Yet every once in a while, it is important to borrow two components of Virgo's nature.

One is their perfectionism and the other is their practicality. If you borrow these, then, when you run into difficulties or you can't seem to weigh whether something is worth pursuing, you will use that method of examining things that may be dull and rather overly practical from your point of view, but it will also enable you to make plans that are based on simple, rather uninteresting yet solid facts. And once you do that, then you won't actually have to think too much more about it.

Borrowing these characteristics will then give you a new freedom to fly in a way that is wonderful for you as a Libra, because in doing that, you have created a firm foundation for what you are thinking about.

This may seem strange to you—and feel a bit odd, and possibly even a bit dull—until you realize just how much you've accomplished. It's a skill that, once learned, will serve you well and in many settings.

You and others

Getting things organized is great and—while by no means as a Libra are you fixed in your habits—when something works, you dislike having to rethink things. Yet the message for you is to embrace change with enthusiasm, by borrowing some of the practicality of your neighboring sign Virgo. Once you do, you'll discover how much you can achieve with ease.

Health and well-being

The outer world is very much a theme for you when it has to do with your physical well-being and how you'll benefit. But when you combine this with the inner world of your ideas as well as your more spiritual side, you will find you have a full circle, a globe, which is glowing with activities both satisfying and worthwhile.

Goals and challenges

It is important that you consider whose goals you are pursuing, because, as a Libra, it's easy to get caught up with others' objectives and even their passions. You understand them and you may even want to support them. Yet the question is, what's happening to your own passions? Every once in a while, you need to review whose passions are number one.

I find that giving love is actually easier than receiving it

L
\
I
/
B
\
R
\
A

18

OCTOBER

You

Every once in a while it is easy to get caught in a vision of that is all about how-to goals: how to plant a garden, how to cook. There are rules about all of this and while those are reassuring, for you as a Libra, it can actually be restrictive.

It is true that certain plants benefit from pruning, and obviously certain meals benefit from being cooked in a particular way, but when it comes to your life, it's vital to ignore those rules and trust another part of your nature. This has to do with the wisdom that comes with being a Libra and somebody ruled by Venus, the planet of beauty and charm, but also of abundance.

This means ignoring those rules and trusting what your heart and your soul say, and even more, trusting your instincts and moving past those formulas.

Once you do that, the odds are good that you'll spot something that inspires you, or recognize what you are already doing is amazing. Yet you've been ignoring it because it doesn't seem exciting enough—because all those things you've been hearing about seem more promising. But they are promising for other people, whereas for you, the trick is to spot what lifts your spirits, then commit to it with a wholeheartedness that allows you to turn those ideas into miracles.

You and others

As a clever Libra you're good at figuring things out, but there are certain individuals whose charisma enables them to seduce people into following them just because they're so exciting. That may be the case, but as a Libra, what appeals to you personally is more important every day.

Health and well-being

When you feel full of energy and optimism, if others begin to prescribe things for you because they think you should have a different variety of energy, thank them very much. Then follow what your own heart, soul, and body tell you. There is no better reference for what's in your best interest than you and you alone.

Goals and challenges

We all talk about what we're doing, about what excites us and about our plans, but when did you last think whether what you're passionate about still matters to you? When did you last dismiss something that seemed rather exciting because you were so wound up in passions from the past? There is no one answer, but these are questions that need to be asked regularly—and dealt with in depth.

THIS DAY FOR EVERYONE

There is a fine line between sidestepping troublesome issues and being dishonest. Obviously, you would prefer to avoid clashes. However, consider this—the insights that result from talking over those tricky situations frankly will more than justify the risk of having to live through and deal with dramas.

Whether it is personal or anonymous, kindness can be life-changing

You

As a Libra, the idea of making a final plan is very appealing. There are two reasons for this. First, as you will know, you have a tendency to debate certain ideas back and forth, sometimes for a very long time, until suddenly it all falls into place. But at the same time you want things to be right. You hate it if you set out to achieve a goal and then discover that you forgot something.

However, there is another approach, and that is to make final plans, but to make them with the knowledge that, with each day, life changes. In fact, with each breath you change, so the idea of anything being final is bizarre.

If you understand that, then you will also understand that with each breath, you alter your chemistry. The world you're living in and what you're doing, and your ideas and even your mind, evolve moment to moment.

This idea of things being final may not make sense. Instead, think of the best option for the moment. Even more than that, this allows you to explore what comes your way so that if you do have some sort of final plan, that doesn't mean you can't explore something else. In fact, that final plan and your new plan may even meet and turn into something amazing. Take that approach and you will make the best of each month, each week, each day, and each hour.

You and others

As a Libra, relationships are important to you, and while you can focus on achieving an accord, it is also important to recognize that the people in your world are different. Inevitably, the links with each of them will differ as well, and that is your lesson: to realize that while some alliances will be very proper, others will be rather rock 'n' roll.

Health and well-being

The debate about what to eat has become a bit of a trend—it is something that becomes a conversation when no one else has anything else to talk about. Yet it's also important because you will listen to others' advice and take it, where actually what is best for you to do is what you feel is right on the day.

Goals and challenges

Occasionally, people want to talk about the biggest goal and the most potential in any situation. While that is appealing to you, you also have a sense of proportion and while biggest is impressive, it's not always best. You don't need to discuss this with others. When you're deciding that what you are going to do with your life, ensure that goal suits you perfectly.

L
\
I
/
B
\
R
\
A

19

OCTOBER

What began as a minor misunderstanding has turned into a seriously complicated mix-up. Tempting as it is to talk issues through now and all at once, it's not that simple. The actual problems go back a long way and will require considerable time and patience to untangle and put to rest.

Mother Nature deserves our love, big time

L
\
I
/
B
\
R
\
A

20

OCTOBER

You

Discussing ideas and plans with others is important, but at the same time it can be confusing. As a Libra and an air sign, what seems your best plan one day isn't the next. Yet, if you chat with others, they'll say, "Oh, but before you said that," and then you'll have to explain to them why changes occurred.

The answer to this is to tell others the minimum. As a Libra, you're not secretive by nature, but if there is a plan you are working on that hasn't yet been dealt with, you might want to think carefully about who you mention it to, especially those individuals who were simply asking because they would be interested.

This is very much about Venus, which isn't just the planet of relationships, but also has to do with the wise use of your resources. In every case, pause and think about whether those plans, or even those passions, are worth discussing with others, and whether you actually care about what they have to say.

Once you are looking at your life from that angle, then you'll begin to realize how important your own values, your own vision, and your own passions are. And in doing that, instead of even caring what other people have to say, you will care most of all about those passions being lit up by your conviction that you are doing the right thing.

You and others

From time to time, everybody clashes with those around them, where someone complains about what they are doing, and you think you could do it better. If so, offer to do it. Similarly, if they try to tell you how to do things, let them give it a try. This will reveal the difference between discussion and reality.

Health and well-being

The discussion here is about a perfect formula: a perfect way to eat, to exercise, or even to live. Many Libras like to figure that out and stick with it forever. However, you're encouraged to try something new. Trying something out won't just be interesting, you'll also learn a lot about yourself.

Goals and challenges

The question is, why would you get involved in a challenge that doesn't interest you? Simply because you will learn from it. If everything you do is fascinating, then it is going to be a repeat performance of the past. Accepting a challenge or going someplace you're not interested in may not work out and you may want to escape right away, which is just fine. Yet when you do escape, you will escape with the knowledge of the experiences you've had.

THIS DAY FOR EVERYONE

For ages you've sidestepped even acknowledging certain misunderstandings, mostly because you knew paying attention to them would lead to lengthy discussions, but now you have no choice. Unappealing as the idea of talking things through is, once you've begun, it will be a huge relief.

Anonymous love is love at its most genuine

L \ I / B \ R \ A

You

For you, Libra—and as somebody who is right next to the sign of Scorpio, you share a bit of that science, deep nature, and focus, and in fact, tendency for obsession that Scorpios have.

As a Libra, when you obsess about something, it is all in your head, because, of course, you are an air sign. But the Scorpio variety of obsession is deeper and more persistent, and also one that, when you are committed to it, is hard to get rid of.

On the other hand, what you learn when you're dealing with this kind of deeper, darker approach to life will be incredibly informative for you. This is the trick. It is to enjoy both sides of your nature, even if one seems a bit strange, odd, or overwhelming, but then it is rather like encountering an amazing scent, or having a meal that is so fragrant, simply the aroma alone it is exciting.

What you are learning now, from yourself and from sharing both sides of your nature—the rather careful measured Libra side and the passionate, if not overwhelming Scorpio side—won't just enhance your life and your wisdom, it will also enhance every day, getting up in the morning, in the middle of the day, and in the evening—and every hour you spend doing what you love with those you love.

You and others

As a Libra, you like to agree with others or absolutely disagree, whereas the idea of having a sort of truce is very strange to you. That's because you are ruled by balance—the scales. Yet this part of your nature is important because it understands not balance but simple passion, and the more you experience that passion, the more exciting life will be.

Health and well-being

There are lots of formulas for health and lots of diets to follow and exercises to do. Yet there is a whole other variety of treatment for health that comes from simple joy. That is, from knowing life's stories, and from breathing it in, whether it is from nature or a connection with something divine that has touched you. The more you are linked to that joy, the better.

Goals and challenges

You have a tendency to worry that if you get something wrong in the plan, then it is really a problem. But actually, life is a big experiment and if you take chances—whether it's ordering something you have never eaten, whether it's falling in love with somebody new, or whether it's a new plan—it's an experiment. And the experiment itself is bound to be profitable.

21

OCTOBER

Scorpio

Ruler Pluto
Element Water

Symbol The Scorpion
Flower Rhododendron

October 22–November 20

Scorpio Compelling by nature and style, as a Scorpio—whose symbol is your namesake, the scorpion—you beguile with your mystery as much as by what you say or do. Whatever your chosen field, your insights will be unique and your capacity for intimacy compelling—perhaps influenced by your ruler, Pluto, who reigns in the underworld. Your flower is rhododendron; your spices are peppers; and your plant, blackthorn. The mysterious opal mirrors your alluring secrets.

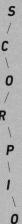

S / C / O / R / P / I / O

GIFTS Passionate, Thorough, Shrewd

CHALLENGES Obsessive, Vengeful, Severe

NUMBER 5

(2+2) + (1+0) = 5

Sometimes listening and saying nothing is the best option

You

If there is any theme for your birthday, it could be "endings and beginnings." That is because your birthday continues the winding up of one season (summer in the northern hemisphere and winter in the southern hemisphere) and the move into another: the beginning of fall in the northern hemisphere and spring in the southern hemisphere. But it is also about a battle between the ruler of the previous sign, Libra, which is Venus, and your own ruling planet, Pluto, or, indeed, Mars. In every case, this is about contrasts.

Still, as a Scorpio you prefer to live life with grace and clarity. When these challenges arise, you will tend to stick with the familiar rather than allow unsettling changes to confuse things. However, as you will increasingly realize, often those changes aren't mere changes. They are breakthroughs that are taking you in new directions. That is very much the theme for your birthday.

While the fixed sign side of your nature is a mark of stability—and it means you know what you can expect and what others will expect from you—the greatest expectation at the moment is your willingness to begin to explore, even if it means venturing into unfamiliar territory. Once you do, you'll not only know why, you will be glad you did.

22

OCTOBER

You and others

There have often been times when you have tried to avoid the ups and downs of life. Yet as you've lived more, you've found that ups are exciting while the downs help you understand the nature of your deepest feelings far better than you would've imagined possible—so much so that you may even begin to embrace them.

Health and well-being

An affection for a regimen is great, because whether it is how you eat or a form of exercise, it means you're taking care of yourself. Yet there is a problem if it's compulsory because you haven't included joy. This is the trick for you; find a way to add that and not only will you feel and look great, you will blossom in your deepest heart.

Goals and challenges

The question is whether it is worth setting higher goals and taking a risk that things won't work out. If you are in doubt about this, think back to when you faced a similar dilemma and went for it. You took a chance. And not only did you do well, you did better than you expected and had the bonus of having a tremendous feeling of victory. Take chances now and you will have the same benefits.

THIS DAY FOR EVERYONE

You have been battling certain individuals about important details, or so they seemed. Now that you're looking back, you are beginning to realize you were sidestepping the real issue. Deep down, you know what it is. The challenge is raising it. Once you do, everything else will be easy.

Being true to others can involve love or loyalty, or both

You

As a Scorpio, you admire those who are able to focus on their goals and stick to that. It's something you value. You're embarrassed by those who plunge into something without planning and who, as a result, suffer—or at least from your point of view they do.

Yet as you've discovered that watching those individuals, while they're floundering around and experimenting and making mistakes, they learn a lot. They learn things you wouldn't have learned had you been following that careful path. When you hang out with them, you learn things that benefit you, too.

In a way, you're both of these. One part of you wants to focus on a direct goal and achieve that without being distracted. Yet another part, the part that's an intuitive water sign, recognizes that the more willing you are to be what might be termed seduced into trying something new and to venturing into unfamiliar territory—whether it is personal, involving relationships, or your activities out in the world—the more you'll learn and the more you'll benefit from what you're doing.

Allowing yourself to grow in this way is one of the biggest challenges for you as a Scorpio. And as you actually begin to thrive as a green plant does in a garden, it will be one of your greatest joys.

You and others

All relationships, from family, friends, or even colleagues, involve a balance between people who are quite simply different, with a range of ideas about how things could be done. Your tendency is to want to correct them so they'll do things the way you know works. However, often they ignore you and have a far better way of doing things than you have ever thought of.

Health and well-being

You used to dislike eating certain foods because of their texture or flavor. Now you're beginning to realize that times have changed, you've changed, or perhaps even that food has changed. But it is also about what you do in elements of your life that you said long ago you would never enjoy. And now, suddenly you find yourself doing them and having a fabulous time.

Goals and challenges

There are a number of phrases that could follow the words "I've always wanted to…" but then haven't because you've found various excuses. This is the golden moment for you. The minute you transform those excuses into an opportunity, your life will become far more exciting today and each and every day.

23

OCTOBER

Somebody is determined to have things their way or you're facing tricky circumstances. You may be better off giving in for now, but conditionally, then negotiating later. Once the current tricky planetary setup has passed, you'll be in a better position to bargain and more likely to achieve your objectives.

GIFTS Intense, Loyal, Protective

NUMBER 7

CHALLENGES Distrustful, Hurtful, Destructive

$(2+4) + (1+0) = 7$

S
/
C
\
O
/
R
\
P
\
I
\
O

24

OCTOBER

One of life's skills is predicting the future based on the past

You

There are those who say that, as a Scorpio, you argue when changes are suggested. From your point of view, when you manage the conversation, if not manipulate it, it is because you know what you are willing to do and what you are not. When others suggest things you have no intention of doing, you will simply but politely change the subject.

However, what they're suggesting may be interesting—partly because you simply never paid attention to it before, or because their enthusiasm about those activities or ideas is contagious, and you're beginning to wonder if instead of sticking to your own views, you might actually benefit from trying things out.

This is a turning point for any Scorpio, and it is one that you will encounter again and again. Because Scorpio is what is termed a fixed sign, you are a creature of habit. Once you get into a habit, budging it is difficult.

This is why these breakthroughs are so important. They allow you not just to make changes, but to make discoveries—discoveries about the world around you, discoveries about the people around you, but probably most importantly, about yourself. You will embrace a new perspective on life around you and its possibilities—but most of all, what you personally can achieve, both now and in the future.

You and others

For you, micromanaging seems normal—simply watching what's going on and, if you see things veering in what appears to be the wrong direction, pulling them back. Yet as you are increasingly aware, that means doing things in the same old way again and again. And not only are you getting a little bit bored, you're realizing that there is a wide world of adventurous experiences waiting for you.

Health and well-being

The idea of a regimen is appealing, especially when it comes to taking care of yourself—how you eat, when you get up, when you exercise, and, even to a certain extent, what you think. However, it doesn't give you a lot of freedom. The more you realize you can have fun if you take chances and venture into new territory, the less appealing that regimen will be and the more appealing an adventurous life is.

Goals and challenges

You like to know where you stand. However, with the world and the people around you changing, it may be better to be a little less clear about your plans and a little more inquisitive, especially when the unexpected arises. It could be that what is least expected today becomes your best friend tomorrow.

THIS DAY FOR EVERYONE

Nobody would blame you for telling a particular individual how much of a nuisance their last-minute changes in plans are for you. Before you say anything, however, do a little investigation. You may well discover those changes weren't their fault and they're as unhappy about them as you are.

Accepting others' shortcomings isn't easy, but accepting mine is another matter

S
/
C
\
O
/
R
\
P
\
I
\
O

25

OCTOBER

You

As a Scorpio, you have a tender heart. You're a water sign, and water signs are more sensitive than others. Of course, you are ruled by the powerful Pluto, so you have a great deal of focus. Yet there are many Scorpios who work in areas that require tenderness—from being involved in fashion to actors, artists, and writers. Whether famous or not, a large portion of their nature is involved, not in following some objective achievement, but in expressing something more artistic.

That is a part of you, too, and it's an essential part of your nature. It is also vital to your relationships with others. It may be that not everyone understands this, which is what's tricky, because, of course, not everyone else is a water sign, and even those who are water signs don't always understand the importance of this soft side of life and of nature.

However, the more you understand it and the more you share it and discuss it with others, the deeper this will become. Not only will it become an important part of your life, it is something that will become an increasingly important part of the lives of those around you. In that sense, you will not only be improving your own existence, you'll be improving the existence and well-being of others and, even to a certain extent, the world.

You and others

Being open and vulnerable about feelings can have a cost. In certain situations, others will be grumpy or difficult, and you might regret having discussed things. That is, until the individual in question begins to tell you how much what you said to them meant, and you'll realize there are few things more powerful than talking about your feelings.

Health and well-being

We are all told stories in childhood about what is good for us and what isn't. Yet there are certain things you decide as an adult you didn't like. The time has come for you to dump all of those stories and decide what feels good to you, in terms of both what to eat and what to do, and to benefit from the joys that come with making those choices.

Goals and challenges

There are two kinds of goalposts that can be put up when it comes to goals and challenges. The kind you see in the playing field are planted firmly on the ground. They are the type that many people live with. However, as an intuitive water sign, it's vital to be aware that you could move your own goalposts, so that what is most important to you, whatever you do and achieve, brings you joy.

THIS DAY FOR EVERYONE

Sometimes obstacles are just difficult situations that need to be overcome. But what you are currently facing is an invitation to delve into and learn about an increasingly tricky matter. While the actual process might be challenging, what you discover will more than justify the effort required.

S
/
C
\
O
/
R
\
P
\
I
\
O

Often others misinterpret my silence as agreement when I meant "No"

26 OCTOBER

You

For you as a Scorpio, the line between what is private and spoken—that is, what you don't discuss and what you talk about easily—is very clear: or at least it is clear to you. However, that line actually moves from day to day and even from subject to subject and mood to mood. Yet at the same time, if you're feeling uptight or concerned, a part of you gets very grumpy and says, "Why would I talk about that to anybody else?"

There are those around you, though—it may be a family member, it may be a close friend, or it may be somebody you trust—who you will reveal more to than anybody else. Gradually, as a Scorpio, one of your journeys is being able to discuss these matters more openly with family and with friends, so they understand you better, but also so that you can begin to realize how long they've known and understood everything anyway.

This is the key to being a Scorpio among those who love you. While you think that what you're hiding are deep, dark secrets that nobody understands, the fact is they do. They are just being patient with you, because they've known you weren't ready to talk about it. The more swiftly you begin to discuss both concerns and your heartfelt passions, the more swiftly you will be able to enjoy time with those closest.

You and others

There are many different kinds of intimacy with others: not so much physical intimacy, although that is important, but how much you trust certain individuals. Just as the Moon goes from the sliver of the New Moon to the Full Moon and back to the sliver of the New Moon, so, too, your feelings of trust evolve.

Health and well-being

These days, there is constant discussion about what's good for you, food-wise. But how do you truly know what's good for you? Well, as a Scorpio and someone who is highly intuitive, you can probably ask your body how it feels when you eat something. That will tell you far more than anyone else ever could.

Goals and challenges

Setting goals and acting on them is important. There will be those who tell you that the minute you're clear about that goal, it is important to act on it, but a part of you as a Scorpio and a fixed sign tends to wait. But then sometimes you wait too long and the moment has passed. How do you know? The best answer is to think whether you would regret not plunging in right now. Usually that will result in you taking action right away.

THIS DAY FOR EVERYONE

Unsettling as recent events seemed at the time, you're beginning to recognize that they were breakthroughs. True, these weren't in the form you've anticipated and could take things in worryingly unexpected directions. Be patient. The more you explore and learn, the more optimistic you'll be.

Loving myself means being true to my desires, despite others' demands

S
/
C
\
O
/
R
\
P
\
I
\
O

You

You were born at the season of the year, if you're in the northern hemisphere, that is fall, and in the southern, the time of spring. In both cases, it is about nature making changes. For you as a Scorpio, this is important to understand, because often you feel responsible for organizing things. Yet when you observe nature, particularly if you have a garden, or even if you are in the grocery store and seeing what is available, you will realize that nature itself changes, and it changes what it offers. In the same way, you, too, are a creature of change.

You don't think of yourself that way. In fact, many Scorpios work hard to be consistent. Yet as a water sign, you are an individual with tides—tides of passion and tides of enthusiasm. Returning to that symbol of nature is not just about nature itself growing, but about what you use of nature, how you eat and what you enjoy.

When you walk in nature, each of these changes are important because the more aware you are of the way that nature around you evolves, the easier it will be for you to deal with the changes that come into your life: changes that might be unsettling initially, but which are beginning a new cycle that will ultimately bring you joy in new experiences and discovery.

You and others

As a Scorpio who tends to be rather private, the idea of discussing doubts is unappealing. True, if there is someone you trust, you may do that. However, the more you talk about these feelings, the more you realize these doubts that so worried you are actually very normal indeed.

Health and well-being

Getting out and about and doing something to feel good is wonderful. As a Scorpio and a fixed sign, you will also tend to stick with one thing until you get really good at it. While this is tempting, it is also a fantastic exercise of another sort to try something else, and then to try something else after that in order to exercise the muscle of growth and discovery.

Goals and challenges

In the past you dismissed certain objectives because you weren't quite sure you could achieve them—and as a Scorpio, you hate the idea of failing. Now, however, you've become more inquisitive and the situations in question seem far more available and accessible to you. Not only are they accessible to you, the potential for learning how to do them and overcoming those doubts is also more accessible. Take a chance and give them a try.

27

OCTOBER

Somebody has decided to point the blame for certain problems in your direction. Tempting as it is to hope everybody's well aware of the facts, you're urged to stand your ground. Mostly, this is about making it clear to the individual in question that you won't tolerate any such maneuvers.

S
/
C
\
O
/
R
\
P
\
I
\
O

Generosity comes from the heart, not the bank account

28

OCTOBER

You

For you as a Scorpio, the difficulty of hanging out with others is that there are things you want to share only with certain individuals. When those around you are asking questions, you will sidestep them, because you feel that either it is none of their business, or they won't understand where you're coming from.

Actually, they probably would understand. It's just that you are so careful about who you share things with that you don't want to let them know what's happening. Part of your journey as a Scorpio is to respect the sensitivity that is so much a part of your nature, but also to share the part that is very perceptive with those who will appreciate that.

Gradually, you will acquire a new viewpoint. It will remove many of those barriers to sharing things with others, but it will teach you to do something you never would have expected to be able to do with others, and that is to laugh—about the ironies of life, and about how concerned you were about being open. After that, you will find that there is an entirely new way of relating.

You may have to do it again and again in different ways with different individuals, but each time you do it, you'll recognize that it is a skill you have acquired and one that brings you a variety of intimacy and friendship you previously hadn't thought possible.

You and others

The question is, how much do you want to tell others? You don't realize how secretive you are until certain individuals ask perfectly ordinary questions that you regard as probing. If you're uncomfortable, discuss it with them. You will soon realize the reason they're asking is they simply want to know more about you.

Health and well-being

There are many formulas for health and well-being, a lot of which have to do with what you eat and the vitamins you take, and even the order in which you take them. It's true, feeling well is a skill. Once, people simply aged and fell apart. But nowadays it's about how you feel each day. For you, those feelings of well-being are perhaps the most important variety of vitamin you could take.

Goals and challenges

Once in a while, you probably make a list of your goals. If you don't actually put pen to paper, every Scorpio will still have those very much in mind. However, it is important to recognize that some of your goals may be relics from the past. So before you begin to write down goals for the future, let these go.

THIS DAY FOR EVERYONE

While you are easygoing about most situations, there are a few you have strong feelings about. Tempting as it is to take a strong stance, at least explore what has come up or what others are suggesting. At minimum, you'll learn something, but what rises could prove to be unexpectedly exciting.

Little is more rewarding than changing another's life, but discreetly

S / C \ O / R \ P \ I \ O

You

Every so often, you face a situation in which you realize you've completely lost your perspective and can't figure out what to do with certain tricky individuals. Then you realize the issue is your desire for control. True, as a Scorpio you were born under the sign that is perhaps the most analytical. Also, being ruled by the planet Pluto, which wants to get all the facts, you feel that if you can just learn enough, you will have control.

However, the irony is that the more you delve into life, the more you realize that no matter how many facts you gather, circumstances themselves will reshape the situations you're dealing with. But not only that, it will reshape your priorities as well. This doesn't just have to do with those rather tricky situations; it has to do with life itself and with those you care about, with close relationships, with your passions—your personal passions and passions involving others.

Once you recognize that, in many cases, you have very little control, you can set a goal or objective. But then you need to yield to it.

You will also find a new joy in being alive. With every breath, instead of worrying about things going your way, you will simply enjoy the fact that you're breathing—because you're living out yet another day, a day that is full of promise.

You and others

Occasionally, you struggle with a situation simply because you want the other individual to do what you want. The problem is that you haven't discussed it openly with them. While those born under the sign of Scorpio are brilliant at manipulating others, and can convince those around them to do what they want, often it is far easier if you simply ask.

Health and well-being

Many Scorpios have a physical health routine and a diet that they follow closely, often for years. However, you are always changing and evolving, and even though you believe you are being true to yourself—that is, to the values you keep—every cell is being replaced over time. So, too, must that perfect formula.

Goals and challenges

It is appealing to have a single clear goal. But why would you do that? The fact is, a big world is out there waiting for you to play with it, waiting for you to come and try out new things. That first step is the most challenging one, but once you've taken it, the world will embrace you with plenty of unexpected opportunities.

29

OCTOBER

I will always review every option before going back to the familiar

S
/
C
\
O
/
R
\
P
\
I
\
O

30

OCTOBER

You

One of the things you may or may not be aware of as a Scorpio is that in 1930, the ruling planet for your sign changed. For most of history, Scorpio has been said to be ruled by the planet Mars, the planet of action, the athlete, the warrior. Then Pluto was discovered, and it became the ruler of Scorpio.

As a planet it has been demoted, but it is still considered to be the ruler of your sign. And Pluto adds a different color to being a Scorpio because it's the planet of secrets; not just secrets as in things that aren't said, but also the kind of secrets that give you power. The Roman god Pluto was considered to be the ruler of the underworld. He knew what no other being could, whether it was a god or a human. Having that complex mythical background, you, of all the 12 signs, probably have the most rewarding journey of self-discovery, but also one in which you go deep within to understand yourself and the world, more than anybody else.

This freedom to explore is important. At times, others won't necessarily understand what you're experiencing, yet often will have a bit of Scorpio in their nature. And when you begin to talk about the depths of awareness that are so much a part of the journey that comes with being a Scorpio, you will find you have found a kindred spirit.

You and others

As a Scorpio, you have a greater understanding of others than most. Remember this, because when others complain about things where you see a solution immediately, you will have to explain it slowly to them. This will give you compassion, but it will also give you a depth of perception very few benefit from.

Health and well-being

As much as you would like to be given a single formula about how you eat and take care of yourself, it isn't that simple. Times change, you change, and even your body changes. Recognize that as an inquisitive and perceptive Scorpio, and you will enjoy the process of discovery that each of those changes takes you on.

Goals and challenges

It's worth reviewing your goals every now and then. Of course, circumstances change, but what you've learned and what excites you are also changing. And the more swiftly you grow, the more swiftly those intriguing developments will change. You have the gift of inquisitiveness when it comes to setting those goals, so not only will you discover a lot, you will enjoy the actual process of discovery as well.

THIS DAY FOR EVERYONE

Ordinarily, when facing an obstacle, you'll confront the situation. Only if that doesn't work will you ask for advice. Now, with Mercury accenting questions, you'll find that you're missing vital details. The more swiftly you seek the guidance of others, the faster you'll get things back on track.

Being willing to admit when I've missed something important isn't just wise, it's vital

S
/
C
\
O
/
R
\
P
\
I
\
O

31

OCTOBER

You

The fact that your birthday is on Halloween, or All Hallows' Eve, the day before the Day of the Spirits, means that you benefit from an awareness of the two worlds: of the everyday world—something most Scorpios are good at handling—but also the world, not merely of spirits of the Halloween sense, but our inner world, our own spirit, our own nature. And finding a balance between this is so important, especially because we're in a period during which there is an emphasis on the practical and scientific side of life, your coruler is Mars, the planet of action.

You dislike hanging around too long and hearing people talk when you could simply go out and gather facts. All of these sides of your nature come together to turn into someone— it's you—who is inquisitive and enjoys discovery. These discoveries aren't necessarily about the world around you, though you could go traveling. They are also about what makes us tick as human beings, what makes us feel what we feel, what brings us both anxiety and joy.

For many Scorpios, that is an important part of your life and journey, especially for someone born on October 31st. Recognize the privilege that is and how much you've learned from it. Not only will you be fascinated by each day, you will enjoy it as well.

You and others

While you benefit from a fascination with the complexity of life, not everyone does. Certain individuals, even those you are close to, are unwilling to talk about those ideas, and are sometimes even spooked by them, while others enjoy going on and on about it. They will be the ones you want to talk to most. The others you'll leave for times when you are talking about other matters.

Health and well-being

As a Scorpio, you are strong, but as a water sign, you can be influenced by the mood of others and your own moods. So it's important to look after yourself physically, but also to undertake activities such as yoga, or perhaps one of the Chinese martial arts that builds your energy, well-being, and resilience.

Goals and challenges

It is rare that anybody thinks that what they're doing is in the hands of the gods. And it isn't necessarily literal. But sometimes it is worth declaring what you'd like to do, standing back, and seeing what the gods deliver to you. For you, as a Scorpio, who's usually out there making things happen, standing back and seeing what comes your way could be exciting.

THIS DAY FOR EVERYONE

For years, you have worked hard to turn one particularly promising idea into a plan and hopefully a lasting arrangement, but not only are things not going well, those plans are falling apart. Don't worry. Let them go. Something is already on the horizon that will be far less of a struggle.

GIFTS Seductive, Intense, Committed

CHALLENGES Distrustful, Spiteful, Grim

NUMBER 3

(0+1) + (1+1) = 3

I've learned how dangerous saying "I'll try" is. Either I commit or I forget it

You

Being born on November 1st, particularly if it's in the northern hemisphere, you are looking at matters of light and dark, perhaps in the world around you, the shorter days and the longer nights. But also, this is light and dark in the terms of your own nature. As a Scorpio and somebody ruled by the planet Pluto, part of you understands that elements of life either can't be explained, or you need to step back and allow the power of nature to take over.

Yet at the same time, part of you wants to ensure that things go in the direction you want, and this is part of the battle of being a Scorpio. At the same time, however, it is crucial for you to stand back and recognize that often what you regard a ideal may not be in the best interests of you or the world around you, those who you care about, or perhaps a project.

It may be that you are being taken on a journey of discovery. What you encounter or learn as a result of that journey will benefit you in wonderful ways, will broaden your horizons, and may even help explore that dark. And that is very much part of this, because you'll realize that by allowing yourself to be taken on that path through the darkness, you'll get a different kind of light: the kind that will illuminate your life, now and throughout the years to come.

You and others

People say you're perceptive, and increasingly, you realize how true that is, that there are certain things you notice that others don't. And that capacity to spot more than others means that often, you will not only be explaining things to certain individuals, you will become their defender or their guide.

Health and well-being

There is a portion of you that feels like if you can figure out what you should do, that is, how you should eat and how you should work out. Everything will be fine. However, ups and downs are normal—just as there is day and night. Your own energy will have its surges, and times when you need to be still. The most important thing is to honor those cycles.

Goals and challenges

When you set goals, they are almost set in stone, because that's your nature. Has it ever occurred to you that if those goals aren't working out, or in fact, if the circumstances in which they're set are shifting, it's fine to change them, and to change them midstream, or even to dump them? Give that some thought, because every once in a while, it will be the best-possible strategy.

THIS DAY FOR EVERYONE

Sometimes mistakes are a nuisance, but often they're minor, and dealing with them requires little thought. While those you are currently facing are more complex, what you learn in the process of untangling them will answer questions or allow you to delve into issues you've been wrestling with for ages.

GIFTS Masterful, Intuitive, Keen

CHALLENGES Malicious, Envious, Hostile

NUMBER 4

$(0+2) + (1+1) = 4$

Truth is absolute. But that doesn't mean I have to tell everybody everything

You

As a Scorpio, you have tender sides. You're a water sign, and of all the water signs—Cancer, Scorpio, and Pisces—you are perhaps the most perceptive. This gives you a nature that is able to notice much more than others. And in fact, many of those born under your sign use elements of it. They may be artists. They may be performers. They may write. While some do it professionally, others do it simply as a way to use that intuitive part of your nature. But it's also a part that relates deeply to others, to those who also have a deeper and more intuitive side. You also connect with those who have no idea about their own feelings, and can be a friend, a guide, and in some cases, a sort of guru to those individuals.

What is most important for you is to exercise what might be termed your imaginative or your creative muscle, which is allowing that part of you that is a visionary to grow so you can experience it deeply. Not just in helping others, although that can be very rewarding, but to do it in a way that is yours and yours alone.

If it involves creating something, perfect. If it involves others, also perfect. But the point of this is to recognize that whether it's on your own or with others, it us a very personal journey that is dictated not only by your needs, but also your joys.

You and others

There is a question that's vital for you go ask: Who do you trust? Also, which individuals do you trust with your feelings? Sometimes you may feel a connection with somebody, but that doesn't mean they should be honored with the trust of your deepest feelings. Think carefully.

Health and well-being

These days, we pay attention to what we eat, and to exercise. But not as much attention is paid to what kinds of thoughts we put into our minds, or what kind of spiritual energy we hang out with. There tends to be an emphasis on science, yet the less material, more intuitive side of you as a Scorpio is just as important, and one that is essential you pay attention to.

Goals and challenges

Have the goals and challenges you're facing truly been chosen by you, or are they the result of the thinking of others? It may well be that those individuals have your best interest at heart, and also are highly intuitive, or it could be that they are simply telling you to do what they would have done. This is an important question, one for you to reflect on now and often in the future.

02

NOVEMBER

THIS DAY FOR EVERYONE

Nobody would blame you for taking offense at the brusque attitude of one particular individual. The real problem is, you are unaware of the pressure they're contending with. Ask if there is another way of approaching this matter. The odds are good that you'll receive a positive response.

**S
/
C
\
O
/
R
\
P
\
I
\
O**

Being lovingly faithful to others is important. Staying faithful to myself is essential

03

NOVEMBER

You

There are two sides to every Scorpio. Basically, there are the focused Scorpios, who are ruled by Pluto and try to be invulnerable. They may even be fighters in whatever arena they're in, as the influence of your original ruling planet, Mars, the warrior, comes in: you will stand up to whatever it is you feel is important.

Yet there is a more vulnerable side to your nature. And even if you are one of those warrior types, there's a portion that is sensitive and also intuitive, that understands what those who are not as strong as you are facing. And at times you may feel that vulnerability.

This is the important thing for you to understand, because when you allow yourself to feel that vulnerability, you also incorporate it into your own being. This means that you understand others better. But when you are close to somebody, it makes them feel comfortable, because they are aware that you know and understand how vulnerable they are.

It may sound strange that the stronger you are, the more vulnerable you're able to be. But this is one of the great paradoxes of being a Scorpio and a water sign in a period during which force is so overwhelmingly favored. The deeper you go, and the more you understand yourself, the stronger you will be.

You and others

Not everybody understands sensitivity of any kind. And because many people learn to focus on their minds over their feelings, they may not even know if they're happy or not. Be aware of that, and if you're talking to somebody who seems to have absolutely no idea what they're feeling, make a careful decision about how much you will discuss with them.

Health and well-being

Physical well-being has to do with having a strong body and eating well. But it's also having a regimen that builds up your sense of balance, that is, your inner being—what some might call your spine. There are many Eastern kinds of training, from yoga to Chinese martial arts, that help, and if you choose one, you will realize how vital it is for someone of your nature.

Goals and challenges

In a culture where everyone is encouraged to do their best, it can be as important to aim low. As a Scorpio, this may seem strange, but giving yourself the gift of not having too much pressure—at least at certain times of your life—also gives you an opportunity to decide if what you are pursuing is what you really want in your life.

THIS DAY FOR EVERYONE

Others are saying you're being stubborn. But from your point of view, certain changes are unrealistic. This is one of those tricky times when it's a matter of sticking with what you believe is best, or relying on those you trust. In this case, go for the latter. Others really do know better than you.

GIFTS Perceptive, Loyal, Passionate

NUMBER 6

CHALLENGES Compulsive, Forbidding, Leery

(0+4) + (1+1) = 6

Sometimes silence is a greater kindness than saying what I think

S
/
C
\
O
/
R
\
P
\
I
\
O

04

NOVEMBER

You

These days, everybody is encouraged to plan ahead. And in fact, it's a good idea, especially for impulsive types—maybe the fire signs Aries and Leo and Sagittarius. But for somebody who thinks things through, and who also will consider a plan carefully, make it, and then stick with it, being told that you need to plan ahead is unnecessary. If anything, what you need is the strength and the courage to change plans when things aren't working. And that can be very challenging indeed. In fact, you can spend so much time debating changes that the opportunity to make those changes vanishes.

And this is where it is important that you do something that is difficult for you, which is put yourself first. One of your excuses for not changing plans is that it will be unsettling for those around you.

However, changes of the type you will often make are a great gift for you and others, simply because, instead of being impulsive, you will have thought everything through so carefully that you and others will benefit from that journey.

In fact, if you recognize that, when the idea of making those changes arises, you're not only encouraged to explore it, you are encouraged to say yes first, then to think of the details later.

You and others

When it comes to making changes, those around you are well aware that you will think them through. They will often wait for you to make decisions so they can benefit from your wisdom. You may not realize how important this is. Your capacity to analyze things and to be visionary at the same time is an extraordinary gift.

Health and well-being

You have a capacity to be too disciplined. If so, life can become a bit joyless, because taking care of yourself becomes a strict regimen. This becomes a pain to others who would love to do something spontaneous, but because you're following your regimen, you can't. The trick? Take a break from time to time. You can go back to it if you decide to.

Goals and challenges

Thinking about how to overcome obstacles is important for you, but if you spend too much time thinking about it, you may never do it. Simply plunge into something new in a way that could be considered to be "un-Scorpio." Then not only will those obstacles vanish, you'll find yourself involved in something as exciting as it is thrilling.

S
/
C
\
O
/
R
\
P
\
I
\
O

05

NOVEMBER

Those who know truly what love is don't try to change us

You

It's rare that you are unaware of what's going on. If so, it is probably because you're ending one cycle and beginning another. This is something you don't often sense, because as a Scorpio and one of the fixed signs of the zodiac—those in the middle of each season— once you're into a plan, you're really into it. And you can tend to have tunnel vision.

Yet occasionally there is a need for things to change. A new cycle is beginning. And the trick for you is to recognize the presence of that new cycle—not so that you can plunge into it, but so you can begin to make adjustments from the old plan and explore the new one and the world involved.

When you're able to do that, not only will you begin to enjoy this process of change and discovery, it will also be helpful, and might even be fun. Better than that, you will get other people involved. And knowing that you're sharing this process, you will learn together and figure out ways to let go of the past.

This has to do with every area of your life. As much as you would like to think of yourself as being a fixed sign, as living a stable life, and having very little change, everybody is in the midst of a cycle of change constantly. The more you recognize that process, and the more you involve yourself with it, the more you'll enjoy it.

You and others

Certain individuals are team players. And once you know who those individuals are in your life, they will be your best friends when it comes to the changes that flow through life— something that you as a Scorpio don't always recognize. Make them your affiliates, your coaches, and often your best friends. Do that, and indeed, as you approach those changes, you will not only survive them, you will enjoy them.

Health and well-being

While you may try to eat right, and do some kind of physical movement, it's even more important to stop. Not as in laying around on the sofa and possibly watching television. It means stilling your mind, and simply being— staring out at a sunrise or sunset, breathing the air, and allowing life to come to you.

Goals and challenges

In modern life, we're taught to think of things in a very scientific way, and that when they're organized, events will proceed as they are intended to. However, life is based on cycles, and if you look at the heavens and, certainly, the cycle of the Moon, you will realize that the more you honor those cycles, the easier life will be.

THIS DAY FOR EVERYONE

Some time ago, you sidestepped even mentioning certain facts or issues, mostly because they are of little significance. But circumstances have changed, and now these matters are of considerable importance. Waste no time figuring out an explanation. Just inform those who need to know right away.

The heart's moods are infinite—but the committed heart never changes

You

One of your greatest gifts as a Scorpio is your capacity to experience joy in what others are experiencing and how they're developing. In some cases, you'll be doing that together, which is even better. And this draws you closer, which is something that is important for you, as a sensitive and intuitive water sign.

However, it is also important to recognize that that closeness won't last: not because there's anything wrong, but because each of you, and each individual in the world, in fact, lives at their own unique rhythm.

There will, however, be other forms of closeness, because when you respect that rhythm, you are able to enjoy watching others grow at their own rate. You are able to observe yourself, and enjoy the rate at which you're developing. You're also learning about different varieties of closeness, and the different varieties of trust that come with this process of growth and development.

Sometimes it really is all about what you are doing. Sometimes it has to do with an emotional or even a romantic connection. But in every case, it's about doing something that is little discussed or noticed in the world today, and that is, honoring the rhythm of life for each of us as human beings. We are all unique, and we all care deeply, and we all connect, but we all do so at our own pace.

You and others

That ideal of being close to somebody, and feeling everything together, is very romantic. And it is peppered throughout poetry, movies, and plays. Yet, it is an ideal, and an unlikely one. Even twins, born with the same genetic programming, live life at different paces, simply because they have individual brains. And this is what keeps things interesting, because if you could predict what everyone would do all the time, life would be fairly dull.

Health and well-being

Vitamins and food are important. However, what is often forgotten is your mood. This is important because it influences how you digest food. If you're in a bad mood or uptight, you don't digest things as well. But your state of mind is important. Pay attention to that, whatever you're eating, and your efforts will pay off.

Goals and challenges

The question is whether what you are doing will be rewarding. Are you sure what you're aiming for will be make you happy? Of course, you can't always tell. Do others believe that you will? There is nothing that proves that will be the case, but your reaction is 100 percent up to you.

Tedious as discussing tricky issues in detail may be, you really have no choice. Once you begin reviewing the actual situation, you will realize that, first, you need to update your own facts. This could so alter your perspective that you'll rethink your views—and in turn, what you have to say to others.

Putting myself and my interests first may be wise, but can confuse others

S
/
C
\
O
/
R
\
P
\
I
\
O

07

NOVEMBER

You

Passion is very much part of your nature as a Scorpio. That passion, of course, has to do with individuals, but it's also about your approach to life in general. You may notice that those around you rarely care much at all. That passion seems unique to you and possibly those who aren't Scorpios, but who have a bit of your sign in their nature. This influences things like relationships, or creative pursuits, yet it also it has to do with your everyday life.

You can be passionate about a job, a particular kind of exercise, about learning to cook, or gardening. It is essential for you, but not everybody feels that way. And the most important thing for you to recognize is that if somebody feels a bit lukewarm about something yet shows interest, they may be interested in their way. Just because they're not showing the passion that you have, it may simply be because they are a different person. And the more you learn about them, the better you will understand what makes them tick.

This journey of understanding how others are may seem a crazy one, but at the same time, you will learn what might be termed the human language: that is, how to deal with those whose way of living is very different, yet who bring something wonderful to life—just like you do.

You and others

An important way to learn about life is to learn from your experiences. And hopefully you will learn from them and won't repeat them. Instead, you may want to take chances with people and in situations that are completely unfamiliar and an adventure—yet will, for sure, prove to be an education.

Health and well-being

Many people take how you live, eat, and exercise very seriously, and it is a good idea to know what nourishes you. But there is another approach to this—to do things for fun, especially when it comes to exercise. You can adopt some kind of dancing that is so exciting and so bizarre, it can only be fun.

Goals and challenges

When you run across something that brings up memories—of difficulties or challenges, of things didn't work out that well—it should highlight what you shouldn't do again. But there is something to be aware of, that is the past. Circumstances have changed and so have you. And maybe what didn't work then would work now, because the fact is, the world has changed—and you've learned a lot.

THIS DAY FOR EVERYONE

While the issues you're dealing with may be significant, there is also a funny side to them. And viewing what you are facing with irony or even humor won't just boost your spirits, it could also bring an entirely fresh and unexpected approach—one that is helpful to the matters in question.

Circumstances may shift gradually, but loyalty remains unchanged for life

S
/
C
\
O
/
R
\
P
\
I
\
O

08

NOVEMBER

You

As a Scorpio, you pride yourself on being a logical individual. And it's true: many Scorpios are just that. In fact, sometimes you're so logical, you depend on the past to assess the present when circumstances change. The world around you and your viewpoint are changing. Individuals you will be talking things over with are changing their viewpoint, too, so basing decisions on discussions alone could actually be unwise.

So if you're making a decision, what do you base it on? As an intuitive water sign and being ruled by Pluto, the planet of truth and vision, you may be better off relying on your intuition, at least initially. Then, once your perspective is clear, you can discuss ideas with others, even those who tend to dominate the decision-making process. Approach these exchanges with reshuffling plans. When you're shuffling cards, the point is to mix them up. This is important because, when organizing changes, you could unwittingly create a new version of what you've done before.

However, it is time for you to approach certain elements of your life in a very different manner than in the past. Your aim? To achieve a balance between sticking with what you know and exploring ways to make changes when it seems you've no options. You will be amazed by what you discover.

You and others

Look around and you'll recognize the world itself is changing so much that sticking with what's familiar will only complicate matters. Instead, take a chance on something quite new and you will benefit far more than you imagined possible. But then that's the point. This is all about discovering something new.

Health and well-being

You know what works for you and stick with it. Once, that was wise. But the world is changing and you are changing, more than you realize. This means being more flexible in your way of living and even thinking. That way, you'll ride out the dramatic changes reshaping your world. Better yet, you won't just accommodate those changes, you will enjoy them.

Goals and challenges

The term "success" is measured in different ways. From family and friends to colleagues or an employer, and then your personal take, the range is huge. However, these extend beyond practical measures and, in fact, have to do with whether you're enjoying life headed in the right direction. Ask those questions, when changes are easy to make.

THIS DAY FOR EVERYONE

Only recently, you hoped one particular issue would resolve itself. Now you realize this isn't going to happen. Others want to talk things through. Yet the problem is, you fear they'll point out what you've done wrong. They will. But what you learn from that will revolutionize your thinking.

GIFTS Enigmatic, Penetrating, Canny

NUMBER 2

CHALLENGES Bitter, Controlling, Paranoid

$(0+9) + (1+1) = 11 = (1+1) = 2$

Friendship is wonderful, family is crucial, but a trusted beloved is like gold

You

Here's a question: is joy earned? Is it magic? As a water sign, you tend to think that feelings sort of occur. Yet, at the same time, as a Scorpio who reflects deeply on things, you realize that those feelings, those moods, have a lot to do with what you do and even how you eat. But also it has to do with how you organize your practical life: your job if you go to one, but also how you organize your day. Yet another component is those who you spend time with and whether those individuals support you.

Of course, we can't always be around people who are lots of fun, or supportive. Yet you can make a point of spending more time with those who think the world of you, and boost your spirits so it balances out the influence of those who are less positive. But what may be most important in a period of growth is to recognize that what worked in the past may not work in the present or the future.

And that journey is very much part of this period of discovery. What's more, this isn't just about you. Ideally, those around you will be equally aware of their challenges, and are looking after their own well-being. If so, then discuss your experiences with them and share the ups and downs of your journey. Of course, it is different for everyone. But you can all learn from each other—and will add to each other's wisdom of your own journeys.

You and others

It may seem a strange question, but who do you trust? Think about this. Generally, family members come as they are, some trustworthy or supportive, and others not. However, there are also your friends. Consider whether they're more trustworthy; you've chosen them, so they should be. This awareness is important for everybody, but especially for you as a Scorpio.

Health and well-being

The big question is: why do you eat? Well, of course, you're hungry, but there are other reasons. Sometimes, you're hungry or, possibly, it's a celebration. Aim to combine those feelings when you eat, and you will turn a meal, even if it's a quick one, into a joyous experience, often to be shared—and the more you will enjoy every single meal you have.

Goals and challenges

As a Scorpio, you are one of the stable, fixed signs of the zodiac. You have a gift for sticking with things. While this is an asset, you'll sometimes struggle to find a new approach to challenges. Yet you don't always spot this. Add inquisitiveness to your armory of insights, and even the greatest obstacles will be easier to deal with.

THIS DAY FOR EVERYONE

The last thing you're in the mood for is a lengthy discussion about an already complicated issue. Much as you are dreading this, the individual in question has realized they've got their facts wrong, but they are too proud to admit it. Be patient. Gradually, the truth will emerge, along with a timely apology.

GIFTS Sensuous, Devoted, Committed

CHALLENGES Compulsive, Covetous, Threatening

NUMBER 3

(1+0) + (1+1) = 3

Talking to those you trust isn't just wonderful, it is a divine gift

S
/
C
\
O
/
R
\
P
\
I
\
O

You

As a Scorpio, you have very clear thoughts about circumstances and certain individuals, but you won't always express your concerns, simply because it seems pointless. It doesn't help. It will confuse things. And unless you have good reason to put your foot down about certain matters, you may shrug your shoulders or make a comment but no more. However, once in a while, you actually need to stand your ground. And it's not so much because you need to have your way but, rather, talking about what matters and standing your ground are important for you as an individual.

It forces you to review your priorities. It's likely the last time you thought about such matters, life was different. Since then, you've grown and changed. Not only that, in talking this over with those who are very different from you, and so think differently, you will be forced to rethink your own views so you can express this in a way others will understand.

As a Scorpio and a water sign, someone who is as intuitive as you are intellectual, this isn't just about communicating with others; it will also help you rediscover who you are now. We all grow and change. Take advantage of discussions of this nature, of both having to stand your ground and challenging others, mostly for the sheer joy of what you discover in the process.

You and others

Every once in a while, it is worth considering whether conversations with others are mere chats or something you can learn from. Certain individuals have a wonderful way of posing a question that results in conversations that enrich everybody concerned—and these individuals are worth keeping in your life.

Health and well-being

Occasionally, it is worth rethinking, then changing, your daily regimen, including how you take care of yourself and how you eat. The big question is, are you responding to your own need to do things differently or is it others' influence? As a Scorpio, you settle into routines, so changes are often the result of others' encouragement. If so, bravo!

Goals and challenges

Changes are normal; they're like breathing. Yet you often put them off. As a Scorpio, you're a fixed sign, so sometimes avoid making changes simply because you can't imagine how they'll work. The secret? Talk to those who encourage you to explore. They'll give you the necessary boost to take the next steps.

10

NOVEMBER

Tempting as it is to give advice to somebody who's struggling, keep your thoughts to yourself, at least for now. Things aren't the way they seem, and despite your good intentions, you could complicate matters. If you must say something, express your support. This will do wonders to boost their spirits.

GIFTS Mysterious, Thorough, Shrewd

NUMBER 4

CHALLENGES Dominating, Jaundiced, Neurotic

(1+1) + (1+1) = 4

S
/
C
\
O
/
R
\
P
\
I
\
O

11
NOVEMBER

You may recognize that special bond with another instantly, but it often takes time

You

Here's a question to think about: Is winning always good? There is an emphasis on it, on getting what you want. But sometimes challenges are about what we can learn.

Whether they're temporary or more lasting, the big question is, what would winning look like? Is it about what you want? What seems your best option today may be no more than doing more of what's familiar. As a Scorpio and somebody who experiences powerful changes from time to time, the battle you're facing may be about moving on from familiar circumstances, shedding an old skin, and becoming a new person.

What's tricky is that you won't necessarily know what that new life is like, at least initially. For you, as someone who tends to be a bit of a control freak, the unfamiliar can be difficult. If so, you probably know people who have the same characteristic; ask them to support you in this process. They won't tell you what to do, but will remind you when you're in the midst of it, that—just like the caterpillar becoming a butterfly—you, too, will turn into a new being, but one you can't yet imagine.

Once that's clear, every other step of this process will be important. And the reason it's important is this won't happen only once in this life; it will happen again and again, yet every time that process will be joyous.

You and others

During periods of transition, do you stick with the familiar, or do you battle what's out there, despite it being in your best interest? While you are probably aware you prefer to stick with what you know, sometimes simply having the courage to break away from the familiar is a vital first step. The rest will come after that.

Health and well-being

There are many ways of taking care of yourself at different times in life. Often, when challenged, Scorpios will choose the toughest approach. However, if ever there were a time to be gentle with yourself, it's now. Allow those around you to support you, and you will find life has as many unexpected beauties as challenges.

Goals and challenges

Every now and then a problem appears that seems a repeat of past challenges. It may be. Consider that possibility first, then explore further. More important, seek guidance from those who know you well and have stood by you during similar dramas in the past. They will be amazingly helpful.

THIS DAY FOR EVERYONE

There are many ways to say "No." While you tend to assume others are aware when things aren't going well, and that a request is unlikely to be agreed to, not everybody picks up on such things. That being the case, you may need to be very clear, if not blunt, about your views.

GIFTS Confidential, Strong, Protective

CHALLENGES Distrustful, Harsh, Envious

NUMBER 5

(1+2) + (1+1) = 5

Being true to yourself seems simple, but Scorpios know how complex it can be

S / C \ O / R \ P \ I \ O

You

Your theme is the difference between intuition and suspicion. As a Scorpio and intuitive water sign, questions of this nature come naturally to you. Yet being ruled by Pluto, the planet of secrets, your intuition can easily drift into suspicious feelings, and you could find yourself wrestling with "shadowy" worries about situations you are aware of, but about which you're also short on facts.

One of your charms is your intensity. Yet these days we're encouraged to trust facts over feelings, so you may have been ignoring that inner wisdom, possibly for a long time.

However, if you base decisions solely on facts, you'll sense that you've missed something important. The trick is to analyze what's coming your way in factual terms while assessing your emotional reaction to those offers. And this takes us back to the power of those feelings and distinguishing between your true intuition and suspicions that rouse questions or, at times, worries.

The trick? Analyze this yourself, but also, seek out the truth in its most basic form, in discussions with those you've always trusted. Remind yourself of that feeling of clarity, then make it part of your everyday thinking. Soon those shadowy doubts will vanish, having given way to the clarity that comes with knowing, and living with, the truth full-time.

You and others

Wondering where you stand with others? Think about what they say—the actual words. Most give this little thought. But for you as a Scorpio, it is vital. On occasion, it's worth thinking about whether those you are spending a lot of time with are just good company or they're speaking from the heart and would be there when you need support.

Health and well-being

Every once in a while, it's important to indulge yourself. And during challenging times, a treat is therapeutic. What's more, knowing it's a treat means that you are taking care of yourself in very special ways. Some believe being fit involves depriving yourself. While discipline is wise, spoiling yourself can be just as important.

Goals and challenges

Thinking things through is vital, but what is even more important sometimes is to take action, just to get the ball rolling. What you do may be impulsive or unwise. It will get you chatting with others and exploring ideas, some of which never crossed your mind. From that point onward, you will learn from and enjoy every step.

12

NOVEMBER

THIS DAY FOR EVERYONE

You seem to be caught in one of those tricky situations in which one individual will go to any length to avoid taking responsibility for something that went wrong. While obviously this isn't your problem, it is essential you make it clear that you had absolutely nothing to do with the matter in question.

Others may joke about truth, but for Scorpio, honesty is a personal matter

S / C \ O / R \ P \ I \ O

13

NOVEMBER

You

Some people think luck means winning the lottery. And that may be the case, but not everyone who wins a lottery is happy. For you, one particular question will come up in a lot of different forms: "What is luck?"

And because there's a focus on luck in your birthday chart, it's essential to think about what that will look like. Especially because for you, as a Scorpio, and somebody who gets into your routine, luck could often mean making changes in your day-to-day life, in your activities and close relationships and even in your thinking.

Notice how that's explained. It's not about making those changes, but simply seeing the circumstances you're in with a different perspective, which means that you may decide something is better than you imagined—and that other things that you had envisioned as being thrilling actually should be given second place.

It's also about perhaps accepting a bigger picture in certain activities that you've assumed wouldn't be rewarding. But most of all, it's about allowing those events to unfold in their own time. You can become addicted to worry and you can over plan. And when you do, that means that it's difficult to be spontaneous and that's the most important lesson of all for you.

You and others

The single big question is who to trust. If someone says what you want to hear, they may be helpful, especially if you're seeking breakthroughs. Those who encourage you to ask questions and to venture into new territory, especially if it's unfamiliar—and especially if those individuals challenge your thinking—are probably the ones you'll want to listen to.

Health and well-being

Many people believe that certain foods are lucky, and that's a wonderful tradition. But other varieties of foods are lucky simply because they do wonders for you. They nourish you in other ways, and add to your well-being. These are always good for you, but especially good during periods of transition. The more balanced you feel, the easier it will be to embrace the unknown.

Goals and challenges

If you want a motto for periods of change and growth, it's "Be bold." While, as a courageous Scorpio, you'll stand your ground, this has to do with breakthroughs, learning something new, venturing into new territory. The more prepared you are to take what seem to be chances, the more swiftly you'll begin to enjoy, and profit from, those changes.

THIS DAY FOR EVERYONE

Having to deal with tedious problems is bad enough, but having to discuss them at length with those who insist on going into these matters in detail is the last thing you're in the mood for. Despite that, these need attention, and the longer you wait, the more troublesome they'll become.

GIFTS Intense, Conscientious, Fascinating

CHALLENGES Melodramatic, Vitriolic, Cruel

NUMBER 7

(1+4) + (1+1) = 7

Generosity is always admirable, but it's at its best when it is done in secret

S
/
C
\
O
/
R
\
P
\
I
\
O

14

NOVEMBER

You

For you, the theme is inner peace. That may sound very spiritual, but actually it's not, because for many people, and especially many Scorpios, the chatter you hear in your brain prevents you from finding peace, simply because you're discussing plans, you're weighing up what will work and what won't, and what you think of other people.

While there is peace spoken of in many forms of spirituality, that single variety of peace has to do with being able to sidestep, if not silence, that chatter. But silencing that chatter is also important because it appears that there will be certain decisions you have to make, and if you will allow that chatter to influence your intuition—which is very powerful for you as a Scorpio—then you could miss the hints, the ideas that come with following that intuition, to call a particular individual to go to a particular place.

But this will also enable you to find a joy in each day and in others' happiness in a way that you may not usually do.

This is important—because exploring what others are happy with will give you an example of the kind of world you could be creating for yourself simply by following your intuition over logic, and by using that hard-won inner peace you require to make decisions.

You and others

During times of transition, it's usual to ask those you trust for advice. However, you actually need to listen to what they have to say. As a Scorpio, you tend to argue with others simply because you'd rather stick with what is familiar. But if you are truly interested in change, listening to that advice is a gift.

Health and well-being

There are a number of special formulas, and no single one works better than another, but what is important is that during periods of transition you take it slowly. This is no time for a harsh routine. Treat yourself with love and with a kind of gentleness that encourages you to take a step into the future.

Goals and challenges

There is a single phrase you should think about, and that is "all forms of change bring chaos." If you're moving into a new home, it's chaotic. If you are changing elements of your life, it's chaotic. Even if you're going on a trip, a much-desired trip, it will still trigger a certain amount of chaos. As a Scorpio and a fixed sign, you like things to stay as they are and you may actually bemoan that chaos. Actually, when you're experiencing that chaos, it's an indication that you are making progress.

THIS DAY FOR EVERYONE

Long ago, you learned that there's little point in arguing with someone who has already made and committed to a decision. Although you don't realize that is exactly what you've done in a range of situations, review existing plans, especially those you regard as unchanging. They could be holding you back.

GIFTS Captivating, Determined, Passionate

CHALLENGES Fanatical, Unapproachable, Cruel

NUMBER 8

$(1+5) + (1+1) = 8$

S / C \ O / R \ P \ I \ O

15

NOVEMBER

True love exists in many ways; at its most powerful, it is unspoken

You

For you as a Scorpio, living with unanswered questions can be difficult, especially because as somebody ruled by Pluto, the planet of truth, you want answers—and reliable facts. However, with the foundation that situations are based on is shifting, and the push and pull of life for many individuals, the kinds of guarantees you want are unlikely.

Yet there is a different kind of truth—and that truth is one you are learning about. It is a truth that steps outside of the plans you have in mind and, in fact, outside of what is normally termed as a battle to get things done. Instead, it forces you simply to look at life from a different angle and to consider what will work in this moment, and the next moment, and then the one after that.

This approach is very different, because it doesn't involve planning. In fact, it's rather like living out each day, unable to guess what the weather will be tomorrow or next week or in a couple of months—but to be in the present. That is a philosophical approach to life, but in your particular case, once you even begin to think about it, much less try to master it, you will discover that the more easygoing you are about decision-making, the easier it will be to be drawn to the right activity in this hour, on this day, tomorrow—and over the coming months and even years.

You and others

If you're living in this unusual world—in which you're not so much trying to make decisions as to do what seems right in the moment—then you're also redefining what achievement means. If you are no longer worrying about succeeding, then a challenge becomes an exciting exercise, one from which you will benefit in wonderful ways—not least for the sheer joy of what you learned.

Health and well-being

Everybody seeks a routine that will make them feel young and healthy. But what will make you feel best during times of transition are those that are adaptable: they accommodate the air and the energy moving through you. The more flexible you are in what you do and the way you take care of yourself, the more fun you will have.

Goals and challenges

Planning ahead is a virtue. But being able to accept what comes your way is a joy, and choosing unpredictability is a superb and rare approach to life. But once you've done that, once you've stopped telling others what you're planning and stopped planning yourself, then whatever arises will be a delightful surprise.

THIS DAY FOR EVERYONE

After battling seemingly insurmountable objects, you've discovered the issue wasn't the situation, but a fundamental misunderstanding of what you were dealing with. Going back to the beginning scenes is aggravating, but what you learn will explain what went wrong, and eliminate that confusion.

Some regard saying you'd do anything for a loved one as extreme, but not to Scorpio

S / C \ O / R \ P \ I \ O

You

As a Scorpio and a water sign, part of you very much wants to be generous with others. Yet another part of you is careful, simply because you know that kind of generosity can often end in unfortunate situations of people being ungrateful or expecting more. However, there is a balance in this, and the real trick is actually to discuss the matter with others.

As a Scorpio, you'd normally think this kind of thing through and decide what's in everyone's best interest, and then put those plans into action. However, the trick is to talk things over, even though you may suspect that not everybody would make decisions as wise as you hope. This may well be the case, but this is part of the point and part of what is important for you. The sooner you get others involved in those decisions and in making those plans, the more swiftly they will begin to take a certain responsibility and take that off your shoulders, which is an important thing.

But even more than that, it will show a growing trust with others, something that is very difficult for you as a cautious and occasionally suspicious Scorpio to achieve.

Take this approach: discussing things stage by stage, including those matters that worry you. Discuss them openly and you will be amazed how worthwhile and often loving those exchanges are.

You and others

The phrase you'll want to use with others is simple: what do you think? As a Scorpio, you often tend to think things through first and then tell others your opinion. In this case, you are encouraged to ask for others' views. You may not always agree with them, but that's the point. This will get you talking and that isn't just important—it will be incredibly helpful.

Health and well-being

For you, the best approach to feeling terrific is to step away from what you've done before and to try something new. That may be the last thing you're in the mood for. Yet if ever there was a time to try new things and break old habits, it's now.

Goals and challenges

There are some things you've said you'd never do. Most Scorpios have this sort of sacred list. And now is the time to begin to do some of those things, because it's essential to burst through those concepts and beliefs about things that either were once unacceptable or that you're actually afraid of doing. In every case, the simple act of saying you'll do them will change things, and in some cases, actually doing them will prove to be miraculous.

16

NOVEMBER

S / C \ O / R \ P \ I \ O

17

NOVEMBER

A Scorpio commitment isn't just for real, it outlasts everything life can deal you

You

Ordinarily, you're setting goals for the future. You think both in the short and long term, which might have seemed sensible. However, with the world changing so swiftly, it may not be the best approach. Of course, as a Scorpio and somebody who dislikes unnecessary changes, you may think in those terms so you can avoid seemingly disruptive changes.

But this is a period during which the structure of many elements of the world around you, and in your own life, are changing, so the more flexible your approach, the better. That means making plans in the short term may not be ideal. It also means being willing to explore in ways that would seem unwise, if not just plain crazy, at other times. But things are changing in so many ways, and the more you explore them, even if just for the fun of it, the better off you'll be.

This variety of inquisitiveness doesn't necessarily come naturally to you as a Scorpio. Yet you indulge in it, and the broader your vision for the future, the better able you'll be to deal with the unexpected twists and turns that are coming your way.

Inevitably, these aren't just for you, but for the world around you. In fact, if there is one single approach you want to embrace now, it's an approach that may be very out of character—and that is being easygoing.

You and others

During this period of change, when questions arise and you may be drawn down unfamiliar avenues, if ever there were a time to listen to what others have to say and their ideas, it's now. While you seek trustworthy people and pay attention to their ideas, take advantage of the ears and eyes of those around you and you may spot something you'd otherwise miss.

Health and well-being

While a routine is reassuring, especially during periods of change, altering various elements of your routine is advisable. Shaking things up actually reprograms your brain, so when those changes do arise, you are ready to make the best of them.

Goals and challenges

Setting new goals is worth doing from time to time. But setting goals that are so far out you can't believe you're even thinking of them is something entirely different, and that is very much the theme. Because you know exactly what you do well and what you dislike, rethinking goals may seem unwise. Yet make a point of doing one new thing every day, and add something unlikely to your list of goals. Then you will not only make the best of this period, you' will enjoy it.

THIS DAY FOR EVERYONE

In your efforts to avoid crossing the fence or seeming to be critical, you've given one particular individual the impression that you've no objection to what they've said or done. That's not the case. This leaves you little choice but to be frank, and in a way that removes all possibility of doubt.

Scorpio love for family, friends, or partner may be largely unspoken, but is unshakable

S
/
C
\
O
/
R
\
P
\
I
\
O

You

As you will notice, you're in a period during which you have a choice. You can fix—that is, deal with—minor difficulties as they arise, in situations you're unhappy that are inconvenient, or which others are finding difficult. Or, you can take another approach—one that will be far more disruptive in the short term, but which will probably work a lot better in the long run—and that is to stand back and look at the big picture and see where changes are necessary.

Here again, as a Scorpio, you will tend to look at details and then, if necessary, the big picture. But because this is a period during which the way a lot of the world works and the way we think are shifting, the more willing you are to let go of reassuring realities and to take chances on doing things in a very new way—in a new setting, altering your routine or your schedule, or even the world in which you live and work—the better off you'll be in the long run.

Again, that may seem crazy and wild. However, it may also be that opportunities come your way, or it could be that you devise something that will enable you to do things in that entirely new manner. This combination is the trick, the most important way, and the most efficient way to deal with this period of change.

You and others

Sometimes others will encourage change, or you'll have an idea, or circumstances will corner you into it. Take that first step. Don't wait until the final moment when you're pushed, but rather, recognize that the more swiftly you get involved in that process of change, the better advantage you will take of it—and the more you will enjoy it.

Health and well-being

Sometimes battling for something is good exercise. It focuses the mind. But there are times when the battle leads to tension, and that's no good. In fact, if there is anything that you want right now, it's not tension, which limits intuition. It is a certain serenity that comes with allowing change to come to you.

Goals and challenges

This is out of character, but for you to pause and simply allow things to unfold isn't weak, it's wise. The reason is that some of what's arising is so unfamiliar, even you, as a canny Scorpio, wouldn't necessarily recognize it. Yet if you borrow the point of view of the sign next to you, Sagittarius, which has a capacity not only to spot but enjoy sudden changes, you'll recognize those and embrace and make the best of them, all within nanoseconds.

18

NOVEMBER

THIS DAY FOR EVERYONE

Change is in the air. While it's clear things can't remain as they are, you've began hoping you could discuss and deal with certain tricky matters gradually, but ironically, the disruption caused by these changes will force others to acknowledge and join you in tackling the issues you have in mind.

S
/
C
\
O
/
R
\
P
\
I
\
O

19
NOVEMBER

There are many ways of sharing life's most precious moments; Scorpios are experts

You

If you notice that what you once regarded as a welcome surprise has become annoying, you will realize just how much you and the world around you is changing. The fact is, those treats are now boring and predictable. Yet at the same time, you're wondering what will surprise you, and this is where it's tricky, because those surprises are appearing, yet you still regard them as difficulties. That is because the world is changing in a way that is requiring you, as a stable Scorpio, to view elements of your life from a very different angle.

However, if you can find that different angle, you will be able to see many of those elements from a fresh perspective, and instead of wrestling with each, that perspective will allow you to move ahead. Yes, it will require a certain amount of faith, and it may seem that you're taking chances, but it is a lot better than struggling with each of those changes.

You'll still have the opportunity to say no if you want to, but the more swiftly you get involved with these unusual circumstances, the better off you'll be. The trick is to realize that, as an intuitive water sign, there is a part of you that already trusts this kind of thing. It's just that your old habits of control are what are holding you back. Recognize that and you will also recognize how powerful that intuitive side of your nature is.

You and others

The question is: how often do you brush off offers or ideas that are intriguing, but you just can't imagine how they will fit? Yet the sooner you say yes and get involved in exploring them, the better off you'll be. It is important now, but even more so as you live out the coming days, weeks, months, and years.

Health and well-being

As a fixed sign of the zodiac, you like your pleasures. In fact, you like certain pleasures regularly and the same way. However, with the world around you changing, it's time for you to change your habits, sometimes because it's good for you, but also because certain things you once enjoyed won't be like they used to be. While you could struggle to find the same products, foods, and activities, you could also plunge in and try something new, and you could do it deliberately.

Goals and challenges

When was the last time you deliberately altered your goals and embraced new challenges? Future events will encourage you to do things in a new way, but the sooner you realize that those occasionally unwelcome challenges are going to make your life more interesting and more rewarding, the better off you will be.

THIS DAY FOR EVERYONE

Having right on your side is reassuring, especially when you're dealing with those you're eager to debate with about existing plans or priorities. Still, before you challenge anybody, double-check even seemingly solid facts. Times have changed—and you're likely to make surprising discoveries.

The deep feelings that make others weep
lead to a Scorpio's emotional core

You

Because this day is related both to Scorpio and to the sign Sagittarius, we're talking about dealing with both energies, and if ever there was an unusual pairing, it is this. While the Scorpio is a reflective and sensitive water sign, Sagittarius is an expansive and impulsive fire sign. However, if you can learn to benefit from the two of them—the breadth of ideas that come with the Sagittarius's inquisitive side and the reflective nature of the Scorpio—you will benefit in many and wonderful ways. In fact, this will be terrific, not just for you but for those around you, for the excitement that you bring to the lives of everybody, from friends and family to colleagues.

But not only that, instead of worrying about how things will go—and the details that are so much a part of the Scorpio life—you will also find that you're able to enjoy things in ways that you never understood or expected. By exploring this spontaneous side of your nature, you will begin to embrace a part of your own being that has always been there, but which you may have held back because the Scorpio side wanted to make very sure that you were in control of everything. But of course, what you're discovering is that there's more than one way of controlling things, and sometimes that spontaneous Sagittarius approach is the best way to live life.

You and others

The idea of being multiple personalities is something that actually is not unusual in the zodiac—take Gemini, which is the twins in one sign. Embrace both sides of your nature—the impulsive fire side and the reflective Scorpio—and you'll enjoy life all the more.

Health and well-being

There are lots of approaches to taking care of yourself, as many as there are signs of the zodiac. But in your case, creating a menu of activities that accommodates the breadth of your character will be an adventure, and one that allows you to experiment. Perhaps the most important commitment you'll want to make is to continue to explore, because this kind of exploration is like taking vitamins.

Goals and challenges

To have your approach to making goals change may seem strange, yet at the same time this balance between your internal nature as a Scorpio and the need to expand, and expand constantly, will make life so much more exciting you will wonder why you didn't think of it before. When you embrace that expansive side of your nature, you will find that every day is much brighter.

S
/
C
\
O
/
R
\
P
\
I
\
O

20

NOVEMBER

You're running up against people who are so opinionated, they're unable to have a civilized exchange of ideas. That's not a surprise. However, it is worth noting that your views on several matters are equally inflexible. Begin reviewing these, and suddenly discussions with others will go better.

Sagittarius

Ruler Jupiter
Element Fire

Symbol The Archer
Flower Dandelion

November 21– December 20

Sagittarius Being half horse, half human—and what's more, an archer—it's no surprise you Sagittarians are restless. The third fire sign, you thrive on new ideas, action, and challenges, and suffer when life is too predictable. While you're risk-takers, you've an instinctive sense that comes from your ruling planet, the fortunate Jupiter. Dandelion is your flower, sharp cinnamon is your herb, and the yew is your tree. Your stone is gold topaz.

S
A
G
I
T
T
A
R
I
U
S

S
/
A
\
G
/
I
\
T
/
T
\
A
/
R
\
I
/
U
\
S

21

NOVEMBER

GIFTS Vivacious, Eager, Articulate

CHALLENGES Restless, Rash, Clumsy

NUMBER 5

(2+1) + (1+1) = 5

Nothing's better than waking up brimming with energy

You

You were born at the beginning of the sign of Sagittarius, so have a balance between the influence of the sign just before yours, Scorpio, and its tendency to be reflective and rather secretive, and your own expansive nature, which is constantly shifting and exploring.

You are always growing and developing in a way that benefits you, because the inquisitive side of your nature finds delving into complex, if not puzzling, questions worthwhile and rewarding. That process of exploration leads to setting goals and exploring ideas, as well as considering how you will look after your own interests. What you learn as a result of that Scorpio tendency to delve into facts, and to gather information. And information that is reliable is very helpful indeed.

The Sagittarius side of your nature is always inquisitive, and needs to expand and grow. Consequently, when you're learning about something, or indeed, somebody, you enjoy and benefit from asking questions.

And then you begin to look at medium-term and long-range plans. This is a secret for you. If you take advantage of that short time you took exploring the very careful side of your nature, then—when you begin to turn those plans into lasting arrangements, and possibly even lifelong plans—you will be sure you're doing the right thing.

You and others

As a fire sign, you are energetic, but at the same time, you have a strong need not only for the stimulation of others' company, but the ideas they bring your way. What you discuss with those around you—everyone from friends and family to colleagues—will add to your life enormously.

Health and well-being

The Sagittarius side of you prefers to eat quickly and have something that's tasty, but that you can also move on from. However, there is another part of you that enjoys a dish you can delve into and learn about. If you manage to add that to your diet once a week, you will be glad you did.

Goals and challenges

As a fire sign, you always need new goals. However, certain of your goals and objectives are important enough that they will become a foundation for years—if not your whole life. Find a balance between those two and you will also find lasting satisfaction.

THIS DAY FOR EVERYONE

The last thing you want is to disappoint anybody, yet sudden changes in circumstances mean you can't adjust to do what you've promised and deal with more recent obligations. Explain that to those you are worried about upsetting. Not only will they understand, they'll do what they can to help.

GIFTS Expansive, Lively, Inquisitive

CHALLENGES Impatient, Explosive, Fickle

NUMBER 6

(2+2) + (1+1) = 6

The world is full of amazing places and people, and I love discovering them

You

As a Sagittarius, you're restless. This is in fact one of your most profitable characteristics, in the sense that between being ruled by the expansive Jupiter and being a fire sign, you're always interested in what's going on around you and, even more, you're eager to learn about it, and when it suits you, take part.

That interest ensures you meet new people, and take advantage of opportunities to go new places, that you broaden your horizons, and that, in turn, leads to news idea and potential new pursuits. However, this can be distracting. In fact, the challenge is to sustain what you have that works in your life—in your relationships, in your habits, and out in the world—yet at the same time, to include these intriguing developments. This is because, as somebody ruled by Jupiter, the planet of growth, ideas, and discovery both via study and travel, it is vital that you always have something new to discover and learn about.

It may involve actual ideas that you study. It may involve getting to know people. It could mean going places: any place from school to travel. In every case, this will add to your life.

As a Sagittarius, those experiences you encounter and what you learn won't just be interesting; they will contribute to your existence and to the rest of your life.

You and others

Most Sagittarians are sociable anyway. But for you, it is especially important that you are around people who you can talk to, and who you can bounce ideas off. In doing this, you'll not only learn a lot, their views will also add to your knowledge.

Health and well-being

One of the advantages of being a Sagittarius is you are full of vital energy. This comes with being ruled by the planet Jupiter. But it also means that you can actually forget to eat or not eat enough or at the right time, and end up being exhausted despite that natural energy. The secret? The challenge of maintaining balance in all things.

Goals and challenges

There is a phrase—moving the goalposts—which speaks to the idea of almost reaching a particular goal and then setting entirely new, and often very distant ones. This is very common to those born under the sign of Sagittarius—and something to be cautious of.

22

NOVEMBER

THIS DAY FOR EVERYONE

The events coming your way will be exciting, but also the odds are good they'll trigger the stubborn side of your nature. Bear this in mind and when you're becoming exasperated, instead of digging your heels in, you will ask others to explain what they have in mind. That will change everything, and soon.

23

GIFTS Quick-thinking, Exuberant, Mirthful

CHALLENGES Erratic, Reckless, Disparaging

NUMBER 7

(2+3) + (1+1) = 7

Exploring new places brings a special kind of excitement

You

While you have a strong physical nature, and need to be out and about, whether on a walk or involved in sports, there is no denying the power of the philosophical side of your nature. This is the side that asks questions about everything—about what works, what's wise, kind, and equally, what isn't. It is associated with your ruling planet, Jupiter, and explains the element of your nature that can get lost both in considering what is best to do in the here and now, and future plans.

Moreover, you will spend hours considering what you can learn more about. While that interest in the world around you is important, it's also essential to balance that inquisitiveness to keep you from focusing on something and, possibly, allowing it to become a real passion. This has nothing to do with age. It is a challenge for Sagittarians of any age, because too much focus can mean excluding other activities, when you are by nature restless.

So the issue isn't what you are focusing on, but finding a balance between your central core enthusiasms and those other activities. You might even ask someone to give you some pointers in organizing those priorities. That won't just be helpful in the here and now, that individual could be helpful over the years to come and add to your life.

You and others

Because your thinking moves swiftly and you connect strongly with people, when you re spending time with those who think equally swiftly it's a tremendous connection. Yet at the same time, there are those who are interesting who simply think and move more slowly. The trick is to understand that and to adjust your own pace in accordance with theirs.

Health and well-being

Taking care of yourself, that is, eating wisely and moving in a way that is useful for you, can be easy. However, you get distracted. Probably the best approach is to indeed choose the easiest thing to do, which includes eating simple but nourishing foods and doing something as simple as taking regular walks.

Goals and challenges

Some of the signs near you, particularly Capricorn, tend to overanalyze everything, but you don't. At the same time, it is important to rethink what you've done recently. Maybe not as frequently as your neighboring signs, but if you put it in your calendar to review what you've done—say, a couple of times a year—you will be glad you did.

THIS DAY FOR EVERYONE

Unsettling as sudden changes may be, what's coming your way now and over the next week isn't just exciting. Those events could be the answer to persistent problems. However, they won't seem that promising when they arise. Make a point of exploring everything. You'll be amazed by what works out.

GIFTS Buoyant, Spirited, Daring

CHALLENGES Fidgety, Outspoken, Disapproving

NUMBER 8

(2+4) + (1+1) = 8

The best challenge is both physical and requires learning something new

24

You

You don't think of it until you're making plans with others and realize how cautious they are—about even the simplest of things—but the fact is, you are a natural optimist. While that makes life easy for you, you have a knack for overcoming the obstacles that would stop others in their tracks. However, not only are certain individuals cautious, even when things are going well, they seem to find something to complain about. While you can sidestep their negative comments, making plans that involve them isn't easy, and they can be difficult to talk to, whatever the nature of the conversation.

It doesn't matter if you have known them for a long time; they might even be family. What is most puzzling is, despite their tendency to complain, they're often helpful and supportive. The trick to dealing with those who seem to find the downside of almost anything is to let them comment and to let them moan, but also to ensure that you have enough kindred spirits around you, those who are optimistic in the way you are, that you can also talk to them.

By having both types of people in your life, you will not only benefit from the balance and the wisdom they bring, their ideas could broaden your own thinking and either encourage you to achieve more, or prevent you from taking action you'd later regret.

You and others

There are clusters of many kinds. Sometimes, if you allow yourself to be intrigued by those who don't really make much sense, they'll add a lot to your life. In fact, it may make life more exciting than those who you know better yet who are predictable.

Health and well-being

Having a regimen that keeps you in shape is wonderful. But if it's something you don't really enjoy and will drop, then it isn't a good idea. The trick for you as a restless Sagittarius is to find something that works, that is probably varied but also gives you plenty of time to do other things.

Goals and challenges

Taking chances on and exploring the world is essential for you as an inquisitive Sagittarius. Yet it is also essential that you think twice about what you get involved in, particularly if those arrangements are long-term. Make that your policy and you won't regret it later.

In some situations, fast action is vital, but in at least one, you're urged to wait until you have the clarity, in terms of both hard facts and your own feelings, that comes with certain moments. If you do that, then you will be sure to explore your options and avoid lasting decisions.

GIFTS Courageous, Wide-ranging, Ebullient

CHALLENGES Judgmental, Flustered, Volatile

NUMBER 9

(2+5) + (1+1) = 9

Sometimes the only cure for feeling down is a bad comedy movie

You

As a Sagittarius and a fire sign, you really enjoy discussions, especially if they're enthusiastic, if not actually heated. Keep in mind, however, that what you enjoy and regard as being an enthusiastic exchange of ideas might seem to other, more timid souls—and probably those who aren't a fire sign—as a battle, one that somebody will win to have the last word.

The real problem is that you don't take these exchanges to heart. All three fire signs—Aries, Leo, and Sagittarius—enjoy such lively conversations. However, if others are loud or trying to prove something to you or to others, including more timid souls, consider whether it's best to talk about something less combative. At the time, that might seem weak, but when things are calmer, you will realize you would have just been drawn into that particular issue when there's so much else to explore and discuss.

Better than that, once you understand this, you will learn the art of recognizing when there's more to be said, when there is something to discuss that you'll learn from, or when you'll learn about others, and about their ideas, views, and passions. And, especially, when it's time to change the subject and go on to something else that is just as interesting, but less controversial.

You and others

As a fire sign, you're a quick thinker, which means you will often dominate discussions, not because you're trying to take control, but you come up with more ideas. However, there are those with whom you have a strong connection and you get together often. If those individuals are slower thinkers, you may need to do exactly that—to take over to ensure that you cover everything that's on your mind.

Health and well-being

Are you feeling tired? As a Sagittarius and a fire sign, sometimes you don't notice fatigue until you are completely exhausted. One of the most important components for you is to recognize when you need to rest. Rather than thinking it a waste of time, see it as an investment in your well-being.

Goals and challenges

Everybody tells you to list what you want to do. Usually it's a good idea. However, as you do, make two columns: one, a list of activities and goals that excite you, and the other, of those that seem worthy but dull. If you want to do something from that dull column, think three times before you commit to it.

THIS DAY FOR EVERYONE

Recently, when discussing plans you sidestepped certain details. You weren't being careless, or as some suggest, secretive; it's just you knew things would change. If others are concerned, explain slowly and in detail. Otherwise, they'll continue to assume that you were being careless.

GIFTS Frank, Cheery, Passionate

CHALLENGES Unstable, Belittling, Defiant

NUMBER 1

(2+6) + (1+1) = 10 = (1+0) = 1

Fighting for what or who I believe in isn't a battle, it's an honor

You

You probably don't think of yourself as being complex or demanding. But you are. This isn't in the sense that you demand things from others, but you are so full of ideas and activities and hopes and enthusiasms, and the accompanying requirements, that it is vital that you think carefully about your priorities.

But, also, you talk things over with others, both those closest and those whose advice you trust. This ensures you have somebody to bounce your ideas off. However, it is also about them knowing enough to give you useful advice. If you don't do this, if you don't outline your hopes and plans, you can overwhelm yourself and leap into making solid plans without thinking things through.

So this isn't just about an update, but a worthwhile discussion with those who are able to ask worthwhile questions and guide you. They may be close to you—family or loved ones or trusted friends.

While organizing yourself in this way may seem overwhelming, it leads to something unusual for you. That's having organized both your thinking and plans well enough in advance so that you and others can consider what you want to achieve, and even better, you can relax. This may not come naturally, but as you'll discover, it's a good habit for you, as an inquisitive Sagittarius, to develop.

You and others

As you move through elements of your life, or activities or interests, it is important to bring some friends from the past, but also to acquire new friends and associates that have to do with what you are pursuing at the moment. Not only will you learn from them, you will be able to chat about what you're exploring and enjoy that all the more as well.

Health and well-being

As a Sagittarius, you're inquisitive. This includes new fads that have to do with the way you eat or how you exercise. While it is worth exploring what arises, also recognize that unless food or a particular kind of exercise is your passion, keeping it simple is probably the best choice for you.

Goals and challenges

Nobody works harder at achieving what means a lot to you than you. However, you also can have a short attention span, which means that if you haven't achieved that goal swiftly enough, you will move on to something else. Think twice before you allow that to happen, particularly if those goals are very dear to your heart.

26

NOVEMBER

The last thing you're in the mood to do is conduct a top-to-bottom rethink of plans you have worked hard to organize. While your feelings of hesitation are understandable, with each day circumstances are also changing and because of this, so, too, must the plans you've organized.

GIFTS   Valiant, Lighthearted, Persuasive

CHALLENGES   Inconstant, Forgetful, Jumpy

NUMBER 2

(2+7) + (1+1) = 11 = (1+1) = 2

Nothing beats waking up knowing I'll be doing something I've never done

You

You'll often jot down ideas of what you want to do. While of course, almost everyone keeps some sort of list of plans and goals, and adds to them from time to time, in your case, those lists are often jotted down here and there, on bits of paper, some of which you discover six months later in a pocket.

However, when you're comparing notes with those around you, you sometimes feel that, despite your enthusiasm, you're missing something. The fact is, as a Sagittarius and somebody ruled by the expansive Jupiter, you are inquisitive by nature, and whatever you're doing or wherever you are, you will also be exploring. For you, it's like breathing. But this can mean many Sagittarians don't have a single goal, or perhaps it reshapes itself over the months and years. This unique part of your nature is what enables you to do something that is extraordinary.

Even better, you manage to shift those goals and redefine them while adding to your current vision. While others may advise you to stick to certain objectives or plans, deep down you know that while this may work for them, it isn't your thing. For you, the more inquisitive you are and the more willing you are to rethink your goals, even frequently, the more likely you are to achieve them and possibly achieve far more than you imagined possible.

You and others

Understandably, you're fascinated by those who focus on one thing and one thing only. While you will talk to them, at the same time you wonder what else they do, and find them a bit obsessive. It is an important lesson in how wonderful your own inquisitive way of living and thinking is.

Health and well-being

Are you feeling grumpy, or are you feeling on edge and ready to bite someone's head off? It may not be your temper. It may be something really simple. Are you hungry? It may be that you're tired and you need to go to bed early and get some rest.

Goals and challenges

Certain individuals are determined to give others advice. In your case, they are advising you to stick with a single focus, to stick with a single goal. The fact is, they aren't Sagittarians and they don't know what makes you tick. Thank them—and then ignore them.

THIS DAY FOR EVERYONE

By no means are you antisocial or secretive. Yet Mercury, the planet of ideas, is accenting the parts of your chart that have to do with talking things over with others. It will become clear that you've sidestepped certain matters. While they're not crucial, the sooner you raise them the better.

The best cure for feeling down is being in nature

You

You have a talent for bringing new ideas and excitement to the lives of others, but then they move on and do their own thing. For you, however, the question is, who brings excitement into your life? While mostly you do it yourself, you don't even think of it, or wonder how it happens.

This is because you're inquisitive by nature. As a fire sign, you are restless and you thrive on learning, so you're always looking for new things to do, experience, and explore. You like learning for the sake of it, doing what might be termed "exercising your brain." If there is any problem, it is that once you've found something interesting, you will still be on the lookout for something else, even if you are absorbed with your current pursuit.

This is the lesson for you: finding that balance between sticking with what you enjoy, yet giving yourself time to continue to explore and discover. You do this in the way that not only comes naturally to Sagittarians, but in a way that is one of your greatest virtues.

The fact that you are interested in others and in the world around you adds to your life, but often that interest adds to the lives of others as well. In some cases, you may turn that interest into something lasting. Whether or not you do, it will always have added to the life of those you've encountered.

You and others

Those around you are often seeking that individual who will change their lives. As a fire sign, you are often the one who does that, not just for yourself but for others as well. Recognize that your role in life is to be you, but also occasionally to add enormously to the lives of others.

Health and well-being

It is important to recognize that the fire sign part of your nature means you are almost always moving and doing something, which means that when you're realizing dreams, and doing things with others, you won't stop and can get exhausted. The trick is to realize that sometimes you can conjure up dreams, but from a seated position.

Goals and challenges

As a Sagittarius you are spontaneous, and often you'll discover something you want to do simply because it pops into your mind. Yet occasionally you need to sit down and review your life. Consider what should go, what's lacking, and what's next—and what is the ideal opportunity you want to come your way.

28

NOVEMBER

THIS DAY FOR EVERYONE

Planning ahead is always wise. But if you do too much of it during this changeable period, you'll only run into problems. The trick is to think carefully about your objectives, and then discuss those with others. After that, talk over how to achieve them—always aware you might need to rethink things.

GIFTS Effervescent, Witty, Brave

CHALLENGES Wild, Eruptive, Demeaning

NUMBER 4

(2+9) + (1+1) = 13 = (1+3) = 4

Curiosity is one of life's greatest gifts; with it, no day is ever dull

You

One of your greatest assets as a Sagittarius is your sense of humor. You can see what's funny in all sorts of settings, often in those that other people ignore, or sometimes even complain about. Spotting this is one thing, but the trick is to find a way to mix this unique perception with the practical side of life. If you need to make money, if you're starting a new project, if you need to figure things out, you will want to blend your inborn enthusiasm with those practical needs.

While initially, this may seem strange, once you begin discussing it with others, you'll find that they, too, have an interest in what you're doing. They love the idea of breaking away from the dull side of life, and they may well have the ideas or even be in a position to support you. But this isn't just about your sense of humor. You can make this a part of your approach to doing anything new, and in fact, to living life.

Ordinarily, you rely on yourself to achieve your goals, and enjoy hanging out with those who are fun. Yet every once in a while, it is useful to pause and consider who could be helpful and perhaps even ask for that help. That will be a new and unusual approach to life for you. But it will also be a skill that will benefit you in many, and often magical, ways.

You and others

The fire sign part of your nature says life should be a party. This is natural to fire signs, but particularly Sagittarians. Also, you don't mind a large proportion of drama in the middle of it all. However, it is important that you hang out with people who support you emotionally, as well as who support your goals.

Health and well-being

Occasionally, you realize that you're overdoing it, that you are juggling far too much. While you are able to do that, the question is, do you actually have the energy to do it at the moment? Or is some of what you're juggling sufficiently unimportant that you could actually put it off till later?

Goals and challenges

As a fire sign, you don't mind sudden changes. In fact, they keep life interesting. If you did everything alone, that would be fine. However, those around you aren't the same, and many of them are not only uncomfortable with sudden changes, they're anxious about them. The most important thing to keep in mind is the more you talk over, the easier it will be.

29

NOVEMBER

THIS DAY FOR EVERYONE

It's true: you are often reluctant to make changes others insist on if you can't understand what you'll get out of them, or why you should bother at all. But the fact is you have no choice. The situation in question involves others as much as it does you—and they're eager to take things to the next stage.

GIFTS Intrepid, Forthright, Avid

CHALLENGES Flighty, Abrupt, Impulsive

NUMBER 5

(3+0) + (1+1) = 5

In those "down" moments, I recall the last real challenge I faced

You

Sometimes you need to take a break—for yourself, and from yourself and some of your habits. The fact is, you're always busy, really busy, often distracted and sometimes late.

This is the Sagittarian side of your nature, the part that enjoys picking up on, trying out, and adding activities and pursuits with each passing day. But it's also worth recognizing that it's good to have time for friends, to do what you enjoy, to explore, and sometimes just to relax or even be still.

Yet if you keep adding to the list of things you are doing and intend to do, this not only gets difficult, it can be overwhelming. The only one who can decide how to use your time is you. Those around you may make suggestions, but as you well know, you will often ignore them.

The question is, how can you deal with this? Ideally, you'll pause, at the beginning or end of the day, and think about what you could let go of, and you'll make that decision before you actually begin.

Certain things you put first don't really matter, while others are important yet are put aside because they don't seem quite as urgent. Do that little mini-review frequently, and instead of rushing from one thing to the next, you will be able to enjoy every element of your day and of your life.

You and others

As a passionate fire sign, you are always moving and you attract people to you. Yet every once in a while, you also need to allow those who are around you to add to your life, by taking you to places that will enhance your existence, by exposing you to interesting people, and perhaps simply by spoiling you.

Health and well-being

Feeling fit is important for you as a fire sign and a Sagittarius. However, you have a tendency to get involved in a fitness regimen that is as complicated as it is boring. Variety is essential for you. If you don't have that, it's time you made it a part of your regimen.

Goals and challenges

Writing down your goals seems dull, especially as someone who would rather be out doing things. However, if you do it, even if you just jot those things down, you will remember them. You may later find a note in a pocket, but when you look at it, it will remind you of what you really wanted to do.

30

NOVEMBER

THIS DAY FOR EVERYONE

You may have thought certain plans were settled and in detail. Since then, however, events have made it clear you must reassess these. As much of a nuisance as it seems, once you begin, you'll realize how much circumstances have changed—and how much your own plans need a rethink.

GIFTS Humorous, Eloquent, Wise

CHALLENGES Ruffled, Nervy, Condescending

NUMBER 4

(0+1) + (1+2) = 4

Even if I have no idea how to do something, I'll give it a try

You

Many think of the pursuit of fun as something that's all about childhood. But for you as a fire sign and particularly as someone ruled by the expansive and playful planet Jupiter, it is natural to want to turn whatever you're doing—even something serious—into fun.

You'll want to bring joy into what you are experiencing. You may even want to get those around you, those individuals who are usually grumpy, to enjoy things and to have a good time, too. In some cases, it requires planning, but in others it is simply a matter of the attitude or the people you get involved, or perhaps the places you go, or what you have in mind.

While others might choose a rather dark or difficult or dull setting, you will find someplace that is itself an invitation to have a good time. And, just as much, it's about spontaneity: taking advantage of the moment.

The point of this is to refuse to let those who regard themselves as practical and, therefore, dull to overshadow your natural joy in life, whatever the nature of the setting or your relationship—whether it's personal, romantic, or has to do with your life in the world or a job. Ensure that whatever you are doing at least gives you the opportunity not just to succeed, but to have a really good time doing it.

You and others

There are two kinds of people. There are the people you know because they're family or colleagues or even neighbors—they may be fun or not. But then there is another group of people: they're pals. They, too, could be family or neighbors, but these individuals add to your life. They add enthusiasm, they add support, and most of all, they add magic.

Health and well-being

As an energetic fire sign, nothing feels better to you than challenging your body, discovering just how far you can push it before you're exhausted. But unless you are an athlete, that's not always wise—or possible. However, what you can do is feel your muscles move and the energy you use with every step, especially if you've some stairs to climb.

Goals and challenges

Everybody knows somebody who's sensible. For you, as a Sagittarius and a resilient fire sign, the sensible people may seem to be speaking a foreign language to you, simply because you tend to rate what you do on the potential for achievement and excitement, not how sensible it is. Listen to those feelings within, not to those very cautious individuals.

01
DECEMBER

THIS DAY FOR EVERYONE

In their enthusiasm to tell you about certain new ideas they think you'd like, one particular individual could be overenthusiastic. They may even seem to be bullying you. Yet what they have in mind could be in your best interests. You won't know until you do a little exploration.

I swear I'll learn something new each day. It doesn't last, but it is fun

You

As one of the three fire signs—Aries, Leo, and you, Sagittarius— it is very much your nature to feel excited about your day, your week, and even your life. The fire signs are all about enthusiasm, and a contagious zest for life.

That excitement comes as naturally to you as breathing, in that you don't really think about it. However, it is worth being aware that certain individuals not only don't understand it, they take a negative view of this upbeat approach to life. Of course, they don't think of it that way—they think they are being "sensible." Getting along with them? There's a trick to that: listen to them, and occasionally take advantage of the advice they give.

However, you may not want to get too close to them, but instead ensure that those you are close to in your life are like you—upbeat, optimistic, and eager to explore new things. Create that balance in your life between those sensible individuals and those who share your natural enthusiasm and you'll be able to make the best of your own enthusiasm.

That way, when you're about to do something that might be a little risky, you'll be able to talk to somebody who will help you balance that and ensure that you achieve exactly what you hope for—in whatever activity you're doing, but also in your life.

You and others

Many people enjoy spending time with friends who go back a long way: sometimes childhood friends, former classmates, or even from the old neighborhood. While they are wonderful, it's also important that you have friends who are linked with who you are at the moment, and who will support your natural enthusiasm. Whatever it is you decide to do, you'll be sure they will back you up.

Health and well-being

For most Sagittarians, sticking to any kind of precise regimen is difficult, but being ruled by the inquisitive Jupiter, you're always interested in learning something new. Make that the core of your well-being regimen, whether it's what you do or what you eat, and you will be continually fascinated by your options.

Goals and challenges

The trick is to blend your life—to blend elements of the past and the present and to use that to make decisions about your goals. Usually, as a fire sign, you'll leap into that activity first and make decisions later. It's worth pausing before you start, even if for a few minutes.

02

DECEMBER

GIFTS Jocular, Exuberant, Hearty

CHALLENGES Damning, Unruly, Flaky

NUMBER 6

(0+3) + (1+2) = 6

Not everybody understands that change is essential to Sagittarians

You

Everybody knows certain people who are very good at giving advice. The trouble is, the advice they give isn't actually of benefit to you. Rather, their thinking is to alter your approach to life so you will be of more benefit to them, so that you'll be more like them as individuals.

They don't actually think about, or have any interest in, what makes you tick, personally. This is one of the most important things for you to remember, especially if somebody makes you feel uncomfortable. If they say they're trying to give you a hand or guide you, but have a very different character—if they aren't a fire sign like you are, as a Sagittarius—they are unlikely to view life the way you do. So while their guidance may be well-meaning, it could actually complicate matters. The trick? Thank them for their advice, then ignore them.

In fact, even more than that, thank them, and then spend a little time with someone else who is an enthusiastic fire sign. Do that, and whatever element of your life it is that you're exploring, you'll find that talking with somebody who boosts your spirits and who agrees with your own viewpoint of life will itself clarify your thinking. That, in turn, will give you that extra boost that allows you to take the next step to turning a potential dream into a reality.

You and others

As a Sagittarius, you rarely stop to assess whether people have some agenda or a story when they're talking to you. But there are certain individuals who are called rescuers, who try to help people and fix them, except their way of fixing them is to do things the way they would. Be aware of them.

Health and well-being

From time to time, people don't feel well physically. Also, everyone has dark moments when things don't seem that promising. There can be several reasons: it may be that you're simply tired and you need to eat, you need a rest or a meal. In every case, think about how to improve on your physical well-being first.

Goals and challenges

Long-term goals are important, but they are often tough for Sagittarians, simply because as a fire sign, you're a bit impatient about seeing progress. The secret? Make a list about the stages needed to achieve that goal. And then, as you progress toward it, you can mark off those achievements and measure how far you've come.

03
DECEMBER

THIS DAY FOR EVERYONE

There are many ways to agree to plans, but at the moment, you're being rushed into arrangements you still question. Say exactly that. The fact is, things are still in transition, and you will be tinkering with whatever is arranged over the weeks, if not the months to come.

Discovering an unwelcome commitment is an adventure in disguise

You

You probably never think of it, but it is vital to be aware of the power of your nature, as a sunny fire sign. While you share this warmth with your fellow fire signs Aries and Leo, yours is different—and distinctive—because it is expansive. You have a unique enthusiasm for life. You approach each day with your own unique joy. You inspire others. Your warmth makes them feel that so much is possible, things they wouldn't regard as being within reach if they weren't around you, and viewing life from your perspective.

What's more, this viewpoint is a bit like taking vitamins. Those who hang out with you begin to absorb your enthusiasm. However, it is vital to recognize this goes both ways, and you need to hang out with people who lift your own spirits. It may be that you don't think of it, but if you spend time with those who are habitually negative, you feel as if you've lost your bounce. Ironically, while you may take vitamins and try to eat well, do you notice how you're nourishing your mood?

Are you hanging out with people who encourage you to believe in yourself? Many Sagittarians don't, because you have a natural resilience and feel that those who encourage you are somehow imposing themselves on you. Reflect on this, because you not only deserve a boost, you'd benefit from it.

You and others

Every once in a while, it's important that you get what might be termed an injection of new people in your life. Not just family or friends, who are rather inescapable, but those individuals you hang out with just for fun, or perhaps who inspire you. Keep that variety going and you will recognize how much you benefit from it.

Health and well-being

There are many varieties of health and many reasons for it, and many reasons for well-being. While you will certainly benefit from taking care of yourself, eating well, perhaps taking vitamins and exercising, for you as a fire sign, achieving a goal may give you the biggest boost of all.

Goals and challenges

Every once in a while, it is useful to have a new challenge. However, it is also important for you to write down that challenge. Why? Because as a fire sign you move on swiftly, and once you've dealt with it, you'll already have the next one in mind. If you have written it down and can mark it off as done, then you will be well aware you have achieved it and can move on to the next with the sense of accomplishment.

04

DECEMBER

THIS DAY FOR EVERYONE

You've been trying to win one particularly stubborn individual over to plans you know they'd enjoy. The problem is, they aren't just being stubborn, they won't even listen to what you have to say. Back off, then get them to ask about your ideas. It will require patience, but it will also work.

GIFTS Lively, Debater, Fluent

CHALLENGES Undependable, Reckless, Clumsy

NUMBER 8

(0+5) + (1+2) = 8

I can't resist saying yes to challenges, often before I know what they are

You

Fire-sign enthusiasm is contagious. It is a wonderful quality, and those who are around you benefit from your inquisitiveness and zest for life. But the question is, do you?

Sometimes you're moving on so quickly from one particular activity, plan, or passion to another, from the people and goals central to your life, that you don't actually stop to think about what you have accomplished. If you don't make a note of what you've done or those encounters—which busy Sagittarians rarely do—you may not recognize or recall, who you've met, what you've accomplished, or indeed, what you learned in the process of achieving those goals.

This isn't just important in terms of boosting your spirits—it is worthwhile knowing what you've accomplished. What's more, when it's time to evaluate the past and consider the skills you've added and what you've done, and assess their influence on your goals, it is worth pausing to consider exactly such matters. You enjoy learning for the fun of it. But maybe it's time to focus on adding a skill. Ask a few questions. Explore. The resulting insights could lead to a rethink of your plans, or even to a new vision of what's next. It isn't just about what you've learned. It's also about what you might want to embrace over the coming weeks, months, and the long-term future.

You and others

As a Sagittarius, and someone who talks a lot about what you're doing, often those around you will show up to be helpful. But the question is, do those connections remain? Or do they come, learn from what you're doing and take off again? It's worth thinking about.

Health and well-being

When you're doing a lot, you'll often prop yourself up in certain ways. For Sagittarius, and somebody ruled by Jupiter, caffeine and especially sugar can't do the trick, which is fine. What's most important is to be aware of what you're wanting next week and next month, too.

Goals and challenges

Every once in a while, you need a new challenge, partly because it's exciting defining it, and achieving it is the best thing possible for a Sagittarius. However, it is also important to pause and consider whether the challenge that you are pursuing is very similar to the past, or something entirely new and exciting.

05

DECEMBER

THIS DAY FOR EVERYONE

If you have already talked about what you'd like to do, and hoped to achieve, and are running out of enthusiasm, then it's time to change the subject. In fact, judging by the rather tricky current planetary activity, you are better off sidelining those plans and savoring each day for the pleasure it offers.

GIFTS Candid, Buoyant, Sporty

CHALLENGES Curt, Rebellious, Jumpy

NUMBER 9

(0+6) + (1+2) = 9

Joy is discovering a new way of thinking, living, speaking, or even eating

You

As a fire sign and as a Sagittarius, your sunny, optimistic nature is what draws people to you. Because of this, being a Sagittarius can be great fun. You think and move swiftly, dealing with life's practicalities as they arise, usually without mentioning it. However, this can also mean that you're so self-sufficient that you don't even notice when others want to lend a hand, and still less, don't stop to enjoy the way certain individuals want to spoil you or what they're offering—attention, support, exciting invitations. What's more, you also either don't notice or brush off the "give and take" that's part of most close relationships. This isn't just about practical matters; it's about someone wanting to spend time with you, to spoil you simply by paying attention to you.

Unless you give thought to your reaction, it can alter the balance in that particular relationship, and to an extent, all of them. In fact, many Sagittarians feel uncomfortable, because it's as if you suddenly owe something to those who are being generous to you.

The fact is you give so much to them, and to everybody, in so many ways and every day, that what those individuals are doing for you, or giving to you, is only balancing the equation. Keep that in mind, and when that lovely and loving energy comes your way, you'll not only enjoy it, you'll embrace it.

You and others

For you, saying yes seems strange, simply because you're the one who's usually making things happen. However, when others offer you support, it is important to say yes, because that will lead to valuable discussions and even bring you closer in ways you couldn't have imagined possible.

Health and well-being

While you can go off and do something that will make you fit on your own, how about making it a game? How about making it playful? How about enjoying it? That's one of the most important things for you as a Sagittarius—to turn even things that are good for you into fun.

Goals and challenges

As someone who thinks and moves swiftly, the idea of sitting down and making a list, even a grocery list, is difficult for you. Yet, if you list your goals, and read that list fairly often, you'll realize how much you have accomplished and realize what a joy it is to make that effort—and see that effort pay off.

06

DECEMBER

THIS DAY FOR EVERYONE

Long ago, you learned to live with, and in some cases, to agree to disagree with, certain individuals. But if you're going to take certain complex plans to the next stage, you have no choice but to find a way to deal with those issues— and in detail. It won't be easy, but it is vital.

GIFTS Vibrant, Bold, Jokey

CHALLENGES Rash, Charged, Madcap

NUMBER 1

(0+7) + (1+2) = 10 = (1+0) = 1

The toughest physical challenges can be mastered. Loving another is another matter

You

Having been born an optimist, you don't really think about whether certain people or certain situations could be risky, or even undermine you. When you notice that you're struggling, you generally just try different solutions, do more, consider options, and work harder.

However, when tricky situations arise, it's worth pausing to consider exactly what's happening, and who's behind them. While it is true that sometimes these can't be avoided, you will simply muster that time, energy, effort, or persistence—and, possibly, facts necessary to deal with the matter in question.

This approach means you will be prepared for what's next. Still, there have been times when those situations involved individuals who, in some way, were taking advantage of you. Being an optimist, you refused to recognize the facts, which could mean they had time to create serious problems. We're all here to learn from such experiences and spot troublemakers before they can do any damage.

That is your lesson, even in minor situations. It could involve family, friends, or colleagues who leave what should be their tasks for you to deal with. The more conscious you are, the more swiftly you can discuss the matter or make your own decision about what to do. Clear this up, and you'll free yourself for those joys that are so important for you.

You and others

Out of character as it may be, you're encouraged to allow those around you, friends, colleagues, or even family, to take the lead. This isn't natural for you, but it will be helpful. Why? Simply because the way they approach things will be very different from the way you do and you might well learn a lot.

Health and well-being

There are all sorts of approaches to well-being—to what you eat, and all varieties of exercise. But here's the secret, one that is especially important for you as a Sagittarius: it is to walk, just to walk. And as you walk, to breathe, to take deep breaths. Do both of those, and you will be amazed how much you benefit from it.

Goals and challenges

It is hard to believe that you actually need new goals from time to time, but in a way you do. It's like vitamins, and this encourages you to get excited, to focus on the future, to make a new plan, and most of all, to develop a new passion and enthusiasm for life.

THIS DAY FOR EVERYONE

Sooner or later, you'll need to take a tough line with somebody who's difficult on the best of days. While it is understandable that you're putting off tackling the issues in question, these won't vanish. You may in fact be better off tackling things in stages. Slowly but surely, you'll get there.

GIFTS Enthusiastic, Honest, Animated

CHALLENGES Inconstant, Superficial, Edgy

NUMBER 2

$(0+8) + (1+2) = 11 = (1+1) = 2$

Some adore routine. The challenge for a Sagittarius is living with such individuals

You

Being ruled by the expansive planet Jupiter, you thrive on anything new. Where others are hesitant about undertaking new plans or challenges, you can't wait. You enjoy going new places, meeting new people and delving into the unfamiliar. This is very much part of your nature as a Sagittarius, and somebody for whom Jupiter is a strong player in your life. However, it also means that you need to find a balance between your existing arrangements, especially those that are long-standing, and any tempting new activities.

This can be tricky. It's not that one is better than another, but in your enthusiasm to learn about what has just come your way, you can easily neglect elements of the past, whether it's habits or activities that are worth your while, or even certain individuals.

Finding that balance isn't just important, it is essential, because the more you have in your life—the more you're juggling—the more significant certain elements of the past will be. They offer stability: certain relationships that are a valuable part of your life. Make achieving that balance one of your goals—an ongoing goal—and instead of feeling that you always need to catch up, as you create your schedule, you will balance those elements that form a basis for your life with the present and the excitement the future holds.

You and others

It's easy to get bored with the same thing. Yet, in order to achieve certain goals, that's exactly what you need. The trick to dealing with this is to do other things that aren't just flexible, they are also changeable. Find that balance and achieve those goals, and you'll have a good time, and quite possibly learn a lot in the process.

Health and well-being

Everybody knows that eating well and sleeping enough is important. However, for you as a Sagittarius, you're always bargaining with destiny, feeling that if you can fit a little more into each day, then it will be fine. It is—in the short term. But it is also important to recognize that your body, like a car, needs fuel and it needs it regularly.

Goals and challenges

The question that's important to ask yourself is, what have you won recently? That may sound strange, and in fact, that's the point. Often you won't even think of what you have achieved. You don't stop to notice. But if you do, you will also be excited about that and might even give yourself a valuable pat on your own back.

08

DECEMBER

GIFTS   Eager, Ebullient, Wide-ranging

CHALLENGES   Restless, Nervy, Capricious

NUMBER 3

$(0+9) + (1+2) = 12 = (1+2) = 3$

Trusting nature is one thing; trusting a human being is quite another matter

You

The impatient fire-sign side of your nature loves fast action, and equally struggles when you're stuck dealing with life's duties and dull details. While these often slow you down and are frustrating, if not aggravating, you also learn a lot from them. In fact, these serve a purpose. While you prefer to move swiftly from one activity or obligation to the next, these painstaking matters—whatever their nature: personal, work-related or otherwise—all slow your pace and force you to examine what you're doing, learning, or achieving.

The fact is, if you weren't cornered into this variety of review, you'd be unaware of what you've done. True, you are sometimes forced to keep track anyway. As a result, when you need to list your achievements to get a job or a license, for example, the details are handy.

That, alone, is an amazing payoff. Better yet, those insights may help you streamline tedious tasks. While this type of organization doesn't come naturally to you, once you begin doing it, you'll find it enables you to enjoy things that you used to ignore, simply because they seemed such a nuisance. This is the trick to being a fire sign and enjoying life's luxuries. Instead of rushing through tasks, take time to do them, and appreciate how sensual the achievement of those tasks is, and how sensual the rest of life can be as well.

You and others

Sometimes the best links in your life are formed with very different types of people, people who ordinarily you wouldn't get along with. But then, this is no surprise. If you've dealt only with those who are exactly like you, you'd already know them. The trick is to let each of those companions teach you something—about the world, and even more, about yourself.

Health and well-being

Because most Sagittarians are chronically short of time, the idea of so-called fast food is very appealing. Except as you know, it often isn't that good for you and can get very boring. But the trick is to make it nutritious and delicious fast food. It can be done.

Goals and challenges

It's important to set up your own challenges. You would think that's obvious, but sometimes you will allow those around you, an organization or certain individuals, to tell you what to do, and it is easier to let them figure it out. Except as you will soon discover, you will have streamlined the way to achieve those goals, and in ways others would never have thought of.

09

DECEMBER

THIS DAY FOR EVERYONE

It is said that you should never go to bed without settling differences, yet if, as is the case now, you want to at least express hope that you're reaching an accord with others, even saying that might be challenging. But when you wake up in the morning, you will be glad you did.

S
/
A
\
G
/
I
\
T
\
T
\
A
/
R
\
I
/
U
\
S

A day without at least a small risk is like a day without sunshine

You

The single word "spontaneity" could be said to be the keyword for all those born under the fire signs. That's you, as a Sagittarius—but also Aries and Leo. You all think and move swiftly. Not only does it come naturally, you enjoy it. Yet as you are aware, not everyone in the world around you—from family or friends to colleagues, if you work—understands or, in fact, appreciates it.

There is a trick to learning to deal with those who think and act more slowly, and it is to take advantage, in the nicest possible way, of their slower pace.

These individuals, especially the earth signs—Taurus, Virgo, and Capricorn—think and move slowly, but are also thorough, and both enjoy and are superb at taking care of the variety of details that you find extremely dull. The problem? In your haste, you often forget to ask for help.

This is not simply about appreciating others. It's about giving those you know a chance to do what they're good at, and for you to focus on what you're best at, and enjoy. That way, you will also avoid the complaints that come with you attempting to deal with the kinds of details others enjoy, and the compliments that come with your ability to make magic happen, and in a way that the other signs simply aren't able to do.

You and others

As you know, there are certain individuals who are allies—your friends—who will be beside you, who will, as some people say, have your back when you're doing something tricky. Or perhaps they will be the earth sign who you need, who will help guide you. Whatever you do, trust these individuals.

Health and well-being

As you're told from time to time as a fire sign, you can get wound up, so wound up that you don't even realize you are exhausted. The lesson is to stop, maybe even if you don't feel tired. It won't be until you do actually stop and take a couple of deep breaths that you realize that irritated mood is nothing but sheer fatigue.

Goals and challenges

Everybody has to set goals—even you do when you're at your most rushed. It's just that those around you tend to set goals that are more detailed than yours. Talking them over may drive you crazy, but it is better to do it at the outset than to try to do it when you're already well into those activities.

10

DECEMBER

THIS DAY FOR EVERYONE

Sometimes, discussions are about an exchange of ideas. At the moment, however, it would seem that your main role in several such discussions is as a listener. Tempting as it is to offer advice, it's not really wanted, or, in fact, helpful. The individual in question needs to talk, and talk, and talk.

GIFTS   Persuasive, Heroic, Frank

CHALLENGES   Demeaning, Defiant, Fiery

NUMBER 5

(1+1) + (1+2) = 5

Understanding others' beliefs isn't easy, but trying to learn about them is fascinating

You

As a Sagittarius and somebody ruled by the inquisitive, philosophically inclined planet Jupiter, you're fascinated by those who talk about new, unfamiliar, or intriguing ways of looking at life. This ranges from how life works here on Earth, to those who discuss ways of thinking, or even realms, that extend beyond our everyday world. They fascinate you, and in some cases, you are drawn into exploring their ideas or even teachings.

This can be tricky for you, because while you can be drawn to those who set themselves up as gurus who give advice, you don't necessarily question their ideas. It is simply that their ideas so intrigue you, you could turn plans into action, and possibly, commitments, without much thought. However, it is important to pause, and ask a few questions.

While some may have worthwhile ideas and good suggestions, others may be demanding or possessive. You may even battle with them. While that may be complicated, and while those individuals who set themselves up as authorities can be as irritating as they are fascinating, the experience is worth your time.

With every encounter you can broaden your horizons and discover interesting ideas or people. Yet while you think of yourself as being inquisitive, you have a stubborn streak, and you could well be facing it here.

You and others

You don't think of yourself as having any particular characteristics because you are simply true to yourself. Yet the fact is, certain individuals find your passionate nature, your intensity, and the fact that you are entirely who you are, attractive and charming. Take advantage of this, in the sense of recognizing how much you add to the lives of others.

Health and well-being

As somebody who is an inspiration to others and full of energy, every once in a while, you have to remember to take care of yourself, to take care of your body and your energy level. This has to do perhaps with pausing and taking a rest, perhaps with eating a little differently, or perhaps with letting those who care so much about you spoil you in the way they'd like to.

Goals and challenges

Occasionally you need to rethink what you're doing—not just your objectives, but how you're approaching them. If you do that, it may be that certain simple changes will prevent you from complicating matters that would require more serious changes along the line.

11

DECEMBER

THIS DAY FOR EVERYONE

The last thing you're in the mood for is disappointing people and leaving situations undone. But certain individuals have ignored your cautious advice and are blaming you for their problems. Explain firmly where you stand, then withdraw from discussions. There really is nothing more to say.

GIFTS Forthright, Droll, Fluent

NUMBER 6

CHALLENGES Blunt, Wacky, Capricious

(1+2) + (1+2) = 6

The best adventure is as challenging as it is unexpected

You

You sometimes think the best gift you could possibly have is some free time—time to relax, time to do what you want, time to think. But, despite those dreams, it seems like you always have too much to do. Yet you also tend to refuse offers of help from those around you, some of whom really enjoy doing exactly that kind of thing. They are not only able to impose order on life's tedious practicalities, they'll happily organize you, then deal with those matters so you don't have to do.

Still, you say "No." Why? Usually, the reason is that you feel explaining what needs to be done would take too much time. But the fact is, you are impatient. Others can probably figure out how to deal with any such matters and with what you're doing—and probably better than you.

That may be a shock. However, at the same time it will create an entirely new relationship, first, with time—you will have more of it. But it will also alter your relationship with those individuals you've simply dismissed as being unable to handle things as well as you do. They can, and actually, better than you. This recognition of their abilities will change your relationship as well. They will know you appreciate them, and trust them with those tasks. Even more than that, you will be able to speak as equals, too.

You and others

Recognizing that some individuals have the same joy you do in being spontaneous, at acting swiftly, yet others don't, is a great gift. In both cases, you'll want to thank them for what they offer, but also you want to recognize who you can trust with those pressing tasks.

Health and well-being

Many people don't think of this. But for you as a Sagittarius, in particular, clearing out your space is as important as exercise. Getting rid of excess stuff, which you look at and which depletes your energy, is as important as doing actual exercise.

Goals and challenges

One of your biggest challenges is keeping track of what you've done. While you may keep a diary, actually noting your achievements is a lot more difficult. Except how else will you remember what you achieved if you don't at least make a note or save a souvenir that will remind you of those achievements?

S / A \ G / I \ T \ T \ A / R \ I / U \ S

12

DECEMBER

Love is a joy and a challenge; understanding another is an endless puzzle

You

As an expansive fire sign and a Sagittarius, you hate regretting what you didn't do, so you try to fit everything you can into any day, any week, or any month—or even any year. While this means you're able to get an amazing amount done, you can be overwhelmed, if not driven crazy by tasks and obligations that pile up. Worse, those obligations are even more overwhelming because you set them for yourself. Of course, when you did, you were confident you had time to fit those tasks in, along with everything else.

The trick? Borrow a characteristic from your neighboring sign, Capricorn, which is a practical earth sign. That may seem dull to you, as a fire sign, yet the exhaustion you feel and the disappointment you experience when you have no time to do what you intend, or to do it properly, isn't worth it.

This is important because your life is about making new friends and encountering people. And if you don't have time to spend with them, then you won't get to know them and deepen that early acquaintanceship into something lasting. This slower pace probably won't come naturally to you as a fire sign and as a Sagittarius, but once you learn that skill, and do it from time to time, it will add enormously to your life, day by day, week by week, and month by month.

You and others

Core to your life are family and friends: people you have been with a long time. But ironically, when you meet new people and don't have time to get to know them, it's difficult to have that feeling of closeness, of trust and intimacy. Regard the time you spend with them as an investment in friendships and in your future.

Health and well-being

Sometimes you get so involved in what you're doing that you regard even going to sleep as a failure. While you're not conscious of that, it does happen and it means you're unable to enjoy all of life because you are exhausted. The trick, of course, is to fall asleep before you collapse in a heap.

Goals and challenges

You set your own pace, you set your own goals, but sometimes you don't realize that because you're in such a hurry, it seems like destiny has done it for you. The trick, and the magic, for you is to realize that you have created those goals—and you can set the pace for them.

THIS DAY FOR EVERYONE

There is a difference between a possible solution for a problem—and you have lots of those—and the kind of solution you can be sure will last. At the moment, nothing quite fits. While others are impatient, your instincts tell you it is vital that you wait until more worthwhile ideas surface.

13
DECEMBER

GIFTS Passionate, Energetic, Excited

CHALLENGES Unreliable, Abrupt, Flustered

NUMBER 8

$(1+4) + (1+2) = 8$

There are physical challenges. Those of an emotional nature are something else

SAGITTARIUS

You

Often, when you're making a plan or promising something to others, in your enthusiasm you'll say that you can do far more than, realistically, you know is possible. But you've done it in the past, although it may have exhausted you and taken far longer than you thought. And because of that, you will be thinking you can do it again.

However, you have another option. You could pause, and simply take a different approach. This involves thinking about what needs to be done, the time those activities and obligations will take, and the hours in the day, and viewing them from an entirely different angle. But it is also about doing something that is completely out of character, and that is asking for the support and help of others. Both of these are very much against your nature as an impulsive, independent fire sign.

Yet you live in a world of people who not only like you, they'll be happy to help you, and better yet, to learn from you. They'd be excited to spend time with you. True, this won't come naturally to you, because despite being sociable you're sure it's easier to do everything yourself. However, not only will these individuals lend a hand, you'll find you're able to get more out of each day and, even more, you'll be able to deepen those relationships in ways you've hoped for, but not yet achieved.

You and others

Even if you're not particularly into astrology, you sense your fire-sign nature, the speed at which you think and the way in which you'll tend to override the activities of those who don't move as swiftly. Even if they may be better skilled at certain activities than you are, think carefully before you do it again.

Health and well-being

Often, it's important that you pause before you begin doing something, and think about whether you actually have the energy to do it, or would benefit from someone else's support, guidance, or perhaps even handing it over to another individual. This won't come naturally, at least at first. But the payoff for making those changes will be huge, if not lifelong.

Goals and challenges

You have a stubborn streak. You don't think of it that way, because you're always enthusiastic about new ideas. But there are certain activities, certain relationships and even certain things you simply don't consider because long ago, you decided it wasn't your thing. If ever there was a time to consider allowing those to be your thing, it's now.

14

DECEMBER

GIFTS Inquisitive, Honest, Spirited

CHALLENGES Delving, Clumsy, Eruptive

NUMBER 9

(1+5) + (1+2) = 9

Laughter is said to cure even the darkest moods. It works for me

You

The fire-sign motto, especially for you as a Sagittarius, is that "life is meant to be fun."

Whatever you're doing—from duties or a job, and even seriously challenging tasks—can be a joy, as long as you approach them in the right way. And that is in the fire-sign manner. While at times that's true, you can also act so swiftly that you forget about important details and unwittingly complicate matters.

The problem is, if you moved at a slower pace, you'd be able to deal with them right away. And if you ignore them entirely, you'll end up having to go back over things, which is, of course, even worse. Yet still, the optimistic side of your fire-sign nature says that life at its best is lived at a swift pace, even if that means ignoring details.

The trick is to find a balance between the two—to occasionally adopt that jet-fueled approach to living when it doesn't matter, but also, when it is necessary, to take time to deal with details, most of which will come up sooner or later.

Equally, focus on spending time with those you care about most, those individuals whose company brings you joy. Find the balance between these every day, and not only will you get as much done as you can, you will enjoy the day itself all the more.

You and others

You may think you know who brings you joy, and what activities lift your spirits. But sometimes, you don't stop to try new ones, simply because you're so busy with the old ones. The message from the heavens is to try something new regularly, if not every week.

Health and well-being

There are two kinds of pushing. There's pushing to make yourself healthy and strong, and there's pushing to get everything done, which means you never get enough done, and you're always exhausted because you're trying to catch up. Give some thought to this approach—to your diary and your schedule.

Goals and challenges

As you well know, you hate rules and regulations. Yet every once in a while, situations demand that, either because it's part of them, or occasionally for someone's safety or well-being. Whatever the case, it's time to choose your battles. You could fight them, or you could simply accept them and move on.

15
DECEMBER

THIS DAY FOR EVERYONE

The planetary activity ahead won't just be exciting. Much of what's coming your way could turn into something worthwhile and often of a long-term nature. However, that won't be clear at the time, which means you owe it to yourself to explore everything, including what seems unappealing.

When others question me, it's not through distrust but genuine curiosity

You

As a Sagittarius you're not only sociable, you're genuinely interested in others, so frequently face the challenge that comes with the desire to talk to those you meet, and hear what they're up to, while always being aware that you have things to do. That awareness that you have dozens of things to do before the end of the day is one thing. But if the person you're talking to isn't a Sagittarius, their conversational style will be more relaxed than yours. When the topic wanders from one thing to another, you will get increasingly uptight.

The trick? Set aside time to have a good chat, enough so that you can exchange ideas and then move on. This may mean juggling your schedule, but that way, you will only have to do it once.

For you, life as a Sagittarius can mean always rushing on to whatever is next—from appointments to work. But it applies as much to simply hanging out with others.

Whatever the case, the trick is to do whatever it is that you need to do, and allow the time you need to do it and without cutting it short, which is your tendency as a Sagittarius and someone who always juggles several things at once. When you achieve this skill—and it is, indeed, a very great skill—not only will you be able to enjoy life, it will be being the best that any Sagittarian can be.

You and others

Those who know you will understand the pace at which you live—and others will learn. But those who care most about you will help you remember that haste doesn't always achieve the most.

Health and well-being

Deep down, you have a feeling that you can outdo the rest of the world and outdo everybody else, whether it has to do with being creative, whether it has to do with what you fit into a day, or what you accomplish in a lifetime. The fact is, even as a Sagittarius, you have your vulnerable points, one of which is the need to stop and assess what you can do.

Goals and challenges

There are two rules for you to remember. One is that it's okay to take on too much. The second is that it is okay to cut back: that is, when you realize that you literally can't do what you thought as the day began. It's all right to say that either you'll do it tomorrow, or perhaps you won't do it at all.

16

DECEMBER

GIFTS Lighthearted, Eager, Athletic

CHALLENGES Impulsive, Cursory, Erratic

NUMBER 2

$(1+7) + (1+2) = 11 = (1+1) = 2$

The best questions can't be answered in a day

You

Being ruled by the planet Jupiter—the planet of growth, expansion, and just plain good fortune—is a real gift. Your life is full of amazing people, and wonderful things come your way. Despite that, you're often impatient, to the extent that you will agree to offers without checking the facts, possibly because you're overly eager or don't have the time to ask questions—or, you simply hope everything will work out.

While this hasty approach to various elements of life and planning is typical for you as a Sagittarius, it is a habit, not an unchanging destiny. You can learn to examine the practical side of things—matters such as timing, finances, and the support you need. Of course, if you wait long enough, you can do that in a hurry, too. And you probably did in the past, possibly more than once.

Or you can begin to approach being a Sagittarius differently. Instead of putting off details until the last minute, which has almost become a habit in your life, you can take one of your best assets, which is your enthusiasm, and share it with others. Ask them to join you in figuring out how to make the best of certain plans, projects, or passions, and then to help you turn that into reality.

It may not be your usual approach, but it will be easier—and a lot more fun.

You and others

You already know how important it is to keep old friends in your life. Also, you have a strong instinct about making new ones. When someone's exciting, you'll draw them closer to you. However, what you don't do is edit those individuals. That is, to recognize that as new ones come into your life, it's time to let go of some. You might still see them out of habit, but actually, it is time to say farewell.

Health and well-being

The ups and downs you face as a Sagittarius can be stressful, and you're resilient. However, it's easier if—instead of draining your energy, as you do with those ups and downs—you find a new balance. Some of that will include trusting those around you with some of the more stressful of those activities.

Goals and challenges

You thrive on challenges: not because you want problems, but because it's a kind of exercise for you. It's like doing a puzzle, but a life puzzle. It is important to recognize that if you have too many challenges going at any one time, you can't do any of them well. The solution? Pick and choose carefully.

17 DECEMBER

THIS DAY FOR EVERYONE

There's a difference between making tentative plans, which is what this period is all about, and lasting commitments. The problem is, one particular individual views arrangements as final. Gently but firmly help them understand that plans that are flexible will be better all around.

Walking faster than I have to makes me feel really alive

You

Considering what you're planning isn't just important, it's vital. You know that, but also you'd rather plunge in and then think about them while you're actually organizing things.

You take this approach because you're convinced that if you're in the midst of it, then you can react swiftly and base plans on recent experience. While that makes sense from one perspective, you are urged to pause regularly and think about what you're organizing—and for two reasons.

One, if you're exhausted or overwhelmed, you can be moody or irritable without really knowing why, and your decisions are unlikely to be wise or sensible. If, on the other hand, you pause or, alternatively, do something that is very out of character and make a list, or even ask others for guidance or assistance, then you can turn those seemingly overwhelming tasks into something that isn't just manageable, it's fun.

In fact, if you take things in stages, you can turn what would otherwise have been a crisis into something creative. This approach may be out of character, and it may seem as if you're compromising. However, shifting from that sense of being overwhelmed, which can be a Sagittarian signature, to a sense of pacing— as if you were doing a dance—isn't just a good idea, it can be a thing of beauty.

You and others

Some people are just good company, but a few very special people are almost like magnets for good luck. They have the ability to spot something exciting, and even more than that, to bring all the pieces together, to turn those exciting concepts into a part of a life that you share with them. Draw them close to you.

Health and well-being

The concept of resting seems very dull and dreary to you. In fact, it almost seems like a compromise. However, for you as a Sagittarius and a fire sign, and somebody who tends to live life full-steam ahead, simple rest is like taking very powerful vitamins.

Goals and challenges

Every once in a while, you need a new challenge to get you going. This is very much part of your nature. However, there is a secret to this, and that secret is to select that new challenge very carefully.

18

DECEMBER

THIS DAY FOR EVERYONE

Few things are more precious than time with loved ones. Now somebody you care about is putting others first. Before you get hurt or angry, ask what's going on. The odds are that they have obligations they haven't mentioned. Once they explain, you'll understand exactly what it is they're dealing with.

GIFTS Courageous, Outspoken, Vibrant

CHALLENGES Reckless, Audacious, Unstable

NUMBER 4

(1+9) + (1+2) = 13 = (1+3) = 4

Joy lives in both life's quiet moments and its most uproarious parties

You

As a Sagittarius and somebody who is a life enthusiast, you will often decide to figure out the perfect plan—for the day, the perfect way to do something, the perfect long-term goal, or even life plan. While very true to your nature as an idealistic Sagittarian, the problem is that you can get addicted to that kind of perfection, when often, what life brings your way isn't quite like that.

This means you have no choice but to start with what you have, or are facing, in the here and now, then do the best you can. If you're being idealistic, that can seem like a compromise. However, if you simply decide to begin with what you have in the present and take each step as it comes, you'll find you experience all sorts of unexpected delights.

You'll be able to go more deeply into certain situations that, otherwise, you'd have given up on. Equally, you'll take time to chat with the people involved, not just about solutions, but instead, about possibilities. And that, in turn, could lead you on a very different path than what you had in mind when you determined to make things perfect—your way.

This doesn't just have to do with your life, your activities, but also your relationships, even your feelings about yourself. The more flexible you are, the more easygoing you are, the more fun you will have being you.

You and others

Very often you're the one who takes the lead. Being a fire sign and being enthusiastic, this comes naturally to you. But there are individuals who are either clearer or perhaps are themselves guides in some way. If they arrive in your life, listen to them. Even if it doesn't come naturally at first, you will soon be glad you did.

Health and well-being

It is terrific to take care of yourself, but as a Sagittarius you can have too much of a good thing—and that would be the case if you take care of yourself too well, by following an obsessive eating regimen, or exercising too much. Being moderate doesn't come naturally to you. But in this particular case, it is vital.

Goals and challenges

You don't always think things through before you take on a goal or face a challenge. Some would be concerned, if not critical, about that. But often the only way you can learn about what you're dealing with is once you're actually in the midst of it. In many cases, this is exactly why it's better to learn about those challenges as you are moving ahead and dealing with them immediately.

19

DECEMBER

THIS DAY FOR EVERYONE

Usually, there's no wrong way to express concern about a matter somebody is struggling with. However, one particular individual is presenting an upbeat facade to the world, and would be very upset if they thought you saw through it. What they will need, however, is somebody to talk to and to trust.

A badly told but funny joke is better than taking life too seriously

You

Your date forms a bridge between the fire and passion of your Sagittarian nature and the cautious, thorough Capricorn. As you're undoubtedly aware, it is an interesting blend to live with. Yet at the same time, when you understand the difference between the two, they achieve an ongoing balance, and life takes on a new order, but not the kind that extinguishes your fiery passion.

Rather, those feelings are more measured, so instead of being overwhelmed, you manage to get things done and dealt with.

It is an amazing combination, one that enables you to find a power and intelligence that you can use in ways you wouldn't have dreamed possible. The trick to all of this is to recognize that the growth that is part of being alive never stops. If you think of yourself as a project, one you're still working on, it won't be about getting things just right on any one particular day. Instead, it will be about continuing to explore your nature, to discover your inner world, and the wider world.

You will discover how your mind works, your intuition, and the creative side of your nature, and bring them all together in a way that allows you to make the best of each day, each relationship, and what the next day offers. Take that approach, and you will also make the best of being the person you are.

You and others

The best way to be inspired by the two sides of your nature is to hang out with equally multitalented, expansive people. They don't need to be the same. But there are certain individuals who have a gift for doing a number of things at once. Spend time with them, and it will teach you how to use your gift better.

Health and well-being

Knowing when you're doing things perfectly is great. Knowing when you're doing a bit too much of perfect things is even more important. It is easy to glide into what might be termed perfection overdrive, but it's more important to look after yourself than being exhausted.

Goals and challenges

Everybody needs new goals, but the trick is not to start them all at once. Line them up and make a list—even though that doesn't sound very exciting. If, when you're finishing one, you know you can tackle the next one, you'll be all the more excited about finishing it.

20
DECEMBER

THIS DAY FOR EVERYONE

For a long time, you've managed to keep one particularly tricky issue under wraps. It hasn't been easy, but you felt strongly that this was nobody else's business. Now it is, and you'll need to ensure that certain individuals are aware of the full facts, including why you said nothing until now.

Capricorn

December 21– January 19

Capricorn As a practical earth sign, whose symbol is the horned goat, you can achieve the impossible, in the form of ascending a mountain, or attaining an ambition. Being ruled by hardy Saturn, you're discreet about your many kindnesses, but glory in your tough exterior. Your flower is the pansy; your plants are hemp and ivy; your trees, elm and yew. Your stones are symbolic of winter's dark days—black pearls, black diamonds, and jet.

C
A
P
R
I
C
O
R
N

GIFTS Ambitious, Vigilant, Respectful

NUMBER 6

CHALLENGES Disciplinarian, Pedantic, Mean

(2+1) + (1+2) = 6

I'll explore ways to blend—and benefit from—my fiery practicality

C
/
A
\
P
/
R
\
I
/
C
\
O
/
R
\
N

21

DECEMBER

You

Being a December 21st Capricorn, you balance the sign just before yours—Sagittarius, a fire sign—with the far more earthy Capricorn. That fiery side is restless and both enjoys, and thrives on, facing challenges. This is also the part of your nature that is easily bored.

However, the earth-sign part—the Capricorn side—is not only able to focus on whatever you're facing, but mostly, because of your inborn discipline, you have a remarkable ability to stick with a battle, and will amaze others by what you achieve simply by employing that Capricorn focus.

Yet every once in a while, you will experience the restlessness that is part of your Sagittarian side. While, initially, you'll try to chase it away, once you are conscious of it, and even more, how you can benefit from it, you will realize what an asset it is.

Each side of your nature brings the other amazingly useful skills and perceptions, and when you blend the two, you will find that not only do you have a greater capacity to adapt to unexpected changes, you will benefit as much from the joy that is very much a part of your Sagittarian nature, as you will from the stability that comes with being a Capricorn.

The more aware of them you are, the more you will enjoy what each adds to your life.

You and others

It's true that you're generous by nature and you will support friends and family, as well as the world, in ways that are often as appropriate as they are unanticipated. However, there is a part of you that's very discreet about this and prefers to keep those gifts a secret. Do so, but also realize that if you do it openly, you will inspire others.

Health and well-being

Being an earth sign, you have an instinctive understanding about the importance of keeping in shape, and will work hard to do that. However, there is a side of your nature that you tend to neglect, and that has to do with the part that's affected by stress. Allow it to take over, and it can undermine you. Underdoing it? You can begin by simply breathing.

Goals and challenges

Normally, as a Capricorn you have endless goals for this week, for this month, for this year, and for your life—and you don't need more of them. What those goals need is an edit. Do that regularly and you will recognize how much you've done, and then be clearer about what's next.

THIS DAY FOR EVERYONE

Ordinarily, what begins as a dispute ends up ideally with a constructive outcome. But what you're facing now could have as much to do with a fundamental misunderstanding of your and others' objectives. Make discussing and untangling any such issues your priority, and those tensions could vanish.

Each day's surprise could become tomorrow's opportunities

C / A \ P / R \ I / C \ O / R \ N

You

The joys of the physical world are a part of what comes with being a Capricorn. As an earth sign, you are aware of nature around you, in all its forms, from its majesty to an understanding of how things grow. You're conscious of the elements that are an everyday part of our lives, from water to light, the air and energy, and how these, plus sunlight, virtually create your world.

While you try to incorporate these into your life, you are sometimes distracted by everyday duties and obligations to others. That's why it is easy to lose that appreciation for the world around you and, in fact, for something larger than yourself. When that happens, you can lose access to that joy. And you'll feel that loss, but won't always realize what it is, or why. Yet it's important for every person, especially for you, as an earth sign.

There is a trick to dealing with it, and, first, it's to notice it, and then to realize that whatever you're doing, you can reconnect with that power.

You don't need to go anywhere. The simple act of pausing and thinking how amazing it is that you are you, and you're living the life you're living at the moment—that is the best place to start. And it is the best way to recover that joy—and in fact, to begin to feel that joy wrap its arms around you.

You and others

As a Capricorn, you have a knack for helping those around you, except sometimes your instincts correctly tell you that those individuals need to help themselves. The trick is to inspire them. This may be more difficult than you anticipate, but once you do it, you will have given them the greatest gift of all.

Health and well-being

You may not feel yourself influenced by fads. However, when it comes to the shape of your body, it's really easy—simply because, while there are some things you can change, there are others you can't. The solution? To love yourself and love yourself unreservedly, whatever shape you are.

Goals and challenges

It's important to be aware that as an earth sign, you will inevitably set worldly goals and they are easy to measure. When it comes to goals that have to do with your own self and your feelings, however, they are much less easy to measure, but feel much better when you have achieved them.

22

DECEMBER

GIFTS Honorable, Guarded, Elegant

CHALLENGES Glum, Downbeat, Over-serious

NUMBER 8

$(2+3) + (1+2) = 8$

Any challenge is an adventure, if I choose to make it one

You

When living your everyday life, you are thinking about what needs to be done and that's pretty much it. However, you will also have a broader sense of the influence of your actions on those around you, from family and friends to the wider world. Personally, you know exactly what needs to be done, each day, week, month, and, probably, year.

Yet as an earth sign, you have a powerful connection with nature itself, from spotting a plant growing to looking up at the sky, although often without realizing it.

What's more, you are drawn to those who inspire you to focus more on this side of life, often as a balance for your drive to get things done. The trick? Recognize that achieving this balance is itself an adventure. And that is juggling your own obligations to others, your work if you go to a job, but also fulfilling life's joys. It's about blending these into your everyday life.

Part of the fun is figuring it out. It's an adventure, sometimes on your own but, just as often, with others. Just like in fairy tales, it helps if you believe miracles are possible.

That may sound like pure fantasy, but the best way to find out how it works is to try it. And that, for you, as someone born on December 23rd, is one of your challenges.

You and others

There are all sorts of people you can spend time with, of course: some of whom you have no choice about and others who are a joy. But one very important type of person is those who break your habits, who keep you from doing the same old thing, and who take you into new and exciting territory.

Health and well-being

Usually, you're the guide for others. You have initiative and you think things through. However, there are certain individuals who have taken the lead. Let them set an example. What you learn about eating and living well from them won't just be helpful, on occasion it could be life-changing.

Goals and challenges

There is a part of you that wants life to be organized and once it is, feels like you can be relieved. However, it's vital that you recognize that nothing is ever static, and life is about the new and, often, unexpected. It's because what is least expected and most disruptive often brings the greatest gifts.

THIS DAY FOR EVERYONE

The principle of being truthful is vital to you and you try not to lie about anything at all. Yet it seems the only way to avoid getting involved in activities you dread. Unappealing as this seems, you'll soon realize how beneficial those activities will be. If you can't say an enthusiastic yes, just don't say no.

GIFTS Mindful, Solicitous, Wily

CHALLENGES Tight-lipped, Stern, Miserly

NUMBER 9

(2+4) + (1+2) = 9

I can stick to plans, or view them as a jumping-off point

C / A \ P / R \ I / C \ O / R \ N

You

You are quite rightly proud of your drive as a Capricorn. However, you've probably noticed it's easy to confuse those worldly goals with your more personal goals and ideals, and the achievements you have in mind with other goals. Those are the kind that you know others will acknowledge, possibly certain individuals you would like to impress.

Defining this drive is part of your journey. While others may have helpful ideas about the best approach, while you will listen to their suggestions, it is vital that you rewrite their suggestions so they suit you. In some cases, it may be doing something a little differently than others suggest. But, just as often, it will be about discovering something that isn't merely different, it is entirely separate from anything anyone around you, including you, would have conceived.

It's about a breakthrough. True, in some cases, it may seem you're rebelling, but there is another way of looking at it. There is a plan for you—one that is taking you in new and often completely unexpected directions.

And, better yet, simply by exploring it, you'll learn something new, exciting, and magical. This new path enables you to make the best of the earth-sign side of your nature, but also allows you to see what the heavens offer you, and that is where the excitement comes in.

You and others

As a Capricorn you will occasionally want to associate with those you look up to so that they will inspire you. However, if you're feeling anxious, you enjoy being around those who haven't done as well as you simply because they will boost your ego. Of course, the secret is to seek out equals who will draw you forward with them.

Health and well-being

You can do all you can to keep yourself in good shape—eating properly and working out—yet there is still one thing that can undermine you if you don't pay attention to it and that is, quite simply, stress. The remedy? You could do fancy meditation and all of that, but simply taking a walk and a few deep breaths is a good start.

Goals and challenges

While people often write lists of what needs to be done, perhaps the most important thing for you to do is simply to stop and rethink what isn't working. That isn't losing the game; it is actually being creative—and just when it's important.

24

DECEMBER

Plans based on experience chain you to the past. Create each day anew

C
/
A
\
P
/
R
\
I
/
C
\
O
/
R
\
N

25

DECEMBER

You

While you are probably aware that your symbol is the Capricorn goat, you may have seen another—not just the goat, but a creature that is half goat, half fish.

This is one of the most ancient of astrological symbols and dates back to Babylonia, thousands of years ago, yet it is still sometimes used today. The fact that it combines these two creatures reflects an intriguing combination in your character.

While you're best known for the practical, earthy goat side, the fish incorporates the more intuitive, flexible part of your nature. This is intriguing because while it survives very well on land, it can move into the sea and swim through the tides of life. If you think about this when you're facing difficulties, instead of trying to figure everything out as an earth sign would, you may begin to rely on your intuition more.

It's balancing the fundamental toughness of Capricorn with the sensitivity that you may not realize or may even have regarded as weak. The trick to all of this, of course, is to embrace both parts of your nature and to realize that each has a powerful role. The more you understand each part, the more you will be able to take advantage of it and the more you will be able to enjoy who you are and the person you're becoming day by day.

You and others

You may not think of it this way, but sometimes you feel that you need to help others and that you're there to inspire them. That's true. But there are other times when actually they inspire you. What may be most important, however, is those close ties with family, who are always who they are for you every day.

Health and well-being

While as a Capricorn, you enjoy a challenge, including a physical challenge, it is worth noting that gentle movements are as important as those that are challenging and you may even learn more about your body and yourself if you take a gentler approach.

Goals and challenges

Everybody lists their goals and most of them also note their challenges, but the trickiest bit is to embrace those challenges with enthusiasm, knowing that each has come your way to teach you something. And the more enthusiastically you embrace them, the more swiftly you'll learn those lessons.

THIS DAY FOR EVERYONE

By no means are you stubborn, yet you are very attached to certain arrangements, mostly because they've been part of your life for a long time and you rather like the challenges they introduce. Still, these really must come to an end. If you're looking for new challenges, you can expect them soon.

GIFTS Economical, Encouraging, Effective

CHALLENGES Stingy, Scornful, Gloomy

NUMBER 2

(2+6) + (1+2) = 11 = (1+1) = 2

Feelings of passion, whatever their nature, balance my practical side

You

Being an earth sign, when you look at life and your goals from a realistic angle, you think carefully about what you've achieved and, especially, what you haven't. In fact, often, you'll have made a list of those objectives, mostly so when each is achieved, you can mark it off and focus on what's next.

If that list isn't actually on paper, there will certainly be one in your mind. While this is helpful, especially when it comes to deciding what to do first, there is something you'll want to keep in mind, and that is to recognize that life itself is always shifting, and therefore juggling, those goals. So however, much as you achieve, there's no perfect moment when it's all done—because, of course, life moves on. Your list will change, and so will you.

There is a trick to dealing with this—it's to see those constantly shifting goals as being part of a drama. However, these aren't appearing for your entertainment, but rather, so you can grow. And once you're viewing them from this angle, and recognizing they are a variety of theater created so you can learn more about life and the world itself, then you won't take it quite so seriously. In fact, you might even enjoy it, and as you do, you will recognize that every twist and turn is there for you to learn from, to be entertained by—and to inspire the creative side of your nature.

You and others

It's easy to get lost in that game of life and, especially, to view those around you, from family and friends to colleagues, as part of that story. However, those moments between you and them when you're each experiencing breakthroughs remind you just how deep this process is and how much each of you is benefiting from it.

Health and well-being

As a Capricorn, you'll always be happy with a regimen that has to do with how you eat or how you take care of yourself. However, there is another activity that will benefit you and it's something called relaxation: stopping and simply enjoying life as it is, taking one deep breath after another.

Goals and challenges

Everybody dreads setbacks as an indication that either you've done something wrong or it's a difficult period, but actually it's a bit like hiking up a rather steep hill—it spurs growth in you. Note that and not only will you go for them, you will grow from them.

26

DECEMBER

CAPRICORN

GIFTS Dependable, Well-mannered, Sound

NUMBER 3

CHALLENGES Authoritarian, Strict, Standoffish

(2+7) + (1+2) = 12 = (1+2) = 3

Taking chances is an art, one that isn't about planning but courage

C
/
A
\
P
/
R
\
I
/
C
\
O
/
R
\
N

You

As a conscientious Capricorn, you are well aware how unwise it is to live life seeking the approval of others. Yet you live in a world where, despite knowing that fact, there are certain individuals you admire for one reason or another. It may be family or friends, somebody who inspires you. Or the setting may be more worldly—somebody who has undertaken a challenge or, as is often the case, an individual in a professional setting whose approval or assistance is vital if you're going to achieve more.

All seem important in their own way. Yet there is something else you can do. Initially, it may seem strange, but give them your approval. You can let them know how much you're learning from them, and now much you appreciate that. Once you shift the balance, their approval isn't quite as important, and in fact you have, in a way, "changed the rules."

Instead of a life of challenges to be met, you will shift from being aware of them to enjoying what's on offer—whatever the setting. While challenges are good, and you grow from them, sometimes the ability to shift the balance is more important. It is a chance not only to grow but to become more creative. Instead of focusing on knowing most, it's about being wise enough to learn from those challenging situations and those around you.

You and others

Humility is a funny thing. However much certain individuals have accomplished, every once in a while they need the support of others, often about simple matters. Not only will that reveal the necessary facts, it's also a reminder that we all have something to learn. And that process of exchanging ideas is more valuable than the facts you already know.

Health and well-being

Feeling fit is one thing. Feeling energetic when you get up in the morning and being the right weight and shape according to your society can be nice, but it depends on what you were born with. What is most important is simply being able to love yourself, to look in the mirror each day and give yourself an embrace.

Goals and challenges

Everybody needs a challenge, especially a Capricorn. As a goat, having a challenge is very much part of your life, but there are many kinds of challenges. Some of them are public, and some of them are very private. And on occasion, you don't even know you're doing them at the time. It's not until they're history that you realize how much you've achieved.

THIS DAY FOR EVERYONE

For days, if not weeks, you've been avoiding a seriously tricky issue that you quite rightly fear could become explosive. Since this isn't going to vanish in an otherwise quiet period, you're urged to raise and discuss this. Do so now and the odds are good that you'll avoid those dreaded dramas.

GIFTS Unflinching, Conventional, Upstanding

NUMBER 4

CHALLENGES Stern, Old-fashioned, Grouchy

(2+8) + (1+2) = 13 = (1+3) = 4

Worldly achievements are terrific, but personal happiness is a better companion

C
/
A
\
P
/
R
\
I
/
C
\
O
/
R
\
N

You

As a Capricorn, you deal with an unusual, in fact rare, combination of drive and desire to achieve in the world you're in. It may not be commercial, it may be your own world.

However, another side of your nature can struggle, if not be amazingly anxious about getting things right. At times you struggle with self-doubt. Some would say that this is the reason you chose to be a Capricorn: to learn from both the challenges and the doubts you are facing. Some question that idea of choosing this.

However, if you choose the way to live, work, and take care of yourself that suits you, it could well be that you'll have been drawn to life as a Capricorn, with its unique gifts and lessons.

Think of this when fears arise, and you will not only learn from them, you may well find you are able to share that wisdom with others as well. And whatever form it takes, this discovery will enable you both to discuss your experiences and recall how much you've benefited from them.

In each case, recognizing that you're not alone in those doubts is one of the secrets of life for you. And when you recognize that, you will be able to deal with your doubts and help others in ways that you can't imagine at the time, as well as bringing a very special variety of support and help to the world.

You and others

Speaking of doubts, you can sometimes think that others have it easy when you don't really know them. But as you become acquainted with them, you realize that they're wrestling with exactly the same kind of doubts you are and that, instead of standing back and looking at each other, you can support each other.

Health and well-being

Yes, food and exercise are important—and getting those right helps you feel well. But the thing that actually makes you feel terrific when you get up in the morning, and just as terrific when you go to bed at night, is simple happiness, and that comes with accepting who you are today: now, in the moment. Learn that skill and everything else will fade away.

Goals and challenges

As a Capricorn, you tend to aim high, which is admirable, but it's vital that you ask the question of whether you actually want this goal. Because you tend to aim so high, the goal is often for something that touches your heart and your soul. Ask yourself this. The answer may surprise you.

28

DECEMBER

THIS DAY FOR EVERYONE

With so much in flux, this hardly seems a logical time to reject certain once-appealing options, but the more you learn, the more aware you are that they really wouldn't be a good idea. What's more, the time has come to narrow your options to those that would work in every setting.

Waiting until you know the outcome before taking chances leads to a very dull life

C
/
A
\
P
/
R
\
I
/
C
\
O
/
R
\
N

You

The question is, are you restless? Do you feel that if you get out and about, see more people and do more things, then you will overcome those feelings? While that might help, the real problem is that for you as a Capricorn, you have too much on your mind and a list of things that need to be done—one that's so long, you're anxious about getting everything done.

This means you're distracted from everyday life and what you achieve each day, in terms of the tasks you actually deal with. Often, you are virtually unaware of the joys you're experiencing, such as spending time with those who matter most to you or, perhaps, helping certain individuals who need a hand.

This is about life's simple joys: taking a slow walk rather than hurrying home. Talking with family or friends. Noting these and savoring them is one of your biggest lessons as a Capricorn.

You have long believed that achievements of various kinds, in a range of settings, would bring that joy. While they're wonderful, as is increasingly clear, the ability to pause and experience joy in what you've accomplished recently, what you're doing no and are planning, is just as rewarding.

Add the joy that comes with doing things for others. Whatever the weather, your life will be filled with sunshine.

You and others

Sometimes it's not easy to trust those who seem to want to spoil you. However, certain individuals have an instinct for taking care of others and the lucky Capricorn will have at least two or three individuals like that in a lifetime. Allow them to fulfill their destiny, let them spoil you, and, just as important, learn to enjoy it.

Health and well-being

There are fitness regimens and there are eating regimens, and while a regimen can be appealing, the most appealing regimen is one that is joyous. If you find something to do or a way to eat that brings you joy, the rest of it will be—if you'll excuse the expression—a piece of cake.

Goals and challenges

Capricorns are famous for their lists: you list what you want to achieve, and you list what you want to do each day, each week, each month, and, sometimes, each year. Those lists are fine, but the secret is to rethink and reorganize them regularly. Do that and not only will you learn a lot, you will rethink your goals as well.

THIS DAY FOR EVERYONE

Watching elements of your life you're fond of, if not very attached to, come undone is no fun. Yet long ago, you realized that these particular pursuits, activities, or even alliances were coming to a natural conclusion. While, understandably, you've battled to keep things going, it is time to say farewell.

GIFTS Solid, Decent, Efficient

CHALLENGES Severe, Grumpy, Melancholic

NUMBER 6

(3+0) + (1+2) = 6

While generosity can be measured, the return it brings is endless.

You

You like to know where you're going and what you'll be doing, so it's your habit to make a list, possibly on paper, but certainly in your mind, of your schedule for the day, the week, the month, and, to a certain extent, for your life.

This is very efficient, but it also can mean you are so busy getting those things done that you ignore the spontaneity that is essential when it actually comes to feeling great. True, achieving your goals is important and that boosts your spirits.

However, the capacity to act spontaneously allows you to do something that excites you in the moment, to be with somebody who lifts your spirits or who touches you in that way few do. And if you can manage to balance the two—achievement and moments of joy—then you will have achieved a rare happiness. While this is what life is about, there isn't a single "right way" to organize your life.

And that is one of the most powerful insights for any Capricorn. It's understanding that it isn't about achieving that list of goals but recognizing that life itself is a creative exercise. So however carefully you plan, you'll probably need to rethink things frequently. And that's the good news, because those last-minute changes in plans will lead you into new, exciting, and possibly unfamiliar territory.

You and others

Certain individuals come into your life for a special reason. You might say they're good friends, or possibly guides; some would call them guardian angels or even gurus. Whoever they are, stay close to them. They are, indeed, there because they're special, and will guide and inspire you.

Health and well-being

Feeling good is subjective. Your muscles may be toned and your digestive system may be working—or, in fact, you may actually have the flu but you could still feel fantastic. The trick for your health and well-being is to learn to have those fantastic feelings whatever is going on with your body.

Goals and challenges

Of course, as a Capricorn, you'd like to have everything outlined and know where you're going. However, sometimes the best challenges are the ones that appear suddenly and the best goals are the ones that get achieved and then vanish. Be willing to revise what you're doing regularly and you'll not only achieve what you want, you'll have a good time doing it.

30

DECEMBER

THIS DAY FOR EVERYONE

This is one of those strange periods during which minor issues aren't just important, they could reveal misunderstandings that go way back. Invest time in asking a few questions or discussing those issues, and take it slowly. What you learn could prove surprisingly informative.

GIFTS Persistent, Go-getting, Resilient

CHALLENGES Wary, Obstinate, Penny-pinching

NUMBER 7

(3+1) + (1+2) = 7

Surprises can be viewed as a disruption, or a breakthrough, if in disguise

C
/
A
\
P
/
R
\
I
/
C
\
O
/
R
\
N

31

DECEMBER

You

Of course, you like things organized and for good reason—so you can plunge in, so you know what you're doing, so you can move swiftly. However, as you've noticed, sometimes life has a different idea and those plans get turned upside down, often instantly.

This is where it's important to recognize those changes as giving you an opportunity to take advantage of a gift you've been given— the freedom to act in the moment. True, this may lead to changes, some disruptive, others demanding. You may have to gather facts, organize plans, find people who'll support you.

For you as a Capricorn, this is challenging simply because you'd rather think ahead, and be organized well in advance. In fact, your independent side likes the idea of not needing anybody else. Yet that can also isolate you.

Instead, situations where you must seek the guidance of someone else are actually a gift that's opening up the world to you. It is also allowing you to do something that doesn't necessarily come naturally to you, and that is to act spontaneously and with joy and trust.

Begin dealing with whatever arises— whether it's personal, involves your life out in the world, or is something new—with an appreciation for those sudden twists and turns, and not only will you handle them wisely, you'll even find yourself enjoying them.

You and others

The capacity to spot people who aren't just friends, but who are guides, who are there to support you, and who do it without expecting anything from you is difficult, simply because as a Capricorn, you live in a world of give and take. Yet once you discover those people, keep them close.

Health and well-being

During tricky periods, everyone exchanges recipes for dealing with stress, whether it's a certain kind of exercise or eating a certain way or even meditation, but there is one really simple one—relax, simply stop, take a few deep breaths, and see what happens.

Goals and challenges

Every Capricorn has a list of things to do. What is most important for you, however, is when you make that list, to do it in pencil and make sure you have an eraser handy. If you are changing that list regularly, you'll know that you're on the right track.

THIS DAY FOR EVERYONE

There are many ways to say the word "No," but the problem is, certain individuals aren't listening to any of them. What's more, this particular group is working together on a goal that they regard as highly possible, but you have doubts. The only solution is to back out—and to do it now.

Calculating the time tasks will require takes longer than simply tackling them

You

Of course, celebrating the New Year and a new life is wonderful, and those Capricorns born on this date often benefit from that sense of celebration and even the resulting resolutions.

But most of all, it is important to recognize that this variety of Capricorn "to-do" list can become restrictive and prevent you from responding to the exciting, if unexpected, events that come your way. However intriguing ideas or offers are, you like to know what you are getting involved in.

Yet when you encounter individuals who are offering things that are beyond anything you know—or opportunities that will take you into new territory in terms of activity, or perhaps mean you'd have to go someplace unfamiliar or learn something new—you'll think about it. Possibly for so long that it's no longer feasible, or, alternatively, you decide that you need to study in order to do it.

The trick to overcoming this resistance to the new and unfamiliar is to recognize that, actually, these activities constitute a variety of vitamins for you. That is, people who you don't know, who draw you into new territory, or activities that force you to learn new things, are all adding to your life and to your mind and to your future. And these, in turn, spur you on to greater growth and discovery.

You and others

Every Capricorn needs people around them they can trust. This isn't easy. In some cases, family will do it; you've known them and you trust them. But in other cases, it is those who you draw to you. Learning to do that, learning to build your own family of friends and supporters, can be one of life's greatest skills.

Health and well-being

Every once in a while, you say to yourself, "I really must relax." And you mean it, but you don't quite know how to do it, simply because you're probably thinking of a very sophisticated course of meditation or going to a spa. But there is a very simple way to relax, and that is to stop your body and your mind, even if it's only for 10 minutes. The technique? Sit down quietly, then breathe.

Goals and challenges

The most important question to ask yourself regularly is when you last set your goals and whether it's time to review them. If you've been sticking with goals that have been around a long time, it may be time to get a new piece of paper and a new set of goals as well.

01

JANUARY

For ages, you've been trying to find a way around a tricky obstacle and form a rather exciting plan. Yet this may be preventing you from getting more involved. Straightforward as this seems, the actual situation is fraught with issues that could turn into serious problems, possibly overnight.

Showing I care makes me feel vulnerable for minutes, but can pay off for a lifetime

C
/
A
\
P
/
R
\
I
/
C
\
O
/
R
\
N

02

JANUARY

You

As you move into the New Year, and further into the sign of Capricorn, you'll become aware that you were born under a sign and during a season when life itself changes. If you're in the northern hemisphere, winter will have settled in. And if you're in the southern hemisphere, it will be all about summer.

Whatever the case, it's as if, with that shift in climate, the rules for life have changed. And that, in turn, will call your attention to the importance of reviewing your own "rules for life" regularly, too. As a Capricorn, once you've thought through your objective, and set a plan, you'll stick with it. And you will regard that persistence as a virtue.

Yet every once in a while, it's important to notice how what might be called the "climate" of your life is changing. And, because of that, it's worth reviewing your priorities, the goals you've set, what you're hoping to say farewell to, and what you're working hard to achieve.

And, as you proceed, you may well note that some of the things you thought should be on their way out actually fit rather well in your life. And, similarly, certain individuals you thought you wanted to say farewell to also fit very well. But most of all, you'll realize that certain goals and passions that once meant a lot to you still do, and still deserve your heartfelt attention.

You and others

Speaking of oppositions, it's important to recognize that in certain situations, you are drawn to the opposite type, not because of anything exotic, but simply because they help you understand yourself. As a driven Capricorn, you don't always pause to go within, but when you spot that inner part of you in another person, you will learn a lot.

Health and well-being

The unexpected could be doing you a big favor if you need to change elements of your life—especially if you have to travel suddenly, or if you've changed your job. It is also time to rethink how you take care of yourself. What you learn in the process won't just be about the present, it will bring powerful insights for the future as well.

Goals and challenges

Every once in a while, it's important to redefine your existing challenges so you can spot more opportunities for the future. That may seem strange, because everyone's encouraged to focus on opportunities, but it may be that the way you've defined your challenges has kept you from exploring certain ideas or offers. At least explore them, and you will discover a new excitement.

THIS DAY FOR EVERYONE

There is a fine line between chatting about what you're planning for the future and actually showing interest in what others suggest. It's tricky, at least at the moment, simply because once you begin discussing ideas with certain individuals, they'll expect to be included in future plans.

Hurling myself into a goal I'm passionate about isn't irrational, it's life at its best

You

As a Capricorn, you probably have at least one list, a list of what you need to do today. However, that list may have sub-lists, things from the past that come to mind, or goals for the week or of a more long-term nature. You may not have written out that list; often it's in your mind, and you repeat it to yourself.

That's how Capricorns get more done that most other signs. Yet there is another kind of list—one that is playful, a fantasy list—a list that describes the things you couldn't possibly do. Why? Because as an earthbound Capricorn, you tend to get so focused on what seems practical and realistic that you don't even consider the possibility of something outlandish. By making two lists, you release the power of your unconscious, the part of you that is not bounded by the practicalities of being a Capricorn.

And in doing that, you open the door to varieties of ideas and exploration, of activity, and joy, and achievement, that wouldn't otherwise have crossed your mind. True, the next step will be taking action on them.

But once you've embraced that fantasy part of your nature, the part that enjoys visualizing what seems "impossible," you'll not only find yourself taking great pleasure in it, you'll discover some of those fantasies are far more possible than you imagined.

You and others

Everybody knows somebody who has a gift that makes life seem magical, and who are themselves an inspiration. Knowing them is one thing, but allowing them to influence your vision of what's possible is another matter. Still, let them help you overcome the sensible side of your nature. You'll be glad you did.

Health and well-being

There is an irony about you as a Capricorn. If you feel unwell, you'll tend to be tough on yourself, thinking that's the best way to overcome either physical ailments or even if you're feeling a bit unsettled. The fact is, a gentle touch is always far better.

Goals and challenges

The question to ask yourself every day is: Do you still really want that goal? In some cases, the answer will be instant and passionate and a big "Yes." In other cases, the answer may be "I don't know," and those are the ones it is time to say farewell to.

CAPRICORN

03

JANUARY

Self-discipline isn't about limiting indulgences, it's about selecting the best of them

You

Occasionally, it's useful to look at those who drift from one plan to another, who seem directionless in a way that bothers you, but who also seem happy. What's more, their lives are functioning smoothly and successfully.

While their approach to life intrigues you, it is also puzzling because it differs from your own more focused way of thinking. As a Capricorn, generally, you will set a goal, carefully organize a plan to achieve it, then stick to it. Yet there is something to be learned from others' more casual approach to life and to achieving goals. This is especially important if you have been struggling with certain plans that seem to be going nowhere.

The trick is to view planning as if it were breathing, which you do naturally—unthinkingly. If you're breathing heavily but, for example, not climbing a steep hill, then it's important to ask a few questions. It is the same with plans. If they aren't working out, it is time to pause and consider whether they'd ever work out, or whether you should put your time, energy, and, in some cases, heart into exploring others. An initial review is a good start. You may spot a fresh approach, or you may immediately realize you have better options, possibly right there, awaiting your attention—plans that would be far better, far more rewarding, and far more fun to achieve.

You and others

Compromise is a difficult thing for a Capricorn who is settled on a goal or made a plan, whatever it is. However, once you recognize that there are moments when letting go of what you have organized and considering others is wise, you will not only do it, but you will be excited to find out what you discover in the process.

Health and well-being

While it's important to take care of yourself, everyone agrees it is also important to do what might be termed spoiling yourself. Every once in a while, it is essential that you have an indulgent date, and with people who will be happy to join you in a little joyous excess.

Goals and challenges

Achieving what you have in mind is one kind of challenge. Another, more difficult one is actually recognizing that certain goals just aren't going to work—then letting go of them. Doing that takes courage, but also it frees space in your mind, in your calendar, and possibly in your heart.

CAPRICORN

04

JANUARY

THIS DAY FOR EVERYONE

It would be easy to assume that others' lack of irritation with current shake-ups means they don't care about these, or the disruption they're causing. Actually this means a lot to them. It's just that they're not nearly as expressive as you are about those feelings of frustration, but they definitely do care.

GIFTS Conventional, Managerial, Decent

NUMBER 6

CHALLENGES Inflexible, Patronizing, Downbeat

(0+5) + (1) = 6

Putting work I love first is easy; doing what I must boosts my self-worth

You

While most Capricorns are rightly proud of being born under your sign, and even more, of your nature—that is, your willingness to work hard, but also your practical generosity and earthy humor—there is another side, too. This element of your nature can almost always find something to worry about, or can experience feelings that go up and down. Alternatively, you're always a bit concerned about things going as they should.

This side of your nature is related to the part that can dwell on life's doubts, and recognizes stability as a way to avoid those. However, the fact is—and something for you to remember, especially as a Capricorn and an earth sign—everything changes. The world around you changes—the seasons, the weather, plants grow. While you recognize those changes as normal and ones to be embraced, you sometimes forget that the seasons in your own life, the ups and downs, are normal. Once you learn to recognize and welcome them, your perspective will improve.

Instead of being anxious when changes arise, you won't just embrace them, it will be with enthusiasm, knowing that something exciting is coming your way and that you're prepared for it. The more optimistic you are, and the more creative you're feeling, the more exciting your embrace of the new will be.

You and others

Bouncing ideas off of others isn't just wise, it opens up a new world to you. Often, you will retreat to figure out plans, then discuss what you have decided, hoping for their approval. However, with the foundation on which many arrangements are based shifting regularly, the more closely you work with others, the more you will learn.

Health and well-being

When you feel unwell, you will often head off to the gym or figure out the best-possible diet. However, those unsettled feelings may have to do with the simple fact that your world is changing and so is your life. These ups and downs are nothing more than your body becoming accustomed to a new way of living, thinking, and doing things.

Goals and challenges

Organizing life is a skill. Organizing a life when things are changing constantly is more than a skill; it's an art and it's one that it is important for you to learn. You probably started out thinking that there would be a single plan. Now that you've learned that a new plan is far more exciting than a single one, being able to embrace change is the skill.

C / A \ P / R \ I / C \ O / R \ N

05

JANUARY

THIS DAY FOR EVERYONE

This is one of those exceptionally tricky periods during which what begins as a modest exchange of ideas could burst into a contentious disagreement within moments. The real issue is unspoken tensions. For now, say nothing. This is likely to blow over as swiftly as it surfaced.

GIFTS Traditional, Solid, Proper

CHALLENGES Fatalistic, Stubborn, Distant

NUMBER 7

(0+6) + (1) = 7

Setting aside pressing tasks to support others benefits me as much as them

C
/
A
\
P
/
R
\
I
/
C
\
O
/
R
\
N

06

JANUARY

You

For you, as a Capricorn, and somebody ruled by the planet of achievement, Saturn—which is known for the focus it brings but, also, its stern nature—you sometimes struggle with the feeling that, somehow, you should have done more or worked harder. But, if you view the actual situations in question logically, you realize you've done all you can, or need to.

Catching this isn't easy, because it's like an automatic recording, one that plays when you have finally dealt with your list of tasks and obligations. The trick is to recognize that these are only ideas—or even worrying questions—and not about your own life or the world around you. The challenge? First pause and look at what you've done. Then, if you still have doubts, ask those you trust to discuss your concerns with you.

Your ruler, Saturn, is not only the planet of focus and achievement, but also accents doubts of this nature. Recognize that while Saturn can be a tough planet, it also is about being able to spot and enjoy the cycles of nature, and you will recognize that there are times when life is meant to be still, there are times when you are meant to learn things, and there are times that are about celebrating what you've achieved.

Embrace this cycle—and everything else will make complete sense.

You and others

Finding balance in life's changes is tough for anybody—it's like walking a tightrope. Yet everybody's life does change. The challenge for you is that you tend to want to control those changes and undertake them according to your own schedule, which, as a logical Capricorn, you realize simply isn't going to happen.

Health and well-being

Fitness is a very good idea. For you as an earth sign, however, well-being is even more important. That is, being able to enjoy yourself, who you are, and what you're doing, simply because you are who you are. Make that your priority, and the rest will fall into place.

Goals and challenges

Every once in a while, when you're working at something—and, as a Capricorn, you're usually working at several things—you will be asked how near you are to achieving that goal. The real question is, how can you measure it as you change and goals change? How much joy are you gaining from the process?

THIS DAY FOR EVERYONE

There's a fine line between sticking stubbornly to long-standing, possibly out-of-date habits or beliefs and giving in to the rather pushy attitude of others. While you'd probably be willing to consider changes, you'd rather do it when and how you want. Explain this to others; they may well back off.

However I may view them, no single one of life's joys is better than another

You

Setting goals and standards for yourself is important for every Capricorn. Being ruled by the planet of order, Saturn, it is vital that you know where you stand, in your life, with others, in your role with family or at work, and even more, in terms of your own goals, objectives, and ideals. But there is another important question, and that is: whose values will you allow to shape your own? Normally, your parents, your background, your community, or your culture will shape those.

But as life has moved on, you may not have given as much thought to who or what is influencing your thinking, values, and priorities. There is plenty to focus on, but are you allowing others' passions to shape yours, personally, professionally, or in terms of a cause that is meaningful to you? Each leads to the question: do these activities link with your own personal goals and values?

As a Capricorn, and as somebody who thrives on having a "mission"—something you can help out with, or a challenge you can meet—it's vital for you to review your mission from time to time. The trick is discovering whether what you're doing means as much as it once did, or possibly needs to grow along with you. As your mission for yourself and the world around you changes, it may be that commitment will change as well.

You and others

The keyword here is "inspire." That's partly about who is inspiring you. But, also, who you're inspiring with your words and action. You may not think about this, but as you do, you'll realize why certain situations are shifting and begin to discuss new ideas with those around you. And, as you do, you'll find you're the one who's doing the inspiring.

Health and well-being

As a Capricorn, you take a certain pleasure in being disciplined, and, in fact, you can get a bit addicted to them simply because they give order to your life. However, one of the themes for you is to learn to ease up on them. Make those activities of health and well-being emphasize the well-being most of all.

Goals and challenges

Many Capricorns have the idea that setting goals and then sticking with them is powerful—it indicates you have a focus. And while sometimes that's true, it is also important to recognize that reviewing and altering those goals isn't weak, it is actually a brilliant idea.

C / A \ P / R \ I / C \ O / R \ N

07

JANUARY

THIS DAY FOR EVERYONE

Somebody seems determined to discuss personal matters that really aren't their business. Your reluctance to get involved is understandable, yet you're urged to make an exception here. The insights that emerge could make a huge difference, and at a time when your guidance would be especially valuable.

Lasting happiness isn't about what I earn or own, but the result of joy within

C
/
A
\
P
/
R
\
I
/
C
\
O
/
R
\
N

08

JANUARY

You

While the idea of feeling joy is wonderful, as a Capricorn, you tend to think such feelings must be earned through a certain amount of focus or effort or achievement.

There is no arguing that both effort and getting things done merit exactly such feelings. Yet it is worth reflecting on your reaction to upbeat feelings of this nature that appear "magically." That is, you can't think of anything you've done to earn them.

Actually, the fact is, joy is there waiting for you at any time. It has nothing to do with what you've achieved—or done for others. It exists. And the challenge for you is to overcome the Capricorn doubt that has convinced you that you aren't allowed to feel sheer joy until you achieve certain things or overcome certain obstacles or, perhaps, have dealt with the task at hand.

This is a kind of guilt that most Capricorns wrestle with for a while—until they have that amazing breakthrough that is about joy, and about the fact that it's always been there waiting to be discovered. It's just the direction you look in and your sense of the right to have it, and to have it at any time.

Once you know that's true, then nothing and nobody can take it away from you. It will always be there walking beside you and shedding its light on you.

You and others

Most people have to live in the world with others and the drama that goes on with them can be a compelling one. Both you and others are judges, but also serving each other in some way. It would be a great play, but because it's real life, you are better off approaching it with compassion.

Health and well-being

Being in shape is great; being able to lift weights, or eating the right thing, or having a trim body, is fabulous. All of that is wonderful, especially being able to zip up those jeans. But what about your inner fitness? Because that influences you 24/7, whether or not you've got your jeans on.

Goals and challenges

While most Capricorns will stick with goals, others will keep altering them in the hope of finding something that flows smoothly. The fact is, life isn't designed to flow well, it is designed to be a bit bumpy, and those bumps will be what you have learned from and value most in retrospect.

THIS DAY FOR EVERYONE

When it comes to the issues you're currently facing, timing is everything. While, admittedly, some can't be stopped and, in fact, are best tackled head on, others can and should wait. Assessing this is easier than you think, especially if you trust your instincts. They'll be unexpectedly reliable.

I can challenge myself to face obstacles solo, or I can accept offers of support

You

Most Capricorns are list-makers, and those lists always contain small goals and big goals and often, in fact, your dreams.

While you can achieve those goals, one by one, life ensures you have a list against which you can measure your success. Yet the fact is that, however many of those goals you achieve, the thing you're looking for isn't on that piece of paper. And it isn't in your thoughts either. It could be said to be seated in your heart, and it is actually what might be termed the joy of achievement.

Achievement can have to do with those goals that you have in mind and with the acknowledgment of using your skills. But at the same time, it can have to do with you personally. It can have to do with simply being who you are, or being loved by another, or giving love to another, or simply pausing to observe, and rejoice in, the majesty of nature.

Those components are the most important. So when you make that list of those goals, bear that in mind. And, as you live out each day, take a few minutes to experience that joy—the joy in nature, the joy in being yourself and knowing what you personally are offering to the world around you—and to life itself.

You and others

Many Capricorns feel they're responsible for supporting, or being an example to, others—whether to family, to friends, or to colleagues. And while often you will inspire people, the question is: Is that your duty? It's something for you to decide, but you may actually find it is somewhat more of a spiritual calling.

Health and well-being

Being fit is fantastic, but if you're joyless, then it doesn't make too much sense. Because fitness includes your inner world, and that's not so much about moving your body or your muscles as putting yourself in a frame of mind that allows you to experience inner peace 24/7.

Goals and challenges

The question is: Are all goals worldly? From a Capricorn point of view, as an earth sign, you might think that. Yet every Capricorn who has lived long enough to know that achieving certain goals gives you only so much is aware that there are other varieties of achievement, and they have very little to do with the outer world.

C
/
A
\
P
/
R
\
I
/
C
\
O
/
R
\
N

09

JANUARY

It would be easy to make the mistake of assuming that, when somebody ignored serious issues you raised, they didn't want to discuss them. Actually, the individual in question has been distracted, and may not even have understood what you were saying. Raise it again, and the sooner, the better.

Doubts are best tackled swiftly; putting them off only allows them to grow

C
/
A
\
P
/
R
\
I
/
C
\
O
/
R
\
N

10

JANUARY

You

Often, when you're figuring out what you want to do, you use your background as a foundation for it. Not only is that logical, we all learned to speak and to think in the language of our background, from family and the community we were in. Since then, of course, we will have experienced other people, other settings, and, for many, a wider world.

And each of those will have added something to what we consider to be possible, worthwhile, and appealing. Yet every once in a while, it is important to pause and consider whether what you want to do and what would bring you joy are related to what you've learned in your background or have an entirely different origin. And if so, then it may be time for you to begin to explore that.

Of course, as a Capricorn, you'll tend to want to analyze this. However, simply paying attention to what you're drawn to, what excites you, and, most of all, what brings you joy, may offer valuable, and possibly unexpected, clues.

After that, you may shift your focus to the here and now, and consider what and whose company inspires you. Then you may think about what you prefer doing anyway and, with very little thought, you'll realize that you're already doing something that enriches your life, and which quite possibly could become a much more important part of it.

You and others

Eventually, everybody realizes that certain individuals in their lives are there because of a relationship, because of an obligation, because they're family and they may not bring much joy, but also they are simply there. And then you realize other individuals have something to give to you, a sort of a gift. You know which ones are the ones that are most important to trust.

Health and well-being

There is a lot around these days about fighting the aging process. However, there is another approach to it, which is simply retraining the mind not to take the idea of "getting old" into account at all, but instead to recognize each day as the new birth that it is.

Goals and challenges

As a Capricorn, you love a good challenge every once in a while. It's sort of like a workout; it may actually be a physical workout or a mental workout. But the important thing is to recognize that, as rewarding as dealing with those challenges is, it is also possible to overdose on them. Enough is enough.

THIS DAY FOR EVERYONE

Annoying as the games others are playing may be—by making, then unmaking plans—it's forcing you to review your thinking about various arrangements. This, in turn, will lead to unexpectedly profitable discussions about what you would like to see happen over the coming weeks and months.

GIFTS Mindful, Solicitous, Economical

CHALLENGES Distant, Cold, Stingy

NUMBER 3

(1+1) + (1) = 3

Sticking with the familiar seems wise but means bypassing unexpected offers

You

Many think of life as being a duty, something that's easier to deal with if you organize your tasks or obligations. Those come first.

Once you have figured them out, you can turn your attention to life's joys, activities that lift your spirits, and the people who bring light to your day.

However, you have a tendency to think that those joys need to be earned, mostly by getting things done. That may seem normal to you, but it's a little like saying breathing is earned. The fact is that creating a balance between duty and joy in life is important, but it's like that in every element of life.

Many parents encourage their children first to behave, and then to be dutiful. Often, however, they make having fun a bonus, added for good behavior. The secret is to begin to rewrite that script, to untangle the notion that joy and fun itself must be earned.

Instead, make those duties fun, and in the process you can incorporate what you need to do for others. This means rethinking things entirely, but then that is the whole core of it.

It means that you will spend more time doing what you love, with those you love, simply because together, you'll be rewriting what might be termed the script for life and its joys, and making those joys the most constructive portion of your life.

You and others

There is a great deal of importance put on being loyal. While that's essential, there is another element. If you can combine being kind—that is, helping others or ensuring their needs are taken care of—along with being loyal, it's even better. And if you can combine being loyal and being kind with partying, then life is as it should be.

Health and well-being

There is something called the deprivation culture—that is, depriving yourself, or having been deprived, is seen as something good, that a tough regimen strengthens you. It is a bit of a Capricorn thing, but there's an even stronger kind of regimen that you can embrace and that is a regimen called loving and being loved.

Goals and challenges

Try setting up temporary goals and seeing what happens. This is totally out of character for you as a Capricorn, but if you want to learn something quickly, it is better to plunge in first, see what happens, and then study your reaction later.

C / A \ P / R \ I / C \ O / R \ N

11

JANUARY

THIS DAY FOR EVERYONE

It is out of character for you to leave decisions up to others when they really should be yours to make. Yet you're tempted. This is partly because you have so much to do, but also a certain individual seems convinced they know more about it than you do. They don't. These matters are your responsibility.

The ability to find joy in the here and now isn't just a gift, it is a passport to freedom

CAPRICORN

12

JANUARY

You

The fact is, almost everybody experiences joy of some variety at some time. It's just because it is not discussed much, and because many cultures and settings don't even mention it, that they don't notice it.

This may actually be the case for you. When was the last time you thought, "What joy I'm feeling!"

However, joy is part of human nature and the more you learn to spot it, the more you will learn to encourage it in your everyday life—simply by noting it, and enjoying it.

And in fact, that might be described as a good kind of viral growth. The small joys can grow to big ones, and those you can share with others, and the more you experience them and the more you talk about them, the more you can make small alterations in your activities in your own life.

You can organize how you do work in a joyous fashion. You can organize time with friends and loved ones in a joyous fashion. And even more than that, you can create a joyous relationship with the elements of the world that need healing, from the planet to the way people are treated in the world. The more joy you bring to each day, the more joy you will spread. It's that simple. In fact, if you look in the mirror and think of joy, you will be improving the world that way, too.

You and others

In the contemporary kind of new-age thinking, there's a notion that if you think a thought, then it automatically spreads, which is an interesting concept to consider. So if you look in the mirror and create a moment of happiness and decide to share it, it might work. There's no reason you shouldn't give it a try.

Health and well-being

Can you say you feel great in the moment, even if, in fact, you don't? Something is creaking or perhaps you've got a runny nose, but still, if you think about everything, if you feel great and can think it and even share it with others, then you will be sharing the best possibility of all.

Goals and challenges

As a Capricorn, you probably have a list of goals, but is that list a vision, or is it specific? Probably the most important goals are those that aren't exactly figured out, but those that encapsulate the miracles you're hoping will be coming your way. Take that approach and the odds are good that they will show up soon.

THIS DAY FOR EVERYONE

Usually, when you're enthusiastically discussing ideas with others, the next thing would be to explore turning them into plans. Try to do it, however, and you'll soon realize that the actual situations in question are still too much in flux to think in lasting terms. For now, enjoy exploring your options.

GIFTS Artful, Polite, Results-oriented

CHALLENGES Cunning, Tight-lipped, Tyrannical

NUMBER 5

(1+3) + (1) = 5

Listening to others' advice is one thing. Knowing whose to follow is quite another

You

As an earth sign, you're very practical and clever, so you tend to make a list of what you intend to do, today, this week, this month, and sometimes, this year. This is powerful and focuses your mind.

However, it can also limit your thinking, because you'll already have defined what you want to do, especially when it comes to long-term plans, goals, and objectives. And if you allow your imagination—not the part that's about daydreams, but the part that can envision new ideas and ventures—to have a role in creating that list, then you begin to think in terms beyond what you'd have imagined on an everyday basis.

This is a skill that allows you to transform the down-to-earth Capricorn side of your nature into being a kind of visionary: someone who can see past the restrictions of the present, who is able not only to envision miracles, but can consciously create them.

True, everybody has the potential to connect to something beyond themselves, and make that happen. However, for you, it's about freeing yourself from refusing to get hung up in the details, and instead, visualizing your goals. Then you should simply plunge in, even as if those events have already come together. Begin to do that, and you will be amazed how swiftly they do.

You and others

As a Capricorn, you're rather good at ensuring you know people who inspire you. But in this case, you're encouraged to spend time with people who play. Yet they must be those who play in a very special way, by taking you to new lands of possibilities and encouraging you to explore new elements of your own mind and new possibilities in your life, which, otherwise, you'd never have considered.

Health and well-being

These days, there are all sorts of things you can do to make yourself feel better, to rejuvenate you, to build your energy, but one of the best ones is simply relaxing. Being able to stop and simply be, perhaps to watch a sunset. Try that. It will be miraculous.

Goals and challenges

As a Capricorn, you were born ambitious. That may have to do with work, but you have a need to achieve what you have in mind. While you may choose those achievements by climbing the highest mountain, why not think of an achievement in your own life, which is much closer and more exciting?

13

JANUARY

THIS DAY FOR EVERYONE

The last thing you're in the mood for is dwelling on the past; however, events are calling your attention to long-standing arrangements and you're being prompted to review these. While times have changed, these haven't. Ask questions and you will soon realize they are holding you back.

Struggling with doubts? Recall those times when you regretted not taking a chance

C
/
A
\
P
/
R
\
I
/
C
\
O
/
R
\
N

14

JANUARY

You

As a Capricorn and a practical earth sign, you tend to question, if not dismiss, those ideas that suggest that if you simply think of or visualize something, it will happen.

As somebody ruled by the sensible Saturn, this seems a bit too magical for you. Yet you are also drawn to it, and of course, not only are you aware of those who seem to make things happen exactly that way, you have done it yourself, although unintentionally—that is, you only realized it after the fact.

Even so, if they are unfamiliar, you could be anxious about tinkering with such matters. The trick to dealing with all of this is to recognize that you are in a period during which events are forcing you to think in a different way, and about many areas of your life.

And the more willing you are to do that, the easier it will be to make the best of a cycle that is all about discovery.

These discoveries will have to do with the practical side of your life, with your everyday insights, with the future, and most of all, with what once seemed distant possibilities. The more willing you are to take chances in that way, the better you will do now and over the coming weeks, months, and years. In fact, it might even transform your thinking—and your life.

You and others

Tempting as it is to go along with what others think is a good idea—and, often, it can be informative—it is also essential that you be true to yourself. But that's what's tricky, because in some cases, it's not until you allow others to tempt you and you say "No" that you realize what being true to yourself actually consists of.

Health and well-being

As an earth sign, you are very sensible. However, that realistic and scientific side of you is also intrigued by certain activities that seem kind of weird, but also seem to work for other people. The secret? It's simply to be interested in them, learn a bit about them, and take it from there.

Goals and challenges

The question is, what brings the greatest rewards? Is it a plan, a plan based on something else that worked? Is it guidance from someone who has achieved? Or is it simply what comes to you when you sit and reflect? Because what plan could be better than the one that you create yourself?

THIS DAY FOR EVERYONE

You're not thrilled that certain arrangements aren't working out as you hoped they would, but judging by the current rather tricky planetary activity, what it reveals will soon lead to things that didn't work out as you hoped. Sudden changes could bring answers for everything, and possibly overnight.

GIFTS Honorable, Industrious, Guarded

CHALLENGES Bitter, Obstinate, Remote

NUMBER 7

(1+5) + (1) = 7

Taking chances is profitable; you learn from the outcome, whatever it is

You

True, being able to cross tasks off your list of things to do is both an achievement and satisfying. But whatever kind of happiness this brings to you, as a Capricorn, it is worth noting there are other, equally rewarding activities, and each brings its own variety of satisfaction and achievement, often in ways you wouldn't expect. That's the reason it is vital you think about and recognize as well.

What's more, it offers an opportunity to focus on a side of your Capricorn nature that is very different from the outer world— the tangible world of duty, action, and achievement that is so important to you. That portion of your nature is what might be called your "inner world": that is, what makes you feel worthwhile, what brings you feelings of accomplishment, and what gives you a sense of inner peace.

While this variety of inner peace is unlikely to have been taught in school, achieving a balance between the two—between the outer and inner worlds—isn't just important, it will enhance your view of life. It will inspire you.

Even better, this will touch those around you—family and friends, possibly colleagues, and perhaps even the world around you. Make achieving that balance your primary goal and even better, the rest will fall into place almost magically.

You and others

You are an expert at organizing your own life and the world around you. Not everybody cares or, in fact, knows about that powerful but very private inner world that is so important. Spotting those who do and making them an important part of your life is one of the most significant steps toward creating that balance, the ongoing balance that will enhance the rest of your life.

Health and well-being

Often, people speak of a battle for well-being, which may sound like fun and makes it exciting. Yet is that actually the way you want to approach your body? You can be kind to it and perhaps love it into well-being. That might be a better approach to take.

Goals and challenges

The dream of lifelong achievements versus everyday goals is something to think about, especially for you as a Capricorn. Often, those goals will dominate your thinking and the choices you make. The fact is, you are only alive in the present, and while achieving those goals in the future may be wonderful, your joy in this day is what is most important.

C
/
A
\
P
/
R
\
I
/
C
\
O
/
R
\
N

15

JANUARY

GIFTS Wily, Unflinching, Efficient

CHALLENGES Devious, Wary, Dogged

NUMBER 8

(1+6) + (1) = 8

Loving others can be challenging, but that's easy compared to loving yourself

C
/
A
\
P
/
R
\
I
/
C
\
O
/
R
\
N

You

Doing what you have in mind and accomplishing it is exciting. However, bizarrely, those achievements can turn into an addiction. This isn't just about your personal sense of achievement, but these become something you can talk about, a conversation you and others enjoy. You can tell them about your goals, they can talk about theirs.

At the same time, though, that achievement can prevent you from exploring other options, things you'd like to do and also activities that take you within. These might be described as more personal goals, such as overcoming doubts or turning tricky issues around. Or this might have to do with your relationship with nature, doing something that benefits the Earth but also satisfies you, possibly in certain ways that are new to you.

What's most important is to realize there is no right way to do this. It is about doing something for the pure joy of it, breaking free from the addiction to achievement that is so important in many people's lives, and especially for you as a Capricorn.

The trick is to seek the joy and the peace that come within that. Once you're close to that, then you'll realize why it is so important to balance doing this with that joy. In fact, the more joy you have, the more you will enjoy all of those achievements as well.

You and others

Pals from the past can be terrific because you know each other inside out. Yet the most important friends to have when you're in a period of development are those who feed the inner you. Once you learn more about them and once they understand what you're doing, a relationship can go beyond anything else you could have imagined.

Health and well-being

Working out is one thing, but working out as if you were fighting with your own body won't achieve much. On the other hand, if you overcome that battle and instead make what you're doing an expression of joy and love for your body, it will be an entirely different and hugely rewarding matter.

Goals and challenges

As a Capricorn, you always set your goals high—it is simply part of your nature. The trick, however, is that once you know what you'd like to achieve, to make them a little lower and a bit more manageable and less intimidating. That way you can mark your steps toward achieving those bigger goals with every passing day.

THIS DAY FOR EVERYONE

Somebody seems to think they can win you over to their plans. This is puzzling because the individual in question doesn't seem to care that much. Your observations are correct, they don't. The fact is, they rather enjoy the game of convincing somebody to go along with their own ideas.

Poetry dwells in the beauties of spring; finding joy in life's darker moments is a real art

C
/
A
\
P
/
R
\
I
/
C
\
O
/
R
\
N

You

As a Capricorn, you're an earth sign, but also, very often, you'll have goals that reach way into what might be termed the heavens—that is, they are inspired by a part of your character that goes beyond the here and now. If so, then you will already understand how important it is to balance the two: the part of you that is an earth sign, which really enjoys the here and now and has a knack for achieving goals of a practical nature.

Yet there is also the side that wants to stretch your take on reality and reach toward feelings some would call joy. There is that amazing feeling that what you're doing, your ideas or plans, are actually coming together. And even though not everything has gone as you intended, what has been least expected has been thrilling, and accomplished perfectly in the here and now.

Better yet, you are learning a new skill as a Capricorn. True, it isn't the kind of skill you go to college to learn. It may be that nature will teach you, or possibly, you will encounter somebody who can help you learn about that.

Or one day, you will simply realize that you've already learned it. Then you will also realize why being able to recognize joy is such an important contribution to your life, both now and in the future.

You and others

Who do you hang out with, and how do they make you feel? While it's wonderful to spend time with people who know you and people who will get you laughing about the past, they don't necessarily lift your spirits, or in fact, add to your self-esteem. Ensure you spend a bit of time with those who don't just inspire you, but who also, indeed, admire you.

Health and well-being

The trick to feeling well is to feel really well deep within, and then have those good feelings emerge from the outside. So, eating is good, exercising is great, but finding that place within that gives you what might be termed energy vitamins—that's the place to go.

Goals and challenges

As your horizons broaden, your goals shift quite naturally. This is often the reverse of what many people have been taught, because you're supposed to sit down and list what you want to do, and then figure out what's easiest. However, there is a trick to this, and it's called inspiration. Allow that part of yourself to be inspired and the rest will be easy.

17

JANUARY

THIS DAY FOR EVERYONE

When there was talk of changes in elements of your domestic or working life, you were concerned. This seemed a pointless disruption, but as you've learned more, you've also begun to realize these are part of a far-reaching pattern of change, influencing and benefiting others as well as you.

Planning ahead is wise; the ability to embrace the unexpected enthusiastically is a gift

C
/
A
\
P
/
R
\
I
/
C
\
O
/
R
\
N

You

As a Capricorn, setting goals is important, but discussing your options beforehand is even more important. You need to organize your mind, and your life, and once you know what you're doing, you can proceed free of concern.

However, as you'll have noticed, sometimes it seems you're not in control—and events almost seem to be telling you what to do. It's as if they're pointing you in a direction that's entirely different from what you had in mind—that may well be the case.

You and the rest of the world are in a period during which you're receiving what might be called coaching from another source, one that is perhaps a little bit larger than your ego and one that wants you to ask for more for yourself. In fact, that's the point: you are about to become a bigger person, a bigger person in the sense of your heart, your feelings, and your mind.

That may sound a bit far out, but as you begin to explore, you'll realize that suddenly the world seems a much more interesting place and you're more confident. And you're willing to take chances on activities and perhaps even on caring for others in ways that simply wouldn't have been possible even only recently. This is no bad thing. In fact, you might even find it's the best variety of addiction you could ever have.

You and others

The trick to making the best cycles that are all about growth is to think about who you hang out with. You may or may not know them well, but what you will notice is that when you're around them, you feel more positive, that what seemed unreachable, suddenly is well within your reach, and that joy becomes a part of everyday life.

Health and well-being

There are stories about fighting aging, people talking about what you can or cannot do, or eat or not eat, or treatments. But there is another way to approach it and that is simply to accept it, and in accepting it, to transcend it, to consider the possibility that if you simply believe it isn't going to happen, it may not.

Goals and challenges

The question is, in achieving your goals, does it just happen or is this a result of careful planning? As a Capricorn, you will think that it's all about that planning, but increasingly, you'll realize that both the success you achieve and the happiness you have are the result of a combination of planning and you're simply deciding that will be the case.

THIS DAY FOR EVERYONE

There have been many times in your life when you've wished somebody could deal with the tricky matters you're facing. But now it's the reverse, and with certain individuals in charge, you're unsure what to think. Despite your concerns, their intentions are good and you will be pleasantly surprised.

Trying to understand others is a challenge; accepting them for what they are brings joy

You

You're a very special type of Capricorn because you share the influence of your neighboring sign, Aquarius. You may not be aware that, for most of history, Capricorn and Aquarius shared Saturn as a ruling planet.

However in 1781, Uranus was discovered, and it became the ruler of Aquarius. This gives you a rare, and powerful, link with this remarkable air sign, and accounts for your equally rare capacity to view matters from that practical perspective that comes with being a Capricorn but, also, from the visionary approach of Aquarius.

You also benefit from that link to the planet of innovation, Uranus. If you sometimes find yourself being inspired by ideas so new you can't imagine where they came from, thank Uranus. Equally, if you're restless or eager to break away from overly sensible pursuits most Capricorns thrive on, you've Uranus to thank.

True, often the practical side of your nature may fret about this adventurous side. Yet, if life's for living, learning from, and exploring, then this rare and wonderful balance of planetary energies isn't just of huge benefit to you, it means that every unexpected venture you take up, or surprising encounter you have, will add to that rich experience of blending these two powerful but very different planets, signs, and ways of looking at, and living, life.

You and others

It would be no surprise if, gradually, you realize that those around you—from family and friends to neighbors and colleagues— all come to you for advice, ideas, and suggestions. This isn't just about making wise decisions, but also how to have fun and enjoy the best of life. You have a talent for it: one that is worth sharing.

Health and well-being

There are many kinds of health. There is physical health and there is emotional and mental health. However, well-being itself is all about having an optimistic feeling about what will happen in the next minute, the next hour, and the next day, and that is what this chapter of your life is all about.

Goals and challenges

Figuring out what you're going to do next may seem complicated, but as you're probably discovering, the more you allow something beyond yourself to inspire you, whether it's an event or an encounter or simply an idea that comes out of nowhere, the more exciting life becomes. Believe in that very special variety of inspiration because it's the way you'll be living as the future unfolds.

CAPRICORN

19

JANUARY

Long ago, you wisely decided that while you and close friends are interested in certain matters, their interest is far greater. So you leave them to deal with them and, mostly, that has worked. Now, tempting as it is to intervene, you'd regret it. Don't even suggest it. You've got plenty of other things to do.

Aquarius

Symbol The Water Bearer

Flower Orchid

Ruler Uranus

Element Air

January 20– February 18

Aquarius   One of the few human zodiac symbols, Aquarius is the water bearer, the third of the clever air signs. While ruled by Saturn for most of history, when the first planet to be discovered in modern times, Uranus, was spotted in 1781, you acquired a new, edgy ruler. Your flower is an orchid, your spice is chili, and your tree is all those bearing fruit. Not surprisingly, your stone is the aquamarine.

A
\ /
Q
/ \
U
\ /
A
/ \
R
\ /
I
/ \
U
\ /
S

GIFTS Innovative, Independent, Stylish

NUMBER 3

CHALLENGES Restless, Adamant, Headstrong

(2+0) + (1) = 3

I will regard what once seemed a nuisance as an opportunity

You

As a blend of your neighboring sign, Capricorn, and your own, Aquarius, you have a rare, unusual, yet wonderful mix of energies. Capricorn is an earth sign and very focused on life's practicalities, whereas, of course, Aquarius, as you probably know, is an air sign. That means your thinking and your ideas are far more important to you than being stuck with so-called grounded realities.

Yet it is the blend of the two that is so exciting. and this takes you into new, and rare, territory. It takes you into ways of thinking and doing things that simply don't even occur to others. This is something you won't fully realize until you encounter those who seem so uninterested in the things that touch you, that excite you, that encourage you to explore.

But even more than that, because of this unique combination of characteristics, you not only benefit from your own canny ability to observe, and understand, your own approach to life, you are a natural advisor to others. You're a visionary who sees what's going on far better than those around you.

It is for this reason that people are drawn to you, and often have questions to ask. While the answers may be obvious to you, they won't always be as clear to others. And this is the reason that, without even realizing it, you signed up to be an advisor in this life.

You and others

Your gift for seeing others probably better than they do themselves makes you good company—simply because even anxious individuals feel comfortable. But you also can be the individual who lights a fire under that person who has something to learn. Better yet, they will benefit from the confidence you give them.

Health and well-being

Unsurprisingly, with your nature, you're drawn to new ways of eating and ways of taking care of yourself. Ironically, however, despite this inquisitive side of your nature, you can be a creature of habit, falling into eating the same things and doing the same activities every day, something that is worth being aware of.

Goals and challenges

Being a bit of a visionary, you set all sorts of goals, some nearby, but others that look years ahead. The irony is that, because you get so involved with them, you don't always notice when you've achieved them. It's worth pausing for an occasional review. There is no need try to do what you've already accomplished.

AQUARIUS

20

JANUARY

THIS DAY FOR EVERYONE

Luck is in the air; it's true. However, there are unexpected twists and turns in the air. And it's unlikely you'll benefit from these once you've dealt with them and any unsettling issues. Knowing that, tackle them now, possibly focusing on one a day. These will prove far easier than you imagined.

GIFTS Unconventional, Rousing, Tolerant

CHALLENGES Contrary, Obstructive, Determined

NUMBER 4

(2+1) + (1) = 4

Each day I discover something new and exciting

You

As a January 21st Aquarius, you're always interested in what's going on around you and what people are doing. They don't just fascinate you, they inspire you to ask questions, and to learn about their ideas, plans, and what's motivating them. This process of learning about others, and their direction and intentions, isn't just intriguing, you'll sometimes make important observations. You may notice they're restless; alternatively, others may seem to get stuck doing the same thing again and again.

Yet the fact is that you, too, can be a creature of habit. This is because you're one of the four "fixed" signs of the zodiac, born in the middle of each season, something you share with Taurus, Leo, and Scorpio. While this gives you stability, you can become such a creature of habit, you don't even realize you could live differently, work differently, or even take care of yourself differently. You'll get into eating the same thing and going to the same places.

But once you spot that habit, while you will benefit from the "stick-to-it-ness" that comes with being a fixed sign, you will also have the luxury of exploring what you could do, going to places, meeting intriguing people, and generally making a point of ensuring that every week and, if possible, every day, you discover something new in life.

You and others

As an Aquarian, you're a natural affiliate. That means you're not just a friend to people, you'll stick by them in a way friends don't during periods of change or challenge. And you will both grow. The important thing to recognize is that they will also be of benefit to you.

Health and well-being

You're intrigued by so much that is going on around you, in terms of what to eat and what to do and how to take care of yourself. Yet another part of you says routine makes life easier. While that's true, try to achieve a balance between the two. In fact, making discovery a part of your routine is the ideal.

Goals and challenges

It may well be that in your youth you learned that is unwise to measure yourself against others. The reason for this is, as an Aquarius you're more inquisitive than most, and more willing to venture into new territory. If you recognize that, then you'll realize you can only measure yourself against the unique you.

A
\
Q
/
U
\
A
/
R
\
I
/
U
\
S

21

THIS DAY FOR EVERYONE

Only days ago, you thought certain plans were settled, and in detail. Since then, however, events have made it clear you must reassess these. As much of a nuisance as this seems, once you begin, you'll realize how much circumstances have changed and, because of that, your own plans need a rethink.

JANUARY

GIFTS Trendsetting, Resolute, Unique

NUMBER 5

CHALLENGES Unresponsive, Impersonal, Withdrawn

$(2+2) + (1) = 5$

I'll rethink my everyday routine and make life an adventure

You

By nature, you are a seeker. You'll get involved in a way of living, working, or even loving that becomes core to your life. Yet because the particular process of discovery you're drawn to—that of being a seeker—is so natural, it seems as if each day you find something else you need to learn about, someone intriguing to meet, or a small change in your life that will become a great discovery.

And that is indeed core to the nature of being an Aquarius. On one hand, it's about finding a routine that allows the fixed-sign part of your nature to experience the variety of stability that is so important for you. But having achieved that, and having learned to maintain it, you'll finally feel that your are able to venture out into new territory, and in a number of ways.

This involves exploration in a range of forms. It's about what you do, and what you learn as a result. It's about the people you meet, and various elements of your activities. Many Aquarians benefit from having what might be described as "a number of lives" in each life. They may have different careers, they may go through different elements of their personal life, or they may even experiment with their own identity. Whatever the case, this is all about a joyous voyage of discovery that was almost designed for you as an Aquarius.

You and others

Most Aquarians always seem to have lots of people around them. That's because you're interested in others, you attract them. It is unique to you, as you'll notice, when few of those around you share your own genuine interest in the world and in discovering the people who are in it.

Health and well-being

One of the most wonderful characteristics of your nature is your inquisitiveness and your joy at discovering life. However, as you may have noticed, it can mean that sometimes you get so involved in that process of exploration you forget to eat and take care of yourself. Of course, the challenge is finding a balance between the two.

Goals and challenges

In childhood, everyone is asked what they want to be when they grow up, even if they don't have any particular interest in a special activity. That is a big question. For you, it is the other way around. You will find one thing you want to do, and as a fixed sign, you could get stuck in it as if you have no option. But for you, the question is as an adult: what do you want to be when you grow up?

THIS DAY FOR EVERYONE

Recently, when you were discussing plans, you sidestepped certain details. You weren't being careless or, as some suggest, secretive. It's just you knew things would change, and that would include precisely these details. If others are concerned, explain slowly and, in fact, in detail.

A
\
Q
/
U
\
A
/
R
\
I
/
U
\
S

22

JANUARY

As much as I value old friends, if they're boring they get only so much time

You

Some of those born under the sign of Aquarius seem fairly conventional and lead what appears, on the surface, to be an ordinary life. Others born under your sign are genuine, if sometimes discreet, rebels. However, deep within the core of your nature is that unconventional, if not rebellious, character.

You are probably not aware that you were born under the rulership of the planet Uranus, the first to be discovered in modern times in 1781. So of course, you will see things in your own, unique angle, and differently from the rest of the world—including the other signs, but even from other Aquarians. That is because, in a way, you're creating an entirely new identity for yourself and for your sign.

This isn't just about what you do and think of yourself, but how you live various elements of your life, from your activities out in the world and your relationships in general to your activities, or work, your view of finances, and your goals and objectives. For this reason, when you make decisions about the present and the future, it's worth regarding them as tentative, if not an experiment.

However, as one of the fixed signs of the zodiac—those stable signs in the middle of each season—you sometimes overcommit to plans. The trick is to recognize that, by nature, you were born to be an explorer.

You and others

Many come to you for guidance and ideas. You don't realize this until you compare notes with those around you. And this is useful for them, not just because you have a rare capacity to spot the potential in others, but also because you learn so much from every conversation you have with them.

Health and well-being

As an air sign, you enjoy feeling well and free. However, the routine of taking care of your body isn't something that comes naturally, so you need an activity that combines mind and body. That may sound strange, but if you find something you can do that will stimulate both your mind and your body, you will enjoy it for a lifetime.

Goals and challenges

Many people figure out a system to live by, values to have, things to go for. But as an Aquarius, because you're inquisitive, that changes, and the system itself needs to be all about discovery. Once you understand that, then instead of trying to find the perfect thing to do, you'll realize that those discoveries are what you are meant to be doing.

A
\
Q
/
U
\
A
/
R
\
I
/
U
\
S

23

THIS DAY FOR EVERYONE

JANUARY

Saying no to something or, indeed, somebody where things won't work has never been a problem. You'll usually explain your thinking and the reason why, and then move on to other topics. But now somebody is determined to change your thinking. Listen once, thank them, then, as before, move on.

GIFTS Inspirational, Zany, Progressive   *NUMBER* 7

CHALLENGES Unforthcoming, Intolerant, Uninterested   *(2+4) + (1) = 7*

Finally, I'll swap my current routine for a new, more adventurous one

You

As an air sign, you are witty by nature. All of the air signs, Gemini, Libra, and Aquarius, enjoy exploring ideas—those that are familiar as well as new concepts. And humor isn't just important; it can be an antidote for the practical side of all those ideas, and often adds a welcome sense of the absurd.

Sometimes it may be just a quiet laugh, but there are other times when actually getting down and feeling hysterical about something— belly laughter as it is often called—isn't just fun; it makes you feel terrific. This capacity to see humor in life is vital.

However, you are always fascinated to discover that not everyone understands— or even appreciates—humor. In fact, some people would rather analyze dull matters in detail than benefit from the variety of laughter that often gives life itself a timely perspective.

Once you're aware of this, you'll also spot those who might be termed "laughing pals": people you can hang out with when you're in that mood. You will also be increasingly aware of certain individuals who, whatever you say, take life very seriously.

The fact is, they probably aren't an air sign like you, and they view life differently, and almost speak a different language than you do. Still, give it a try. The irony is that, for them, the conversation could prove life-changing.

You and others

You have a rare capacity to celebrate life's oddities and the quirks that you experience. But also, you've probably learned that not everybody can, and that capacity to spot irony in even very difficult situations doesn't exist in everyone's personality. In those cases, you may even have to learn to be sympathetic.

Health and well-being

The idea of eating well is useful, and many Aquarians do. However, the idea of getting up and moving vigorously is a little less interesting for most air signs, and less of that movement sparks your intuition or excites you, which may have to do with dancing, dancing of any kind. how about the tango? Have you ever given it a try?

Goals and challenges

You have a low boredom threshold. Once you know how to do something, you often see no reason to stick with it, which means that you need to alter your goals. This is not something you share with others, which means also you need to find those with whom you can discuss exploring new goals and do it regularly.

A
\
Q
/
U
\
A
/
R
\
I
/
U
\
S

24

JANUARY

THIS DAY FOR EVERYONE

There are many ways to agree to plans, and at the moment you're being rushed into arrangements you still question. The fact is, you'll be tinkering with things that are still in transition, and whatever is arranged over the weeks, if not the months to come is bound to evolve.

GIFTS Contemporary, Clever, Easygoing

CHALLENGES Hermit-like, Erratic, Unapproachable

NUMBER 8

(2+5) + (1) = 8

Suddenly, I realize somebody who seemed dull is amazing

You

The irony of being an air sign is that you're inquisitive about everything. You love observing the world around you, especially what others are doing, their characteristics, what they go for, and equally what they avoid and their oddities.

However, you often don't stop to observe your own characteristics in the same way. You like what, and whom, you like, and you dislike what doesn't suit you, and that's that. Why would you want to challenge or change that? You have observed other restless individuals as they set out to broaden their horizons in ways they find exciting, yet often you've regarded it as just plain odd.

This is indicated by the fact that Aquarius is one of the four fixed signs, those born in the middle of the season. While this gives you amazing stability, you can settle into a pattern and become so familiar with it that you'll avoid making changes—when actually they'd lead to something new and, often, beneficial.

And this is exactly what you'll spot in somebody else and is one of your own lessons. It's about a new variety of inquisitiveness. Once you learn it, a whole new world of options will open up before you.

Discover that fixed side of your nature, begin to "jiggle it" a bit, and the world will become a far more interesting place.

You and others

Of the 12 signs of the zodiac, the circle composed of friends or, probably, your family and even colleagues isn't just important. The time you spend with them is nourishing to you. They support you, but also, it's their voices you trust when you have questions and, equally, it's their capacity to reassure you that's crucial.

Health and well-being

These days, there's a lot of talk about body, mind, and spirit and finding the balance for you. This isn't just a good idea. It is actually vital, because you wander off in your thoughts and forget about your body and taking care of it. But you can also forget about the part of yourself that knows inner peace.

Goals and challenges

Even setting goals is odd for someone like you, who is restless and inquisitive by nature. Yet because the world shifts, and often those goals shift, that's you, too. And the trick is to find those goals that do naturally shift, because it prevents you from getting stuck.

A
\
Q
/
U
\
A
/
R
\
I
/
U
\
S

25

THIS DAY FOR EVERYONE

JANUARY

You've been trying to win one particularly stubborn individual over to the plans you know they'd enjoy. The problem is, they aren't just being stubborn, they won't even listen to what you have to say. Back off. Force them to ask you about your ideas. It will require patience, but it will also work.

GIFTS Quick-thinking, Empathetic, Sociable

CHALLENGES Forceful, Unnerving, Formal

NUMBER 9

(2+6) + (1) = 9

Those who are fun to talk to will now have priority

You

As you've probably noticed, you don't just have an active and inquisitive mind. There are times when you're not merely in an inquisitive mood, your mind seems to escape and is all over the place—you're thinking about so much that you can't concentrate on any single thing. However, it is important for your mind to work that way, simply because being ruled by Uranus, the first of the newly discovered planets, you as an individual are always discovering things yourself.

And often, these sudden insights are the result of those nearly overwhelming moments of enthusiasm and exploration. Some of what arises will be important to you, but some may be important to those around you—your circle, if not the world. And this is the trick to discover: that while you are always intrigued by the now as well as by what you're doing, very often what you discover, what you enjoy, will be important to you and to the wider world as well.

Most of all, you are here to learn to live life anew every day. While habits may streamline what you do, if you decide to do a single thing differently every day, to alter a minor habit or even a major one, then you avoid falling into the rituals that prevent you from the kind of discovery that you, as an Aquarius, were born to experience, and on a regular basis.

You and others

You are fiercely loyal to those closest, maybe family, but also to friends. This is an important and valuable characteristic, but something that is essential for you to review from time to time. Check it out. Not everyone is as reliable, and you may discover that certain individuals, particularly friends, aren't as loyal to you as you are to them.

Health and well-being

Most Aquarians understand the importance of being physically fit. They like being able to get up and move around quickly. But boredom is a problem, simply because many regimens are exactly that—boring. The trick is to include in your activities body, mind, and spirit. That takes a lot of fitting in, but it is worth the effort.

Goals and challenges

In order to have goals, you need to set them. However, many Aquarians stumble over what they're doing in life, whether it's at home or with family or a career, only later discovering that what they are doing has discovered them, which may actually be the best approach.

26

JANUARY

THIS DAY FOR EVERYONE

If you've already talked about what you'd like to do and hope to achieve and are running out of enthusiasm, it is probably time to change the subject. In fact, judging by the rather tricky planetary activity you're facing, you are better off sidelining those plans and savoring each day for the pleasures it offers.

I've run out of excuses for not making long-overdue changes

You

You have a love-hate relationship with habits. They allow you to organize life in such a way that you don't have to think about every single thing you're doing. At the same time, as an inquisitive air sign, you need to explore. Ideas are like a kind of vitamin for you. The trick, therefore, is to ensure that those habits involve things that keep life going smoothly.

Ironically, you might have to develop a "habit" of breaking habits. That is, from time to time, you think about whether there is anything you do regularly—so regularly that it would prevent you from getting to know somebody interesting or exploring something new. The "habit-breaking" method is simple. It is about ensuring that you always do something new and unaccustomed, at least every couple of days.

This also will allow you to stumble across new ideas, intriguing people, and possibly even activities that otherwise wouldn't have crossed your mind. As an inquisitive Aquarius, you are also one of the fixed signs, so can easily get caught in the kind of habits that are restrictive. Those are the ones you want to watch out for.

Once you find that balance between the habits that stabilize you and the habit of exploration, you will have organized a life that allows you to be efficient, yet also to discover something new regularly, if not every day.

You and others

Who is the ideal friend for an Aquarius? Those who say to you, "Come along with me. Let's explore this. Let's try this. Here is a new idea." While you are inquisitive about everything, someone coming to you with something you haven't stumbled across isn't just a good idea. Those individuals are a gift.

Health and well-being

By now, you have probably come to realize that just because healthy is printed on the label of something, that doesn't mean it is good for you. However, how do you discover what is healthy? Actually, it doesn't have so much to do with what you eat or drink as how you take care of yourself.

Goals and challenges

Every once in a while, it is important to review your goals, simply because what once seemed important isn't any more. When you discover that, you can chuck out those goals, slim down your list of objectives, and pursue what you care about most with passion.

A
\
Q
/
U
\
A
/
R
\
I
/
U
\
S

27

JANUARY

THIS DAY FOR EVERYONE

Long ago, you learned to live with and, in some cases, to disagree with certain individuals. But if you are going to take various complex plans to the next stage, you have no choice but to find a way to deal with the issues and conflicts that arise—and in detail. This won't be easy, but it is a vital skill.

GIFTS Even-handed, Inventive, Quirky

NUMBER 2

CHALLENGES Single-minded, Wacky, Rebellious

$(2+8) + (1) = 11 = (1+1) = 2$

If I'm the most interesting person in a conversation, I need new friends

You

You delight in the world around you—people and what they do fascinate you. But it also fascinates you how some people seem to complain with every breath. It is almost as if that is their perspective on life. They get up each morning and push the "Start" button on their complaint mode. When others, and indeed, you, are joyous, they are complaining, if not miserable.

As an Aquarius, what might be referred to as your "joy temperature" goes up and down, depending on your mood. That's normal. However, those around you who aren't very joyous are a big lesson in how to organize your life, and also how to shape your thinking, because often that joy has to do with how you approach life itself. As an air sign, it is easy to fall into analyzing what you do, as opposed to paying attention to the ups and downs that actually give you a sense of purpose and enthusiasm about life, particularly during those moments when challenges, life's "uphill climbs," are a bit overwhelming.

Once you have mastered that skill, then when you encounter those challenging moments, or longer periods, you will recognize that while they may seem overwhelming at the moment, dealing with this is a skill. And that is making the best of each day—with its uphill climbs and twists and turns.

You and others

It is said that you discover your true friends during periods of challenge. And while that is true, you also discover your true friends when they are challenged, because if they settle into doing nothing but complaining, there isn't much you can do for them as a friend. Choosing those closest is about the character of each of you.

Health and well-being

As an inquisitive Aquarius, you are always experimenting, not only with what you do, but with how to feel well, how you eat, with fitness, with diet. But what is most important is actually your viewpoint about your well-being. If you put that first, everything else will fall into place.

Goals and challenges

As an Aquarius, you need new challenges regularly. You need something to keep that active mind of yours going. However, you also need enough stability that you are able to enjoy being yourself each and every day, because of the 12 signs, you are probably the best at doing exactly that.

A \ Q / U \ A / R \ I / U \ S

28

JANUARY

THIS DAY FOR EVERYONE

Sooner or later, you will need to take a tough line with somebody who is difficult on the best of days. While it is understandable that you are putting off tackling the issues in question, these won't vanish. You may in fact be better off taking things in stages. Slowly but surely you will get there.

GIFTS Neutral, Championing, Unwavering

CHALLENGES Impersonal, Impatient, Iron-willed

NUMBER 3

(2+9) + (1) = 12 = (1+2) = 3

Same plans again this weekend? It's time for a complete change

You

You may not notice this—at least, you may not notice it right away—but of course, you have always been you. The fact is you are more inquisitive than others—and more observant. You discover more simply by observing the world around you, by looking at nature. But, even more, you learn about people by watching them, those you may see on the street and those you see regularly—family, friends, neighbors, or colleagues.

In fact, often you might know more about them than they do themselves. However, turning that mirror on your own life and on what and who you put first is what is most important—and not quite as easy.

Initially, you may not find yourself particularly interesting, but if you fall into the rather typical Aquarian habit of doing the same thing, of a routine, then it is essential that you use your wisdom to examine your own life and to break the habits that could settle into what often are termed "the habits of a lifetime." Instead, make a point of breaking a habit a week, if not a habit a day.

Once you begin doing that, then you will give yourself the freedom that you, as an air sign want. In addition, that freedom will make life itself all the more exciting—exciting enough that you will wake up each day with a sense of eager anticipation.

You and others

Many Aquarians don't notice a difference between those around them because it is not in their nature to compare or judge people. Yet occasionally in conversations, you notice others doing just that. Don't judge or compare, but make a note of how wonderfully able you are to enjoy those around you, whatever their quirks.

Health and well-being

The feeling of being at one with yourself—that is, so settled in who you are that you don't feel the need to change anything—is rare and wonderful. And it is something that, as an Aquarius, is within your grasp. The challenge, however, is to ignore those who say, "If you change X or do Y in your life, you will feel much better." For you, it is simply not necessary.

Goals and challenges

The fact is, you need a new challenge from time to time. This is by no means negative, but it is almost as if you were taking vitamins. Having a small challenge—not something overwhelming or negative—will give you an opportunity to exercise your muscles of being inquisitive and being clever in a way that is very useful indeed.

A
\
Q
/
U
\
A
/
R
\
I
/
U
\
S

29

THIS DAY FOR EVERYONE

Tempting as it is to sidestep dull facts and even more tedious rules and regulations, these really can't be ignored. It may seem like you got away with it, but things are likely to catch up with you. So invest time in dealing with these now, before they become any more complicated.

JANUARY

GIFTS Steadfast, Team Player, Tolerant

NUMBER 4

CHALLENGES Iron-willed, Unresponsive, Contrary

(3+0) + (1) = 4

I won't wait for others to believe in my ideas. I'll just plunge in on my own

You

The phrase "the joy of discovery" is a wonderful one. And to say that is something you have, something you were born with, is even better. This means that you're interested in others in a way that they sometimes aren't themselves. And you are interested in the world around you in a manner that not everybody is. Occasionally, you are shocked—and surprised—to discover how little interest those around you have in the world, from the people in it to the events taking place.

You may try to get them excited about things—and a few may, indeed, respond, but not always for long. The fact is, you were born to be the person you are. And that means inquisitive—interested in others and curious about their lives and activities. This innate interest is not only your greatest asset. It is something that allows you a variety of joy that is rare and wonderful. And it comes with being an Aquarius, perhaps the most inquisitive sign of the zodiac and also the sign that is ruled by the planet Uranus—the first planet to be discovered in modern times.

This itself is a symbol of your nature. Enjoy who you are simply for who you are. And while it isn't your habit to compare yourself to others, if you begin to do so, realize that actually, it is not only unwise, it is unnecessary.

You and others

It may take you a while to recognize, but you will soon discover that there are two groups of people. There are those who are inquisitive, like you, and then there are those who don't particularly care about anybody else. It is not difficult for you to figure out who you should be hanging out with.

Health and well-being

When it comes to taking care of yourself, variety is important. Many people get into a routine, both with what they eat and what they do to feel fit. But while the routine itself is not a bad idea, you need something to challenge that vital mind of yours. And if that means changing those routines, all the better.

Goals and challenges

As you have noticed when you are chatting with others about what you have in mind to do, their idea of a goal is very different from yours. Compare notes if you want, but recognize that you, as an Aquarius, are seeking something very different from most of the world—and what you are seeking has to do with having a broader and brighter horizon.

A
\
Q
/
U
\
A
/
R
\
I
/
U
\
S

THIS DAY FOR EVERYONE

It is said that you should never go to bed without settling differences. And, just as is the case now, at the very least you want to express hope that you will reach an accord with others. Even saying that might be challenging, but when you wake up in the morning, you will be glad you did.

It's time I freed the adventurer in me to explore

You

As an air sign, you have a restless mind and, sometimes, a restless body, too. You have a powerful need to get out and about, possibly merely in your neighborhood, but it may be to explore the wider world. And when you do, you're often surprised, if not shocked, by what others seem happy to settle for.

This makes you aware of how little interest many people have in broadening their horizons, even slightly. But it also makes you realize that, oddly, in certain areas of your own life, you can be very predictable.

This is, of course, because you are born under one of the four fixed signs of the zodiac—Leo, Taurus, Scorpio, and Aquarius. And, in fact, once you develop certain habits, while it seems they streamline your life, they also feel very comforting—except that you can personally begin to feel stifled or suffocated by them as well.

The trick is to develop certain habits that benefit you at the same time as developing the habit of always exploring something new, every week if not every day. Balance those two, and that fixed side of your nature will lend you a stability that is very useful for you as an inquisitive air sign. It will also mean that you are always making very sure that you are not allowing yourself to get stuck in any restrictive habits or ways of thinking.

You and others

As an Aquarius, you need people in your life. But what you mostly need are individuals who have restless minds, who ask you why you are doing what you are doing, who encourage you to explore and who will inquire with you about what is new. They are not only good friends, they are assets.

Health and well-being

There is nothing better than getting up in the morning and knowing what you are going to eat and knowing what kind of physical activity you will undertake during the day. However, for you as an Aquarius, variety is an especially important kind of vitamin, along with what you do and what you eat. Ensure that you have got lots of options.

Goals and challenges

Most children are asked what they want to be when they grow up—as if somehow, as a child, you would know. But for Aquarians in particular, life is itself a voyage of discovery. Make that voyage your priority, and instead of trying to settle on one destination, you will enjoy each and every place you go.

A
\
Q
/
U
\
A
/
R
\
I
/
U
\
S

31

JANUARY

THIS DAY FOR EVERYONE

It's true: you're often reluctant to make changes, especially if you can't understand why you should bother or what you will get from them. The fact is, you have no choice. The situation in question involves others as much as you and, ironically, they are eager to take things to the next stage.

I will do something new at least once a week, but try for every day

You

You are naturally inquisitive. You don't think of it until you're talking with others and realize how little they observed about a particular place, about somebody you both met, or an event of some variety. However, your interest in the world, and life itself, is part of being an Aquarius. Of course, not everybody born under your sign takes advantage of this special variety of curiosity. What's more, even a single change in plan can be an invitation to look at life differently.

True, initially you may be irritated, which is simply the fixed sign side of your nature struggling with change. Yet as an Aquarius and an air sign, you thrive on new ideas, meeting new people, solving new problems. This is what comes with organizing a life that brings you its own twists and turns. If those aren't part of your daily routine at home or in your job, then you can invite those twists and turns into your experience of exploring something new.

It doesn't have to be a single way or a single regimen and ideally, you'll experience different reasons for different twists and turns over the years of your life. What is most important is, as they arise, instead of worrying and saying, "Oh no: not another change," you embrace them with the enthusiasm that comes with knowing this is yet another life-adventure.

You and others

One of the great turning points in your life is understanding that those around you truly don't see things like you do and, in fact, have no interest in viewing things from your perspective. As an Aquarius, you are always fascinated to know how other people think, but it is a characteristic that the rest of the world doesn't necessarily share with you.

Health and well-being

It is easy for an Aquarius to be seduced by exotic physical routines and diets. In fact, the more complicated they are, the better. And you can become obsessed with them, but the fact is, that is a kind of seduction that distracts you from the most important thing, which is how well you are feeling.

Goals and challenges

On occasion, when others are talking about what they are doing in their lives, you aren't just intrigued, you are envious. You want to be drawn into their lives and their goals. But there is an important thing to remember. It is that, as thrilling as their activities are for others, the individuals in question are not you.

THIS DAY FOR EVERYONE

Sometimes discussions are about an exchange of ideas. At the moment, however, it would seem that your main role in several such situations is as a listener. Tempting as it is to offer advice, it is really not wanted or, in fact, helpful. The individual in question needs to talk and talk and talk.

I'll listen to what others expect me to do, and deliberately do something else

You

The phrase "joy of discovery" is an appealing one, but it is important to remember that what others enjoy discovering isn't the same as your own variety of joy. However, you may share a restless appreciation of the new, and those individuals may be perfect companions with whom to explore, to pursue new ideas, to meet people. And when you connect with somebody like that, it's great.

At the same time part of your life is about discovering that each individual is truly taking a unique journey: one that is designed for their own character, and what they are meant to learn. While all Aquarians are inquisitive, each of you benefits from that unique path and, as a result, may end up somewhere very different, doing something very different.

There are those who say they have done it all, explored it all, and now they know where they are going, and it is unnecessary for them to ask any more questions. And for certain individuals, that is true.

For you, however there is always something more to discover. It may be out in the world around you. It may be about humanity, or it may be about yourself. Whatever it is, for you, life isn't just a journey; it is an exquisite journey of discovery, one that has gems waiting for you every day.

You and others

It is a very rare Aquarius who is meant to go through life on their own. Some will be surrounded by family, some by friends, some by colleagues, even occasionally by those you encounter here and there. In every case, these individuals aren't just companions; they are there for you to bounce ideas off and learn from.

Health and well-being

As an air sign, you love nothing more than a quick fix for your well-being, whether it is an eating regimen or activities—and the more complicated it is, the better. But the big discovery is actually paying attention to what makes you feel well. There is no better regimen than that.

Goals and challenges

As an Aquarius and somebody who might be termed "an original," it is vital for you to be true to yourself. Simply defining the term "goal" may be one of life's greatest challenges. It will take time, but what you learn will remain with you all of your life, and bring rewards each and every day.

A
\
Q
/
U
\
A
/
R
\
I
/
U
\
S

02

THIS DAY FOR EVERYONE

The last thing you want is to disappoint people and leave situations undone. But certain individuals have ignored your advice and are now blaming you for their problems. Explain once, and firmly, where you stand, then withdraw from discussions. There really is nothing more to say.

FEBRUARY

GIFTS Equitable, Humanitarian, Laid-back

CHALLENGES Unorthodox, Hermit-like, Obstinate

NUMBER 5

$(0+3) + (2) = 5$

Joy isn't in knowing what's coming, it's about making life an adventure

You

One of the gifts of being an Aquarius is your genuine interest in others. On occasion, you realize that most people pay little attention to those around them, even family and loved ones. Your inquisitiveness comes naturally. And not only do you listen to what they have to say, think about it, and ask questions, you actually pay attention and are fascinated with elements of their lives.

While you tend not to compare yourself to others, you learn about yourself from the differences between your approach to life and theirs. This, in turn, allows you to think about doing things in a new way and about exploring new activities. Yet certain individuals may also provoke you into asking questions about yourself—and this is where it is worth pausing to consider whether that is necessary.

Many Aquarians have managed to find an inner balance, one that is rare and allows you to be who you are without spending hours of pointless poking at your own psyche or your ego, which so many do. This is because having been born under perhaps the most inquisitive sign of the zodiac and the sign that is all about exploration, you do that naturally.

Appreciate this element of your character, and when others are struggling, you will realize why you are not and that you don't need to. Then you can appreciate yourself all the more.

You and others

Most Aquarians love having people around them, whether it is family—if you have an extended one, or they are nearby—or neighbors, colleagues, or pals. But being able to brush up against others isn't just fun, it reminds you of the beautiful diversity that life offers in the form of the people around you.

Health and well-being

There are all sorts of ways to take care of yourself, but one of the best ones has to do with actually hanging out with friends and seeing what they are doing. They will take you into new territory, not just in terms of fitness, but in terms of how you eat and what you think. And often, a few days spent with pals will constitute a proper workout.

Goals and challenges

It is important that, as one of the fixed signs of the zodiac, you are aware that you can easily repeat the same challenge in a different form. Be alert to that, because if you are thinking about doing something differently, you might as well learn something new, too.

03

FEBRUARY

A
\
Q
/
U
\
A
/
R
\
I
/
U
\
S

THIS DAY FOR EVERYONE

There is no tidy way to make sudden, and in some cases dramatic, changes in long-standing arrangements. Others may complain, but they, too, are being influenced by the changes triggered by this period. Unsettling as these changes are, there is no arguing the fact that things must move on.

GIFTS Popular, Resolute, Current

CHALLENGES Lone Wolf, Adamant, Repetitive

NUMBER 6

(0+4) + (2) = 6

Instead of complaining that life is predictable, I'm going to spice it up

You

Those around you may be complaining about "challenges" in their own lives. These days, this term is used to mean that things are difficult and actually others are seeking not merely your advice, but your help in some form. However, it is most important for you to think about whether this is merely a matter to be discussed, or if you can or should do anything to help them.

In some cases, these individuals need to deal with their own challenges; that's the point for them. In other situations, it is about you pointing them in a particular direction, then leaving them to deal. But also it is essential for you to recognize that being distracted by others may be preventing you from looking at your own restlessness and need to begin the next chapter of your life.

As one of the four fixed signs of the zodiac born in the middle of each season, along with Taurus, Leo, and Scorpio, you can get stuck in your own habits. And if you find yourself drawn in to others' crises, it may well be that actually it is an invitation for you to begin to explore and to shake things up in your own thinking and life. Begin to do so and you will discover a whole new world of activities, ideas, and people worth waiting for.

You and others

Most Aquarians have a gift for making friends, whether it's neighbors, or being close to family, or colleagues. It is important, however, that you make a point of linking up with those who are always interested in the world around you and always out there discovering something new and interesting. While that is your instinct. They will encourage that in you.

Health and well-being

There are many ways of assessing you health, and of course you can watch how you eat and how you exercise. Yet there is also the influence of an unsettled mind and how much it can disrupt things. If that's the case, you don't need to do a major meditation course. What might be termed mini-meditations—that is brief ones—can do the trick.

Goals and challenges

Being somebody who's inquisitive by nature, it is easy for you to line up a set of goals. This gives you not only a sense of purpose, but enthusiasm and variety. However, it's worth ensuring that those goals are realistic, otherwise you also risk being overwhelmed.

A
\
Q
/
U
\
A
/
R
\
I
/
U
\
S

THIS DAY FOR EVERYONE

There's a difference between a possible solution for a problem, and you have lots of those, and the kind you can be sure will last. At the moment, nothing quite fits. While others are impatient, your instincts are correctly telling you that it is vital for you to wait until more worthwhile ideas surface.

Agreeing may build friendships, but clashing with them makes me think

A \ Q / U \ A / R \ I / U \ S

You

You may have set goals or resolutions recently, long ago, or, possibly, every New Year. Whatever form these take, for you as an air sign and someone who has an instinctive sense of the future unfolding—perhaps greater than any other sign—whatever form this process takes, it is an important one.

While this vision is about what you could be doing over the coming months, or even the coming years, it is also vital to discuss your existing ideas and objectives. Some may go back a long time, yet you haven't reviewed them. These may no longer be relevant to who you are now, or today's world. The trick is to do a clear-out. You may be clinging to once-cherished but unrealistic objectives. As you declutter, consider whether your current goals need an update, too. This may lead to a rethink of what setting goals looks like. You may regard them more as an experiment, taking you into unknown but exciting territory.

Most of all, it is about being flexible. The more you explore, the more you will discover. Make discovery your theme, and instead of worrying about setting the right goal or achieving it, you will enjoy every twist and turn of the voyage, simply because of what you've experienced, who you've met, and what you've learned.

You and others

There are certain people you click with and life is easy, but it is also important for you to recognize that certain individuals have a capacity to prevent you from settling into habits in the way that you'd like to at times, and encourage you to come along with them on new journeys of discovery.

Health and well-being

Knowing what you are going to do the next day and the next week may be reassuring, but it doesn't necessarily mean it's good for your mind or your body. In fact, sometimes surprises are the best possible gift, whatever form they take.

Goals and challenges

It is good to have the perfect setup, but in some ways it actually hampers you, simply because if you're sticking with that perfection, you're prevented from exploring. For you as an inquisitive Aquarius, exploration of that nature is like taking a deep breath.

05

FEBRUARY

THIS DAY FOR EVERYONE

Welcome as current ideas or offers coming your way may be, inevitably they'll be disruptive. While in some cases it's about having to rethink the timing of plans, in others, changes are seriously unsettling. Although, obviously, you've no complaints, you can't help wishing things weren't so rushed.

GIFTS Objective, Unswerving, Lenient

CHALLENGES Impersonal, Unyielding, Unresponsive

NUMBER 8

(0+6) + (2) = 8

It may be tiny or a big deal, but each day I will do something very different

You

As one of the three air signs—Gemini, Libra, and Aquarius—you're fascinated by what is going on in the world around you and in your own life, and learn from what you observe.

But when it actually comes to making changes, it's not so easy. This is partly because you want to ensure that you have freedom in your own life, which in turn means that if you commit to one avenue of activity, you would be missing out on others.

Yet every once in a while, it's important not only to make a change, but also to break away from a path so familiar that you know exactly what awaits you, and around every twist and turn. This is one of the tricky issues for you as one of the fixed signs of the zodiac—born in the middle of each season. You fear that in taking that first step in a new direction, while you're breaking old—and often restrictive—patterns, you're plunging into the unknown.

In a way, you are. That is the point. For you, the world of discovery is vital. In fact, as an air sign and as an Aquarius discovery, experimentation, and growth are as natural to you as breathing. Sticking with what you know seems safe, but it's like remaining in a stuffy room when you could throw open the door and walk outside into the fresh air. The more skilled you become at discovery in life, the more you will enjoy life itself.

You and others

Most Aquarians have a large circle of friends and enjoy the company of others. The tricky bit is how much time you spend listening to what they're doing and their dramas versus the time you spend exploring together. Think carefully about that, and then think carefully about who you put first when making plans.

Health and well-being

Discussing dilemmas is easy, and in fact many people enjoy the process. Allowing them to take over your thinking and to turn into ongoing anxiety, however, is something that is important to watch out for. Choose what you discuss, who you discuss it with, and most of all, what you put your mind to.

Goals and challenges

It is easy to set things up that will impress everybody else. Not that you do so for that reason, but simply because their enthusiasm brings enthusiasm out in you. The trick is discovering what really excites you. As an Aquarius, you're a unique individual, and that process of discovery may take a while, but it's worth the patience and the effort.

A
\
Q
/
U
\
A
/
R
\
I
/
U
\
S

06

FEBRUARY

THIS DAY FOR EVERYONE

The planetary activity ahead won't just be exciting. Much of what's coming your way could turn into something worthwhile and of a long-term nature. However, that won't be clear at the time, which means you owe it to yourself to explore everything, including what seems unappealing.

GIFTS Rebellious, Inspiring, Trendspotting

NUMBER 9

CHALLENGES Intolerant, Unrelenting, Disconnected

(0+7) + (2) = 9

Instead of complaining that life is predictable, I'll turn it into an adventure

A
\
Q
/
U
\
A
/
R
\
I
/
U
\
S

You

As an Aquarius, you benefit from an inquisitive mind, a powerful imagination, and a rare sense of vision. Even more than that, you have a restless and very real interest in the world around you and in others. You will talk with others, and learn about them and what they are doing.

Yet ironically, that doesn't necessarily trigger an interest in making changes in your own life. On the contrary, you compare what you're doing to the activities of others, then are pleased with certain elements of your life—and this can lead to you becoming a creature of habit.

Spend time with those individuals. Yet if you also make a point of ensuring that what you're doing isn't merely interesting but is rewarding for you personally, you will realize that certain individuals may talk a lot and discuss interesting ideas, but these don't in any way involve you.

As a fixed sign, born in the middle of each season of the year, you'll happily settle into routines, often inspired by others' interests. As a result, it doesn't occur to you to explore, even in matters that mean a lot to you. It may be you're unaware of what you're missing until, suddenly, you're longing for them. This is one of the most important journeys for you: to acknowledge and embrace your passions.

You and others

Being able to discern between individuals who are interesting and warm and those who are focused on their own missions and have no interest in yours, is one of the greatest skills you can develop. When you've learned to find and spend time with those who are passionate about you, then life will take on a new joy.

Health and well-being

There are many who say that your well-being is all in your head, that it has to do with how you think about yourself. And in some cases, that's really true. If you allow yourself to get involved in worries or dwell on anxieties, then it 's unlikely you will feel great. The trick is to begin with loving who you are and what you are doing.

Goals and challenges

Everybody needs a new challenge. If you don't have one, it will simply appear. If, on the other hand, you set your challenge for yourself—or possibly even make a list of what you'd like to do or achieve—then you can tick them off, one by one, knowing each has been your own selection.

07
FEBRUARY

THIS DAY FOR EVERYONE

Admitting that you're wrong is no problem. However, certain individuals insist that their facts are right and you need to apologize. The problem is, they're looking for a fight and have chosen the topic, which involves you. Say nothing. Those individuals will soon turn their attention elsewhere.

GIFTS Empathetic, Neutral, Fair

CHALLENGES Uninterested, Distant, Bigoted

NUMBER 1

$(0+8) + (2) = 10 = (1+0) = 1$

Today I'll rearrange my day, just for the fun of it

You

As an air sign, you love thinking about ideas, discussing what's going on in the world around you with others. You'll touch on all sorts of possibilities, some familiar, others so new you're still learning about them.

For you, as an Aquarius, being up-to-date is both exciting and makes you think about what you could do next. However, once you begin thinking about the practical side of embracing those possibilities, your enthusiasm dies down, mostly because getting involved would mean making changes you regard as overwhelming, if not just plain impossible.

So those discussions remain exactly that— an exchange of ideas. The trick? It's to recognize that it is impossible to discuss a future that is as unfamiliar as it is exciting. This is where, in the past, you've backed out of promising plans, personal or otherwise.

However, certain individuals have a knack for being guides. You may not be able to do it alone. Trust them. At least talk to them. They will help you imagine how those changes could work. In the past, often you've said, "Yes, but ..." then done nothing. It's the same with relationships. Here, too, you tend to look for what you know. But as an Aquarius, your life is about experiencing a broader world, and once you decide to do it, not only will you learn, you'll enjoy every step of the journey.

You and others

You enjoy meeting people who are interesting and settling into habits that might be termed the rituals of meeting. But that alone can be restrictive. The trick is to have at least one person who kicks you out of those habits and corners you into doing something new.

Health and well-being

There is a concept circulating about healthy addictions: the ones that encourage you to undertake activities, ways of thinking, or even ways of eating that will benefit you and which you don't even have to think about every day. Focus on those and you will notice the difference.

Goals and challenges

You tend to repeat different versions of the same activities, whether they're professional activities or the way you organize your life. The trick is to become interested in truly new ones. Find a friend who will join you in that pursuit. You will never regret it.

A
\
Q
/
U
\
A
/
R
\
I
/
U
\
S

08

THIS DAY FOR EVERYONE

FEBRUARY

There is a difference between making tentative plans and lasting commitments. The problem is, one particular individual views every arrangement as final. Gently but firmly help them understand that, at the moment anyway, plans are flexible and that will be better for everybody concerned.

GIFTS Unbiased, Collective, Clever

CHALLENGES Formal, Unpredictable, Confrontational

NUMBER 2

$(0+9) + (2) = 11 = (1+1) = 2$

Each day I'll think of something I would "never" do—and do it

You

You have the rare situation of being one of the signs that acquired a new ruling planet—the first in modern history. That planet was Uranus, which was discovered in 1781. This means that, along with its new planetary influence, your own sign has developed new characteristics, and is continuing to do so.

While once you were ruled by the cautious Saturn, now life is about discovery—and in many ways. Even more, it is about doing what some would refer to as "reinventing yourself." In the past, if you found an approach to doing things that worked, and that streamlined life, you'd stick with it.

However, you feel restless—and you should. Being an Aquarius is about discovery, both as you explore the world around you and, just as much, rethinking elements of your own life. And if things become too predictable, you may just make a few changes for the fun of it.

And for you as an inquisitive air sign, you need at least one or two activities that shake you out of those habits and challenge you to solve problems, to do things in a new way and encourage you to meet people—possibly the kind of people you wouldn't otherwise have encountered. Make that your single objective in life, and the rest of what follows will not only make life more interesting, it will make it more rewarding as well.

You and others

You have a natural ability to connect with those who will bring a sense of warmth to you, family and friends and, if you work, colleagues. However, it is important to ensure that this circle broadens—and broadens gradually. The new individuals in your life will enrich you as you add them to your circle.

Health and well-being

Many people get into a fitness regimen when they're young and they stick with it through the rest of their life. Yet you as an individual have changed—and how you take care of yourself, how you eat, what you do should change as well. The ideal is to adopt a new fitness regimen and possibly even a new sport every couple of years.

Goals and challenges

As an inquisitive Aquarius, you have many options in life, options to do new things and reinvent yourself. The question is, do you? There may be a part of you that prefers to stick with what you know, the new being so disruptive. But the part that's in your best interest is someone who will always embrace the new and unfamiliar.

THIS DAY FOR EVERYONE

Few things are more precious than time with loved ones and family. Now, suddenly, somebody you care about is putting others first. Before you get hurt or angry, ask what's going on. Yet they have an obligation they haven't mentioned. Once they explain, you'll understand exactly what they're dealing with.

GIFTS Innovative, Contemporary, Edgy

CHALLENGES Eccentric, Provocative, Impudent

NUMBER 3

(1+0) + (2) = 3

If I can't change my entire wardrobe, I'll begin with one new color

You

No one is more interested in others, in the world around you, in life and what people are doing in the community than those born under the sign Aquarius. Yet at the same time, all those interests can become a distraction, one that prevents you from doing something even more important, and that is focusing on your relationship with yourself. That may sound like psychobabble, but it is the best way to describe the importance of pausing regularly to reflect on how you feel in the moment, whatever the setting, and whoever you're with.

You probably don't think of it this way, which is the reason it's important to pause and consider who it is you're spending time with, and the places you're going, and whether they add to your life. This may seem selfish, but the fact is those activities, those thoughts, and even those companions constitute a variety of vitamins for your mind and spirit.

They may also introduce you to new activities or pursuits you wouldn't otherwise encounter, and in that way, add to your life. As an intellectually restless Aquarius, allowing those individuals to bring new ideas to you isn't just efficient. It means that you're broadening your horizons and will be able to do so in return with others, creating a circle of growth and development—one that, in certain cases, will last a lifetime.

You and others

There are all sorts of reasons to have companions. Some are fun. Some are relaxing. But ensure that you always have at least one individual in your life who encourages you to break habits. You don't notice that, indeed, you are a creature of habit, until that individual asks you why you're doing the same thing yet again.

Health and well-being

It's worth taking a few moments to consider what kind of fit you are. You may eat well. You may walk a lot. But there are other kinds of fitness that have to do with your resilience and your zest for life. Ensure that you include in your activities those that add that particular variety of vitamin to your life as well.

Goals and challenges

Any new goal is a challenge, and any new challenge is worthwhile. The point isn't whether it will be successful or not, although if you would like it to be, that's good. The simple act of breaking patterns when you embrace a new challenge will add to your life.

A \ Q / U \ A / R \ I / U \ S

10

Usually there is no wrong way to express concern about a matter somebody is struggling with. However, one particular individual is presenting an upbeat facade to the world and would be upset if they thought you saw through it. What they will need is somebody to talk to. That person could be you.

FEBRUARY

GIFTS Championing, Independent, Remarkable

CHALLENGES Righteous, Inflexible, Bizarre

NUMBER 4

(1+1) + (2) = 4

I'll surprise my friends, and myself, when they ask if I want "the usual" and I say no

You

Obviously, experiencing joy as an everyday part of your life is an appealing idea. But as an air sign, you'll easily get lost in analyzing the past, its influence, and you'll consider what worked and what didn't.

Yet as you will be aware, it is vital that you broaden your horizons in terms of what you do and the people you're meeting in the here and now. The fact is, every element of your life—from the individuals you spend time with, to the activities you pursue, and especially, your goals—is like a form of vitamin. They nourish you in a unique way, and for that reason, you need a "dose" of them regularly, if not every day. And every once in a while, you need a different formula.

If things aren't working, then it isn't about just simply exchanging one activity for another. It is about facing what hasn't worked and recognizing some tough facts before you begin to consider your options.

Otherwise, you will simply do the same thing again. It's a little bit like getting fit, that is, using new muscles. It aches initially, and you may even have to be taught to do it. But in this case, the muscle you're using is about being inquisitive about life, people, and places in a new way. Once you understand that, if what you're doing aches a little, you'll also know you're doing exactly the right thing.

You and others

During times of change, certain individuals may seem to be unsympathetic, if not just plain bullying. Ordinarily, that's not welcome, but in certain situations, it is those true friends who are preventing you from settling into old patterns, forcing you to do things in a new way and introducing you to those new activities.

Health and well-being

Many people are encouraged to get in the habit of taking care of themselves in a particular way—eating in a particular manner and working out in a particular way. But life changes. Your body changes. And so must the way you take care of yourself.

Goals and challenges

Even if you're happy with what you're doing, every once in a while a shake-up is important. Not because there is anything wrong, but what it does is it helps you spot what's working, what isn't, and even more than that, it helps you to spot what you want to reach for next.

11

FEBRUARY

THIS DAY FOR EVERYONE

You've managed to keep a particularly tricky issue under wraps. It hasn't been easy, but you've felt strongly that this was nobody else's business. But now, it is the business of others. And you need to ensure certain individuals are aware of the full facts, including why you've said nothing until now.

A
\
Q
/
U
\
A
/
R
\
I
/
U
\
S

GIFTS *Supportive, Impartial, Surprising*

CHALLENGES *Unforthcoming, Dispassionate, Erratic*

NUMBER 5

(1+2) + (2) = 5

Changing the first thing I do in the morning seems pointless—until I actually try to

You

As a chatty and friendly Aquarius, it is amazingly easy for you to get caught up in talking about "doing." That may sound strange, but talking about what you could be doing, or might be doing soon, isn't the same as actually undertaking new those activities.

It isn't about changing habits. It's about the "idea" of doing it. And again, for you as an air sign—and especially as an Aquarius—ideas can be incredibly stimulating.

However, if your objective is to alter elements of your life, you actually also have to be prepared to make those changes—whatever their nature, whether it's in habits, how you live, your routine, the clothes you wear, or the places you go. And, of course, it may have to do with your activities out in the world, or your job, if you go to one.

The trick is understanding that this isn't about a major change. Sometimes a minor alteration that will jar your habits will begin the process of shaking things up, which in turn gets you considering options that, only recently, you never would have thought of.

This isn't about a single occasion. It's about developing the habit of exploring regularly. Once you begin doing that, life will suddenly become a much more exciting thing, one full of opportunities and adventures that previously you hadn't spotted.

You and others

Hanging out with old friends and family can be wonderful, but new individuals add spice. Those that are the most important, however, are the ones who challenge you to go some place new, do something new, and perhaps break those reassuring yet restrictive habits.

Health and well-being

The emphasis is often on what you eat and how you work out. The single idea of learning a new skill regularly is brilliant. It not only gets you interested in things, it is a type of mental push-ups. It exercises your mind in ways you might not otherwise be doing.

Goals and challenges

Many people have long-standing goals in their lives. Some have to do with an aspect of their career. Others are personal, but particularly for you, as an Aquarius, that goal may be shining in front of you. It may be also that it's something you actually no longer care about. If so, it is time to say farewell to that and think about something entirely different.

A
\
Q
/
U
\
A
/
R
\
I
/
U
\
S

12

THIS DAY FOR EVERYONE

Obviously you're not thrilled about admitting you made an unwise decision. This is especially the case because this involves a matter where you'd battled to have things your way. However, the actual circumstances have changed. Acknowledge you got it wrong, apologize, and move on.

FEBRUARY

GIFTS Inventive, Tolerant, Progressive

CHALLENGES Withdrawn, Strange, Unstable

NUMBER 6

(1+3) + (2) = 6

Instead of expecting others to be passionate about what I love, I'll explore their passions

A
\
Q
/
U
\
A
/
R
\
I
/
U
\
S

13
FEBRUARY

You

As an Aquarius, you enjoy getting to know about people, and for that reason, you are also confident you're good company. Most Aquarians have a natural understanding of others. And your genuine interest in them makes you charming. What's more, you enjoy exploring ideas and talking to people.

Yet, there's one small issue, and that is, as broad-minded and inquisitive as you are about others, you can get stuck in certain situations that aren't just repetitive, they are so predictable that even you are getting bored. The problem is, you are unsure what to do about it. This comes from being one of the four fixed signs of the zodiac, those born in the middle of each season—Taurus, Leo, Scorpio, and Aquarius.

While you benefit from amazing stability, once you get into a habit you can either be comfortable with it and never even try to change it, or, if you do try to break it, you struggle—and to a puzzling extent.

This is both your challenge and your opportunity. The trick isn't to figure it out, but merely to make one change: a single alteration in the hour you get up, in the way you eat, perhaps even in the order in which you do things in the morning, which will begin to alter how you use your mind. That's the first step, not toward changing your routine, but toward beginning a new chapter of your life.

You and others

Note that there are certain individuals in your life who encourage you to take chances. Spend time with those individuals on occasion, because they are not only there for fun. They are there to help usher you into the next chapter of your life.

Health and well-being

Familiar activities are comforting, but they can also lead to a trap. They can lead to powerless feelings versus the excitement of taking chances, altering the way you live, the way you eat, the way you think—and even the way you love.

Goals and challenges

The big question for you is, how long ago did you set the goals you're living by? If it was a while ago, maybe the time has come for a revision. In fact, maybe the time has come for a proper top-to-bottom revolution.

THIS DAY FOR EVERYONE

There is a distinction between facts—that is, things that are true—and what is often termed the full facts, which means every element of a situation. Acknowledge this, and you will realize why some discussions seem to turn into battles. It's not about who's right or wrong, but about your perspective.

I'll create a "discover something new" club, then act on my commitment

You

Your birthday is Valentine's Day, which, in many parts of the world, is about the ideal of the perfect romance. However, as everybody knows, while there may be a few of those around, life living with other human beings can have its ups and downs. And even the most perfect romance may be the result of dealing with, and finding a way around, those difficult points that arise when dealing with any other human being over a long period of time.

However, the notion of romance complicates it, because the simple phrase "falling in love" suggests that it is pure destiny, and the individuals in question have no responsibility to make things work in practical terms. In fact, it isn't that easy to deal with those in your life, from family and friends and colleagues to those you meet. With each, it is about discovering what they're like.

This interest in individuals is natural. It comes with being an Aquarius. And for you, one of the most disillusioning days is the moment you realize that many people have little interest in those around you—including you. When you come across someone who shares an interest in humanity, and in you, not only is that an individual to value, it is someone to cherish. Whatever the relationship, keep them close to you and cherish them.

You and others

There are those individuals who are easy to deal with. And then there are those who always challenge you, who ask why you're doing what you're doing, who encourage you to make changes, and who even, in some cases, badger you to do something new. They are your true friends and allies.

Health and well-being

It's easy to get lost in the regimen of taking care of yourself, of eating well, and particularly the kind of exercises that go on in gyms, where there are all sorts of machines. However, it is easy to get lost in those machines and let your Aquarian mind wander. If so, you might as well not be exercising, but living in a dream.

Goals and challenges

Some say that sticking with the same goals your entire life is wise. However, it's worth noting that, what with the world around you changing, what you're seeking must change, too. There are many kinds of growth. And the growth that has to do with allowing your goals to grow is one of the most important.

A
\
Q
/
U
\
A
/
R
\
I
/
U
\
S

14

THIS DAY FOR EVERYONE

Recently, life has been so demanding and so complicated that each day has felt like a battle. And equally, it has meant that you've had little time to think of yourself, or your own plans and arrangements. Review these now. Ironically, all that you've already dealt with will mean this is surprisingly easy.

FEBRUARY

I will admit familiar habits are holding me back—then I will change them

You

Most Aquarians are sociable by nature. People fascinate you, and often simply observing them will keep you interested for hours. However, being on your own is quite another matter, and as much as you enjoy your own company, actually facing life without family nearby, a companion, or even roommates can be a challenge for you.

Yet it also gives you a chance to think. As an air sign and somebody who thrives on bouncing ideas off of others, often you will learn most from those around you, or so it will seem. But it isn't until you're able to sit and reflect on those insights that you will gain clarity about where they're taking you. This is an important thing to be aware of, because as somebody who is one of the four fixed signs of the zodiac—Taurus, Leo, Scorpio, and Aquarius, the signs in the middle of each season—you can settle into a routine. That may be reassuring, but it also prevents you from sticking your head up above the parapet and looking around to see what's out there.

Ideally there will be certain individuals in your life who don't just encourage you to explore but challenge you to do new things, to break patterns, to break habits that seem reassuring yet have actually become a bit of a trap. For you as an Aquarius, those individuals are more precious than diamonds.

You and others

It is easiest to stick with the familiar. Sticking with those who encourage you to break habits won't be quite as easy, but they are the ones who will turn your life into a journey of growth, joy, and discovery.

Health and well-being

Your theme is discovery. And as you know, as an Aquarius and an air sign, you can either forget to eat or stick with pretty much the same menu, even for weeks on end. Yet at the same time, you love to discover—you thrive on new experiences. It is essential that some of those discoveries have to do with your daily routine.

Goals and challenges

Thinking about what you intend to do is one thing, but it's essential you write goals down. Not so much so you can achieve them in a metaphysical way, but so you can read what you wrote down a week later and revise those goals. Then continue to revise them as you broaden your goals and your horizons.

15

AQUARIUS

FEBRUARY

THIS DAY FOR EVERYONE

It isn't that you mind others making decisions in situations that involve you. Actually, often it is a relief. However, you prefer to take part in discussions, mostly because others lack your knack for telling those around you what's up. While this is tricky, you'll soon find a way to deal with those problems.

Once, joy was meeting the same person, same place. Now it's about exploration

You

For you, those around you—family, friends, and occasionally colleagues—aren't just people you know, they are what might be termed provocateurs. They are vital accessories in your life, simply because, from time to time, one will ask a question or another will point out something you've been doing the same way for a very long time. And in each case, they are gently but firmly challenging you to change habits that are familiar. So familiar, that in a way they numb your mind.

Even if it doesn't seem to be the case at the time, they prevent you from exploring in ways that are so important for you, as an Aquarius and an air sign. Yet while others' words may be irritating, deep down you know they're doing you a favor. If they didn't provoke you, or didn't point out what you said you wanted to do but haven't taken action on, they wouldn't be true friends or family members.

Remember this when you're annoyed with them. Instead of flaring up, as you have in the past, you might even thank them.

But even more than that, if possible, get them to join you in those adventures. For you as an Aquarius and an air sign, life is about discovery, and every time you do something in a new way, every time you break a familiar habit, you are taking another step toward delightful discovery.

You and others

Some place deep in your mind, you have a feeling that those who are true friends should be people you can hang out with and simply enjoy without any kind of conflict. But of course, the point is, those who are true friends or family members who love you will actually challenge you. They're concerned about your being stuck. This may not be welcome, but it is the biggest favor they could do you.

Health and well-being

There are all kinds of ways to ensure that you feel better. There are various kinds of exercise, from walking to yoga to jogging to things you haven't even heard of. And there are different ways of eating. But there is another trap that you, as an Aquarius and an air sign, can often fall into, and that is called daydreaming. It it may feel good if you do it, but it probably won't do your body much good.

Goals and challenges

Tempting as it is to revive goals from your past that once meant a great deal to you, deep down, you know they are indeed from the past. The trick is to pay attention to those that are in the present and in the future, that glimmer in front of your eyes. Those are the ones to go for.

A
\
Q
/
U
\
A
/
R
\
I
/
U
\
S

16

FEBRUARY

THIS DAY FOR EVERYONE

In their enthusiasm to tell you about certain new ideas or offers, one particular individual could be overly zealous. They may even seem to be bullying you. Despite that, what they have in mind would actually be in your best interest, but you won't know that until you do a little exploration.

GIFTS Resolute, Uncommon, Fair

CHALLENGES Unrelenting, Rebellious, Autocratic

NUMBER 1

(1+7) + (2) = 10 = (1+0) = 1

Do I say "No" before I even realize it? That's an invitation for a breakthrough

You

As an Aquarius, you often have several plans or projects on your mind, some of which are actually happening, and others you're only thinking about. Yet as somebody ruled by Uranus, the planet of innovation, life is about breakthroughs. And it is vital to consider whether what you're doing and planning has to do with the past, and past successes, and is similar to what others around you are doing, or is actually about taking an entirely different approach to some element of life.

Those new pursuits may involve a range of activities, but they all share something in common—what might be described as a form of "vision." That is, they are not about things that you have already done or have already experienced, but are new.

And that is the most important thing about them for you—they inspire you. Some may have to do with work, some may be practical, some may be social.

But in every case, they remind you that there's a world out there that you can change—in small ways and in big ways. And for you, as an Aquarius and somebody who not only has vision, but who can be a visionary, this is important.

Undertake that—ideally with those you care about—and life won't just be exciting, it will be extraordinarily satisfying.

You and others

Nothing is better than hanging out with people who spur on your thinking and get you going. That may be family, associates, or people you are involved in. Whatever the case, this process of exchanging ideas isn't just stimulating, it's about taking steps into the future.

Health and well-being

It is worth bearing in mind that, as much as you enjoy getting focused on ideas and ideals, it's easy to forget about taking care of your body. Yet you will need that body in order to take things to the next stage. Taking care of it is just as important as looking after those exciting changes.

Goals and challenges

Be wary of those around you who describe what you're doing as idealistic. As an Aquarius, you were born to be exactly that. While you may have a fairly boring day job, some element of your life needs to have that idealistic thread running through it. For you, that's like vitamins.

THIS DAY FOR EVERYONE

In some situations, fast action is vital, but in at least one, you are urged to wait until you have clarity, in terms of both hard facts and your own feelings, and that comes with having dealt with things and thought them through. Until then, explore your options, but avoid lasting decisions.

Certain places and people bring me joy, and so I stick with them. But others might, too

You

You are always ready to explore and try new things. In fact, there is a part of you that rather enjoys doing something that isn't just a bit of an experiment but that will, in some way, change the world. It may be modest; in fact, it may be your very private experiment. You may have fantasies about it leading to exciting things.

Yet there is another part of you that enjoys having a routine. It's familiar, and as an air sign and somebody who is easily distracted, knowing what is next grounds you. During times of transition, it is essential that you give yourself what might be termed elbow room: a chance to alter that routine, or perhaps even create a new one.

In doing so, that will reprogram the way you use your mind and your brain, and allow you to think about those goals and activities in a new way as well. This is probably the reverse of your thinking. You feel that if you can stick to the same routine at home, say in the morning, or when you go to bed, then you can venture out further. But actually it is the opposite. This is one of the greatest skills for you, to learn not only to play games with your mind, but to train your mind as if you were taking it to a gym, to exercise it and to work with new ideas. Do that regularly, and you will be amazed by how much fun you have.

You and others

Don't be surprised if those around you are suddenly asking you a lot of questions, or perhaps even referring to you as someone who is guiding them. This isn't necessarily what you set yourself up to be. But the fact is you are often more observant and closer to the trends that need to change than others, and your guidance will indeed be helpful for them.

Health and well-being

There is a phrase that is important for you to edit from your thinking and your habits: "I always need to." Whether it's what you eat or what you do, this is what might be termed an addiction. And even if it is a healthy addiction, exercising in a certain way, or eating in certain foods, at this point in your life, flexibility is more important than habits.

Goals and challenges

There are many kinds of goals, but for you, the most important one is discovery. And that means not setting the goal itself, but simply deciding you are on a journey during which, every week, every day, or as often as possible, you will encounter something new, something inspiring, and something that reassures you that you are on the right path.

A
\
Q
/
U
\
A
/
R
\
I
/
U
\
S

18

Unsettling as sudden changes may be, what's coming your way now and over the coming weeks isn't just exciting. Those events could be the answer to persistent problems. However, they won't seem that promising when they arise. Make a point of exploring everything. You'll be surprised what works out.

FEBRUARY

Pisces

February 19– March 19

Pisces Symbolized by a pair of fish, you, as a Pisces, born under this often charismatic and highly intuitive water sign, can view almost any situation from two angles. While you were originally ruled by Jupiter, Neptune's discovery in 1846 changed that. Your flower is water lily, your food and flavors are moss and lime, and your tree is the fig. Your stone is misty, blue-green jade.

P
I
S
C
E
S

GIFTS Intuitive, Liberal, Spontaneous

NUMBER 3

CHALLENGES Unworldly, Pipe-dreamer, Detouring

$(1+9) + (2) = 12 = (1+2) = 3$

Dawn is a reminder of nature's capacity to forgive humanity

You

You were born on a very special day—the first day of the sign of Pisces, a sign that has reinvented itself. You are probably aware of your symbol, which is two fish swimming in different directions. And those fish actually saved the goddess Aphrodite when she was born in the sea and brought her up into the air.

But also your sign has reinvented itself because in 1846, it acquired a new ruling planet, Neptune, which, of course, is appropriate for your sign. It could also be said to inspire you to be the Piscean you are today, whereas before, Pisces seemed to live a life that depended on circumstances. With Neptune, you have stepped out as someone who is very interested in having a positive impact on those around you, from those closest to the world itself. And that impact has to do with helping people be the best selves they can be.

This is a wonderful mission, but at times can lead to confusion in relationships and friendships. And that is the balance you're seeking: to be able to inspire others yet encourage them to be independent. It's as if you're watching an infant learn to walk—first, you let them take their first few steps while holding your hand, then you back off and leave it to them. This is one of the best gifts you can give others—your support. And there is nothing like the support from a Pisces.

You and others

A lingering friendship between an individual and a Pisces is a great treasure. You're an inspiration, and your presence in the life of another can help them turn a good idea into something wonderful, something which inspires others, and on occasion, could even benefit the world as well.

Health and well-being

As you're aware, as a Pisces, you can get so involved in what you're doing, you simply forget to eat or even sleep. Finding that balance—between being an inspiration to others and for them, in turn, to inspire people themselves—can be challenging. However, when you manage to do it, you will increase what you're able to give to the world.

Goals and challenges

Having the ability to care for others is a gift, but being able to care for yourself and deal with what you need to do at the same time can be a challenge. However, it is a challenge that, in some ways, you almost designed for yourself as a Pisces. While it won't always be an easy one, it is one you are equal to, and will profit from.

P
\
I
/
S
\
C
/
E
\
S

19

FEBRUARY

THIS DAY FOR EVERYONE

It's not that you've been trying to escape certain burdens and responsibilities, but rather you didn't know which to tackle first, so did nothing. However, now events have kick-started a cycle of action, each day will bring something new, exciting, and wonderful to focus on and to deal with.

GIFTS Redemptive, Extrasensory, Flowing

CHALLENGES Unreachable, Naive, Vague

NUMBER 4

(2+0) + (2) = 4

Even a seemingly minor gesture, done at the right moment, touches a Pisces heart

You

While you're sympathetic by nature, when the moment calls for it, you can be very firm, if not actually tough—with others and with yourself. What's more, you also benefit from a powerful practical streak. In fact, when it comes to big matters, it is amazing how clear you can be.

However, the sympathetic streak that is also a part of your nature surfaces from time to time, and can distract you. That means, when you're doing something, however modest, the real challenge isn't figuring out what to do. You can rely on your instincts for that. It is balancing that vision with the portion of your nature that gets so obsessed with tiny details or which can, at times, be so hurt by someone else's unthinking behavior, you're distracted from your objective.

As a water sign, while you're idealistic, you can take things personally—from others' unwitting comments to the peculiar attitude of certain individuals. Most Pisceans learn to spot this and, before you take things to heart, either speak up or, if that isn't possible, make a decision to ignore them.

This is a skill—but then all of life is a skill. And the better you get at dealing with such distractions, whatever their nature, the better you'll be able to use your extraordinary ability to touch others—and to transform the world around you that comes with being a Pisces.

You and others

While dramas around you can be distracting, once you learn to spot these, you'll learn to ask the question, "When is enough?" It's as if you were enjoying the warmth of the sun, but then realize if you stay out too long, you're likely to get burned. Dealing with those who could undermine your confidence is the same. The trick? Ignore them.

Health and well-being

As a water sign, while you take care of yourself, you sometimes forget about the toll being around those who have a tendency to undermine you can take. This not only causes concern, it can also lead to worry about other things. The trick is to discuss the matter clearly and firmly and in a way that you, as a Pisces, wouldn't usually do.

Goals and challenges

Every once in a while, you pause and organize yourself, your thinking and your life, so you know what is working and what isn't. And that will last for a while. However, one individual will then draw your attention and pull your balance away. The trick is to go back, as swiftly as you can, to that balance—because that balance is one of the most precious elements of your life.

P
\
I
/
S
\
C
/
E
\
S

Understandably you are in no mood to argue with somebody who, on the best of days, is difficult to deal with. But if you don't tackle the issue in question now, it will be assumed you're happy with things as they are, when that is by no means the case. Speak up now. You won't regret it.

20

FEBRUARY

A spring leaf, an infant, a new love, all remind us of life's promise

P
\
I
/
S
\
C
/
E
\
S

You

You take great joy in being able to make the world better, whether it is one person at a time, one situation at a time, or even bigger projects. For you as a Pisces, it isn't easy to maintain this as your main activity.

With the world around you changing— and with what might be those who're involved shifting—there are bound to be many twists and turns, and of many varieties. Even those whose main profession is doing exactly this variety of humanitarian work know they need to balance that with other activities in their own life and, equally, with family or hobbies.

So it is important for you to be aware of the need for that balance. These individuals and activities are an essential part of your life. They are, in fact, like a variety of emotional vitamin—just as you'd take actual vitamins, in this case, those activities and those individuals help you keep your perspective, and when necessary, realign your thinking and remind you what is actually in your best interests.

They help you rediscover your core, your center. Not only do these individuals benefit you, they give you the strength you need to go on to the next day, the next week, and the next month, and to make the world better in the way that you like to, but to do so without having to pay a price yourself.

You and others

You're probably aware you are sentimental, but you don't notice how much the attitude of others matters to you. And if they're uncaring, it can be hurtful. It is important to be aware of this and steer clear of those who are thoughtless. Instead, ensure those closest support you in the way they, and you, know is vital.

Health and well-being

While some Pisces are naturals at working out, most aren't. And if you are one of the latter, then finding ways to move that aren't really exercise is vital. And it can be fun. Seek out something that is magical and, ideally, musical. Do that, and you will appreciate the next time you can get out there and shake with those vibes, exercising your body at the same time.

Goals and challenges

Setting goals is one thing. Pursuing them is another matter. However, list those goals, ideally on paper, and you know what you expect to do. But actually, combining these with your own personal desires can be an even bigger challenge. The solution? Ask someone to stand beside you when you need that support. It is worthwhile.

21
FEBRUARY

THIS DAY FOR EVERYONE

While you'd have every right to be annoyed with certain thoughtless individuals, the fact is they are unaware of the impact of their words or actions. Raise this gently, but frankly, and invest time in the process. The resulting discussions will be astonishingly informative for everybody concerned.

Discern between those in need and complainers, who are louder and more persistent

You

You are, of course, living by your own set of ideals. This is something that you, as a Pisces, will have figured out probably from your earliest days. And as you've lived over the years, these ideals have become clearer.

You have also tended to assume that others have ideals, too. But gradually, you've come to realize that not only do others not have ideals, many don't even care. This is disillusioning, but this also explains quite a lot about certain people in your life and why, when you're talking about something you hope to do because it is an ideal, they look at you blankly.

Once you understand that, then you will understand why certain individuals are easier to live with, work with, and do things with. Others may require more time and effort—until you reach the point of simply telling them what you expect them to do and not explaining why it's good for them, or the world.

This variety of insight—this variety of being able to deal with others—is one of the greatest skills for you as a Pisces. It means you will stop trying to get those who have no capacity for empathy toward others to be that way. And equally, you will recognize who has earned your attention, your friendship, and in some cases, your love.

You and others

You're beginning to understand that certain individuals hear what you say in different ways. Some totally get your vision, and what you're describing is steps toward that. But others just see life as a long list of things to do. Once you realize that, then simply tell them, and don't expect them to share that vision, because it is unlikely they will.

Health and well-being

The idea of stopping to take care of yourself is difficult for Pisces, partly because, as a water sign, you don't really notice if you're hungry or tired until you are almost falling over. But also, taking care of yourself in terms of activities may seem strange. Yet if you begin to question how you feel about it, then it may be quite different. Fall in love with some kind of activity and eating well. The rest will be easy.

Goals and challenges

As a Piscean, you're a visionary. And for that reason, you may have had a sense of exactly what you wanted to be when you grew up. But even if you didn't, you will still have been drawn toward certain activities. Stick with them. Even if you have to redefine them every couple of years, they will still become key to your sense of achievement and of who you are.

P
\
I
/
S
\
C
/
E
\
S

Usually, rethinking plans at the last minute is no problem. In fact, you rather enjoy the challenge. But reorganizing arrangements when they're advanced—as is the case now—is complicated, disruptive, and time-consuming. Once you've begun, you will realize how necessary these changes are.

22

FEBRUARY

GIFTS Fluid, Self-sacrificing, Charitable

CHALLENGES Cryptic, Martyr-like, Profligate

NUMBER 7

(2+3) + (2) = 7

Nobody is better at spotting those who need help and knowing exactly what to do

You

If you're into astrology, then you'll know that as a Pisces, you are one of the three water signs, along with Cancer and Scorpio. And that, as a water sign, you have the power to understand the feelings of others often better than they do, and to recognize that your own feelings and emotions can be very powerful.

Not only that, you're idealistic. And you feel—and hope—that if you can work out a way to make your own life and the lives of others better, you can also have a greater impact on those around you, or maybe even the world.

While this is irrational and emotional, it is also visionary. And, very often, vision can override obstacles simply because you leap over the practicality that so many others live with, and begin to work away at turning that vision into a reality.

If there are those who question your capacity to achieve that, thank them for telling you. But go on doing what you believe in, because, as a Pisces, some would say you were born as that sign to benefit from that vision in whatever form it takes.

And it is true. That form may shift over time, but that doesn't matter. As you grow, it will change as well. But most of all, the important thing is never, ever to give up believing that miracles are possible. If anyone can make them happen, it's a Pisces.

You and others

All Pisces have an intuitive side and a belief in others. The funny the thing is, often you will have more belief in those around you than they do in themselves. Avoid arguing with them about what you see, but simply be there as they begin to recognize the characteristics that you long ago spotted. This is something you will do regularly and throughout your life. And many will thank you for it.

Health and well-being

One of your greatest gifts is your capacity to commit to a person, a cause, or a plan. And you do it so much, you forget about your own energy and even your body. The trick is to catch it before you go too far. Hurl yourself into something with passion—but at the same time, know when to stop.

Goals and challenges

Most Pisces have a list of goals you want to achieve. If there is a problem, it's a tendency to line up new ones too soon. While on one level, that makes sense—because you want to be preparing for the next—it can also mean that goals seem relentless. The secret? Celebrate each one as it is achieved.

P
\
I
/
S
\
C
/
E
\
S

THIS DAY FOR EVERYONE

There have been all sorts of excuses for the increasing distance between you and somebody who was once an important part of your life. While it's true you've been busy and so have they, the fact is, you simply haven't made time for them. Do it now. Once you're together again, you'll be glad you did.

FEBRUARY

GIFTS Generous, Idealistic, Spiritual

NUMBER 8

CHALLENGES Reckless, Inefficient, Unworldly

(2+4) + (2) = 8

Often, simple gestures say more about feelings than grand gifts

You

In most areas of life, you have an ideal, a vision for yourself, for others, or possibly for an organization. It may be simple or ambitious. But in every case, there will be a phrase that is involved with them, which is, "One day when ...."

This may have to do with work, or relationships, or something that you care deeply about. However, if you are waiting until that one day when things are a certain way, then you aren't able to enjoy it in the here and now. And the odds are good that when you get there, wherever there is with that plan or project, you will already be thinking about something else new.

For many Pisceans, this is tricky. And for many Pisceans, being in the here and now—and enjoying what you're doing with the people that you're with—is a real challenge.

Yet, if you can manage to do this—that is, manage to enjoy the incomplete plans and the not-quite-done goals that you are working on—and if you can manage to enjoy the presence of the people you're with, again the relationship may not be perfect, but you will still enjoying them. That is a victory, and it, too, will add to what might be called your joy vitamins. Goals move along, but if you ensure you have your joy vitamins every day, then you will be fine.

You and others

Pisceans tend to gather others for support when necessary. While mostly that's good, it is about who is reliable or trustworthy. The challenge? Recognize that, while certain individuals are supportive, they don't do much. Others may not be good company, but are reliable. Once that's dealt with, you'll have exactly the kind of support you need.

Health and well-being

It's easy to meet someone and grab a cup of coffee or a drink. But that's not really spending time with them. Yet with life ever more complicated, when is there time? The secret? Make a "grown-up" playdate to set aside quality time with others. This isn't just pleasant, it gives you a very special variety of emotional vitamin.

Goals and challenges

Pisceans are the dreamers of the entire zodiac, but that doesn't mean you should completely ignore reality, even though that is something you often hope is the case. The trick is to recognize that one day, reality will hit—and you need to welcome it, because the insights it gives you will enable you to ensure that your dream does become reality.

P
\
I
/
S
\
C
/
E
\
S

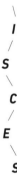

24

FEBRUARY

THIS DAY FOR EVERYONE

It would be easy to assume the silence of others means they disagree with you, dislike your plans, or perhaps are angry and unwilling to communicate at all. Or equally, it could be a simple misunderstanding. But you won't know if you don't ask. Do exactly that—ask. And the sooner, the better.

Pisces understanding is infinite, unless faced with cruelty. That's a game-changer

You

You don't think of yourself as an idealist until you talk to others and realize they don't care nearly as much as you do about the world, or about people, well-being, or individuals being happy. While you've assumed others also cared about such matters, the fact is, they live in very different worlds, and their feelings aren't the same as yours.

Once you get over being disillusioned, the trick is to learn to speak their language. If you want their support in some way, you need to be very clear, because they won't be swept up in the way you are by your passion for those situations. Yet, if you tell them exactly what you need, they will probably be not only be happy to help, but may even give you advice.

Ironically, this will also help you broaden your own contacts and interests, because when people don't respond to your Piscean enthusiasm for what matters to you, you assume they're not interested. Yet when you take another approach, then you will learn a lot about that. This isn't just about those activities you're passionate about. It is about almost any kind of relationship with others.

Those in the world around you speak a very different language from the language of Piscean idealism. And once you realize that, then you'll understand them far better—and they will understand you far better as well.

You and others

Most of us are born surrounded by family or friends who remain part of life but don't necessarily understand us. It is about longevity, being part of our lives. That also clarifies why they may not share your views. Ironically, they may be most informative when they disagree. Talk about why and you'll learn a great deal about the viewpoint of others.

Health and well-being

Everybody has ideas about eating well and the right kind of exercise and ways to achieve physical perfection. But there is something exciting you can do that will suit you whatever the season, and wherever you are—simply walk. Take a short walk, take a long walk, walk on your own, or walk with a friend. But doing that will remind you just how magnificent the world itself can be.

Goals and challenges

Achieving the goals you want at the level you want isn't going to be easy, and others have no idea what you are thinking of. Their view of something done well is only about 75 percent of what you have in mind. Once you understand that, instead of being shocked by them, you will simply realize that they are just being themselves.

P
\
I
/
S
\
C
/
E
\
S

25

FEBRUARY

THIS DAY FOR EVERYONE

You haven't exactly been patient, but you have been forced to recognize that no matter how unfair circumstances have been, there is no single solution. While sudden events will eliminate obstacles, these matters still can't be rushed. Continuing to be patient won't be easy, but it will pay off—and big time.

GIFTS Free-flowing, Instinctual, Supportive

NUMBER 1

CHALLENGES Wasteful, Unrealistic, Distant

(2+6) + (2) = 10 = (1+0) = 1

Sometimes the kindest thing you can do for another is accept their generosity

You

Life as a Pisces can be complex. In fact, it is an ironic part of your nature that if things are going too well, you begin to feel guilty. And if you're having too much fun, you may even unconsciously undermine certain things you're doing so you have to work harder. In fact, that means you have to rethink your timing and do more for duty and relax less.

Of course, this side of your nature keeps changing, so it is hard to spot it. Yet, if you recognize those moments when what was going smoothly gets undermined, then think about whether there was something that you committed to suddenly, or someone you've gotten close to who takes a lot of time, then you recognize the part of you that can undermine progress. You will also learn how to organize things in a very different way, and possibly even sideline that side of your nature and those individuals.

As a Piscean, you have a unique vision, one that is often beneficial to the world in many ways. Apply that vision to your own everyday life, excluding those individuals, those activities, or those obsessions that could undermine things and prevent them happening.

Not only will you be able to contribute to the world in the wonderful ways that you do as a Pisces, but you'll be able to do so without drama and with ease.

You and others

Defining "joy" may be challenging. But it is simply knowing you're happy with what you did yesterday, you are pleased with today, and you're pretty excited about tomorrow. The trick? Not to allow anything to disrupt that joy. It isn't easy, but it's up to you alone to determine this. It may sound complicated, but, actually, it's very simple.

Health and well-being

Currently, there is an obsession about getting things done. But for you as an intuitive Piscean, it is clear what you need. Despite that, you sometimes get so involved in what you're doing, you forget about eating or sleeping. It's easy to get back on track. Just sit quietly, reflect, and remember who you are and what's in your best interests.

Goals and challenges

Every Pisces has the notion, deep in their mind, that they can achieve amazing goals—what others would call fantasies. However, some say you must sacrifice something. That is an old story. But, actually, as a Piscean, you were born to have that vision. All you need to do to achieve it is ignore those who either try to undermine it or laugh at it.

P
\
I
/
S
\
C
/
E
\
S

There is a fine line between discussing the best option and having an exchange of ideas that descends into a battle about who's right and who's wrong. Neither you nor anybody else is likely to give in. The solution? Allow the evaluation process to unfold as it must—then wait and watch.

26

FEBRUARY

Usually, trust must be built slowly. Except when it bursts on the scene like fireworks

You

Every sign of the zodiac is said to have a ruler, a heavenly body that is linked with it, mythically and astrologically. This practice goes back thousands of years. Yet over the past couple hundred years, three signs have acquired new ruling planets, including yours.

Until 1846, Pisces was considered to be ruled by Jupiter. Yet that year the appropriately named Neptune was discovered, and it became your ruler. This is especially appropriately because your symbol is two fish, swimming in opposite directions. And that is one of your big lessons as a Piscean. Neptune is not only about vision but also intuition; it's helping you align those two fish, one of which is going in a practical direction, and the other of which is going in an intuitive direction.

Learn to balance the two: that is, the practical side that needs to align with your intuition, and the side that is more about feelings. As a Pisces, you have rare access to both. You can create a beautiful life in the physical world, but also reach to the heavens, and sometimes deep into humanity's core.

Certain individuals have a role to play in others' lives, whatever the setting. It may be among family—or in the wider world. And it may change at times. Whatever it is you are doing, you will bring a special touch, which is your Piscean capacity for caring.

You and others

Urgent as remedying others' problems seems, the fact is, they probably aren't yours to deal with at all. Some people are born knowing what they want to do, while others develop that vision over life. Many have family and friends guiding them, and sometimes telling them what to do. Be cautious of others becoming too dependent on you.

Health and well-being

As a Piscean, you are easily touched by others, and if there is tension—if they have tension in their own lives, or if there's tension between you that you can feel deeply—the trick is not to try to solve it. Instead, you need to realize that if there isn't anything you can do at the moment, so back off and let things be as they are.

Goals and challenges

Setting goals can be difficult. Yet, being true to yourself is essential. And as you understand yourself better, those goals are likely to change. Don't feel you have to stick with the same ones when you've shifted; those goals should shift then as well.

P
\
I
/
S
\
C
/
E
\
S

27

FEBRUARY

THIS DAY FOR EVERYONE

Few things annoy you more than trying to organize plans with somebody who refuses to focus on the big picture, but instead thinks only about details. Actually, this is ideal. You dread fine-tuning matters of this nature, but are superb at dealing with the overview—and now, you can split your duties.

GIFTS Calming, Insightful, Compassionate

CHALLENGES Escapist, Assumptive, Unreadable

NUMBER 3

$(2+8) + (2) = 12 = (1+2) = 3$

Quiet joys go deepest and are the longest-lasting

You

As a water sign, you are influenced by your feelings, of course. However, you are also influenced by the world around you, by the people you're talking to, and by circumstances.

And all of those can mean that you rethink what once were very clear plans, a vision for what you want to do and achieve. But even more than that, if you talk to others too much about your own goals, it's very easy to allow them to influence you, simply because they want to understand your vision.

But then of course, they aren't you. Even if they are Pisceans, your own vision is very much an extension of yourself. It may seem antisocial when others talk about things to say, "Well, I totally disagree with you." However, it is worth noting that many Pisceans are actual artists—they are actors or performers—and they use that intuitive side to create roles.

In your case, if you find others are always trying to tell you what to do, it may be that it's important for you to dig deeper into your own nature and discover what your role is in life.

Equally, it is important to recognize that what is the right role at one point can evolve over time. Because, of course, we all grow over time. When you recognize that, then, instead of worrying about getting it right, you will enjoy the process as it unfolds.

You and others

Discussions can sometimes be difficult because others don't seem to understand that your views are completely different from theirs. However, if you run into one of those rare individuals who not only celebrates the unique character of your views, but encourages you to nurture them, then keep that person close to you. They're the one you want nearby as you're exploring your options.

Health and well-being

There are those who feel that if you have your health well in hand, then life will run smoothly. But as a Pisces and a water sign, for you ups and downs are natural. There will be times when you eat enthusiastically and sleep well and others when you're restless or not hungry. That's all about being a Pisces, experiencing the ebb and flow of being a water sign.

Goals and challenges

Basically, there are two ways to achieve what you want. One is to set a goal and go after it. But there's another that is far more Piscean, and that is to wake up and sense what you should do next. Gradually, you'll learn how powerful intuition can be, and how following it can shorten the path to achieving those goals.

P
\
I
/
S
\
C
/
E
\
S

Life would be a lot easier if you could sidestep certain obligations that are as tricky as they are tedious. However, as tempting as it is to put these off, they won't just vanish. In fact, they could become more complicated. The sooner you tackle them the better—and the easier that will be.

28

FEBRUARY

GIFTS Telepathic, Imaginative, Positive

CHALLENGES Evasive, Suffocating, Careless

NUMBER 11

(2+9) = 11

This rare and special date accents unique gifts and charms

P
\
I
/
S
\
C
/
E
\
S

You

This is a very special birthday—not only because it occurs only every four years, but also because in numerology, your number February 29th, two and nine add up to 11, which is considered to be one of the master numbers. This indicates that you showed up for a special reason.

And as you live through life, all sorts of intriguing opportunities will arise. It may also be that you have your own particular vision—many Pisceans do, but you may be drawn to a certain activity. You may have a certain talent, a gift or a characteristic that adds not only to your life but to the lives of those around you—and possibly even to the lives of those on the planet.

In many cases, you may sense this when you're young. In others, it will come about and in some cases it will morph, it will reshape itself as you live out the days of your life. But what is most important for you to realize is that, while each of us comes into this life with a gift, as someone who is a February 29th Piscean, you have a very special gift—one that is important to share with the world, but also one that is even more important to embrace and enjoy as the individual that you are.

Simply being you will add to the environment you're in—every day and in more ways than you can imagine possible.

You and others

Feeling you have something special to offer may seem bizarre, or even arrogant, but the fact is, you do. You don't need to define it or say it, but talking to certain individuals will leave them changed—and you as well. Every time you do it, you'll be contributing to the well-being of others and of the planet—and you'll bring greater joy to your own life as well.

Health and well-being

Finding ways to take care of yourself can be difficult because often you are sensitive or perhaps have unusual energies, so it's different from everybody else. All you need to do is check in with yourself on any particular day and sense what you need. It may be you need to rest. It may be you need food. It might even be you need a large ice-cream cone. Whatever the case, give yourself that gift on that day and listen in the same way every day.

Goals and challenges

Many in the world want to make things better. The practical earth signs have one set of ideas and the air signs have another. But as a special Pisces, you have what might be described as a golden touch. And when you make a suggestion, it might work out to be nothing short of miraculous.

THIS DAY FOR EVERYONE

You are in no mood to take care of tasks or obligations as boring as they are rewarding. However, these aren't just your responsibility. Once you're involved, you'll realize how much you have to learn from them. That alone will justify the time and effort required, but also you'll soon begin to enjoy them.

Most arguments are mere differences, but a few are a way of showing love

You

Part of your nature as a Pisces is that of the searcher. You're searching for all sorts of things. You're searching for that vision that is yours, but you will also be searching in other ways, in practical ways and personal ways, that have to do with friendships—that special gift for somebody, something that will make their life easier, or even an introduction that you can make, the right person meeting the other right person at the right time.

And that element of perfection is also core to your life. There is a tendency to feel that if you can just line up the energies, then things will fall into place. And that would be true if you were in a world where everyone else had that intention. But as you have seen, some people almost have an instinct for turning what are relatively smooth arrangements upside down, and they do it all on their own.

If you take responsibility for that, then you'll be distracted from who you are, which is someone who's there to align events and the thoughts of others and to make things happen.

The trick is to continue to search, but to forget about it being perfect. Then, you'll draw to you those individuals who somehow always manage to turn things upside down, and instead you will make the best of every day and every hour and every moment that you do, simply because that is your intention.

You and others

Every once in a while, you'll come across somebody who's quite special. In fact, those individuals might become what you might call co-searchers: they, too, have a sense that there's something to be discovered, not through struggle but through a quiet intention to encounter something wonderful. You might spend a day with them, or a lifetime. But you will change each other's lives.

Health and well-being

There is one characteristic of the true searcher and that is someone who has a vision. Your energy extends into the world, looking for what you can do and how you can share those experiences with others. There's no formula for it, but there is a formula for enjoying it: realize that each morning when you wake up, you will be experiencing something new.

Goals and challenges

Many people have no understanding about you. It's as if you speak a different language. The fact is, you do. They don't understand about vision or about search. They only understand about today and tomorrow, and life's practicalities. Acknowledge that simple fact and the rest will be easy.

P
\
I
/
S
\
C
/
E
\
S

Obviously, you'd rather not stand your ground with somebody who's difficult in the best of circumstances, but not only is it wise, the individual in question knows they're in the wrong, yet is too proud to admit it. Gently, but firmly, challenge them and they'll not only respond positively, they will thank you.

01

MARCH

If somebody is being demanding, do nothing until you observe how they treat others

You

The word "idealism" is so often used when talking about Pisceans. Of course, certain individuals insist they are idealists, but they're probably a little bit different from your brand, simply because their idea of things going well has more to do with politics and economics than it does with yours. It is the sense that there is a vision, a way of living life, where, instead of things being a struggle, they can work out and, in some cases, fall into place.

And that is entirely possible, except that it's mostly only Pisceans, or those for whom the sign is very strong in their astrological chart, who can deal with that. It's also important for you to recognize the difference between those who share your vision and those whose version of idealism might be more, shall we say, practical or even academic.

When you understand that, then you'll also understand there are actually two languages you must use: the one you use with the fellow true idealists, and the one used with those who are trying to live up to their version of that.

And when you understand that there are two brands of idealism, then also, you'll be more relaxed about it. The fact is, with those who are following their "not quite Piscean" brand of idealism, their hearts are good, as are their intentions. Embrace that—and the rest will be easy.

You and others

Finding a way to talk things over with those whose view is very different can be tricky, until you realize it's as if you're speaking different languages. When that's clear, you'll realize that their values, ethics, and objectives are very different. Then you'll be able to talk about things the way they understand them, and may even be able to add a few intriguing thoughts to their approach to life.

Health and well-being

As a Piscean, the possibility of catching something from someone isn't just about a cold; you can catch someone's bad mood. However, it's easy to shake off, because if you remember what is the best of your vision for the world, you will quickly reshape your mood.

Goals and challenges

Explaining to somebody else what you'd like to achieve can be difficult. As a Piscean, even if you are in the same business, you still have your own unique values and viewpoints. Understand that, and then, when you're talking with others, you will realize that occasionally you need to say things in a different way if they are to understand the vision you have in mind.

P
\
I
/
S
\
C
/
E
\
S

02

MARCH

THIS DAY FOR EVERYONE

You are facing a range of decisions. Some are minor and easy to deal with. Others are so complex, you have no idea where to begin. Urgent as things seem, there's no rush to deal with these. Invest time in asking questions. What you learn will clarify matters more swiftly than you'd imagined possible.

Nobody understands the power of love better than a Pisces

You

What does it take for you to say life is good? You'd think you know that. Many want a home, love, jobs, friends—and those are important. But for you, as a Pisces, in particular, while of course those matter a great deal, there is also a part of you that wants those around you, or possibly the entire world, to be free from pain and struggles. That is your Piscean idealism.

And if you can't remedy them, then you might have a tendency to say you can't be happy until the world is free of whatever it is that is worrying you.

It is worth thinking about that, because it means that you won't be able to add your personal happiness to the world until certain issues are dealt with..

If you had infinite powers, then that would be understandable. But the odds are that you haven't. Therefore, the trick here is to recognize that there are things going on in the world that you are definitely not happy about, but their existence doesn't need to, and shouldn't, undermine your own contentment.

It's a tricky thing to remember when you say you won't be happy until X problem or Y situation is solved, but it will also bring powerful insights about the way certain parts of your mind can undermine your own joy.

You and others

We all have a gift to give to the world. In some cases it has to do with family, loved ones, or friends. It may be raising children. It may be being a valuable friend to others. But in every case, it's essential to think about what you can do and give each day. It may seem so ordinary to you that you don't realize how actually, truly extraordinary it is.

Health and well-being

There are lots of ways we are advised to maintain our health: vitamins, the right food, and exercise. But there is another way that is important for you as a Piscean, and that is to have a good time. When you're having fun, when you're relaxed, when you're happy, you are calling on the best and the most healing elements of your nature. They will comfort you and scare away any shadowy thoughts fast. Try it and you'll see how well it works.

Goals and challenges

Certain individuals dismiss you as not being very practical—because they are realists. However, some would say that each of us has created our own world with our own vision, at least in terms of how we see things. That as an entirely different view, but it's one that, for you as a Pisces, is well worth reflecting on.

P
\
I
/
S
\
C
/
E
\
S

MARCH

GIFTS Romantic, Diverting, Reflective

NUMBER 7

CHALLENGES Gullible, Sidestepping, Wishful

$(0+4) + (3) = 7$

Love, at its purest, is life-changing.
The trick? Recognizing that purity

You

Many Pisceans believe in miracles—or what might be termed "amazing possibilities" if you're not into religion or words like that. Whatever the case, you'll have had experiences, small and large, where what seemed to be impossible situations were dealt with magically. That's another word you can use.

It is the capacity for there to be a leap of events, something completely unexpected that shows up and seems to follow you around. Actually it is possible for everybody. Yet as a Pisces and someone who is intuitive, with a gift for drawing this kind of, shall we say, magical event into your life, it seems to occur more often for you.

As you're aware, there are those around you who think it is wonderful and are delighted to hear you talk about it. Yet there are others whose reaction could only be defined as a "harrumph" and who simply won't discuss it, if you insist on being illogical.

The fact is, you are who you are. And you have that vision. You also have a knack for picking up a situation with that Piscean energy, and transforming it in some magical or miraculous way. If there are those who don't believe in it, that is up to them. For you, the capacity is something that you not only have every right to enjoy, you also have every right to exercise as frequently as you like.

You and others

You like to talk about what goes on in your life, and there are those around you who sometimes hear about what some would call abnormal occurrences—those very special miraculous events. Talk about them all you want, simply because the more you talk about them, the more normal they become—and quite possibly, the more frequently they will occur. That is what being a Pisces is all about.

Health and well-being

There are all sorts of ways to feel great. There are fitness and eating the right thing, both of which are very important. However, as a Piscean and a water sign, you'll know the way to feel the best is to be in a sunny mood. Even if the day isn't sunny, if your mood is, you will find that you have a bounce in your step.

Goals and challenges

There are those who regard themselves as real intellectuals, who live a life based on facts. It is hard to tell when they fall in love, because that is difficult to prove with facts. But when you talk about your own view of the world, which can range from scientific facts to the more intuitive side of your nature, their vocabulary is stretched. You need to consider just how long you want to chat with these doubters.

P
\
I
/
S
\
C
/
E
\
S

04

MARCH

THIS DAY FOR EVERYONE

Few things are more disappointing than being let down by someone you've trusted. In the past, you've accepted an apology without discussion. It is now time for this to change. Ask what's behind these sudden developments. What you learn and ultimately talk over will be amazingly informative.

Ignore those who question your vision. Trust your instincts over others' doubts

You

The word "promise" means different things to different people and signs. For instance, to a Gemini or Sagittarius, "I promise" means "Maybe" or "I hope so." But for you as a Pisces, when you promise to do something, you mean it absolutely and you will do all you can to make that happen. It comes from the heart as much as from the mind.

However, this perspective, more of a belief than an idea, reflects your own unique way of looking at life. While many regard facts as unchangeable, as a Piscean, you believe deeply that your intention—your vision of what is possible—accompanied by hard work or effort is what makes life happen.

While this isn't just different from most signs, it is unique to your nature as a Pisces. What is more, your perspective often clashes with the reality others live with, which leads to ongoing confusion between you as a Piscean and the rest of the world—it's as if you are speaking two different languages.

And in fact, it's true. Of course, every once in a while, you will come across those born under other signs but whose personal chart is strongly influenced by Pisces, and this is how they think, too. Recognizing this special vision of life and of what is possible is important, because it isn't just your way of looking at life—it embraces the magic of being a Pisces.

You and others

While your idealism is core to your way of thinking and living, it is vital that you recognize the rest of the world doesn't think this way. So if things aren't falling into place, acknowledge that you will need to take an approach that allows you to make plans without the drama.

Health and well-being

Being disappointed by others is inconvenient. Equally, when you are unable to live up to commitments, you suffer from knowing others have to reschedule. But everybody has a different attitude toward such commitments, and often you care more than most. Of course, you can't change the world right away, but you can learn to understand others better.

Goals and challenges

Whatever you're doing, you always aim high. You don't even think about it, it comes so naturally. But you aren't always prepared for twists and turns and surprises, the result of unexpected events, or even the fact that those who say they will absolutely be there for you and then aren't. The problem? Their idea of loyalty is simply very different from yours.

P
\
I
/
S
\
C
/
E
\
S

Certain individuals don't really care about facts, even when getting things wrong would inconvenience others. While ordinarily this doesn't matter, current arrangements involve the two of you and perhaps others as well. Explain that it will be easier if you deal with the details, then do exactly that.

05

MARCH

GIFTS Sparkly, Inventive, Supportive

CHALLENGES Distant, Harebrained, Avoidant

NUMBER 9

(0+6) + (3) = 9

While giving love is easier than accepting it, receiving it changes everybody's life

P
\
I
/
S
\
C
/
E
\
S

You

It's a question you ask yourself again and again—who comes first? Many signs simply act in their own best interest and don't even think about it. But as a Pisces, that is another matter, one connected to your symbol of two fish, swimming in different directions.

You're always conscious of the circumstances of others and how you can help them or support them, but what do you need to do for yourself? And that leads to confusion. Often, there s your loyalty to others. Whether it's family, offspring, or close friends, it is fierce. What's more, you are proud of those values. It could be said that, as you swim through the waters of life, your focus is intense. You are looking after your own interests and, just as much, focusing on those of others.

However, every once in a while, you need to pause and question who and what you're putting first, and especially, whether those activities and those goals are as important or meaningful as they once were. As a Piscean, you can commit deeply to goals; yet life changes, times change, and so do you. Sometimes your focus on certain goals needs to change, if not come to an end. If there is anything that is become an obstruction or isn't falling into place for you, it's worth examining the situation. Try it. What comes to light could begin an exciting new cycle.

You and others

Very often you're the one rescuing others when they're facing difficulties, and when they need support, you're there. But there are times when you need others to rescue you—not in the sense of the same kind of drama, but in the sense of helping. This is something that you face from time to time. And when you do, it's important to recognize that their support isn't just valuable, it is essential.

Health and well-being

As a Pisces, you'll be aware that life can involve emotional ups and downs that can be draining, which means if you've been through a period like that, you may not be as clear as you could be. This is when the support of others is so important: not necessarily to resolve the problems, but simply to help you find that center, the core of your being again.

Goals and challenges

Putting yourself first sounds simple, and many signs are good at it. However, for you as a Pisces, it can be difficult, because you can often feel guilty when you tell others they will have to wait because you have something you need to think about in your own life. Yet there are also times when there is nothing more important than that. Still, do it.

THIS DAY FOR EVERYONE

Few things are more boring than dealing with practicalities, but as you know, ultimately you'd regret leaving these in the hands of somebody else. Once you're involved, you'll realize how exciting this is and how creative you can be, both with existing arrangements and plans for the future.

GIFTS Extrasensory, Empathic, Dazzling

CHALLENGES Diverting, Lost, Irresponsible

NUMBER 1

(0+7) + (3) = 10 = (1+0) = 1

Little is better than making a life-changing suggestion and everything working out

You

As a Piscean, you're a natural organizer. Many people don't recognize this, because you're very discreet in your approach. While certain signs are heavy-handed, you have a way of making others feel important and, in fact, you'll get them to shoulder responsibilities in a way that will boost their confidence.

What's more, you are also superb at fitting in, so even if there's chaos, you will inspire others. Suddenly they'll realize they can help get things organized or even contribute to imposing order on chaos.

And that is your gift as a Piscean. It is not just your capacity to connect with and inspire others to stand up for themselves. Better yet, you encourage them to discover, and offer, the best of who they are.

This has to do with life, with what is being organized, but also it has to do with all sorts of relationships, with family, with loved ones, with friends, and with the wider world.

And this gift you have is something that is meant to be used. Even though you may not think of it as that much of a gift, it enables you to encourage or guide others to be the best they can be.

But even more than that, encouraging them to grow allows you to grow, too, and in satisfying ways. In modern terms, it could be said to be a "win-win" for everybody.

You and others

There are certain individuals who will decide that you are responsible for what they do. They'll play a game with you, they'll ask your advice, and then they'll ask even more advice, and before you know it, you will be in charge. Watch out for that. Of course, you'll know what to do—which is, quite simply, back off.

Health and well-being

As you know, from time to time, you can get so involved in doing something, partly because it's fun, that you don't realize you're overdoing things and ignoring your energy levels and effort. This is particularly important when you're doing something where you recognize that others are benefiting. It seems obvious, but it doesn't always occur to you.

Goals and challenges

The ability to exit from an arrangement is a rare skill. There are certain individuals who will pick a fight to make it happen, while others will just fade away. For you, however, because you have the gift of being able to turn what are often rather unworkable situations into something remarkable, it is also vital that you acquire that skill of saying a gracious but firm farewell at the right moment.

P
\
I
/
S
\
C
/
E
\
S

THIS DAY FOR EVERYONE

While you don't particularly enjoy changes in long-standing arrangements, you have accepted that they are sometimes unavoidable. Changes in close alliances with family and loved ones are another matter, but here, too, things are moving on. Embrace even unwelcome changes—they are vital.

07

MARCH

Hoping for magical events is one thing, but a surprise appearance is something else

You

As you're aware, your symbol—the fish swimming in two directions—can indicate confusion. It's true that, at times, as a Pisces, you can be indecisive. Yet at the same time, you have an amazing ability to deal with a range of situations, some practical, others sentimental and dramatic. This capacity to juggle tricky circumstances is one of your Piscean skills.

Yet others can become dependent on you for dealing with such matters. This is where it gets problematic, because while this skill is rare, you can impart this ability to others, and gradually hand the responsibility over to them.

True, they may not be quite as good at it as you are, but that doesn't matter. They will be adept enough that they can deal with tricky situations wisely and creatively. This capacity to create happy situations and opportunities for growth aren't just important. You will be giving yourself a way out of arrangements where others have been dependent on you.

While they will have been rewarding, each must change as circumstances move on. If the sense of intimacy you've developed makes everyone feel like they want to hang out longer, that can be easily done. The skill? Learn when, and how, to walk away with a fond farewell and you'll have learned a skill that will benefit you for a very long time.

You and others

The fact is, you have a magic touch, and when you remember to use it, it is very powerful. The trick is to use it with intention, then stop. Otherwise, certain individuals will assume that you will continue to organize their life in a way that is just as magical as what you've done recently. Make it very clear that this isn't a service that can be rented, whatever the cost.

Health and well-being

As a water sign, you are somebody who concentrates more on their feelings than their body. It is vital that you take care of yourself, even though it doesn't come naturally. Enough sleep, the right kind of food, and getting away from people who drain you all seem simple, but when you're in the midst of something that is exciting, you tend to forget it. The trick is to say farewell at the right moment.

Goals and challenges

There is a difference between knowing what you want to do and setting goals. As a Piscean, sometimes you are able to "magic up" the situation you need. However, if you put a little thought into defining what you'd like to do—that goal, and how you would like it to happen—then that magic can occur all the more swiftly.

P
\
I
/
S
\
C
/
E
\
S

08

MARCH

THIS DAY FOR EVERYONE

You are by no means a control freak, yet you dislike allowing others to make decisions that really should be yours to decide. For now, leave things to them. What they opt for may be very different from what you would have chosen. But you can reorganize everything later.

GIFTS Kind, Meditative, Rescuing

CHALLENGES Neglectful, Detouring, Interfering

NUMBER 3

$(0+9) + (3) = 12 = (1+2) = 3$

Anonymous generosity is typically Piscean— but it causes both confusion and joy

You

From time to time, you're faced with a range of dilemmas, each of which is chaotic in some way. While intuitively, you sense you can put them in order, it is bound to be complicated.

Yet, with your trademark intuition and with the two Piscean fish being able to view the situation from two directions, you'll soon spot where there are yeses and noes to be dealt with. Equally, you recognize where issues are the fault of certain individuals while others will simply be the result of circumstances.

But in every case, it seems that where others are unable to examine the facts or make a grounded analysis, you will be able to. This is one of your greatest gifts as a Pisces.

However, your challenge is to get involved, talk about the facts, examine matters in detail, but at the same time make it clear you're involved only to a certain extent. You will also ensure others are aware you are not going to monitor the circumstances forever, nor will you babysit any tricky individuals involved.

This may disappoint those who see you as being the great rescuer, but the fact is you are there to help the individuals in question deal with, and learn from, these and any other tricky matters, and that's that.

And, just as much, you will be there to help them be clear in their own minds about what they must, and need, to do.

You and others

There is a part of your nature, and a part of the nature of others, which doesn't just thrive on a variety of chaos, it enjoys it. There is an intellectual challenge and there is an emotional challenge. Most of all, it requires a kind of vision you rarely get to employ in life. Use it, and use it wisely, and encourage others to use theirs so when you've got everything sorted out, you can walk away with a clear mind.

Health and well-being

It may seem strange to say you need sleep, but when you are involved in something, you almost forget. But the fact is you're still living in a human body and you still will allow those worries to make your mind work overtime. So even if you're in bed, your mind will keep on dancing around. Being able to stop is always important, and when you're in the midst of something overwhelming, it is essential.

Goals and challenges

As an idealist, you're only really interested in something if it offers inspiration to the people involved. Yet, sometimes the challenge is so appealing you can't resist getting involved. While you may be able to do wonders, it could mean it's more about ego than the kind of vision that is your Piscean trademark.

P
\
I
/
S
\
C
/
E
\
S

THIS DAY FOR EVERYONE

Every once in a while, you need to stand up to somebody. While you did this before, it was about a particular matter. Now the issue has to do with the arrogant and often dismissive manner of certain individuals. The point is to register a complaint and that's all. Within days, you'll see why.

09

MARCH

Even the most eloquent Pisces will struggle to explain generosity to somebody unkind

You

You say you are longing for an ordered life, to have things going the way you expect, to have balance. Yet at the same time, there's a part of you, that part which is the two fish swimming in different directions, that gets a bit bored if what you're doing or those you're dealing with are too predictable. For you, as a Piscean, the disruption, the feelings that come with it, and the process of finding the solutions for the resulting disarray are part of the drama of our life. Fixing things, finding the potential for perfection in disarray—whether it's in your work, day-to-day life, or close relationships—is all hugely rewarding to you.

However, the trick is to have something else that's a little bit dramatic, whether it's rescuing a situation or perhaps supporting somebody who needs to learn and to deal with everyday life. Why? Because this prevents you from being drawn into the unconscious dramas that are familiar to those who know you: the sudden dramas that are the Pisces signature.

They occur frequently, especially when you're bored. Take that approach, and you will keep the two Piscean fish well occupied, because they will both have to paddle madly to keep up. Meanwhile, you can deal with the dramas that are necessary to keep your watery, rather emotional, rather dramatic, Piscean nature happy.

You and others

If you're trying to figure out what makes you tick and learn about the elements of your character that are very much part of what's going on, the fact is you won't necessarily be ready to analyze things. Yet at the same time, it is all about looking at who you're drawn to, the kind of person who is giving you the kind of fun you love, which, if it is serious drama, means you're kind of enjoying it.

Health and well-being

The art of taking care of yourself in the midst of upheaval is a skill, and it is one that, as a Piscean, you sometimes ignore. For you, living out the ups and downs is exciting, especially in a world that seems to try so hard to walk on a level playing field and to live a life that is unimaginative. As a Piscean, you are not just a visionary, you have a strong, dramatic streak. Think carefully about how you use it. There are many arts to negotiating life

Goals and challenges

Deciding what to say to certain individuals you know are going to be difficult is seriously challenging . Ordinarily as a Pisces, you would already be calculating ways to work around them. However, there's another approach, and that is to say an uncompromising "No."

THIS DAY FOR EVERYONE

Usually there is no point in debating issues you have strong views about, as do others. Yet judging by the planetary activity ahead, which accents discussion, and even more, expansive thinking, you could achieve a shared perspective on even serious differences.

GIFTS Innocent, Imaginative, Sympathetic

CHALLENGES Naive, Impractical, Sidestepping

NUMBER 5

$(1+1) + (3) = 5$

In so many settings, simply saying "Yes" is life-changing. A "No" shatters joy in seconds

You

As a Piscean, you're designed for multitasking. As one of the mutable water signs—the signs born at the end of each season, who have a talent for juggling a range of interests and tasks, but also as a water sign and somebody who is able to tune into others in a rare way—you're able to use your skills in a range of settings. What's more, you are adaptable, so can deal with even rather difficult people, although you may not want to do it full-time.

However, you're also easily bored, and for this reason, you often move from one task or setting to another. Even if you're in business, you will begin doing one thing, then another, and often the next after that. All of this is fine, except certain situations and individuals place great value on sticking with things.

As a clever and tactful Pisces, you are usually able to find a way around such dilemmas. This is, in fact, one of your greatest gifts—and in every area of your life.

You have a knack for rethinking elements of your life, yet making others feel important. That way, you're always doing something new, but it makes life itself much more fun.

The trick to all of this, therefore, is to ignore those who give solid business advice and tell you to stick to one thing. Instead, use your imaginative Pisces vision. It is one of the best allies you'll ever have.

You and others

There are many kinds of friendships and love, and as a Pisces, you know many people who have experienced a range of feelings about you. Some of them will declare their feelings, some of them will simply hang around a lot, but this kind of devotion, appealing as it is, may not be in your best interests, especially because you can get drawn into drama. Finding somebody who cares about you—and finding friends and family members who have that quality—isn't just wise, it is essential.

Health and well-being

If there is a single phrase that is part of your approach to life, it is "overdoing it." When you have a passion about an individual or a project, you'll hurl yourself into it. That is your nature as a Pisces. However, the trick is to also be aware when enough is enough.

Goals and challenges

While you may stick with the same way of living, even the same job, for a long time, it is important that your goals shift, because you thrive on finding new ways to do things, and the trick is to be flexible. That means you're able to tackle new activities, meet new people, and go to new places, all of which feed that inquisitive side of your nature.

P
\
I
/
S
\
C
/
E
\
S

THIS DAY FOR EVERYONE

Thinking back, it was only a while ago that you felt you had no choice but to stand your ground against ideas, events, or changes that would create nothing but disruption. These happened anyway, and you've realized how thrilling they are now, and will be in the future.

11

MARCH

GIFTS Psychic, Peaceful, Hypnotic

CHALLENGES Invasive, Dreamy, Easily Distracted

NUMBER 6

(1+2) + (3) = 6

While Piscean kindness is infinite, receiving is another, far less comfortable, matter

P
\
I
/
S
\
C
/
E
\
S

You

As a Pisces, your enthusiasm is a trademark. It emerges from your inquisitive nature and it is in your approach to everything—from the circumstances you're dealing with to the individuals you meet or the ideas that excite you. You respond to these naturally and deeply.

Sometimes those feelings are emotional, but they will also be creative or even intellectual. They constitute a variety of vitamins, in that they make you feel better and stronger, and that life's more exciting, more worth living. Of course, the trick to dealing with this, whatever the setting, is to bring it your idealism.

As a Piscean and a water sign, you go with the flow. Imposing order on a situation or others doesn't come naturally. Yet in certain matters, you have no choice, especially when practical obligations, money, or commitments are involved. These aren't fun, but ignoring them only leads to complications. So if you deal with that practical side of things early on, and organize them in a way that seems very dull indeed, you'll be glad you did.

You will, in fact, discover that you're free to be all the more creative and encourage others to be as well. This is one of the great paradoxes of being a Piscean. While some of your greatest gifts have to do with being highly intuitive, if not a little crazy, one of the greatest safeguards for you is quite strong organization.

You and others

Pure Pisces energy is about inspiration. Where you take that and how you use it is up to you, and that has to do with figuring things out in practical terms. If you don't, you will continue to bounce ideas off others, which has its own particular kind of high, but often doesn't compensate you in terms of time or money.

Health and well-being

Pisces tend to overdo, and this can occur in lots of ways. You can get too enthusiastic, not enough sleep, give too many ideas, spend too much time with somebody. Only later do you realize you're exhausted and quite possibly haven't been compensated for your efforts. Figure out the practicalities first—that is a message from the heavens.

Goals and challenges

Aiming impossibly high is very much part of your Piscean nature. But so that you can enjoy the ride—and as you do, are able to look down on what you're doing from the point of view of being on a high—you will realize that certain things need to change and improve. And that's the best approach—turning something that's already exciting into something absolutely amazing.

12

MARCH

THIS DAY FOR EVERYONE

Not only is planning ahead wise, organizing your schedule lets you relax and focus on what you're doing in the here and now. Still, however carefully you've planned, the current twists and turns make you rethink things, often at the last minute. Ironically, what's least expected could be the most exciting.

GIFTS Self-effacing, Spontaneous, Flexible

CHALLENGES Escapist, Irresponsible, Irrational

NUMBER 7

(1+3) + (3) = 7

Discreet gestures, backed by deep love, can bring life-transforming change

You

As a restless Piscean, someone who is intuitive by nature, and someone who enjoys drama, it is possible for you to get involved in situations where all of those are happening at the same time. You may even lend a hand to others who are struggling. It's not just about people; you even nurse struggling plants back to health. In each case, that drama is appealing.

Still, it is essential that you balance it with situations that allow you to use your remarkable creative energy, your kindness, and your generosity without the price that comes with those dramas. Initially it may seem rather dull, until you begin to recognize that without the drama, it is far easier to concentrate on what you are doing.

While people often think of this in terms of the arts, many Pisceans are fantastic at business, too, and will excel—as long as they're not distracted by those dramas. The trick? Being able to spot difficulties before you get involved. That has to do not only with the circumstances, but also the people involved. Certain individuals seem perfectly rational until you get involved, then their dramas become yours to deal with, and sometimes you have to take care of them, too. The trick? Using that Piscean intuition as best you can. You will not only benefit from it, you'll avoid yet more unnecessary drama.

You and others

Spotting those who can give to you—friends who can support you and help you block out those who are realistic or demanding—is difficult. But it's a skill that is worth developing, because as you become ever more creative and ever more the marvelous Pisces you are, those who depend on you will be drawn to you. And saying "No" can be rather difficult.

Health and well-being

It's easy to say you'll rest later. It is something you have done as life becomes more fulfilling, more demanding and more exciting. But it requires time and organization. You can't save up sleep like you can money in a bank account. The trick is to learn how to balance it, even if it's having someone close to you tell you when it's time to go to bed.

Goals and challenges

It doesn't have to be a big business—it could be something small, like a local theater—but when there is a lot going on, when those around you are very creative, they can take over and use your own creative abilities. This is where it gets tricky, because it means setting your own goals that may not make you popular in the short term. However, it is essential for you in the long run.

P
\
I
/
S
\
C
/
E
\
S

THIS DAY FOR EVERYONE

Unsettling as sudden changes may be, they are often clearing the way for something better. This applies to links with those individuals who have been part of your life for a long time, but who recently have been more of a burden than a joy. Saying farewell won't be easy, but it may be for the best.

13

MARCH

Being generous once is noble. Frequent generosity with the same person is worrying

You

Some people are argumentative and enjoy battling because it's fun. It's like breathing. But as a Piscean, when you fight for something or somebody it is usually because you believe in it, so you take it more personally than others. In fact, you are intuitive and it is quite difficult for you to have the kind of argument that many do when they're sitting around, don't have much to talk about, and perhaps have a drink in their hands.

In your case, you'll battle for something or somebody you're passionate about. And if you get caught in those situations, you can end up in a war, simply because the other individual doesn't care about the matter in question— they're just making noise and enjoying the action. Backing out of such situations is, however, surprisingly difficult for you.

And that is one of your major lessons. It is to differentiate between what you really care about and other less important matters. Yet what you learn will also lead you to other activities and people who light up your day, your life, and even your soul, in the sense that once you are involved with them, you'll realize their passion doesn't come from enjoying an argument. If they differ from you, it's only because they care just as much as you do about whatever it is you're working on. And that alone will light up your life.

You and others

Dealing with drama is your choice. But even more than that, your choice enables you to learn more about joy. In some cases, those dramas aren't joyous at all, but you realize that behind that, there is the promise of something deeper and more rewarding. And that is what will make the difference.

Health and well-being

When you're in the midst of exciting things, exciting discussions, exciting dramas, or doing something you care passionately about, stopping seems a waste of time. Except in your case, as a Piscean and somebody who is more vulnerable than you like to admit, stopping won't just be important. It will allow you to make the best of what you're dealing with over the weeks, months, and even years ahead.

Goals and challenges

Other people rate achievements in terms of how much they will impress others. Except the only real achievement that is important is something that matters to you as a Pisces and an idealist. It may not have to do with anything artistic or imaginative. It may have to do with pure business. But if it is something that lights up your life and touches your soul, then that's exactly what you should be doing.

P
\
I
/
S
\
C
/
E
\
S

14

MARCH

THIS DAY FOR EVERYONE

Theoretically, facts are reliable. However, certain things you believe to be true for a long time are being challenged by recent discoveries, or certain individuals are embracing new ideas. Tempting as it is to dismiss these, ask what they're about. What you learn will be interesting, if not life-changing.

GIFTS Softhearted, Comforting, Empathic

CHALLENGES Fainthearted, Assumptive, Fragile

NUMBER 9

$(1+5) + (3) = 9$

Those who question your faith in others should look in the mirror

You

The question you need to answer as a Pisces is, why do you struggle to please others, those who want you to make a single plan, when, in fact, your symbol is two fish swimming in different directions.

There's another sign that is similar to yours: Gemini, which is the twins. Both signs have the same rare capacity to look at any situation from at least two different angles.

While that is a gift, it isn't necessarily recognized by the other individuals who are in your world. They simply want you to make a plan and then stick with it. That may be easy for the Capricorns and Virgos of this world, but your nature is always to see both sides of something.

And it is a great gift. If others are unhappy with it, very politely tell them that you will inform them when and how you can commit, but you can't transform yourself.

And this is very much part of the realization of your own gift, as well. Then you realize that those who don't appreciate your vision are actually at a loss—and it's too bad for them.

While you can't, and shouldn't, explain what they can't see, you can and will help them as best you can. And then, having done that, you can quietly back off, spend time with those who appreciate you, and enjoy being yourself. That is the greatest gift of all.

You and others

The simple fact of recognizing that others can't see as much as you can—and even more than that, don't care that they can't see—is difficult. Yet at the same time, there are few things that will free you as much as a simple realization that your vision of the world is far broader and far more inspiring than many of those who think they know more than you do.

Health and well-being

Dealing with periods when you are overwhelmed is tricky. The exhaustion is one thing, but then there are the demands of others who refuse to acknowledge you need to take a break. Do what you can, but no more. Then put yourself in a setting that is free of demands of that nature. This is all about rest and recovery.

Goals and challenges

Choosing your own goals and deciding what you want to do seems easy. But if you happen to be in a world of those whose view of life is based on a struggle and a perspective that is alien to yours, then it will be tricky. What is most important, however, is that in choosing a goal, you are absolutely sure it is yours and yours alone.

P
\
I
/
S
\
C
/
E
\
S

THIS DAY FOR EVERYONE

You are in an uncomfortable position of having to confront somebody about their facts being wrong. In this case, the individual in question tends to speak without thinking. And the matter in question involves you. Address this firmly, and as out of character as it may be, don't apologize.

15

MARCH

Pisces often help out those who're struggling, but prior investigation is worthwhile

You

To say that happiness is fluid may sound very strange to other signs, but as a water sign, you understand that very well. You understand that on one hand, circumstances shift—some work, some don't—but your own mood has its ups and downs as well. So what seemed great one day doesn't seem so great the next, and is the last thing you want the day after that.

However, those around you don't understand, because these less imaginative individuals have the same definition of happiness day in, day out and year in, year out. And from your point of view, that is absolutely fine.

At the same time, however, you're dealing with others, and your relationships also have their ups and downs. It's not so much negativity, but with a world in flux and with the ups and downs of modern life, it is natural that there are moments when things flow and others when they don't.

And this is something that is obvious to you as a Pisces, who also has as your symbol the two fish swimming in opposite directions. Yet every once in a while, you have to explain it. Using the fish as an example might not work, but you will have enough examples in the world that it will be very clear to others that the kind of stability they are demanding simply is unlikely to happen in today's world.

You and others

What you understand that others don't seem to is that, in a world of change, when life is redefining itself, relationships themselves shift. This doesn't mean you care any more or less. It just means the way you communicate with others, the way you see them and the time you spend with them, changes. And in many cases, the world's shifting only deepens those relationships.

Health and well-being

As a Piscean, a water sign, and somebody who has a fascination for drama, a regular regimen can be dull, but it doesn't have to be the case. It's simply that with so much happening, with the changes swirling around you, it is vital that you rest enough, that you eat well, and that you do things that let your body thrive.

Goals and challenges

Life used to be a lot simpler; goals could be clearly defined and ways could be figured out around challenges. But with every passing year, that version of what is a challenge and what is an opportunity is itself changing. The fact is, what are challenges to others may actually be gifts to you. Recognize that and, when others talk about difficult circumstances, they may well be the ones you're thriving on.

PISCES

16

MARCH

THIS DAY FOR EVERYONE

It's not that you've been secretive, despite what certain individuals suggest. But between changes in circumstance and your own equally changeable feelings, you simply didn't know what to say. Fortunately, now that things have reached a turning point, you have a clear sense of those feelings.

GIFTS Elevating, Compassionate, Spiritual

CHALLENGES Infatuated, Quixotic, Ungrounded

NUMBER 2

(1+7) + (3) = 11 = (1+1) = 2

The concept of "quiet joy" is Pisces at its purest and most inspiring

You

It is easy to get drawn into discussions and visions about the goals of others as well as your own. And it's something you quite enjoy as a Pisces and someone who is a bit of a visionary. You also enjoy comparing notes.

However, when it comes to getting things organized, that is completely different. In fact, it's two different processes. Once others simply made a plan and stuck to it, but when the foundation on which their plans are based is itself shifting, that is ideal for you.

As a Pisces, with your two fish swimming in different directions, you have a broader view of what is possible than others do. And those who insist on making a complete and detailed plan of whatever is going to be done can often be distracting. But, of course, the trick is to avoid those conversations and instead, just recognize that each step will need to be taken as you take it, and then the next one after that. And with each step, you will learn a lot.

And if others learn something, that's great. But if others are determined to travel with you, it is essential you make it clear to them that it will be on your terms. That may sound pushy, but many individuals who are accustomed to achieving may well insist on doing things their way. That could be the old way. And it may be a way that will hold you back. As a Pisces, be loyal to one thing—and that is to your vision.

You and others

Are you facing a cynic? Somebody who laughs at others, especially those who care deeply and have vision? You don't have to deal with them, but if you do deal with them, you don't have to like them. You need to set goals that are as clear as theirs. And be as tough. Ironically, that encounter may transform your perspective.

Health and well-being

There is one single four-letter word for you: it's "stop." That's difficult, because when you have a lot to do, it is always just one more thing—an experience, discussion, or task. And that's not stopping. It is taking on more when you need simply to say "Enough." If there is one motto you will want to live by as you go through life's twists and turns, it is "Keep it simple."

Goals and challenges

Every once in a while, it is important to question for whom you're achieving your goals. It may be that you're involved with an organization or a business, or even a family, and you've set goals that are in accordance with theirs. If so, pause and think a little more about those goals. Are they truly yours—in your heart and your soul as well? If so, continue. If not, it's time to rethink them.

P
\
I
/
S
\
C
/
E
\
S

THIS DAY FOR EVERYONE

When sudden changes arose they seemed unsettling but also relatively uncomplicated. Since then, you realize this involved far more than you anticipated, and that they're taking you into new and exciting territory. Yet you almost rejected them. Make a mental note of this, so you can recall it in the future.

17

MARCH

Every Pisces knows they have healing power, and they will use it without a word

You

Pisces often live a life of extremes, not so much that others would see, but more gentle extremes of joy and disappointment, of recognizing what you could do—and what others could do. And while at times there is excitement, there are also dramatic changes. The trick here is to know when to make those changes and what demands to make.

There will be those around you who will think they can remedy your difficulties by making them more like theirs. But unless they are a Pisces, they probably won't understand why you've chosen to organize elements of your life in the way you have. You needn't explain it to them. All you need to do is sidestep those individuals who are quite sure they know far better how to be you than you do. This is a particularly important challenge for you as a Pisces, simply because those around you do have good intentions, but they don't realize that everybody is an individual, and that in being true to yourself, you're able to be the best you can be.

As a Pisces, you are instinctively aware of that. You will have had to argue that point a lot, yet you'll also have learned more about the importance of that personal truth. Make that your goal—far beyond achieving the kind of goals that others go for—and you will always make the right decision.

You and others

Those who have in mind some other project are thinking in terms of their own goals, not yours. Don't argue; just do something that you as a Pisces are so good at, and that is withdraw quietly to another setting. Perhaps you won't pick up the phone for a while— whatever it takes to be true to yourself—but if ever there were a time to do it, it's when others are trying to tell you how to live your life.

Health and well-being

There are many ways of being fit and perhaps the most important one, during periods when you are experiencing growth and change, is to do what feels best to you. There are those who will offer various regimens—walking, dieting, certain foods or supplements—but none will give you the strength in the core of your soul that doing what you feel is best will achieve.

Goals and challenges

If anyone can achieve astronomically high goals, you can. But if you don't feel like doing what those around you are encouraging you to do, then avoid the subject. The fact is, your vision is extraordinary. And what seems not particularly exciting one day will turn into something remarkable, because as a Piscean, you have an instinct for that sort of thing.

THIS DAY FOR EVERYONE

Joy comes in many forms. It can be organized and scheduled. However, what is coming your way is likely to be as surprising as it will be delightful. Because they're unexpected, you might not recognize events for what they are when they first appear. The secret to spotting them is whatever lifts your spirits.

P
\
I
/
S
\
C
/
E
\
S

The biggest challenge? Believing in yourself.
The biggest reward? Also believing in yourself

You

Your birthday is a celebration of balance, between going from the subtle nature of the water sign Pisces to the fiery Aries. In the northern hemisphere, it's about waking from winter's chill and darkness and going into spring, while the southern hemisphere also calls attention to the power of nature's cycles.

The move by the Sun from Pisces to Aries is about a shift in your viewpoint as well. As a Piscean, you're a visionary. But throw in a little of the fire of Aries and you change the game entirely. You have a rare gift of being able to turn the subtlety of the Piscean vision into something that moves swiftly and brings powerful insights.

The trick is to believe entirely in yourself. If those around you want to reassure you, that's fine. However, you will be increasingly aware that you know better than anybody else what you should be doing with your time, your energy, your passions, your love, and your creativity. There are many who are born around your time of year who have done remarkable things.

And whether what you achieve is visible to the world or not, you will be one of them. Believe in yourself in this extraordinary way, because to be born on this date gives you a rare gift: a gift that you will use in many ways, and in many settings throughout your life.

You and others

While it's important to discuss your ideas, be careful not to share too much with others. It is not so much that they will steal them as the clarity you get that is essential. While others may make suggestions, that doesn't mean they will be helpful. If anything, you can use them for contrast and gain greater confidence about the ideas you've come up with.

Health and well-being

If you're going to be in good health, there is a single word that will make all the difference, and that word is joy. It is the joy that comes from doing what you want, recognizing you're being the person you're meant to be, and not allowing anything or anyone to draw you from that truth. It may sound pretty dramatic. But for you as an individual, being able to live out that truth isn't just vital, it will be thrilling.

Goals and challenges

Goals are important because they allow you to define what you want to do. Yet, in fact, you may not even define them to yourself until you look back later and realize certain decisions you made weren't just important, they were life-changing. What is significant, however, is that as you live out each minute of your life, you are true to yourself.

P
\
I
/
S
\
C
/
E
\
S

THIS DAY FOR EVERYONE

Having had to defend yourself from blame for others' badly made decisions, you're increasingly cautious. You have also been comparing notes with those involved. This isn't so much for their advice as to ensure that everybody is aware of your objectives and long-term plans and are happy with them.

19

MARCH

About Shelley

I was born and grew up in Hollywood, and while my parents weren't in show business, it was around me from my earliest days. Although I recognized the glamour of it, I was fascinated by philosophy, and read about and studied it long before I reached my teens.

My recollection of my introduction to the heavens, in terms of both astrology and astronomy, is vivid. I was about eight years of age, at the Griffith Park Observatory in the hills above Los Angeles, waiting to go into a planetarium show on the heavens. In the foyer, there was a pendulum, and above it were frescoes—paintings of the images of the gods, signifying each of the planets.

At that moment, I knew they'd be part of my life. It was clear. The ancient myths, the subtleties of astrology, and even the science of astronomy—about which I am knowledgeable enough to hold my own in an exchange of ideas with experts—have become a joy and a passion. They are central to my life, as a career, and—as anybody who looks at my social media accounts will know—my passion about the heavenly bodies is as enthusiastic as it is extensive.

Today's distractions, on all sorts of screens, mean that even astrological enthusiasts don't actually look up at the heavens; they may note the power of the Full Moon, but they won't have a chat with the heavenly body—that luminous magnet, which, in ancient times, was herself regarded as a goddess. Even today, we honor the Moon with a range of names—Selene, Diana, Artemis, and Phoebe—and it is the same with most of the planets.

Similarly, we cite the planets every time we speak of somebody being unpredictable or mercurial (Mercury), or jolly and generous and jovial (Jupiter). They are woven into our culture and way of thinking, even for those who don't "believe" in astrology.

These days, it has become as much a tool for self-reflection and gaining an awareness of others as about prediction, although many columns, including mine, feature that.

But we are living in a time that balances the knowledge of science with several forms of ancient wisdom, including astrology. It is, after all, the study of cycles, of the rhythms of nature, around us, and our lives, collectively and individually.

And I hope, when visiting this book and its entries, you will not only recognize an accurate and insightful portrait of yourself and others, but also a testimony to this ancient art that honors the year's cycle, day by day.

Today, books like this are only part of the conversation. In addition to writing for publications, I speak to groups and talk on matters from personal awareness to business; recently this has focused on untangling—and making sense of—the dramatic changes reshaping our world.

Some would say (and I agree) that this is the beginning of a new cycle, the Age of Aquarius we've heard so much about. While it may indeed lead to a more peaceful era, on the way to creating it, humanity will have to grapple with a few of the most disruptive characteristics.

Also, some astrologers, including me, suggest that the clearer your own self-awareness is, the greater your power will be to usher in a new, more harmonious and productive way of thinking, being, living—and running a planet.

If you're interested to know more, about yourself or about astrology, I've listed publications and organizations that would be a good place to start.

Questions about the dates of the signs? Find out more at shelleyvonstrunckel.com.

References

First, if you want to know more about yourself, visit my website, shelleyvonstrunckel.com, where you can read your own daily, weekly, and monthly stars.

You can also order your own personal chart, a map of the heavens for the exact date, year, and time (if known) you were born, and the exact place. The resulting astronomically accurate map of the heavens is your personal birth chart and is regarded as a "mirror" of your nature. It comes with an interpretation about your character, written by a trained professional, for your chart—or that of a family member, child, or even your boss.

These are wonderfully easy to read and understand. I've had amazing feedback. Order them from my website.

Astrological charts about children are also available; parents have told me how helpful they are—but they're also a great gift. You can also order charts and a yearly analysis of your own chart. All are done to order, just for you.

If want to know more about astrology itself, there are some great magazines you can read, books to delve into, and organizations that are worth getting to know.

Do you want to learn more?

An excellent website for books is wessexastrologer.com. Those seeking guidance about what to read or where to study and learn more can email info@wessexastrologer.com

The Mountain Astrologer is a terrific journal, published in the US, but of international interest. For subscriptions/inquiries in the UK and Europe:
wessexastrologer.com/product-category/the-mountain-astrologer/

And for inquiries in the US and ROW, as well as digital subscriptions:
mountainastrologer.com/tma/

There is also a Wessex Astrologer YouTube channel, which is being added to all the time:
youtube.com/channel/UCLYJ58jI-5MwkNNa47ClhMw

Schools

London School of Astrology
General: londonschoolofastrology.co.uk
Online courses: londonschoolofastrology.com

The Faculty of Astrological Studies
astrology.org.uk/

The Mayo School, led by Wendy Stacey
mayoastrology.com/

American Federation of Astrologers
astrologers.com/

Kepler College
keplercollege.org

International Society for Astrological Research
isarastrology.org/en-gb/

National Council for Geocosmic Research
geocosmic.org/

The Astrology University
astrologyuniversity.com/

DK UK

Publishing Director Katie Cowan
Senior Acquisitions Editor Stephanie Milner
Editor Alison Thomson
Art Director Maxine Pedliham
Managing Art Editor Christine Keilty
Designer and Illustrator Abi Read
Senior Production Editor Tony Phipps
Production Controller Rebecca Parton

DK DELHI

Pre-production Manager Sunil Sharma
CTS Designer Umesh Singh Rawat

First American Edition, 2020
Published in the United States by DK
Publishing
1450 Broadway, Suite 801, New York, NY
10018

Published in Great Britain by
Dorling Kindersley Limited

A catalog record for this book
is available from the Library of Congress.
ISBN 978-0-7440-2444-9

DK books are available at special discounts
when purchased in bulk for sales promotions,
premiums, fundraising, or educational use.
For details, contact: DK Publishing Special
Markets, 1450 Broadway, Suite 801, New York,
NY 10018
SpecialSales@dk.com

Printed and bound in Canada

For the curious
www.dk.com